Everyman, I will go with thee,
and be thy guide

William Penn

THE PEACE OF EUROPE,
THE FRUITS OF SOLITUDE
AND OTHER WRITINGS

Edited by
EDWIN B. BRONNER
Haverford College, Pennsylvania

EVERYMAN
J. M. DENT · LONDON
CHARLES E. TUTTLE
VERMONT

Critical apparatus © J. M. Dent 1993
First included in Everyman's Library, 1915
This edition first published in Everyman in 1993
All rights reserved

J. M. Dent
Orion Publishing Group
Orion House, 5 Upper St Martin's Lane,
London WC2H 9EA
and
Charles E. Tuttle Co. Inc.
28 South Main Street,
Rutland, Vermont 05701, USA

Typeset in Sabon by CentraCet Limited, Cambridge,
Printed in Great Britain by
The Guernsey Press Co. Ltd, Guernsey, C.I.

British Library Cataloguing-in-Publication Data
is available upon request.

ISBN 0 460 87302 4

CONTENTS

NOTE ON THE AUTHOR

WILLIAM PENN was born in London on 14 October 1644, during the early years of the Civil War in England. His father, Captain William Penn, was an officer in Parliament's navy and rose rapidly in rank. His mother, Margaret van der Schuren Penn, headed the household during the war years. In 1653 the boy enrolled in Chigwell School, after the family moved to Wanstead in Essex. After 1656, however, young Penn studied with tutors, for the family went to live in Macroom Castle, west of Cork in Ireland, after Admiral Penn got into trouble with Oliver Cromwell, Lord Protector.

Admiral Penn was one of many who supported Charles II when he was restored to the throne, and young Penn enrolled in Christ Church, Oxford, in the autumn of 1660. He fell in with nonconformists and two years later was expelled from his college. Sent to France to forget his radical ideas, Penn arranged to study with Moses Amyraut at his Protestant Academy at Saumur. He returned from the continent in late 1664 and enrolled the following February in Lincoln's Inn to study law. Forced to leave London by The Plague, Penn went to Ireland early in 1666 to oversee his father's affairs. Late in the summer of 1667 he heard the Quaker Thomas Loe speak in Cork, and immediately became part of that controversial group.

As a well educated, wealthy young man, Penn became extremely active in Quaker affairs, writing and speaking to further the cause of the new movement. His first publication, *Truth Exalted*, was issued in 1668, and, in December of that year, he was accused of blasphemy and placed in the Tower of London for another of his pamphlets. After his release young Penn returned to Ireland where he published *The Great Case of Liberty of Conscience* in 1670. Later that year he was jailed by London authorities and brought before the courts in what is called the Penn-Mead Trial. His testimony in that case was published in *The People's Ancient and Just Liberties Asserted*, a pamphlet which went through many printings in the following months and years.

In 1672, Penn married the beautiful, wealthy young Quaker woman, Gulielma Springett, and he continued to work actively for Friends, as they preferred to be called. He became involved with affairs in West New Jersey in 1675 and spent much time on the development of that Quaker colony. In 1681 he received his charter for Pennsylvania and was caught up in recruiting settlers and writing promotional pamphlets. He sailed for Pennsylvania in August, 1682, and spent two years organizing the government, settling real estate claims and serving as the spiritual leader of the province. In 1683 he wrote *A Letter from William Penn, Proprietary and Governour of Pennsylvania*, which called for more colonists and described the life of the native Americans in the province.

Shortly after he returned to England Charles II died, and his brother took the throne as James II. Admiral Penn had been a close colleague of the restored monarch, and the younger Penn became a friend and adviser of the new ruler. James II, a staunch Catholic, was soon in trouble with his subjects over religious matters and Penn found he could do little to help him. In 1685 Penn wrote another tract advocating religious liberty, *A Perswasive to Moderation to Dissenting Christians*, urging toleration for Catholics as well as others who opposed the Church of England. After James was driven from the throne late in 1688 by William and Mary of Orange, Penn fell under suspicion and was charged with treason three times in the next two years. By 1691 an informal agreement was reached that Penn would not be harassed any more if he would withdraw from public view. During two years of hiding, Penn published a number of titles including *An Essay Towards the Present and Future Peace of Europe*, and *Some Fruits of Solitude*. He also wrote a Preface for George Fox's *Journal*, which was published in 1694 as *A Brief Account of the Rise and Progress of the People, Called Quakers*.

Not long after Penn began to appear in public once more his wife Gulielma died. Two years later, in 1696, he married the wealthy, capable Bristol woman, Hannah Callowhill, who handled his affairs when he was not able to do so himself. He also published *Primitive Christianity Revived* that same year. Hannah Penn and Penn's daughter Laetitia accompanied him on a second visit to Pennsylvania which lasted two years. Back in England, in 1702, he published *More Fruits of Solitude* and found himself welcome at court when Queen Anne ascended the throne.

However, Penn's financial difficulties with the family of his former agent, Philip Ford, eventually landed him in debtor's prison. In 1712 he suffered a series of strokes and became childlike for the remainder of his life, with Hannah Penn managing affairs. Penn died in July, 1718, nearly 74 years old, and he was buried at the Jordans meetinghouse, near Beaconsfield, England. Hannah Penn died in 1726, and that same year Sir John Rodes published a small book which he entitled *Fruits of a Father's Love*, probably written by Penn in 1699. The two volume *Collection of the Works of William Penn* was also released in 1726.

NOTE ON THE EDITOR

EDWIN B. BRONNER, Professor of History emeritus at Haverford College, has specialized in Quaker history, including the life of William Penn, during his entire career at Temple University and Haverford College. Author of two major books about Penn, he has published numerous volumes, pamphlets, and articles on Quaker history, including several on Anglo-American Quaker relations in the nineteenth century. He served on the Advisory Board for the William Penn publications project and has been president of the Friends Historical Association in the United States and the Friends Historical Society in England. An active Quaker, he was Chairman of the worldwide organization called the Friends World Committee for Consultation for six years. He has received grants from the National Endowment for the Humanities, the American Philosophical Society, the Old Dominion Fund, and the Barra Foundation. He and his wife live on the Haverford campus, outside of Philadelphia, where he was Curator of the Quaker Collection for twenty-eight years.

CHRONOLOGY OF PENN'S LIFE

Note: Dates of years appear in New Style, but precise dates in Old Style. (The Gregorian Calendar, called New Style, adopted in 1582 by Catholic countries, was not used in English speaking areas until 1752. The Old Style, or Julian Calendar began on March 25, and was ten days behind; after 1700, eleven days behind.)

Year	Age	Life
1644		14 October: born in London
c. 1653	9	Begins studies at Chigwell Grammar School, Essex
1656–60	12–16	Penn family at Macroom Castle, County Cork, Ireland
1660	16	October: enters Christ Church College, Oxford
1662	18	Expelled from Christ Church for religious nonconformity; goes to France

CHRONOLOGY OF HIS TIMES

Year	Artistic Events	Historical Events
1644		Ming dynasty ends in China. Descartes, *Principles of Philosophy*
1648		Peace of Westphalia ends 30 Years War
1649		Execution of Charles I in England
1651		Thomas Hobbes, *Leviathan*
1652		Capetown, South Africa, founded
		George Fox, founder of Quakers, has great success in north of England
1653	Taj Mahal built at Agra in India	Oliver Cromwell establishes Protectorate
1655		Cromwell readmits Jews into England
		Dutch annex New Sweden (Delaware)
1656	Harrington, *Commonwealth of Oceana*	Dutch enter China trade
1658		Cromwell dies
1660	Pepys begins his diary	Restoration of Charles II
1661		John Eliot translates New Testament into Algonquin
1662		Royal Society of London receives charter
		Louis XIV begins to build Versailles

Year	Age	Life
1663	19	Begins studying at Moses Amyraut's Protestant Academy at Saumur, France
1664	19	August: returns to London
1665	20	February: enters Lincoln's Inn to study law
1667	22	Late summer: becomes a Quaker in Cork, Ireland; is arrested
1668	24	December: imprisoned in Tower of London for blasphemy
1669	24	July: released from Tower after writing *Innocency with Her Open Face, and No Cross, No Crown*
1670	26	In Ireland, writes *The Great Case of Liberty of Conscience*. September: the Penn-Mead Trial in London *The People's Ancient and Just Liberties Asserted* published His father, Admiral Sir William Penn dies
1671	26	February–July: imprisoned at Newgate for preaching
1672	27	4 April: marries Gulielma Springett and moves to Rickmansworth in Hertfordshire
1674	30	Lobbies against the persecution of Quakers in Charles II's court
1675	30	January: son Springett Penn is born, first surviving child. January–February: arbitrates dispute between two Quakers over New Jersey; becomes trustee of West New Jersey
1676	32	Arranges for settlement of West New Jersey. Autumn: moves to Warminghurst in Sussex
1677	33	July–October: second journey to Holland and Germany; keeps journal published in 1694

Year	Artistic Events	Historical Events
1663		Carolina granted to eight proprietors
1664		Dutch purchase Swedish colonies in Africa and Gold Coast
1665		First cases of bubonic plague in London
1666	Molière, *Le Misanthrope*	Great Fire sweeps London
1667	Milton, *Paradise Lost*	
1668		Isaac Newton invents reflecting telescope
1669	Death of Rembrandt	Venetians surrender Crete to Turks
1670	Pascal, *Pensées*, published posthumously	Hudson Bay Company created
1672		Charles II issues Declaration of Indulgence
1673		Test Act enacted by Parliament against Catholics. Marquette and Joliet explore Mississippi
1674		John Sobieski becomes King of Poland
1675	Sir Christopher Wren begins to rebuild St Paul's Cathedral	King Philip's War in New England
1676		Innocent XI named Pope. Bacon's Rebellion in Virginia
1677	Spinoza, *Ethics*	Marriage of William of Orange and Mary (daughter of James, Duke of York)

Year	Age	Life
1678	33	March: daughter Laetitia Penn born
1679	34	March–July: tries to secure election of Algernon Sidney to Parliament
1681	37	4 March: receives his charter for Pennsylvania and begins promotion of new province. 14 March: son William Penn, Jr, born. Publishes *A Brief Account of Pennsylvania* October: writes a letter of friendship to the chiefs of the Delaware Indians
1682	38	c. 1 March: his mother, Lady Margaret Penn, dies. Publishes a new version of *No Cross, No Crown*. 30 August: sails for America on the *Welcome*; 28 October: lands at New Castle, Delaware
1683	38	His Second General Assembly approves a revised *Frame of Government*. August: writes *A Letter from William Penn in Pennsylvania*
1684	39	18 August: sails for England from Lewes, Delaware
1685	41	Writes pamphlets to advance religious toleration including *A Perswasive to Moderation*
1686	42	Travels to Holland for James II, and to see Friends
1687	43	Arranges publication of *Excellent Priviledge*

Year	Artistic Events	Historical Events
1678	Bunyan's *Pilgrim's Progress*	Popish Plot in England. Robert Barclay, *Apology*, Quaker classic, published in English
1679		Habeus Corpus Act enacted in England
1680		Penny Post established in England by William Duckwra Spanish driven out of New Mexico by Native Americans
1681		Treaty of Radzin, Turks give up much of Ukraine
1682		La Salle claims area of Louisiana for France
1683		Rye House Plot against Stuarts. Vienna saved from Turks van Leeuwenhoek discovers bacteria
1684		Puppet play theatre opens in Tokyo
1685		Death of Charles II and Crowning of James II Revocation of the Edict of Nantes. Monmouth's Rebellion
1686		Dominion of New England created Louis XIV annexes Madagascar
1687		Declaration of Indulgence by James II Venetians bomb Athens, destroying Parthenon Newton, *Principia*
1688		War of the League of Augsburg begins James II driven from throne; William and Mary take over in Glorious Revolution

Year	Age	Life
1689	45	Arrested and accused of treason by new government of William and Mary
1691	47	Death of George Fox. Penn goes into hiding for two years
1693	49	Publishes *An Essay Towards Peace* and *Some Fruits of Solitude*
1694	50	Death of Gulielma Springett Penn Writes a preface for George Fox's *Journal*, reprinted as *A Brief Account of the Rise of Quakers*
1696	52	5 March: marries Hannah Callowhill in Bristol. Death of Springett Penn. Publishes *Primitive Christianity Revived*
1697	53	Proposes a Union of the American Colonies to Board of Trade
1699	55	3 September: sails for Pennsylvania, accompanied by Hannah Penn and daughter Laetitia; 2 December: arrives in Philadelphia
1700	55	January: birth of John Penn, 'the American', in Philadelphia
1701	57	Agrees to Charter of Privileges for Pennsylvania. November: sails for England
1702	58	March: son Thomas Penn is born Publishes *More Fruits of Solitude*

Year	Artistic Events	Historical Events
1689		Bill of Rights enacted in England. Peter the Great becomes Tsar of Russia
1690		Battle of the Boyne, victory for Protestants in Ireland John Locke, *Essay Concerning Human Understanding* and *Two Treatises on Government*
1692	Purcell, *The Fairy Queen*	Salem witchcraft trials, Massachusetts Opening of Russia–China trade
1694		Death of Queen Mary II William and Mary College opens
1695	Congreve, *Love for Love*	
1696		Board of Trade created to administer colonies
1697		Peter the Great visits western Europe Treaty of Ryswick ends War of League of Augsburg
1700		Great Northern War begins
1701		War of Spanish Succession begins. Act of Settlement provides for Hanoverians to succeed Stuarts. Founding of Yale College
1702		Death of William III, crowning of Queen Anne. New Jersey united as a royal colony Founding of *Daily Courant* as first daily newspaper

Year	Age	Life
1704	60	November: daughter Margaret Penn is born
1706	61	January: son Richard Penn is born
1708	64	After legal battles Penn spends time in debtor's prison
1712	68	Suffers serious strokes and is incapacitated for balance of life
1718	73	30 July: dies and is buried in Jordans meetinghouse burial ground
1726		Hannah Callowhill dies. *Fruits of a Father's Love* is published by John Rodes. *A Collection of the Works of William Penn*, 2 volumes, edited by Joseph Besse, is published

Year	Artistic Events	Historical Events
1704		British take Gibraltar
		Boston News-Letter appears.
		Thomas Newcomen improves
		steam engine
1705		Edward Halley predicts return
		of Halley's Comet
		Founding of Husseinite dynasty
		in Tunis
1706		Birth of Benjamin Franklin
1707		Union of England and Scotland.
		Last eruption of Mt Fuji in
		Japan
1708		First accurate map of China
		made by Jesuits
1709	Joseph Addison and Richard	Battle of Poltava, victory of
	Steele, *The Tatler*	Peter the Great over Charles XII
	Birth of Samuel Johnson	
1711		South Sea Company
		incorporated
1713		Peace of Utrecht ends War of
		Spanish Succession
		Asiento Treaty gives England
		monopoly on slave trade
1714	Pope, *The Rape of the Lock*	Death of Queen Anne, crowning
		of George I, of Hanover
		Fahrenheit invents mercury
		thermometer
1715		Death of Louis XIV
1718		New Orleans founded
		Death of Charles XII of Sweden

INTRODUCTION

William Penn is remembered not only as a man who advocated new, liberal ideas, but as one who sought to carry them out in his life. He is also hailed as a person of great charm who drew both men and women to him in every aspect of his life and as a man of courage who was willing to oppose those he thought were wrong, and to suffer the consequences when his actions brought down the law against him. There are only two portraits of him which are accepted as authentic, and in both of them it is apparent that he was handsome and vigorous.[1]

Penn is more highly regarded in the United States than in Great Britain, as he stood out more clearly in the American colonies at the end of the seventeenth century than he did amid the political turbulence of England. He is particularly known in Pennsylvania, the province which he founded in 1682, which was named not for Penn the Quaker but for his father, the admiral Sir William Penn, at the insistence of Charles II. A statue of Penn stands on top of City Hall in Philadelphia, looking toward Shackamaxon where, according to tradition, Penn signed treaties with the Lenni Lenape chiefs. His name is associated with integrity and quality and has been adopted by hundreds of companies and products, not only in Philadelphia, but in the state and nation. He is remembered especially for his practice of religious toleration in the 'Holy Experiment' he founded on the west side of the Delaware River, but he is also honored for his liberal government in the province, even though it was not quite as democratic as tradition would suggest.

Penn began to write and publish when he was less than twenty-five years old, and continued until he suffered serious strokes in 1712. He published one hundred titles and contributed to three dozen others during his career.[2] While many of these were written to defend Quakers from attacks by their opponents and have almost never appeared in print again, a number of his titles have been highly regarded and have remained in print ever since. For example, *No Cross, No Crown* (1682), has gone through fifty printings, has been translated into Dutch, French, and German, and Professor Hugh Barbour edited a new edition in 1981 in preparation for the tercentenary of its first appearance. Four of the titles included in this volume are in print, and none of the other six would fall into the category of writings not worthy of remembering.

Many of Penn's titles were written not only in reaction to a particular controversy with enemies of Friends, but they were written and printed so rapidly that Penn did not go over them before they appeared. Some were even sent to the printer a few pages at a time before the manuscript was completed. In contrast, several of the essays in this volume were written during periods of withdrawal when he had time to rewrite and refine his thoughts and words. It is clear in such pieces as *An Essay Towards the Present and Future Peace of Europe*, *Some Fruits of Solitude*, and *A Brief Account of the Rise and Progress of the People, Called Quakers* that Penn was able to produce enduring prose if he took the time and effort.

William Penn benefited from a superior education, and he had the money to pay for publishing anything he wrote. Born in 1644, almost within the shadow of the Tower of London, to parents who had a comfortable income, Penn received a classical education at Chigwell School in Essex before he was ten and continued to study until his twenty-first year. By that time his father, who had a distinguished career in the navy, had been knighted and rewarded with lands in Ireland for his support of Charles II when the monarch returned to England in 1660 to take the throne vacated by Charles I, who was beheaded in 1649. In addition to Penn's classical study – evidenced in many of his writings by frequent references to Greek and Roman authorities – he was introduced to ideas about both religious and political liberty during his study with Moses Amyraut at his Protestant Academy in Saumur in western France in 1663–4. His knowledge of English constitutional history, which he exhibited in the Penn-Mead Trial, was gained while studying law in Lincoln's Inn in 1665. One is also able to discern, from his writings, that he continued to read and expand his knowledge during the remainder of his life.

Penn's ideas and beliefs were also influenced by his fellow Quakers. He joined Friends in 1667 while living in Ireland, and he was soon accepted by the leaders of the movement as an equal. As such, he came under the influence of the foremost Friend, George Fox, the mystical thinker Isaac Penington, and, a bit later, the theologian Robert Barclay and his lifelong associate George Whitehead. One should also remember that Penn, like his contemporaries, relied heavily on the Scriptures. While we do not see the influence of the Bible as clearly in the ten titles in this book as would be the case in a complete collection of his writings, it may be taken for granted that he referred to both the Old and New Testaments, but especially the latter, in his writings on religious subjects. For example, there are numerous references to the scriptures in *Primitive Christianity Revived* (omitted here), which were printed in the margin in Penn's *Works*, from which the text was taken.

Notes on the Essays

An Essay Towards the Present and Future Peace of Europe has an important place 'in the history of the ideas concerning peace and international organization', in the estimate of Peter van den Dungen, professor in the School of Peace Studies at the University of Bradford.[3] In this work Penn proposes a Diet in which the countries of Europe are represented in proportion to their economic power – ninety members in all. He advocates the use of secret ballots, and calls for a three-fourths majority for action. In order to prevent controversy over precedence, he suggests a circular room with multiple doors so that delegates can enter as they please. Furthermore, he argues for the admission of both the Ottoman Empire and Russia in this parliament. This idea is particularly noteworthy because the Turks had only been pushed back from Vienna a decade before and were still a threat in eastern Europe and Russia was not yet regarded as a part of Europe; Peter the Great, who had just taken power, had not yet started to 'open windows to the west'.

The Latin motto on the essay's title page, which may be translated as 'let parliaments rather than arms decide', is perhaps the key to Penn's proposal. He stresses the economic advantages which would come from international peace, and calls for an end to killing which is 'Offensive to God'. He denies that bringing an end to armed service would lead to effeminacy in young men, saying a rigorous education system would prevent that from happening. Penn hoped that his proposal would achieve peace with justice.

While this essay was ignored for two centuries it has been reprinted repeatedly since World War I and represents an important step in the development of international understanding. This year marks the three-hundredth anniversary of the publication of the *Essay*.[4]

Some Fruits of Solitude, issued in the same year as the *Essay*, is Penn's most readable publication, for many of the maxims are not only charming but they are as relevant today as they were three centuries ago – 'Never marry but for love, but see that thou lovest what is lovely', 'If thou thinkest twice before thou speakest once thou wilt speak twice the better for it', 'The humble, meek, merciful, just, pious, and devout souls are everywhere of one religion; and when death has taken off the mask, they will know one another, though the diverse liveries they wear here make them strangers'. Penn had apparently been collecting sayings, ideas, and pithy thoughts for some time, as he writes of an 'Enchiridion', or notebook, in his preface.

While the paragraphs followed one another without any subject headings in the original publication, such headings appeared early in the eighteenth century and are found in the 1726 collection. In addition, eighty-nine more paragraphs were added during the intervening decades, and we realize that Penn continued to improve the original text as new editions appeared. He writes about such practical things as education, children, family and marriage, as well as such abstract ideas as justice, industry, patience, temperance and truthfulness. He also warns against sins of pride, luxury, avarice, and jealousy. He describes the advantages of country living over city life and the importance of proper respect for the environment. He expresses concern for practical education despite his own classical preparation, saying 'We press their memory too soon, and puzzle, strain, and load them with words and rules; to know grammar and rhetoric, and a strange tongue or two . . . leaving their natural genius to mechanical and physical or natural know-ledge uncultivated and neglected . . .' Frederick B. Tolles called *Some Fruits* the product of Penn's 'matured philosophy of life in the form of maxims and aphorisms – droplets of clear wisdom, as it were, distilled from a lifetime of sober thought and dedicated action'.[5]

*

More Fruits of Solitude contains a number of valuable maxims, but it often lacks the concise, crisp epigrammatic quality found in the earlier collection. Penn was caught up in a great many activities in 1702, and could not polish this manuscript as he had the 1693 volume. While this title appeared as a separate publication originally, it has subsequently been published along with the earlier *Fruits*, often with *Fruits of a Father's Love* added. There are 299 entries in *More Fruits*, divided into twenty-six topics. A few gems appear in this collection such as, 'They that soar too high, often fall hard; which makes a low and level Dwelling preferable'. Writing about speaking, Penn says, 'Enquire often but Judge rarely, and thou wilt not often be mistaken'.

Fruits of a Father's Love is divided into three chapters, and it is Chapter II, containing forty-five paragraphs, which most resembles the two previous essays. In *Works* the title is given as *The Advice of William Penn to his Children*, but the original printing of the manuscript, from 1726, begins with *Fruits of a Father's Love*, indicating that the editor hoped it would be classed with the other two collections of maxims. Sir John Rodes who looked to Penn as his mentor, to use a modern expression, prepared an introduction, which was omitted in *Works*, in which he explained that Penn had given the manuscript to him some twenty years earlier. He added that he had prepared the text for publication as an expression of appreciation for Penn and as a service to 'the World in general'. He included a brief sketch of Penn's life and referred to the controversy with his father, Admiral Penn. Rodes did not say when the manuscript had been completed, but it is believed that Penn prepared it for his children in 1699 before setting off for his second voyage to Pennsylvania. The tone of the paper suggests that Penn was making a special effort to influence his son William, sometimes called Billy, who seemed to be heading away from Quakers and into a dissolute and useless life.

In the first Chapter Penn urges his children to be open to the 'Christ Within', to stay close to Friends and to read the Bible regularly. The second chapter contains advice about achieving the goals outlined in the first. Penn not only urges daily scripture reading and meditation, but stresses the need to seek good company and good conversation. He advocates simple living, and he suggests that his own children live on one-half of their income and be willing to give generously to others. Once more he emphasizes the advantages of living in the country rather than the city. He writes 'Envy none; it is God that maketh Rich and Poor, Great and Small, High and Low'. It is amusing to read paragraph 40 – 'Meddle not with Government; never speak of it; let others say or do as they please' – in view of his lifelong involvement with government, including his service as Governor of Pennsylvania.

In Chapter III Penn stresses the value of humility, meekness, patience, charity, integrity, and frugality, qualities he often failed to achieve in his own life. He concludes with suggestions for further reading, especially in the classics, of works by persons he referred to as 'virtuous Gentiles', and he also mentions his own volume *The Christian Quaker*, written with George Whitehead in 1673. There is a 'preachy' quality to this essay which does not seem apparent in the other two *Fruits* volumes.

A Letter from William Penn, Proprietary and Governour of Pennsylvania is the most informative of all of Penn's promotional pamphlets. He wrote a number himself, beginning in 1681, and arranged for others to prepare additional ones. He had been in Pennsylvania for ten months and could now write from personal experience. This *Letter* not only contains much useful information about the province, but it includes a map of Philadelphia, prepared by Thomas Holme, and a valuable description of the life and customs of the native Americans.

Penn begins by reporting that he is a live Quaker, not a dead Jesuit, as one of his enemies in England had been reporting. He was often accused of being a Catholic because of his defense of religious toleration and his friendship with James, Duke of York. He describes Pennsylvania, repeating the one untruth he usually incorporated in his promotional writings, that there were fifty-pound wild turkeys in the woods.

Penn writes at length about the Lenni Lenape, or Delaware Indians, describing their appearance, language, marriage customs, home life, and other aspects of their lives. He also outlines their religious beliefs, and their government. Clearly he admired the Native Americans and hoped that they could live side by side with their new neighbors. He explains his provision for juries made up of six Indians and six whites when one of them was in legal difficulties. He includes his theory that the Native Americans are part of the lost ten tribes of Israel, dispersed after Assyria defeated

Israel; earlier he had written that they looked either Jewish or Italian.

The proprietor describes the European settlers already living in the Delaware Valley as well as the constitution and laws of the new province. After reporting that there are eighty houses in Philadelphia, he lists some of the businesses already started, expressing the hope that a tannery, a sawmill, glass works, docks, and other projects will be started. He also plans to introduce wine grapes, flax for linen, and whaling.

The People's Ancient and Just Liberties Asserted is a stirring description of what is called the Penn-Mead Trial which led to a landmark decision by Chief Justice Sir John Vaughan establishing the freedom of juries from intimidation. Penn and William Mead had been arrested outside of the Gracechurch Street meetinghouse in August 1670, and were accused of creating an unlawful assembly and disturbing the peace. The trial was held at the Old Bailey with a bench of men sitting in judgment and a jury of twelve men handing down a decision. The judges were determined to find the two Quakers guilty, and thwarted every attempt on their part to prove their innocence. Penn did most of the speaking, not only because he had studied at Lincoln's Inn, but because he had been the person preaching when the authorities arrested them outside of the meetinghouse, which had been locked by court order. Penn's testimony is particularly noteworthy for exhibiting a sense of humor which rarely appears anywhere else in his published or unpublished writings.

Even though the Quaker wrote later that he was not the author of this tract, many of the words, taken down in shorthand, are his, and it is usually included in Penn's writings. The transcript reveals the prejudice of the authorities against Quakers and the unwillingness of the court to accept the verdict of the jury. There is a quality to the text which lends itself to dramatizations of Penn's life, and the trial almost always appears in plays, or filmed descriptions of the Quaker colonizer and pioneer of liberal ideas.

The Great Case of Liberty of Conscience, written in Ireland early in 1670, was Penn's first of two dozen essays advocating religious toleration. The exact number of these pieces is not known, for many were unsigned because of the stringent laws of the period. Hugh Barbour calls this tract 'the most comprehensive of all of

Penn's writings on religious toleration'.[6] However, it does not mention toleration for Roman Catholics, a provision Penn began to include in his essays on this issue in 1680, especially in *A Perswasive to Moderation*, the next title in this volume.

While the original pamphlet was written and published in Dublin, the text used in *Works* is copied from a 1671 revision prepared by Penn when he was once more in Newgate. He had been seized for preaching at the Wheeler Street meetinghouse near Spitalfields, and sentenced to six months in jail. An introductory section, addressed to Charles II, asked that the Conventicle Act, which made it illegal for more than five persons to hold religious services outside of the established Church, be set aside. The main text is divided into six chapters in which Penn outlines his reasons for advocating religious liberty. He claims that persecution denies citizens the freedoms they are entitled to 'by English Birthright', and rejects the idea that dissenters are a threat to security. Penn provides copious references to passages in the Scriptures which defend toleration, and he also turns to the laws of nature and reason for support. He had already concluded that toleration was good for business, using Holland as an example, and he quotes a poem by Chaucer, though he apologized for this (Quakers were opposed to the arts in that period) and draws attention to the substance of his writing. In his final chapter Penn cites various authorities from ancient to modern times to find support for liberty of conscience, and he assures authorities that they have nothing to fear from dissenters who 'lead peaceable, just and industrious lives'.

A Perswasive to Moderation was written after James II had ascended to the throne in 1685 and had openly acknowledged his adherence to Catholicism. He pledged to support the Church of England despite his own personal beliefs, but many were uneasy about this arrangement. While Penn did not print his name on the title page of the first printing, he refers to himself as 'one of the Humblest and most Dutiful of his Dissenting Subjects'. He asserts that moderation really requires liberty of conscience, and he calls upon members of the Church of England to be tolerant of all who are not members of the State Church. He refers to both Dissenting Catholics and Dissenting Protestants.

Penn gives examples from past and present of nations which practiced toleration and benefited from it. He refers to the Romans who lived comfortably with many different religious sects, and points to Holland as the prime example of the success of religious toleration. Seeking to quiet the fears of Anglican authorities, Penn writes of the Anglican and dissenting officers who served loyally under James, Duke of York, despite the King's Catholic commitment, and suggests that it would be no different now. The Quaker also suggests that it might be an advantage to have both Catholics and dissenters in England, for the Anglican Church could sit in the middle and balance the power of one against the other, thus keeping the state Church in control. At the same time he rejects the idea that either of these groups represents a threat to the tranquillity of society.

Despite his discussion of various practical reasons for advocating religious liberty, Penn's two main points are that Christian teachings call for toleration and that James II could be trusted to respect the Anglican Church and refrain from any attempt to foist Catholicism on the English people. Unfortunately, Penn did not prove to be a good prophet, for James did seek to advance some Catholics at the expense of Anglicans, and he rejected some of the safeguards of parliamentary power which had been put in place in the decades since his father had been beheaded. While Penn tried valiantly to dissuade the monarch from some of his actions, he was unsuccessful, and James was overthrown before the end of 1688.

Primitive Christianity Revived, in the Faith and Practice of the People Called Quakers seeks to convince readers that Friends are truly part of the mainstream of Christianity even though some of their beliefs and practices are different from those of other denominations. Earlier in his career Penn had engaged in numerous debates with members of other churches, but he had become more tolerant over the years, and he stresses the positive aspects of Quakerism in this essay without attacking the beliefs of others. He places great emphasis on the 'Light of Christ' in this pamphlet, one of the names used for the divine spark which is found in each human being. Friends valued 'that of God in everyone', and sought to point out the positive, while acknowledging that there was evil in the world as well as good.

Even though Quakers believe that the 'Light of Christ' is eternal and universal, present in all human beings, not just believers, Penn does appeal to the Scriptures to support the concept of the 'Light Within', as it was sometimes called. He sought to show that 'The Light' was an important part of Christ's teachings, and that it was crucial in Apostolic Christianity, hence the title. While Friends tended to look forward rather than backward, and to stress experience rather than doctrine, this did not prevent Penn from citing the history of the Church in this publication as well as in the following one.

In the latter part of this brief pamphlet Penn uses examples of the way in which 'The Light' led to the various testimonies of Friends, such as opposition to paying tithes, to oaths, to war, and to salutations addressed to 'superiors'. He discusses positive practices such as simplicity, using the 'plain language', and seeking marriage partners exclusively among the membership. He points out that these testimonies prevented Friends from engaging in recreations which distract a person from righteous living and from celebrating holy days and public celebrations. In short, Penn sought in this slender publication to outline the faith and practice of Friends. While it was not widely read, it went through three printings in the next six years and was later translated into German and Welsh.

A Brief Account of the Rise and Progress of the People, Called Quakers has been much more popular, with thirty printings over the years, and is currently in print. It has also been translated into French, German, Welsh and Danish. Although it was written as a Preface to George Fox's *Journal*, it does not focus on him until the penultimate chapter. Penn begins with a brief survey of the history of Christianity up to, and including, the various Protestant sects in English history. The second chapter is given over to a description of the rise of Quakerism in which Penn tries again to show how it developed in the mainstream of Christianity. He writes once more of the 'Christ Within' and of the importance of continuing revelation. He also relates the various testimonies of Friends.

In the third and fourth chapters he discusses the Friends' beliefs and practices more fully, including the belief that all may respond to the 'Inward Light', and thus all may minister to others, not only those ordained by church authority. He also describes the organization and structure of Quaker business meetings, beginning at the local meeting and working up to the yearly meeting. However, he stresses that these are meetings for worship in which business is conducted, that decisions are made under divine guidance and not by mere human authority. He also explains the way in which such sessions might discipline those who fail to live in accordance with the faith and practice of Friends.

In Chapter V Penn concentrates on George Fox, outlining his early life before describing his part in the beginning of the Quaker movement. He expresses great admiration for Fox's character, integrity, bravery, and good judgment. In many ways Fox was a father figure for Penn, filling the void left by his natural father whose own strong personality often went completely counter to that of the Quaker. Penn emphasizes Fox's knowledge of the Scriptures and his power in prayer. He concludes the chapter with the phrase, 'Dear George, Thou excellest them all'. In his final chapter Penn exhorts both Friends and others to be guided by the words he has written, by the spirit which lay behind the words, and by the example of the life of this good man, chosen by God to lead and inspire.

EDWIN B. BRONNER

NOTES ON THE INTRODUCTION

1. For biographies of Penn, see: William I. Hull, *William Penn: A Topical Biography* (London, 1937), and Catherine Owens Peare, *William Penn* (Philadelphia, 1956).

2. Much of this section relies on ' "Truth Exalted" Through the Printed Word', in Volume 5 of *The Papers of William Penn*, by Edwin B. Bronner and David Fraser, *William Penn's Published Writings, 1660–1726* (Philadelphia, 1986), pp. 25–45.

3. *William Penn An Essay Towards the Present and Future Peace of Europe* (Hildesheim, Germany, 1983), p. viii.

4. For additional bibliographical information see: Bronner and Fraser, Volume 5, *The Papers of William Penn*, a) *An Essay*, #95, p. 396; b) *Some Fruits*, #96, p. 401; c) *More Fruits*, #125, p. 493; d) *Fruits of a Father's Love*, #134, p. 514; e) *A Letter from Penn*, #67, p. 298; f) *The People's Liberty*, #10, p. 118; g) *Great Case of Liberty*, #9, p. 112; h) *Perswasive to Moderation*, #72, p. 316; i) *Primitive Christianity Revived*, #105, p. 454; j) *Brief Account*, #98, p. 413. These entries have been used in writing these paragraphs.

5. Tolles and Gordon A. Alderfer (eds), *The Witness of William Penn* (New York, 1957), pp. 163–165.

6. *William Penn on Religion and Ethics* (Lewiston, Maine, 1991), p. 413.

NOTE ON THE TEXTS

Each of the ten essays included in this volume was printed as a separate title between the years 1670 and 1702 except for *Fruits of a Father's Love*, which first appeared in 1726, although it was probably written in 1699. All of them were printed by Andrew Sowle, or his descendants, except for *An Essay Towards the Present and Future Peace of Europe*, which Penn did not regard as a Quaker publication.

However, the texts in the present book were taken from a two-volume folio set edited by Joseph Besse in 1726 entitled *A Collection of the Works of William Penn* . . . (London), who used the latest printing, believing he would get the best text that way. (We actually used a 1974 reprint of these volumes, published by the AMS Press.)

The essays in Part I were copied without any changes. While *The Essay Towards Peace* was not listed in the Table of Contents in *Works*, it is printed in Volume II, 838–848. In Part II, the Appendix in *The People's Ancient and Just Liberties* is omitted, the Postscript of *The Great Case of Liberty of Conscience* is omitted, and the Conclusion of *A Perswasive to Moderation* is also omitted. These sections do not add greatly to the body of the texts. The two essays in Part III are printed exactly as they appeared in *Works*. *A Brief Account of the Rise and Progress of the People, Called Quakers* was originally written as the Preface to the *Journal* of George Fox, founder of the Quakers. We have modernized capitalization, punctuation, and spelling.

THE PEACE OF EUROPE,
THE FRUITS OF SOLITUDE
AND OTHER WRITINGS

Part I
Essays for the General Reader

An ESSAY towards the *Present* and *Future* Peace of *Europe*, by the Eftablifhment of an *European* DYET, PARLIAMENT, or ESTATES.

Beati Pacifici.   *Cedant Arma Togæ.*

TO THE READER

Reader,

I have undertaken a subject that I am very sensible requires one of more sufficiency than I am master of to treat it, as, in truth, it deserves, and the groaning state of Europe calls for; but since bunglers may stumble upon the game, as well as masters, though it belongs to the skilful to hunt and catch it, I hope this essay will not be charged upon me for a fault, if it appear to be neither chimerical nor injurious, and may provoke abler pens to improve and perform the design with better judgment and success. I will say no more in excuse of my self for this undertaking but that it is the fruit of my solicitous thoughts for the peace of Europe, and they must want charity as much as the world needs quiet to be offended with me for so Pacific a proposal. Let them censure my management so they prosecute the advantage of the design; for 'till the millenary doctrine be accomplished, there is nothing appears to me so beneficial an expedient to the peace and happiness of this quarter of the world.

I. Of PEACE, and its Advantages

He must not be a man, but a statue of brass or stone, whose bowels do not melt when he beholds the bloody tragedies of this war, in Hungary, Germany, Flanders, Ireland, and at sea. The mortality of sickly and languishing camps and navies, and the mighty prey the devouring winds and waves have made upon ships and men since '88. And as this with reason ought to affect human nature, and deeply kindred, so there is something very moving that becomes prudent men to consider, and that is the vast charge that has accompanied that blood, and which makes no mean part of these tragedies; especially if they deliberate upon the uncertainty of the war, that they know not how or when it will end, and that the expense cannot be less, and the hazard is as great as before. So that in the contraries of peace we see the beauties and benefits of it; which under it, such is the unhappiness of mankind, we are too apt to nauseate, as the full stomach loathes the honey-comb; and like that unfortunate gentleman, that having a fine and a good woman to his wife, and searching his pleasure in forbidden and less agreeable company, said, when reproached with his neglect of better enjoyments, that he could love his wife of all women, if she were not his wife, though that increased his obligation to prefer her. It is a great mark of the corruption of our natures, and what ought to humble us extremely, and excite the exercise of our reason to a nobler and juster sense, that we cannot see the use and pleasure of our comforts but by the want of them. As if we could not taste the benefit of health, but by the help of sickness; nor understand the satisfaction of fulness without the instruction of want; nor, finally, know the comfort of peace but by the smart and penance of the vices of war: And without dispute that is not the least reason that God is pleased to chastise us so frequently with it. What can we desire better than peace, but the grace to use it? Peace preserves our possessions; we are in no danger of invasions: our trade is free and safe, and we rise and lie down without anxiety. The rich bring out their hoards, and employ the poor manufacturers: buildings and diverse projections, for profit and pleasure, go on: it excites industry, which brings wealth, as that gives the means of charity and hospitality, not the lowest ornaments of a kingdom or common-wealth. But war, like the frost of '83, seizes all these comforts at once, and stops the civil channel of society. The rich draw in their stock, the poor turn soldiers, or thieves, or starve: no industry, no building, no manufactury, little hospitality or charity; but what the peace gave, the war devours. I need say no more upon this head, when the advantages of peace, and mischiefs of war are so many and sensible to every capacity under all governments, as either of them prevails. I shall proceed to the next point. What is the best means of peace, which will conduce much to open my way to what I have to propose.

II. Of the Means of Peace, which is Justice rather than War

As justice is a preserver, so it is a better procurer of peace than war. Though pax quæritur bello, be an usual saying, peace is the end of war, and as such it was taken up by O.C. for his motto: yet the use generally made of that expression shows us, that properly and truly speaking, men seek their wills by war rather than peace, and that as they will violate it to obtain them, so they will hardly be brought to think of peace, unless their appetites be some way gratified. If we look over the stories of all times, we shall find the aggressors generally moved by ambition; the pride of conquest and greatness of dominion more than right. But as those leviathans appear rarely in the world, so I shall anon endeavour to make it evident they had never been able to devour the peace of the world, and engross whole countries as they have done, if the proposal I have to make for the benefit of our present age had been then in practice. The advantage that justice has upon war is seen by the success of embassies, that so often prevent war by hearing the pleas and memorials of justice in the hands and mouths of the wronged party. perhaps it may be in a good degree owing to reputation or poverty, or some particular interest or convenience of princes and states, as much as justice, but it is certain, that as war cannot in any sense be justified, but upon wrongs received, and right, upon complaint, refused; so the generality of wars have their rise from some such pretension. This is better seen and understood at home; for that which prevents a civil war in a nation, is that which may prevent it abroad, viz. justice; and we see where that is notably obstructed, war is kindled between the magistrates and people in particular kingdoms and states; which, however it may be unlawful on the side of the people, we see never fails to follow, and ought to give the same caution to princes as if it were the right of the people to do it: Though I must needs say, the remedy is almost ever worse than the disease: the aggressors seldom getting what they seek, or performing, if they prevail, what they promised. And the blood and poverty that usually attend the enterprise, weigh more on earth, as well as in heaven, that what they lost or suffered, or what they get by endeavouring to mend their condition, comes to: which disappointment seems to be the voice of heaven, and judgment of God against those violent attempts. But to return, I say, justice is the means of peace, betwixt the government and the people, and one man and company and another. It prevents strife, and at last ends it : for besides shame or fear, to contend longer, he or they being under government, are constrained to bound their desires and resentment with the satisfaction the law gives. Thus peace is maintained by justice, which is a fruit of government, as government, is from society, and society from consent.

III. GOVERNMENT, its Rise and End under all Models

Government is an expedient against confusion; a restraint upon all disorder; just weights and an even balance: that one may not injure another, nor himself, by intemperance.

This was at first without controversy, patrimonial, and upon the death of the father or head of the family, the eldest son, or male of kin succeeded. But time breaking in upon this way of governing, as the world multiplied, it fell under other claims and forms; and is as hard to trace to its original, as are the copies we have of the first writings of sacred or civil matters. It is certain the most natural and human is that of consent, for that binds freely (as I may say) when men hold their liberty by true obedience to rules of their own making. No man is judge in his own cause, which ends the confusion and blood of so many judges and executioners. For out of society every man is his own king, does what he lists, at his own peril. But when he comes to incorporate himself, he submits that royalty to the conveniency of the whole, from whom he receives the returns of protection. So that he is not now his own judge nor avenger, neither is his antagonist, but the law, in indifferent hands between both. And if he be servant to others that before was free, he is also served of others that formerly owed him no obligation. Thus while we are not our own, every body is ours, and we get more than we lose, the safety of the society being the safety of the particulars that constitute it. So that while we seem to submit to, and hold all we have from society, it is by society that we keep what we have.

Government then is the prevention or cure of disorder, and the means of justice, as that is of peace: For this cause they have sessions, terms, assizes and parliaments, to over-rule men's passions and resentments, that they may not be judges in their own cause, nor punishers of their own wrongs, which as it is very incident to men in their corrupt state, so for that reason, they would observe no measure; nor on the other hand would any be easily reduced to their duty. Not that men know not what is right, their excesses, and wherein they are to blame,: by no means; nothing is plainer to them: but so depraved is human nature, that without compulsion, some way or other, too many would not readily be brought to do what they know is right and fit, or avoid what they are satisfied they should not do: which brings me near to the point I have undertaken; and for the better understanding of which, I have thus briefly treated of peace, justice and government, as a necessary introduction, because the ways and methods by which peace is preserved in particular governments, will help those readers, most concerned in my proposal, to conceive with what ease as well as advantage the peace of Europe might be procured and kept; which is the end designed by me, with all submission to those interested in this little treatise.

IV. Of a General Peace, or the Peace of Europe, and the Means of it

In my first section, I showed the desirableness of peace; in my next, the truest means of it; to wit, justice, not war. And in my last, that this justice was the fruit of government, as government itself was the result of society, which first came from a reasonable design in men of peace. Now if the sovereign princes of Europe, who represent that society, or independent state of men that was previous to the obligations of society, would, for the same reason that engaged men first into society, viz. love of peace and order, agree to meet by their stated deputies in a general diet, estates, or parliament, and there establish rules of justice for sovereign princes to observe one to another; and thus to meet yearly, or once in two or three years at farthest, or as they shall see cause, and to be styled, the sovereign or imperial diet, parliament, or state of Europe; before which sovereign assembly, should be brought all differences depending between one sovereign and another, that cannot be made up by private embassies, before the sessions begin; and that if any of the sovereignties that constitute these imperial states, shall refuse to submit their claim or pretensions to them, or to abide and perform the judgment thereof, and seek their remedy by arms, or delay their compliance beyond the time prefixed in their resolutions, all the other sovereignties, united as one strength, shall compel the submission and performance of the sentence, with damages to the suffering party, and charges to the sovereignties that obliged their submission: to be sure Europe would quietly obtain the so much desired and needed peace, to her harrassed inhabitants; no sovereignty in Europe, having the power, and therefore cannot show the will to dispute the conclusion; and, consequently, peace would be procured, and continued in Europe.

V. Of the Causes of Difference, and Motives to Violate Peace

There appears to me but three things upon which peace is broken, viz. to keep, to recover, or to add. First, to keep what is one's right, from the invasion of an enemy; in which I am purely defensive. secondly, to recover, when I think my self strong enough, that which by violence, I, or my ancestors have lost, by the arms of a stronger power; in which I am offensive: or, lastly, to increase my dominion by the acquisition of my neighbour's countries, as I find them weak, and my self strong. To gratify which passion, there will never want some accident or other for a pretence: and knowing my own strength, I will be my own judge and carver. This last will find no room in the imperial states. They are an unpassable limit to that ambition. But the other two may come as soon as they please, and find the justice of that sovereign court. And considering how few there are of those sons of prey, and how early they show themselves, it may be not once in an age or two, this expedition being established, the balance cannot well be broken.

VI. Of Titles, upon which those Differences may arise

But I easily foresee a question that may be answered in our way, and that is this; what is right? or else we can never know what is wrong: it is very fit that this should be established. But that is fitter for the sovereign states to resolve than me. And yet that I may lead a way to the matter, I say that title is either by a long and undoubted succession, as the crowns of Spain, France and England; or by election, as the crown of Poland, and the Empire; or by marriage, as the family of the Stewarts came by England; the Elector of Brandenburgh, to the Dutchy of Cleve; and we, in ancient time, to divers places abroad; or by purchase, as hath been frequently done in Italy and Germany; or by conquest, as the Turk in Christendom, and Spaniards in Flanders, formerly mostly in the French hands; and the French in Burgundy, Normandy, Lorrain, French-County, etc. This last, title is, morally speaking, only questionable. It has indeed obtained a place among the rolls of titles, but it was engrossed and recorded by the point of the sword, and in bloody characters. What cannot be controlled or resisted, must be submitted to; but all the world knows the date of the length of such Empires, and that they expire with the power of the possessor to defend them. And yet there is a little allowed to conquest to, when it has the sanction of articles of peace to confirm it: though that hath not always extinguished the fire, but it lies, like embers under ashes, ready to kindle so soon as there is a fit matter prepared for it. Nevertheless, when conquest has been confirmed by a treaty, and conclusion of peace, I must confess it is an adopted title; and if not so genuine and natural, yet being engrafted, it is fed by that which is the security of better titles, consent. There is but one thing more to be mentioned in this section, and that is from what time titles shall take their beginning, or how far back we may look to confirm or dispute them. It would be very bold and inexcusable in me, to determine so tender a point, but be it more or less time, as to the last general peace at Nimeguen, or to the commencing of this war, or to the time of the beginning of the treaty of peace, I must submit it to the great pretenders and masters in that affair. But something every body must be willing to give or quit, that he may keep the rest, and by this establishment, be for ever freed of the necessity of losing more.

VII. *Of the Composition of these Imperial States*

The composition and proportion of this sovereign part, or imperial state does, at the first look, seem to carry with it no small difficulty what votes to allow for the inequality of the princes and states. But with submission to better judgments, I cannot think it invincible: for if it be possible to have an estimate of the yearly value of the several sovereign countries, whose delegates are to make up this august assembly, the determination of the number of persons or votes in the states for every sovereignty, will not be impracticable. Now that England, France, Spain, the Empire, etc. may be pretty exactly estimated, is so plain a case, by considering the revenue of lands, the exports and entries at the custom houses, the books of rates, and surveys that are in all governments, to proportion taxes for the support of them, that the least inclination to the peace of Europe, will not stand or halt at this objection. I will, with pardon on all sides, give an instance far from exact; nor do I pretend to it, or offer it for an estimate; for I do it at random: only this, as wide as it is from the just proportion, will give some aim to my judicious reader, what I would be at: remembering, I design not by any computation, as estimate from the revenue of the prince, but the value of the territory, the whole being concerned as well as the prince. And a juster measure it is to go by, since one prince may have more revenue than another, who has much a richer country: though in the instance I am now about to make, the caution is not so necessary, because, as I said before, I pretend to no manner of exactness, but go wholly by guess, being but for example's sake. I suppose the empire of Germany to send twelve; France, ten; Spain, ten; Italy, which comes to France, eight; England, six; Portugal, three; Sweedland, four; Denmark, three; Poland, four; Venice, three; the Seven Provinces, four; The Thirteen Cantons, and little neighbouring sovereignties, two; dukedoms of Holstein and Courland, one: and if the Turks and Muscovites are taken in, as seems but fit and just, they will make ten a piece more. The whole makes ninety. A great presence when they represent the fourth; and now the best and wealthiest part of the known world; where religion and learning, civility and arts have their seat and empire. But it is not absolutely necessary there should be always so many persons, to represent the larger sovereignties; for the votes may be given by one man of any sovereignty, as well as by ten or twelve: though the fuller the assembly of states is, the more solemn, effectual, and free the debates will be, and the resolutions must needs come with greater autority. The place of their first session should be central, as much as is possible, afterwards as they agree.

VIII. Of the Regulation of the Imperial States in Session

To avoid quarrel for precedency, the room may be round, and have divers doors to come in and go out at, to prevent exceptions. If the whole number be cast into tens, each choosing one, they may preside by turns, to whom all speeches should be addressed, and who should collect the sense of the debates, and state the question of a vote, which, in my opinion, should be by the ballot, after the prudent and commendable method of the Venetians. Which in a great degree, prevents the ill effects of corruption; because if any of the delegates of that high and mighty estates could be so vile, false, and dishonourable, as to be influenced by money, they have the advantage of taking their money that will give it them, and of voting undiscovered to the interest of their principals, and their own inclinations; as they that do understand the balloting box do very well know. A shrewd stratagem, and an experimental remedy against corruption, at least corrupting: for who will give their money where they may so easily be cozened, and where it is two to one they will be so; for they that will take money in such cases, will not stick to lie heartily to them that gave it, rather than wrong their country, when they know their lie cannot be detected.

It seems to me, that nothing is this imperial parliament should pass, but by three quarters of the whole, at least seven above the balance. I am sure it helps to prevent treachery, because if money could ever be a temptation in such a court, it would cost a great deal of money to weigh down the wrong scale. All complaints should be delivered in writing, in the nature of memorials; and journals kept by a proper person, in a trunk or chest, which should have as many differing locks, as there are tens in the states. And if there were a clerk for each ten, and a pew or table for those clerks in the assembly; and at the end of every session, one out of each ten, were appointed to examine and compare the journal of those clerks, and then lock them up as I have before expressed, it would be clear and satisfactory. And each sovereignty if they please, as is but very fit, may have an exemplification, or copy of the said memorials, and the journals of proceedings upon them. The liberty and rules of speech, to be sure, they cannot fail in, who will be the wisest and noblest of each sovereignty, for its own honour and safety. If any difference can arise between those that come from the same sovereignty, that then one of the major number do give the balls of that sovereignty. I should think it extremely necessary, that every sovereignty should be present under great penalties, and that none leave the session without leave, till all be finished; and that neutralities in debates should by no means be endured: for any such latitude will quickly open a way to unfair proceedings, and be followed by a train, both of seen, and unseen inconveniencies. I will say little of the language in which the session of the sovereign estates should be held, but to be sure it must be in Latin or French; the first would be very well for civilians, but the last most easy for men of quality

IX. Of the Objections that may be Advanced Against the Design

I will first give an answer to the objections that may be offered against my proposal: and in my next and last section, I shall endeavour to show some of the manifold coveniences that would follow this European League, or Confederacy.

The first of them is this, that the strongest and richest sovereignty will never agree to it, and if it should, there would be danger of corruption more than of force one time or other. I answer to the first part, he is not stronger than all the rest, and for that reason you should promote this, and compel him into it, especially before he be so, for then, it will be too late to deal with such an one. To the last part of the objection, I say the way is as open now as then; and it may be the number fewer, and as easily come at. However, if men of sense and honour, and substance, are chosen, they will either scorn the baseness, or have wherewith to pay for the knavery: at least they may be watched so that one may be a check upon the other, and all prudently limited by the sovereignty they represent. In all great points, especially before a final resolve, they may be obliged to transmit to their principals, the merits of such important cases depending, and receive their last instructions: which may be done in four and twenty days at the most, as the place of their session may be appointed.

The second is, that it will endanger an effeminacy of such a disuse of the trade of soldiery: that if there should be any need for it, upon any occasion, we should be at a loss as they were in Holland in '72.

There can be no danger of effeminacy, because each sovereignty may introduce as temperate or severe a discipline in the education of youth, as they please, by low living, and due labour. Instruct them in mechanical knowledge, and in natural philosophy, by operation, which is the honour of the German nobility: This would make them men: neither women nor lions: for soldiers are the other extreme to effeminacy. But the knowledge of nature, and the useful as well as agreeable operations of art, give men an understanding of themselves, of the world they are born into, how to be useful and serviceable, both to themselves and others; and how to save and help, not injure or destroy. The knowledge of government in general; the particular constitutions of Europe; and above all, of his own country, are very recommending accomplishments. This fits him for the Parliament, and Council at home, and the courts of princes and services in the Imperial States abroad. At least, he is a good commonwealthsman, and can be useful to the public, or retire, as there may be occasion.

To the other part of the objection, of being at a loss for soldiery as they were in Holland in '72. The proposal answers for it self. One has war no more than the other; and will be as much to seek upon occasion. Nor is it to be thought that any one will keep up such an army after such an Empire is on foot, which may hazard the safety of the rest. However, it if be seen requisite, the question may be asked, by order of the sovereign states, why such an one either raises or keeps up a formidable body of troops, and he obliged forthwith to reform or reduce them; lest any one, by keeping up a great body of troops, should surprise a neighbour. But a small force in every other sovereignty, as it is capable or accustomed to maintain, will certainly prevent that danger and vanquish any such fear.

The third objection is, that there will be great want of employment for younger brothers of families; and that the poor must either turn soldiers or thieves. I have answered that in my return to the second objection. We shall have the more merchants and husbandmen, or ingenious naturalists, if the government be but any thing solicitous of the education of their youth: Which, next to the present and immediate happiness of any country, ought of all things, to be the care and skill of the government. For such as the youth of any country is bred, such is the next generation, and the government in good or bad hands.

I am come now to the last objection, that sovereign princes and states will hereby become not sovereign; a thing they will never endure. But this also, under correction, is a mistake, for they remain as sovereign at home as ever they were. Neither their power over their people, nor the usual revenue they pay them, is diminished: it may be the war establishment may be reduced, which will indeed of course follow, or be better employed to the advantage of the public. So that the sovereignties are as they were, for none of them have now any sovereignty over one another: and if this be called a lessening of their power, it must be only because the great fish can no longer eat up the little ones, and that each sovereignty is equally defended from injuries, and disabled from committing them: cedant arma togæ is a glorious sentence; the voice of the dove; the olive branch of peace. A blessing so great, that when it pleases God to chastise us severely for our sins, it is with the rod of war, that, for the most part, He whips us: and experience tells us none leaves deeper marks behind it.

X. *Of the real Benefits that flow from this Proposal about Peace*

I am come to my last section, in which I shall enumerate some of those many real benefits that flow from this proposal, for the present and future peace of Europe.

Let it not, I pray, be the least, that it prevents the spilling of so much human and Christian blood: for a thing so offensive to God, and terrible and afflicting to men, as that has ever been, must recommend our expedient beyond all objections. For what can a man give in exchange for his life, as well as soul ? And though the chiefest in government are seldom personally exposed, yet it is a duty incumbent upon them to be tender of the lives of their people, since without all doubt, they are accountable to God for the blood that is spilt in their service. So that besides the loss of so many lives, of importance to any government, both for labour and propagation, the cries of so many widows, parents and fatherless are prevented, that cannot be very pleasant in the ears of any government, and is the natural consequence of war in all government.

There is another manifest benefit which redounds to Christendom, by this peaceable expedient, the reputation of Christianity will in some degree be recovered in the sight of infidels ; which, by the many bloody and unjust wars of Christians, not only with them, but one with another, has been greatly impaired. For, to the scandal of that holy profession, Christians, that glory in their Saviour's name, have long devoted the credit and dignity of it, to their worldly passions, as often as they have been excited by the impulses of ambition or revenge. They have not always been in the right : nor has right been the reason of war : and not only Christians against Christians, but the same sort of Christians have embrewed their hands in one another's blood : invoking and interesting, all they could, the good and merciful God to prosper their arms to their brethren's destruction : yet their Saviour has told them, that He came to save, and not to destroy the lives of men : To give and plant peace among men : and if in any sense He may be said to send war, it is the holy war indeed ; for it is against the devil, and not the persons of men. Of all His titles this seems the most glorious as well as comfortable for us, that He is the prince of peace. It is His nature, His office, His work and the end and excellent blessing of His coming, who is both the maker and preserver of our peace with God. And it is very remarkable, that in all the New Testament He is but once called lion, but frequently the Lamb of God ; to denote to us His gentle, meek and harmless nature; and that those, who desire to be the disciples of His Cross and Kingdom, for they are inseparable, must be like Him, as St Paul, St Peter and St John tell us. Nor is it said the Lamb shall lie down with the lion, but the lion shall lie down with the lamb. That is, war shall yield to peace, and the soldier turn hermit. To be sure, Christians should not be apt to strive, nor swift to anger against any body, and less with one another, and least of all for the uncertain and fading enjoyments of this lower world: and no quality is exempted from this doctrine. Here is a wide field for the Reverend clergy of Europe to act their part in, who have so much the possession of princes and people too. May they recommend and labour this pacific means I offer, which will end blood, if not strife; and then reason, upon free debate, will be judge, and not the sword. So that both right and peace, which are the desire and fruit of wise governments, and the choice blessings of any country, seem to succeed the establishment of this proposal.

The third benefit is, that is saves money, both to the prince and people; and thereby prevents those grudgings and misunderstandings between them that are wont to follow the devouring expenses of war; and enables both to perform public acts for learning, charity, manufactures, etc. The virtues of government and ornaments of countries. Nor is this all the advantage that follows to sovereignties, upon this head of money and good husbandry, to whose service and happiness that short discourse is dedicated; for it saves the great expense that frequent and splendid embassies require, and all their appendages of spies and intelligence, which in the most prudent governments, have devoured mighty sums of money; and that not without some immoral practices also: such as corrupting of servants to betray their masters, by revealing their secrets; not to be defended by Christian, or old Roman virtue. But here, where there is nothing to fear, there is little to know, and therefore the purchase is either cheap, or may be wholly spared. I might mention pensions to the widows and orphans of such as die in wars, and of those that have been disabled in them; which rise high in the revenue of some countries.

Our fourth advantage is, that the towns, cities and countries, that might be laid waste by the rage of war, are thereby preserved: a blessing that wuld be very well understood in Flanders and Hungary, and indeed upon all the borders of sovereignties, which are almost ever the stages of spoil and misery; of which the stories of

England and Scotland do sufficiently inform us without looking over the water.

The fifth benefit of this peace, is the ease and security of travel and traffic: an happiness never understood since the Roman Empire has been broken into so many sovereignties. But we may easily conceive the comfort and advantage of travelling through the governments of Europe, by a pass from any of the sovereignties of it, which this league and state of peace will naturally make authentic. They that have travelled Germany, where is so great a number of sovereignties, know the want and value of this priviledge, by the many stops and examinations they meet with by the way: But especially such as have made the great tour of Europe. This leads to the benefit of an universal monarchy, without the inconveniences that attend it: for when the whole was one Empire, though these advantages were enjoyed, yet the several provinces, that now make the Kingdoms and States of Europe, were under some hardship from the great sums of money remitted to the imperial seat, and the ambition and avarice of their several proconsuls and governors, and the great taxes they paid to the numerous legions of soldiers, that they maintained for their own subjection, who were not wont to entertain that concern for them (being uncertainly there, and having their fortunes to make) which their respective and proper sovereigns have always shown for them. So that to be ruled by native princes or states, with the advantage of that peace and security that can only render an universal monarchy desirable, is peculiar to our proposal, and for that reason it is to be preferred.

Another advantage is, the great security it will be to Christians against the inroads of the Turk, in their most prosperous fortune. For it had been impossible for the port, to have prevailed so often, and so far upon Christendom but by the carelesness, or wilful connivence, if not aid, of some Christian princes. And for the same reason, why no Christian monarch will adventure to oppose, or break such an union, The Grand Seignior will find himself obliged to concur, for the security of what he holds in Europe: where, with all his strength, he would feel it an over-match for him. The prayers, tears, treason, blood and devastation, that war has cost in Christendom, for these two last ages especially, must add to the credit of our proposal, and the blessing of the peace thereby humbly recommended.

The seventh advantage, of an European, imperial diet, parliament, or estates is, that it will beget and increase personal friendship between princes and states, which tends to the rooting up of wars, and planting peace in a deep and fruitful soil. For princes have the curiosity of seeing the courts and cities of other countries, as well as private men, if they could as securely and familiarly gratify their inclinations. It were a great motive to the tranquility of the world, that they could freely converse face to face, and personally and reciprocally give and receive marks of civility and kindness. An hospitability that leaves these impressions behind it, will hardly let ordinary matters prevail, to mistake or quarrel one another. Their emulation would be in the instances of goodness, laws, customs, learning, arts, buildings; and in particular those that relate to charity, the true glory of some governments, where beggars are as much a rarity, as in other places it would be to see none.

Nor is this all the benefit that would come by this freedom and interview of princes: for natural affection would hereby be preserved, which we see little better than lost, from the time their children, or sisters, are married into other courts. For the present state and insincerity of princes forbid them the enjoyment of that natural comfort which is possessed by private families: insomuch, that from the time a daughter, or sister, is married to another crown, nature is submitted to interest, and that, for the most part, grounded not upon solid or commendable foundations, but ambition, or unjust avarice. I say, this freedom, that is the effect of our pacific proposal, restores nature to her just right and dignity in the families of princes, and them to the comfort she brings, wherever she is preserved in her proper station. Here daughters may personally intreat their parents, and sisters, their brothers, for a good understanding between them and their husbands, where Nature, not crushed by absence, and sinister interests, but acting by the sight and lively entreaties of such near relations, is almost sure to prevail. They cannot easily resist the most affectionate addresses of such powerful solicitors, as their children, and grandchildren, and their sisters, nephews, and neices: and so backward from children to parents, and sisters to brothers, to keep up and preserve their own families, by a good understanding between their husbands and them.

To conclude this section, there is yet another manifest privilege that follows this intercourse and good understanding, which methinks should be very moving with princes, viz. that hereby they may choose wives for themselves, such as they love, and not by proxy, merely to gratify interest; an ignoble motive; and that rarely begets, or continues that kindness which ought to be between men and their wives. A satisfaction very few princes ever knew, and to which all other pleasures ought to resign. Which has often obliged me to think, that the advantage of private men upon princes, by family comforts, is a sufficient balance against their greater power and glory: the one being more in imagination, than real; and often unlawful; but the other, natural, solid, and commendable. Besides, it is certain, parents loving well before they are married, which very rarely happens to princes, has kind and generous influences upon their offspring: which, with their example, makes them better husbands, and wives, in their turn. This, in great measure, prevents unlawful love, and the mischiefs of those intrigues that are wont to follow them: what hatred, feuds, wars, and desolations have, in divers ages, flown from unkindness between princes and their wives? What unnatural divisions among their children, and ruin to their families, if not loss of their countries by it? Behold an expedient to prevent it, a natural and efficacious one: happy to princes, and happy to their people also. For nature being renewed and strengthened by these mutual pledges and endearments, I have mentioned, will leave those soft and kind impressions behind in the minds of princes, that court and country will very easily discern and feel the good effects of: especially if they have the wisdom to show that they interest themselves in the prosperity of the children and relations of their princes. For it does not only incline them to be good, but engage those relations to become powerful suitors to their princes for them, if any misunderstanding should unhappily arise between them and their sovereigns: thus ends this section. It now rests to conclude the discourse, in which, if I have not pleased my reader, or answered his expectation, it is some comfort to me I meant well, and have cost him but little money and time; and brevity is an excuse, if not a virtue, where the subject is not agreeable, or is but ill prosecuted.

THE CONCLUSION

I will conclude this my proposal of an European, sovereign, or imperial diet, parliament, or estates, with that which I have touched upon before, and which falls under the notice of every one concerned, by coming home to their particular and respective experience within their own sovereignties. That by the same rules of justice and prudence, by which parents and masters govern their families, and magistrates their cities, and estates their republics, and princes and kings their principalities and kingdoms, Europe may obtain and preserve peace among her sovereignties. For wars are the duels of princes; and as government in kingdoms and states, prevents men being judges and executioners for themselves, over-rules private passions as to injuries or revenge, and subjects the great as well as the small to the rule of justice, that power might not vanquish or oppress right, nor one neighbour act an indepen-dency and sovereignty upon another, while they have resigned that original claim to the benefit and comfort of society; so this being soberly weighed in the whole, and parts of it, it will not be hard to conceive or frame, not yet to execute the design I have here proposed.

And for the better understanding and perfecting of the idea, I here present to the sovereign princes and estates of Europe, for the safety and tranquility of it, I must recommend to their perusals, Sir William Temple's account of the United Provinces; which is an instance and answer, upon practice, to all the objections that can be advanced against the practicability of my proposal: nay, it is an experiment that not only comes to our case, but exceeds the difficulties that can render its accomplishment disputable. For there we shall find three degrees of sovereignties to make up every sovereignty in the general states. I will reckon them backwards: first, the states general themselves; then the immediate sovereignties that constitute them, which are those of the provinces, answerable to the sovereignties of Europe, that by their deputies are to compose the European diet, parliament, or estates, in our proposal: and then there are the several cities of each province, that are so many independent or distinct sovereignties, which compose those of the provinces, as those of the provinces do compose the states general at the Hague.

But I confess I have the passion to wish heartily, that the honour of proposing and effecting so great and good a design, might be owing to England, of all the countries in Europe, as something of the nature of our expedient was, in design and preparation, to the wisdom, justice, and valour, of Henry the Fourth of France, whose superior qualities raising his character above those of his ancestors, or contemporaries, deservedly gave him the style of Henry the Great. For he was upon obliging the princes and estates of Europe to a politic balance, when the Spanish faction, for that reason, contrived, and accomplished his murder, by the hands of Revilliac. I will not then fear to be censured, for proposing an expedient for the present and future peace of Europe, when it was not only the design, but glory of one of the greatest princes that ever reigned in it; and is found practicable in the constitution of one of the wisest and most powerfull states of it. So that to conclude, I have very little to answer for in all this affair; because, if it succeed, I have so little to deserve: for this great king's example tells us it is fit to be done; and Sir William Temple's history shows us, by a surprising instance, that it may be done; and Europe, by her incomparable miseries, makes it now necessary to be done; that my share is only thinking of it at this juncture, and putting it into the common light for the peace and prosperity of Europe.

Some Fruits of SOLITUDE,

IN

Reflections and Maxims. relating
to the Conduct of Human Life.

THE PREFACE

Reader,

This enchiridion I present thee with, is the Fruit of Solitude: A school few care to learn in, though none instructs us better. Some parts of it are the result of serious reflection: others the flashings of lucid intervals: written for private satisfaction, and now published for a help to human conduct.

The author blesseth God for his retirement, and kisses that gentle hand which led him into it: for though it should prove barren to the world, it can never do so to him.

He has now had some time he could call his own; a property he was never so much master of before: in which he has taken a view of himself and the world; and observed wherein he hath hit and missed the mark: what might have been done, what mended, and what avoided in his human conduct: together with the omissions and excesses of others, as well societies and governments, as private families, and persons. And he verily thinks, were he to live over his life again, he could not only, with God's grace, serve Him, but his neighbour and himself, better than hath done, and have seven years of his time to spare. And yet perhaps he hath not been the worst or the idlest man in the world, nor is he the oldest. And this is the rather said, that it might quicken, thee, reader, to lose none of the time that is yet thine.

There is nothing of which we are apt to be so lavish as of time, and about which we ought to be more solicitous; since without it we can do nothing in this world. Time is what we want most, but what, alas! we use worst; and for which God will certainly most strictly reckon with us, when time shall be no more.

It is of that moment to us in reference to both worlds, that I can hardly wish any man better, than that he would seriously consider what he does with his time: how and to what ends he employs it; and what returns he makes to God, his neighbour and himself for it. Will he never have a ledger for this? This, the greatest wisdom and work of life.

To come but once into the world, and trifle away our true enjoyment of it, and of our selves in it, is lamentable indeed. This one reflection would yield a thinking person great instruction. And since nothing below man can so think; man, in being thoughtless, must needs fall below himself. And that, to be sure, such do, as are unconcerned in the use of their most precious time.

This is but too evident, if we will allow our selves to consider, that there's hardly any thing we take by the right end, or improve to its just advantage.

We understand little of the works of God, either in nature or grace. We pursue false knowledge, and mistake education extremely. We are violent in our affections, confused and unmethodical in our whole life; making that a burden which was given for a blessing; and so of little comfort to our selves or others: misapprehending the true notion of happiness, and so missing of the right use of life and way of happy living.

And until we are persuaded to stop, and step a little aside, out of the noisy crowd and incumbering hurry of the world, and calmly take a prospect of things, it will be impossible we should be able to make a right judgment of our selves, or know our own misery. But after we have made the just reckonings which retirement will help us to, we shall begin to think the world in great measure mad, and that we have been in a sort of Bedlam all this while.

Reader, whether young or old, think it not too soon or too late to turn over the leaves of thy past life: and be sure to fold down where any passage of it may affect thee: and bestow thy remainder of time, to correct those faults in thy future conduct: be it in relation to this or the next life. What thou wouldst do, if what thou hast done were to do again, be sure to do as long as thou livest, upon the like occasions.

Our resolutions seem to be vigorous, as often as we reflect upon our past errors; but, alas! they are apt to flat again upon fresh temptations to the same things.

The author does not pretend to deliver thee an exact piece; his business not being ostentation, but charity. It is miscellaneous in

the matter of it, and by no means artificial in the composure. But it
contains hints, that may serve thee for texts to preach to thy self
upon and which comprehend much of the Course of Human Life:
since whether thou art parent *or* child, prince *or* subject, master *or*
servant, single *or* married, public *or* private, mean *or* honourable,
rich *or* poor, prosperous *or* improsperous, *in* peace *or* controversy,
in business *or* solitude: *whatever be thy inclination or aversion,*
practice or duty, thou wilt find something not unsuitably said for
thy direction and advantage. Accept and improve what deserves thy
notice; the rest excuse, and place to account of good will to thee
and the whole creation of God.

REFLECTIONS AND MAXIMS

1. **Ignorance.** It is admirable to consider how many millions of
people come into, and go out of the world, ignorant of themselves,
and of the world they have lived in.

2. If one went to see Windsor Castle, or Hampton Court it will
be strange not to observe and remember the situation, the building,
the gardens, fountains etc. that make up the beauty and pleasure
of such a seat: and yet few people know themselves: no, not
their own bodies, the houses of their minds, the most curious
structure of the world; a living walking tabernacle: nor the world
of which it was made and out of which it is fed; which would
be so much our benefit, as well as our pleasure, to know. We
cannot doubt of this when we are told that the invisible things of
God are brought to light by the things that are seen, and consequently we read our duty in them, as often as we look upon them,
to him that is the great and wise author of them if we look as we
should do.

3. The world is certainly a great and stately volume of natural
things; and may be not improperly styled the hieroglyphics of a
better: but, alas, how very few leaves of it we do seriously turn
over! This ought to be the subject of the education of our youth,
who, at twenty, when they should be fit for business, know little or
nothing of it.

4. **Education.** We are in pain to make them scholars, but not
men! To talk, rather than to know; which is true canting.

5. The first thing obvious to children is what is sensible: and
that we make no part of their rudiments.

6. We press their memory too soon, and puzzle, strain and load

them with words and rules; to know grammar and rhetoric, and a strange tongue or two, that it is ten to one may never be useful to them; leaving their natural genius to mechanical and physical or natural knowledge uncultivated and neglected; which would be of exceeding use and pleasure to them through the whole course of their life.

7. To be sure, languages are not to be despised or neglected. But things are still to be preferred.

8. Children had rather be making of tools and instruments of play; shaping, drawing, framing and building, &c. than getting some rules of propriety of speech by heart: and those also would follow with more judgment, and less trouble and time.

9. It were happy if we studied nature more in natural things; and acted according to nature; whose rules are few, plain and most reasonable.

10. Let us begin where she begins, go her pace, and close always where she ends, and we cannot miss of being good naturalists.

11. The creation would not be longer a riddle to us: the heavens, earth and waters, with their respective, various and numerous inhabitants: their production, natures, seasons, sympathies and antipathies; their use, benefit and pleasure, would be better understood by us: and an eternal wisdom, power, majesty and goodness, very conspicuous to us; through those sensible and passing forms: the world wearing the marks of it's maker, whose stamp is every where visible, and the characters very legible to the children of wisdom.

12. And it would go a great way to caution and direct people in their use of the world, that they were better studied and knowing in the creation of it.

13. For how could men find the confidence to abuse it, while they should see the great creator look them in the face, in all and every part thereof?

14. Therefore ignorance makes them insensible, and that insensibility hardly misusing this noble creation, that has the stamp and voice of a deity every where, and in every thing, to the observing.

15. It is pity therefore that books have not been composed for youth, by some curious and careful naturalists, and also mechanics, in the Latin tongue, to be used in schools, that they might learn things with words: things obvious and familiar to them, and which would make the tongue easier to be attained by them.

16. Many able gardeners and husbandmen are yet ignorant of

the reason of their calling; as most artificers are of the reason of their own rules that govern their excellent workmanship. But a naturalist and mechanic of this sort, is master of the reason of both, and might be of the practice too, if his industry kept pace with his speculation; which were very commendable; and without which he cannot be said to be a complete naturalist or mechanic.

17. Finally, if man be the index or epitomy of the world, as philosophers tell us, we have only to read our selves well to be learned in it. But because there is nothing we less regard than the character of the power that made us, which are so clearly written upon us and the world he has given us, and can best tell us what we are and should be, we are even strangers to our own genius: the glass in which we should see that true instructing and agreeable variety, which is to be observed in nature, to the admiration of that wisdom and adoration of that power which made us all.

18. **Pride.** And yet we are very apt to be full of our selves, instead of him that made what we so much value; and, but for whom we can have no reason to value our selves. For we have nothing that we can call our own, no, not our selves. For we are all but tenants, and at will too, of the great lord of our selves, and the rest of this great farm, the world that we live upon.

19. But methinks we cannot answer it to our selves as well as our maker, that we should live and die ignorant of our selves, and thereby of Him and the obligations we are under to Him for our selves.

20. If the worth of a gift sets the obligation, and directs the return of the party that receives it: he that is ignorant of it, will be at a loss to value it and the giver, for it.

21. Here is man in his ignorance of himself. He knows not how to estimate his creator, because he knows not how to value his creation. If we consider his make, and lovely compositure; the several stories of his lovely structure. His divers members, their order, function and dependency: the instruments of food, the vessels of digestion, the several transmutations it passes. And how nourishment is carried and diffused throughout the whole body, by most innate and imperceptible passages. How the animal spirit is thereby refreshed, and with an unspeakable dexterity and motion sets all parts at work to feed themselves. And last of all, how the rational soul is seated in the animal, as its proper house, as is the animal in the body: I say, if this rare fabric alone were but considered by us, with all the rest by which it is fed and comforted,

surely man would have a more reverent sense of the power, wisdom and goodness of God, and of that duty he owes to him for it. But if he would be acquainted with his own soul, its noble faculties, its union with the body, its nature and end, and the providences by which the whole frame of humanity is preserved, he would admire and adore his good and great God. But man is become a strange contradiction to himself; but it is of himself: not being by constitution, but corruption such.

22. He would have others obey him, even his own kind; but he will not obey God, that is so much above him, and who made him.

23. He will lose none of his authority: no, not bate an ace of it: he is humorous to his wife, he beats his children, is angry with his servants, strict with his neighbours, revenges all affronts to extremity; but, alas! forgets all the while that he is the man; and is more in arrear to God, that is so very patient with him, than they are to him with whom he is so strict and impatient.

24. He is curious to wash, dress and perfume his body, but careless of his soul. The one shall have many hours, the other not so many minutes. This shall have three or four new suits in a year, but that must wear its old clothes still.

25. If he be to receive or see a great man, how nice and anxious is he that all things be in order? And with what respect and address does he approach and make his court? but to God, how dry and formal and constrained in his devotion?

26. In his prayers he says, Thy will be done: but means his own: at least acts so.

27. It is too frequent to begin with God and end with the world. But He is the good man's beginning and end; his alpha and omega.

28. **Luxury.** Such is now become our delicacy, that we will not eat ordinary meat, nor drink small, palled liquor; we must have the best, and the best cooked for our bodies, while our souls feed on empty or corrupted things.

29. In short, man is spending all upon a bare house, and hath little or no furniture within to recommend it; which is preferring the cabinet before the jewel, a lease of seven years before an inheritance. So absurd a thing is man, after all his proud pretences to wit and understanding.

30. **Inconsideration.** The want of due consideration is the cause of all the unhappiness man brings upon himself. For his second thoughts rarely agree with his first, which pass not without a

considerable retrenchment or correction. And yet that sensible warning is, too frequently, not precaution enough for his future conduct.

31. Well may we say, our infelicity is of our selves; since there is nothing we do that we should not do, but we know it, and yet do it.

32. **Disappointment and Resignation.** For dissappointments, that come not by our own folly, they are the trials or correction of heaven: and it is our own fault, if they prove not our advantage.

33. To repine at them does not mend the matter: it is only to grumble to our creator. But to see the hand of God in them, with an humble submission to His will, is the way to turn our water into wine, and engage the greatest love and mercy on our side.

34. We must needs disorder our selves, if we only look at our losses. But if we consider how little we deserve what is left, our passion will cool, and our murmurs will turn into thankfulness.

35. If our hairs fall not to the ground, less do we or our substance without God's providence.

36. Nor can we fall below the arms of God, how low soever it be we fall.

37. For though our Saviour's passion is over, his compassion is not. That never fails his humble, sincere disciples: in him, they find more than all that they lose in the world.

38. **Murmuring.** Is it reasonable to take it ill, that any body desires of us that which is their own? All we have is the almighty's: and shall not God have his own when he calls for it?

39. Discontentedness is not only in such a case ingratitude, but injustice. For we are both unthankful for the time we had it, and not honest enough to restore it, if we could keep it.

40. But it is hard for us to look on things in such a glass, and at such a distance from this low world; and yet it is our duty, and would be our wisdom and our glory to do so.

41. **Censoriousness.** We are apt to be very pert at censuring others, where we will not endure advice our selves. And nothing shows our weakness more than to be so sharp-sighted at spying other men's faults, and so purblind about our own.

42. When the actions of a neighbour are upon the stage, we can have all our wits about us, are so quick and critical we can split an hair, and find out every failure and infirmity: but are without feeling, or have but very little sense of our own.

43. Much of this comes from ill nature, as well as from an

inordinate value of our selves: for we love rambling better than home, and blaming the unhappy, rather than covering and relieving them.

44. In such occasions, some shew their malice and are witty upon misfortunes; others their justice, they can reflect apace; but few or none their charity; especially if it be about money matters.

45. You shall see an old miser come forth with a set gravity, and so much severity against the distressed, to excuse his purse, that he will, ere he has done, put it out of all question. That riches is righteousness with him. This, says he, is the fruit of your prodigality (as if, poor man, covetousness were no fault) or, of your projects, or grasping after a great trade: while he himself would have done the same thing, but that he had not the courage to venture so much ready money out of his own trusty hands, though it had been to have brought him back the Indies in return. But the proverb is just, vice should not correct sin.

46. They have a right to censure, that have a heart to help: the rest is cruelty, not justice.

47. **Bounds of Charity.** Lend not beyond thy ability, nor refuse to lend out of thy ability; especially when it will help others more than it can hurt thee.

48. If thy debtor be honest and capable, thou hast thy money again, if not with encrease, with praise: if he prove insolvent, don't ruin him to get that, which it will not ruin thee to lose: for thou art but a steward, and another is thy owner, master and judge.

49. The more merciful acts thou dost, the more mercy thou wilt receive; and if with a charitable employment of thy temporal riches, thou gainest eternal treasure, thy purchase is infinite: thou wilt have found the art of multiplying indeed.

50. **Frugality or Bounty.** Frugality is good, if liberality be joined with it. The first is leaving off superfluous expenses; the last bestowing them to the benefit of others that need. The first without the last begins covetousness; the last without the first begins prodigality: both together make an excellent temper. Happy the place where that is found.

51. Were it universal, we should be cured of two extremes, want and excess: and the one would supply the other, and so bring both nearer to a mean; the just degree of earthly happiness.

52. It is a reproach to religion and government to suffer so much poverty and excess.

53. Were the superfluities of a nation valued, and made a

perpetual tax or benevolence, there would be more alms-houses than poor; schools than scholars; and enough to spare for government besides.

54. Hospitality is good, if the poorer sort are the subjects of our bounty; else too near a superfluity.

55. **Discipline.** If thou wouldst be happy and easy in thy family, above all things observe discipline.

56. Every one in it should know their duty; and there should be a time and place for every thing; whatever else is done or omitted, be sure to begin and end with God.

57. **Industry.** Love labour: for if thou dost not want it for food, thou mayest for physic. It is wholesome for thy body, and good for thy mind. It prevents the fruits of idleness, which many times comes of nothing to do, and leads too many to do what is worse than nothing.

58. A garden, a laboratory, a work house, improvements and breeding, are pleasant and profitable diversions to the idle and ingenious: for here they miss ill company, and converse with nature and art; whose variety are equally grateful and instructing; and preserve a good constitution of body and mind.

59. **Temperance.** To this a spare diet contributes much. Each therefore to live, and do not live to eat. That's like a man, but this below a beast.

60. Have wholesome, but not costly food, and be rather cleanly than dainty in ordering it.

61. The receipts of cookery are swelled to a volume, but a good stomach excels them all; to which nothing contributes more than industry and temperance.

62. It is a cruel folly to offer up to ostentation so many lives of creatures, as make up the state of our treats; as it is a prodigal one to spend more in sauce than in meat.

63. The proverb says that enough is as good as a feast: but it is certainly better, if superfluity be a fault, which never fails to be at festivals.

64. If thou rise with an appetite, thou art sure never to sit down without one.

65. Rarely drink but when thou art dry; nor then, between meals, if it can be avoided.

66. The smaller the drink, the clearer the head, and the cooler the blood; which are great benefits in temper and business.

67. Strong liquors are good at some times, and in small propor-

tions; being better for physic than food, for cordials than common use.

68. The most common things are the most useful; which shows both the wisdom and goodness of the great Lord of the family of the world.

69. What therefore He has made rare, don't thou use too commonly: Lest thou shouldst invert the use and order of things; become wanton and voluptuous; and thy blessings prove a curse.

70. Let nothing be lost, said our Saviour: But that is lost that is misused.

71. Neither urge another so that thou wouldst be unwilling to do thy self; nor do thy self what looks to thee unseemly and imtemperate in another.

72. All excess is ill; but drunkenness is of the worst sort: it spoils health, dismounts the mind, and unmans men: it reveals secrets, is quarrelsome, lascivious, impudent, dangerous and mad: in fine, he that's drunk is not a man; because he is so long void of reason, that distinguishes a man from a beast.

73. **Apparel.** Excess in apparel is another costly folly: the very trimming of the vain world would clothe all the naked one.

74. Choose thy clothes by thine own eyes, not another's. The more plain and simple they are, the better. Neither unshapely nor fantastical; and for use and decency, and not for pride.

75. If thou art clean and warm, it is sufficient; for more doth but rob the poor, and please the wanton.

76. It is said of the true Church, the king's daughter is all glorious within: let our care therefore be of our minds more than of our bodies, if we would be of her communion.

77. We are told with truth, that meekness and modesty are the rich and charming attire of the soul: and the plainer the dress, the more distinctly, and with greater lustre, their beauty shines.

78. It is a great pity such beauties are so rare, and those of Jezebel's forehead are so common: whose dresses are incentives to lust; but bars, instead of motives, to love or virtue.

79. **Right Marriage.** Never marry but for love; but see that thou lovest what is lovely.

80. If love be not thy chiefest motive, thou wilt soon grow weary of a married state, and stray from thy promise, to search out thy pleasures in forbidden places.

81. Let not enjoyment lessen, but augment affection; it being the

basest of passions to like when we have not, what we slight when we possess.

82. It is the difference between lust and love, that this is fixed, that volatile. Love grows, lust wastes by enjoyment: and the reason is, that one springs from an union of souls, and the other springs from an union of sense.

83. They have divers originals, and so are of different families: that inward and deep, this superficial; this transient, and that permanent.

84. They that marry for money, cannot have the true satisfaction of marriage; the requisite means being wanting.

85. Men are generally more careful of the breed of their horses and dogs, than of their children.

86. Those must be of the best sort, for shape, strength, courage and good conditions: but as for these, their own posterity, money shall answer all things. With such, it makes the crooked straight, sets squint-eyes right, cures madness, covers folly, changes ill conditions, mends the skin, gives a sweet breath, repairs honours, makes young, works wonders.

87. O how sordid is man grown! Man, the noblest creature of the world, is a god on earth, and the image of Him that made it; thus to mistake earth for heaven, and worship gold for God!

88. **Avarice.** Covetousness is the greatest of monsters, as well as the root of all evil. I have once seen the man that died to save charges. What! Give ten shillings to a doctor, and have an apothecary's bill besides, that may come to I know not what! No, not he: valuing life less than twenty shillings. But indeed such a man could not well set too low a price upon himself; who, though he lived up to the chin in bags, had rather die than find in his heart to open one of them, to help to save his life.

89. Such a man is *felo de se*, and deserves not Christian burial.

90. He is a common nuisance, a weyer cross the stream, that stops the current: an obstruction to be removed by a purge of the law. The only gratification he gives his neighbours, is to let them see that he himself is as little the better for what he has, as they are. For he always looks like lent; a sort of lay-minim. In some sense he may be compared to Pharoah's lean kine, for all that he has, does him no good. He commonly wears his clothes till they leave him, or that nobody else can wear them. He affects to be thought poor, to escape robbery and taxes: and by looking as if he wanted an alms, excuses himself from giving any: he ever goes late to markets, to

cover buying the worst: but does it because that is cheapest. He lives off the offal. His life were an insupportable punishment to any temper, but his own: and no greater torment to him on earth, than to live as other men do. But the misery of his pleasure is, that he is never satisfied with getting, and always in fear of losing what he cannot use.

91. How vilely has he lost himself, that becomes a slave to his servant; and exalts him to the dignity of his maker; gold is the God, the wife the friend of the money-monger of the world.

92. But in marriage do thou be wife; prefer the person before money, virtue before beauty, the mind before the body: then thou hast a wife, a friend, a companion, a second self; one that bears an equal share with thee, in all thy toils and troubles.

93. Choose one that measures her satisfaction, safety, and danger, by thine; and of whom, thou art sure, as of thy secretest thoughts: a friend as well as a wife, which indeed a wife implies: for she is but half a wife that is not, or is not capable of being such a friend.

94. Sexes make no difference; since in souls, there is none: and they are the subjects of friendship.

95. He that minds a body and not a soul, has not the better part of that relation; and will consequently want the noblest comfort of a marriage life.

96. The satisfaction of our senses is low, short, and transient. But the mind gives a more raised and extended pleasure, and is capable of an happiness founded upon reason; not bounded and limited by the circumstances that bodies are confined to.

97. Here it is we ought to search out our pleasure, where the field is large and full of variety, and of an enduring nature: sickness, poverty or disgrace, being not able to shake it, because it is not under the moving influences of worldly contingencies.

98. The satisfaction of those that do so, is in well doing, and in the assurance they have of a future reward. That they are best loved of those that love most, and that they enjoy and value the liberty of their minds above that of their bodies; having the whole creation for their prospect; the most noble and wonderful works and providences of God, the histories of the ancients, and in them the actions, and examples of the virtuous; and lastly, themselves, their affairs and family, to exercise their minds and friendship upon.

99. Nothing can be more entire and without reserve; nothing more zealous, affectionate and sincere; nothing more contended

and constant, than such a couple; nor no greater temporal felicity than to be one of them.

100. Between a man and his wife, nothing ought to rule but love. Authority is for children and servants; yet not without sweetness.

101. As love ought to bring them together, so it is the best way to keep them well together.

102. Wherefore use her not as a servant, whom thou wouldst perhaps have served seven years to have obtained.

103. An husband and wife that love and value one another, show their children and servants, that they should do so too. Others visibly lose their authority in their families, by their contempt of one another: and teach their children to be unnatural by their own examples.

104. It is a general fault not to be more careful to preserve nature in children, who at least in the second descent, hardly have the feeling of their relation; which must be an unpleasant reflection to affectionate parents.

105. Frequent visits, presents, intimate correspondence and intermarriages, within allowed bounds, are means of keeping up the concern and affection that nature requires from relations.

106. **Friendship.** Friendship is the next pleasure we may hope for: And where we find it not at home, or have no home to find it in, we may seek it abroad. It is an union of spirits, a marriage of hearts, and the bond thereof virtue.

107. There can be no friendship where there is no freedom. Friendship loves a free air, and will not be penned up in straight and narrow enclosures. It will speak freely, and act so too; and take nothing ill, where no ill is meant; nay, where it is, it will easily forgive, and forget too, upon small acknowledgements,

108. Friends are true twins in soul; they sympathize in every thing, and have the same love and aversion.

109. One is not happy without the other, nor can either of them be miserable alone. As if they could change bodies, they take their turns in pain as well as in pleasure; relieving one another in their most adverse conditions.

110. What one enjoys, the other cannot want. Like the primitive Christians, they have all things in common, and no property but in one another.

111. **Qualities of a friend.** A true friend unbosoms freely, advises justly, assists readily, adventures boldly, takes all patiently, defends courageously, and continues a friend unchangeably.

112. These being the qualities of a friend, we are to find them before we choose one.

113. The covetous, the angry, the proud, the jealous, the talkative cannot but make ill friends, as well as false.

114. In short, choose a friend as thou dost a wife, till death separate you.

115. Yet be not a friend beyond the altar: but let virtue bound thy friendship. Else it is not friendship, but an evil confederacy.

116. If my brother or kinsman will be my friend, I ought to prefer him before a stranger, or I show little duty or nature to my parents.

117. And as we ought to prefer our kindred in point of affection, so too in point of charity, if equally needing and deserving.

118. **Caution and Conduct.** Be not easily acquainted, lest finding reason to cool, thou makest an enemy instead of a good neighbour.

119. Be reserved, but not sour, grave but not formal, bold but not rash, humble but not servile, patient not insensible, constant not obstinate, cheerful not light, rather sweet than familiar, familiar than intimate, and intimate with very few, and upon very good grounds.

120. Return the civilities thou receivest, and be ever grateful for favours:

121. **Reparation.** If thou hast done an injury to another, rather own it than defend it. One way thou gainest forgiveness, the other thou doublest the wrong and reckoning.

122. Some oppose honour to submission: but it can be no honour to maintain, what it is dishonourable to do.

123. To confess a fault, that is none, out of fear, is indeed mean: but not to be afraid of standing in one, is brutish.

124. We should make more haste to right our neighbour, than we do to wrong him, and instead of being vindictive, we should leave him to judge of his own satisfaction.

125. True honour will pay treble damages, rather than justify one wrong by another.

126. In such controversies, it is but too common for some to say both are to blame, to excuse their own unconcernedness, which is a base neutrality. Others will cry, they are both alike; thereby involving the injured with the guilty, to mince the matter for the faulty, or cover their own injustice to the wronged party.

127. Fear and gain are great perverters of mankind, and where either prevail, the judgement is violated.

128. **Rules of Conversation.** Avoid company where it is not profitable or necessary, and in those occasions speak little and last.

129. Silence is wisdom; where speaking is folly, and always safe.

130. Some are so foolish as to interrupt and anticipate those that speak instead of hearing and thinking before they answer; which is uncivil as well as silly.

131. If thou thinkest twice, before thou speakest once, thou wilt speak twice the better for it.

132. Better say nothing, than not to the purpose. And to speak pertinently, consider both what is fit, and when it is fit to speak.

133. In all debates, let truth be thy aim, not victory, or an unjust interest: and endeavour to gain rather than to expose thy antagonist.

134. Give no advantage in argument, nor lose any that is offered. This is a benefit which arises from temper.

135. Don't use thy self to dispute against thine own judgment, to show wit, lest it prepare thee to be too indifferent about what is right. Nor against another man, to vex him, or for mere trial of skill; since to inform or to be informed, ought to be the end of all conferences.

136. Men are too apt to be concerned for their credit, more than for the cause.

137. **Eloquence.** There is a truth and beauty in rhetoric, but it oftener serves ill turns than good ones.

138. Elegancy is a good mein, and address given to matter, be it by proper or figurative speech: where the words are apt, the allusions very natural, certainly it has a moving grace: but it is too artificial for simplicity, and oftentimes for truth. The danger is, lest it delude the weak, who in such cases may mistake the handmaid for the mistrels, if not error for truth.

139. It is certain, truth is least indebted to it, because she has least need of it, and least uses it.

140. But it is a reproveable delicacy in them that despise truth in plain clothes.

141. Such luxuriants have but false appetites; like those gluttons, that by sauces force them, where they have no stomach, and sacrifice to their palate, not their health: which cannot be without great vanity, nor that without some sin.

142. **Temper.** Nothing does reason more right, than the coolness of those that offer it: for truth often suffers more by the heat of its defenders, than from the arguments of its opposers.

143. Zeal ever follows an appearance of truth, and the assured are too apt to be warm; but it is their weak side in argument; zeal being better shown against sin, than persons or their mistakes.

144. **Truth.** Where thou art obliged to speak, be sure to speak the truth: for equivocation is half way to lying; as lying, the whole way to hell.

145. **Justice.** Believe nothing against another, but upon good authority: nor report what may hurt another, unless it be a greater hurt to others to conceal it.

146. **Secrecy.** It is wise not to seek a secret, and honest not to reveal one.

147. Only trust thy self, and another shall not betray thee.

148. Openness has the mischief, though not the malice of treachery.

149. **Complacency.** Never assent merely to please others. For that is beside flattery, oftentimes untruth; and discovers a mind liable to be servile and base: nor contradict to vex others, for that shows an ill temper and provokes, but profits no body.

150. **Shifts.** Do not accuse others to excuse thy self; for that is neither generous nor just. But let sincerity and ingenuity be thy refuge, rather than craft and falsehood: for cunning borders very near upon knavery.

151. Wisdom never uses nor wants it. Cunning to wise, it as an ape to a man.

152. **Interest.** Interest has the security, though not the virtue of a principle. As the world goes, it is the surer side: for men daily leave both relations and religion to follow it.

153. It is an odd sight but very evident, that families and nations of cross religions and humours, unite against those of their own, where they find an interest to do it.

154. We are tied down by our senses to this world; and where that is in question, it can be none with worldly men, whether they should not forsake all other considerations for it.

155. **Inquiry.** Have a care of vulgar errors. Dislike, as well as allow reasonably.

156. Inquiry is human, blind obedience, brutal. Truth never loses by the one, but often suffers by the other.

157. The usefullest truths are plainest: and while we keep to them, our differences cannot rise high.

158. There may be a wantonness in search, as well as a stupidity in trusting. It is great wisdom equally to avoid the extremes.

159. **Right Timing.** Do nothing improperly. Some are witty, kind, cold, angry, easy, stiff, jealous, careless, cautious, confident, close, open, but all in the wrong place.

160. It is ill mistaking where the matter is of importance.

161. It is not enough that a thing be right, if it be not fit to be done. If not prudent, though just, it is not adviseable. He that loses by getting, had better lose than get.

162. **Knowledge.** Knowledge is the treasure, but judgment the treasurer of a wise man.

163. He that has more knowledge than judgment is made for another man's use more than his own.

164. It cannot be a good constitution, where the appetite is great and the digestion weak.

165. There are some men like dictionaries; to be looked into upon occasion, but have no connection, and are little entertaining.

166. Less knowledge than judgement will always have the advantage upon the injudicious knowing man.

167. A wise man makes what he learns his own, the other shows he's but a copy, or a collection at most.

168. **Wit.** Wit is an happy and striking way of expressing a thought.

169. It is not often, though it be lively and mantling, that it carries a great body with it.

170. Wit therefore is fitter for diversion than business, being more grateful to fancy than judgment.

171. Less judgment than wit, is more sail than ballast.

172. Yet it must be confessed, that wit gives an edge to sense, and recommends it extremely.

173. Where judgment has wit to express it, there's the best orator.

174. **Obedience to Parents.** If thou wouldst be obeyed, being a father; being a son, be obedient.

175. He that begets thee, owes thee; and has a natural right over thee.

176. Next to God, thy parents; next them, the magistrate.

177. Remember that thou art not more indebted to thy parents for thy nature, than for their love and care.

178. Rebellion, therefore, in children, was made death by God's law, and the next sin to idolatry, in the people; which is renouncing of God, the great parent of all.

179. Obedience to parents is not only our duty, but our interest.

If we received our life from them, we prolong it by obeying them: for obedience is the first commandment with promise.

180. The obligation is as indissoluble as the relation.

181. If we must not disobey God to obey them, at least we must let them see, that there is nothing else in our refusal. For some unjust commands cannot excuse the general neglect of our duty. They will be our parents, and we must be their children still: and if we cannot act for them against God, neither can we act against them for our selves or any thing else.

182. **Bearing.** A man in business must put up many affronts, if he loves his own quiet.

183. We must not pretend to see all that we see, if we would be easy.

184. It were endless to dispute upon every thing that is disputable.

185. A vindictive temper is not only uneasy to others, but to them that have it.

186. **Promising.** Rarely promise. But, if lawful, constantly perform.

187. Hasty resolutions are of the nature of vows; and to be equally avoided.

188. I will never do this, says one, yet does it: I am resolved to do that, says another; but flags upon second thoughts: or does it, though awkwardly, for his word's sake: as if it were worse to break his word, than to do amiss in keeping it.

189. Wear none of thine own chains; but keep free, whilst thou art free.

190. It is an effect of passion that wisdom corrects, to lay thy self under resolutions that cannot be well made, and worse performed.

191. **Fidelity.** Avoid all thou canst being entrusted: but do thy utmost to discharge the trust thou undertakest: for carelessness is injurious, if not unjust.

192. The glory of a servant is fidelity; which cannot be without diligence, as well as truth.

193. Fidelity had enfranchised slaves, and adopted servants to be sons.

194. Reward a good servant well: and rather quit than disquiet thy self with an ill one.

195. **Master.** Mix kindness with authority; and rule more by discretion than rigour.

196. If thy servant be faulty, strive rather to convince him of his error, than discover thy passion: and when he is sensible, forgive him.

197. Remember he is thy fellow creature, and that God's goodness, not thy merit, has made the difference betwixt thee and him.

198. Let not thy children domineer over thy servants: nor suffer them to slight thy children.

199. Suppress tales in the general: but where a matter requires notice, encourage the complaint, and right the aggrieved.

200. If a child, he ought to entreat, and not to command, and if a servant, to comply where he does not obey.

201. Though there should be but one master and mistress in a family, yet servants should know that children have the reversion.

202. **Servant.** Indulge not unseemly things in thy master's children, nor refuse them what is fitting: for one is the highest unfaithfulness, and the other, indiscretion as well as disrespect.

203. Do thine own work honestly and cheerfully: and when that is done, help thy fellow; that so another time he may help thee.

204. If thou wilt be a good servant, thou must be true, and thou canst not be true if thou defraudst thy master.

205. A master may be defrauded many ways by a servant: as in time, care, pains, money, trust.

206. But, a true servant is the contrary: he's diligent, careful, trusty. He tells no tales, reveals no secrets, refuses no pains: not to be tempted by gain, nor awed, by fear, to unfaithfulness.

207. Such a servant serves God in serving his master; and has double wages for his work, to wit, here and hereafter.

208. **Jealous.** Be not fancifully jealous: for that is foolish; as, to be reasonably so, is wise.

209. He that superfines upon other men's actions, cozens himself, as well as injures them.

210. To be very subtle and scrupulous in business is as hurtful, as being over-confident and secure.

211. In difficult cases, such as temper, is timorous; and in dispatch irresolute.

212. Experience is a safe guide: and a practical head is a great happiness in business.

213. **Posterity.** We are too careless of posterity, not considering that as they are, so the next generation will be.

214. If we would amend the world, we should mend our selves;

and teach our children to be, not what we are, but what they should be.

215. We are too apt to awaken and tune up their passions by the example of our own; and to teach them to be pleased, not with what is best, but with what pleases best.

216. It is our duty, and ought to be our care, to ward against that passion in them, which is more especially our own weakness and affliction. For we are in great measure accountable for them, as well as for ourselves.

217. We are in this also true turners of the world upside down. For money is first, and virtue last, and least in our care.

218. It is not how we leave our children, but what we leave them.

219. To be sure virtue is but a supplement, and not a principal in their portion and character: and therefore we see so little wisdom or goodness among the rich, in proportion to their wealth.

220. **A Country Life.** The country life is to be preferred; for there we see the works of God; but in cities little else but the works of men: and the one makes a better subject for our contemplation than the other.

221. As puppets are to men, and babies to children, so is man's workmanship to God's: we are the picture, He the reality.

222. God's works declare His power, wisdom and goodness; but man's works, for the most part, his pride, folly and excess. The one is for use, the other, chiefly, for ostentation and lust.

223. The country is both the philosopher's garden and library, in which he reads and contemplates the power, wisdom and goodness of God.

224. It is his food as well as study; and gives him life, as well as learning.

225. A sweet and natural retreat from noise and talk; and allows opportunity for reflection, and gives the best subjects for it.

226. In short, it is an original, and the knowledge and improvement of it, man's oldest business and trade, and the best he can be of.

227. **Art and Project.** Art, is good, where it is beneficial. Socrates wisely bounded his knowledge and instruction by practice.

228. Have a care therefore of projects: and yet despise nothing rashly, or in the lump.

229. Ingenuity, as well as religion, sometimes suffers between two thieves; pretenders and despisers.

230. Though injudicious and dishonest projectors often discredit art, yet the most useful and extraordinary inventions have not, at first, escaped the scorn of ignorance; as their authors, rarely, have cracking of their heads, or breaking of their backs.

231. Undertake no experiment, in speculation, that appears not true in art; nor then, at thine own cost, if costly or hazardous in making.

232. As many hands make light work, so several purses make cheap experiments.

233. **Industry.** Industry is certainly very commendable, and supplies the want of parts.

234. Patience and diligence, like faith, remove mountains.

235. Never give out while there is hope; but hope not beyond reason, for that shows more desire than judgment.

236. It is a profitable wisdom to know when we have done enough: much time and pains are spared, in not flattering our selves against probabilities.

237. **Temporal Happiness.** Do good with what thou hast, or it will do thee no good.

238. Seek not to be rich, but happy. The one lies in bags, the other in content; which wealth can never give.

239. We are apt to call things by wrong names. We will have prosperity to be happiness, and adversity to be misery; though that is the school of wisdom, and oftentimes the way to eternal happiness.

240. If thou wouldst be happy, bring thy mind to thy condition, and have an indifferency for more than what is sufficient.

241. Have but little to do, and do it thy self: and do to others as thou wouldst have them do to thee: so, thou canst not fail of temporal felicity.

242. The generality are the worse for their plenty. The voluptuous consumes it, the miser hides it: it is the good man that uses it, and to good purposes. But such are hardly found among the prosperous.

243. Be rather bountiful, than expensive.

244. Neither make nor go to feasts, but let the laborious poor bless thee at home in their solitary cottages.

245. Never voluntarily want what thou hast in possession; nor so spend it as to involve thy self in want unavoidable.

246. Be not tempted to presume by success: for many that have got largely, have lost all, by coveting to get more.

247. To hazard much to get much, has more of avarice than wisdom.

248. It is great prudence both to bound and use prosperity.

249. Too few know when they have enough; and fewer know how to employ it.

250. It is equally adviseable not to part lightly with what is hardly gotten, and not to shut up closely what flows in freely.

251. Act not the shark upon thy neighbour; nor take advantage of the ignorance, prodigality or necessity of any one: for that is next door to fraud, and, at best, makes but an unblessed gain.

252. It is oftentimes the judgment of God upon greedy rich men, that he suffers them to push on their desires of wealth to the excess of overreaching, grinding or oppression, which poisons all they have gotten: so that it commonly runs away as fast, and by as bad ways, as it was heaped up together.

253. **Respect.** Never esteem any man, or thy self, the more for money; nor think the meaner of thy self or another, for want of it: virtue being the just reason or respecting, and the want of it, of slighting any one.

254. A man, like a watch, is to be valued for his goings.

255. He that prefers him upon other accounts, bows to an idol.

256. Unless virtue guide us, our choice must be wrong.

257. An able bad man, is an ill instrument, and to be shunned as the plague.

258. Be not deceived with the first appearances of things, but give thy self time to be in the right.

259. Show is not substance: realities govern wise men.

260. Have a care therefore where there is more sail than ballast.

261. **Hazard.** In all business, it is best to put nothing to hazard: but where it is unavoidable, be not rash, but firm and resigned.

262. We should not be troubled for what we cannot help: but if it was our fault, let it be so no more. Amendment is repentance, if not reparation.

263. As a desperate game needs an able gamester, so consideration often would prevent what the best skill in the world cannot recover.

264. Where the probability of advantage exceeds not that of loss, wisdom never adventures.

265. To shoot well flying is well; but to choose it, has more of vanity than judgment.

266. To be dextrous in danger is a virtue; but to court danger to show it, is weakness.

267. **Detraction.** Have a care of that base evil detraction. It is the fruit of envy, as that is of pride; the immediate off-spring of the devil: who, of an angel, a Lucifer, a son of the morning, made himself a serpent, a devil, a Beelzebub, and all that is obnoxious to the eternal goodness.

268. Virtue is not secure against envy. Men will lessen what they won't imitate.

269. Dislike what deserves it; but never hate: for that is of the nature of malice; which is almost ever to persons, not things, and is one of the blackest qualities sin begets in the soul.

270. **Moderation.** It were a happy day if men could bound and qualify their resentments with charity to the offender: for then our anger would be without sin, and better convict and edify the guilty; which alone can make it lawful.

271. Not to be provoked is best: but if moved, never correct till the fume is spent: for every stroke our fury strikes is sure to hit our selves at last.

272. If we did but observe the allowances our reason makes upon reflection, when our passion is over, we could not want a rule how to behave ourselves again on the like occasions.

273. We are more prone to complain than redress, and to censure than excuse.

274. It is next to unpardonable, that we can so often blame what we will not once mend. It shows, we know, but will not do our master's will.

275. They that censure, should practice: or else let them have the first stone, and the last too.

276. **Trick.** Nothing needs a trick but a trick, sincerity loaths one.

277. We must take care to do right things rightly: for a just sentence may be unjustly executed.

278. Circumstances give great light to true judgment, if well weighed.

279. **Passion.** Passion is a sort of fever in the mind, which ever leaves us weaker than it found us.

280. But being intermitting, to be sure, it is curable with care.

281. It more than any thing deprives us of the use of our judgment: for it raises a dust very hard to see through.

282. Like wine, whose lees fly up being jogged, it is too muddy to drink.

283. It may not unfitly be termed the mob of the man, that commits a riot upon his reason.

284. I have oftentimes thought that a passionate man is like a weak spring that cannot stand long locked.

285. And it is as true, that those things are unfit for use, that cannot bear small knocks, without breaking.

286. He that won't hear can't judge, and he that can't hear contradiction, may, with all his wit, miss the mark.

287. Objection and debate sift out truth, which needs temper as well as judgment.

288. But above all, observe it in resentments; for there passion is most extravagant.

289. Never chide for anger, but instruction.

290. He that corrects out of passion raises revenge sooner than repentance.

291. It has more of wantonness than wisdom, and resembles those that eat to please their palate, rather than their appetite.

292. It is the difference between a wise and a weak man; this judges by the lump, that by parts and their connection.

293. The Greeks used to say, all cases are governed by their circumstances. The same thing may be well and ill as they change or vary the matter.

294. A man's strength is shown by his bearing. *Bonum agere et male pati, regis est.*

295. **Personal Cautions.** Reflect without malice but never without need.

296. Despise no body, nor no condition; lest it come to be thine own.

297. Never rail, nor taunt. The one is rude, the other scornful; and both evil.

298. Be not provoked by injuries, to commit them.

299. Upbraid only ingratitude.

300. Haste makes work, which caution prevents.

301. Tempt no man; lest thou fall for it.

302. Have a care of presuming upon after-games: for if that miss, all is gone.

303. Opportunities should never be lost, because they can hardly be regained.

304. It is well to cure, but better to prevent a distemper. The first shows more skill, but the last more wisdom.

305. Never make a trial of skill in difficult or hazardous cases.

306. Refuse not to be informed: for that shows pride or stupidity.

307. Humility and knowledge in poor clothes excel pride and ignorance in costly attire.

308. Neither despise, nor oppose, what thou dost not understand.

309. **Balance.** We must not be concerned above the value of the thing that engages us; nor raised above reason in maintaining what we think reasonable.

310. It is too common an error, to invert the order of things; by making an end of that which is a means, and a means of that which is an end.

311. Religion and government escape not this mischief: the first is too often made a means instead of an end; the other an end instead of a means.

312. Thus men seek wealth rather than subsistence; and the end of clothes is the least reason for their use. Nor is the satisfying of our appetite our end in eating, so much as the pleasing of our palate. The like may also be said of building, furniture, etc. where the man rules not the beast, and appetite submits not to reason.

313. It is great wisdom to proportion our esteem to the nature of the thing: for as that way things will not be undervalued, so neither will they engage us above their intrinsic worth.

314. If we suffer little things to have great hold upon us, we shall be as much transported for them, as if they deserved it.

315. It is an old proverb, *maxima bella ex levissimis causis*: the greatest feuds have had the smallest beginnings.

316. No matter what the subject of the dispute be, but what place we give it in our minds. For that governs our concern and resentment.

317. It is one of the fatalest errors of our lives, when we spoil a good cause by an ill management: and it is not impossible but we may mean well in an ill business; but that will not defend it.

318. If we are but sure the end is right, we are too apt to gallop over all bounds to compass it; not considering that lawful ends may be very unlawfully attained.

319. Let us be careful to take just ways to compass just things; that they may last in their benefits to us.

320. There is a troublesome humour some men have, that if they may not lead, they will not follow, but had rather a thing were never done, than not done their own way, though otherwise very desirable.

321. This comes of an over-fulness of our selves, and shows we are more concerned for praise, than the success of what we think a good thing.

322. **Popularity.** Affect not to be seen, and men will less see thy weakness.

323. They that show more than they are raise an expectation they cannot answer; and so lose their credit, as soon as they are found out.

324. Avoid popularity. It has many snares, and no real benefit to thy self; and uncertainty to others.

325. **Privacy.** Remember the proverb, *Benè qui latuit, benè vixit*, they are happy that live retiredly.

326. If this be true, princes and their grandees, of all men, are the unhappiest: for they live least alone: and they that must be enjoyed by every body, can never enjoy themselves as they should.

327. It is the advantage little men have upon them; they can be private, and have leisure for family comforts, which are the greatest worldly contents men can enjoy.

328. But they that place pleasure in greatness, seek it there: and we see rule is as much the ambition of some natures, as privacy is the choice of others.

329. **Government.** Government has many shapes: but it is sovereignty, though not freedom, in all of them.

330. *Rex & Tyrannus* are very differing characters: one rules his people by laws, to which they consent; the other by his absolute will and power. This is called freedom, this tyranny.

331. The first is endangered by the ambition of the populace, which shakes the constitution: the other by an ill administration, which hazards the tyrant and his family.

332. It is great wisdom in princes of both sorts, not to strain points too high with their people: for whether the people have a right to oppose them or not, they are ever sure to attempt it, when things are carried too far; though the remedy often-times proves worse than the disease.

333. Happy that king who is great by justice, and that people who are free by obedience.

334. Where the ruler is just, he may be strict; else it is two to

one it turns upon him: and though he should prevail, he can be no gainer, where his people are the losers.

335. Princes must not have passions in government, nor resent beyond interest and religion.

336. Where example keeps pace with authority, power hardly fails to be obeyed, and magistrates to be honoured.

337. Let the people think they govern, and they will be governed.

338. This cannot fail, if those they trust are trusted.

339. That prince that is just to them in great things, and humours them oftentimes in small ones, is sure to have and keep them from all the world.

340. For the people is the politic wife of the prince, that may be better managed by wisdom than ruled by force.

341. But where the magistrate is partial and serves ill turns, he loses his authority with the people and gives the populace opportunity to gratify their ambition, and so lays a stumbling-block for his people to fall.

342. It is true that where a subject is more popular than the prince, the prince is in danger: but it is as true, that it is his own fault: for no body has the like means, interest or reason to be popular as he.

343. It is an unaccountable thing that some princes incline rather to be feared than loved; when they see, that fear does not oftener secure a prince against the dissatisfaction of his people, than love makes a subject too many for such a prince.

344. Certainly service upon inclination is like to go farther than obedience upon compulsion.

345. The Romans had a just sense of this, when they placed *optimus* before *maximus*, to their most illustrious captains and cæsars.

346. Besides, experience tells us, that goodness raises a nobler passion in the soul, and gives a better sense of duty than severity.

347. What did Pharoah get by increasing the Israelites' task? Ruin to himself in the end.

348. Kings, chiefly in this, should imitate God: their mercy should be above all their works.

349. The difference between the prince and the peasant is in this world: but a temper ought to be observed by him that has the advantage here, because of the judgment of the next.

350. The end of every thing should direct the means: now that

of government being the good of the whole, nothing less should be the aim of the prince.

351. As often as rulers endeavour to attain just ends by just mediums, they are sure of a quiet and easy government; and as sure of convulsions, where the nature of things are violated, and their order over-ruled.

352. It is certain, princes ought to have great allowances made them for faults in government; since they see by other people's eyes, and hear by their ears. But ministers of state, their immediate confidents and instruments have much to answer for, if to gratify private passions, they misguide the prince to do public injury.

353. Ministers of state should undertake their posts at their peril. If princes over-rule them, let them show the law, and humbly resign: if fear, gain or flattery prevail, let them answer it to the law.

354. The prince cannot be preserved, but where the minister is punishable: for people, as well as princes, will not endure *imperium in imperio*.

355. If ministers are weak or ill men, and so spoil their places, it is the prince's fault that chose them: but if their places spoil them, it is their own fault to be made worse by them.

356. It is but just that those that reign by their princes should suffer for their princes: for it is a safe and necessary maxim, not to shift heads in government while the hands are in being that should answer for them.

357. And yet it were intolerable to be a minister of state, if every body may be accuser and judge.

358. Let therefore the false accuser no more escape an exemplary punishment, than the guilty minister.

359. For it profanes government to have the credit of the leading men in it subject to vulgar censure; which is often ill-grounded.

360. The safety of a prince, therefore, consists in a well chosen council: and that only can be said to be so where the persons that compose it are qualified for the business that comes before them.

361. Who would send to a tailor to make a lock, or to a smith to make a suit of clothes.

362. Let there be merchants for trade, seamen for the Admiralty, travellers for foreign affairs, some of the leading men of the country for home business, and common and civil lawyers to advise of legality and right who should always keep to the strict rules of law.

363. Three things contribute much to ruin government: looseness, oppression and envy.

364. Where the reins of government are too slack, there the manners of the people are corrupted: and that destroys industry, begets effeminacy, and provokes heaven against it.

365. Oppression makes a poor country and a desperate people, who always wait an opportunity to change.

366. He that ruleth over men must be just, ruling in the fear of God, said an old and wise king.

367. Envy disturbs and distracts government, clogs the wheels, and perplexes the administration: and nothing contributes more to this disorder, than a partial distribution of rewards and punishments in the sovereign.

368. As it is not reasonable that men should be compelled to serve; so those that have employments should not be endured to leave them humorously.

369. Where the state intends a man no affront, he should not affront the state.

370. **A Private Life.** A private life is to be preferred; the honour and gain of public posts bearing no proportion with the comfort of it. The one is free and quiet, the other servile and noisy.

371. It was a great answer of the Shunamite woman, I dwell among my own people.

372. They that live of their own, neither need, nor often list to wear the livery of the public.

373. Their subsistence is not during pleasure, nor have they patrons to please or present.

374. If they are not advanced, neither can they be disgraced. And as they know not the smiles of majesty, so they feel not the frowns of greatness, or the effects of envy.

375. If they want the pleasures of a court, they also escape the temptations of it.

376. Private men, in fine, are so much their own, that paying common dues, they are sovereigns of all the rest.

377. **A Public Life.** Yet the public must and will be served; and they that do it well, deserve public marks of honour and profit.

378. To do so, men must have public minds as well as salaries; or they will serve private ends at the public cost.

379. Governments can never be well administered, but where those entrusted make conscience of well discharging their places.

380. **Qualifications.** Five things are requisite to a good officer; ability, clean hands, dispatch, patience, and impartiality.

381. **Capacity.** He that understands not his employment, whatever else he knows, must be unfit for it; and the public suffers by his inexpertness.

382. They that are able, should be just too; or the government may be the worse for their capacity.

383. **Clean Hands.** Covetousness in such men prompts them to prostitute the public for gain.

384. The taking of a bribe or gratuity should be punished with as severe penalties as the defrauding of the state.

385. Let men have sufficient salaries, and exceed them at their peril.

386. It is a dishonour to government that its officers should live of benevolence; as it ought to be infamous for officers to dishonour the public, by being twice paid for the same business.

387. But to be paid, and not to do business, is rank oppression.

388. **Dispatch.** Dispatch is a great and good quality in an officer; where duty, not gain, excites it. But of this, too many make their private market and overplus to their wages. Thus the salary is for doing, and the bribe for dispatching the business: as if business could be done before it were dispatched: or they were to be paid a part, one by the government, the other by the party.

389. Dispatch is as much the duty of an officer, as doing; and very much the honour of the government he serves.

390. Delays have been more injurious than direct injustice.

391. They too often starve those they dare not deny.

392. The very winner is made a loser, because he pays twice for his own; like those that purchase estates mortgaged before to the full value.

393. Our law says well, to delay justice is injustice.

394. Not to have a right, and not to come at it, differs little.

395. Refusal or dispatch is the duty and wisdom of a good officer.

396. **Patience.** Patience is a virtue every where; but it shines with greatest lustre in the men of government.

397. Some are so proud or testy, they won't hear what they should redress.

398. Others so weak, they sink or burst under the weight of their office, though they can lightly run away with the salary of it.

399. Business can never be well done, that is not well understood: which cannot be without patience.

400. It is cruelty indeed not to give the unhappy an hearing, whom we ought to help: but it is the top of oppression to browbeat the humble and modest miserable, when they seek relief.

401. Some, it is true, are unreasonable in their desires and hopes: but then we should inform, not rail at and reject them.

402. It is therefore as great an instance of wisdom as a man in buisness can give, to be patient under the impertinencies and contradictions that attend it.

403. Method goes far to prevent trouble in business: for it makes the task easy, hinders confusion, saves abundance of time, and instructs those that have business depending, what to do and what to hope.

404. **Impartiality.** Impartiality, though it be the last, is not the least part of the character of a good magistrate.

405. It is noted as a fault, in Holy Writ, even to regard the poor: how much more the rich in judgment.

406. If our compassions must not sway us; less should our fears, profits, or prejudices.

407. Justice is justly represented blind, because she sees no difference in the parties concerned.

408. She has but one scale and weight, for rich and poor, great and small.

409. Her sentence is not guided by the person, but the cause.

410. The impartial judge, in judgment, knows nothing but the law: the prince no more than the peasant, his kindred than a stranger. Nay, his enemy is sure to be upon equal terms with his friend, when he is upon the bench.

411. Impartiality is the life of justice, as that is of government.

412. Nor is it only a benefit to the state, for private families cannot subsist comfortably without it.

413. Parents that are partial are ill obeyed by their children; and partial masters not better served by their servants.

414. Partiality is always indirect, if not dishonest: for it shows a bias where reason would have done; if not an injury, which justice every where forbids.

415. As it makes favourites without reason, so it uses no reason in judging of actions: confirming the proverb, the crow thinks her own bird the fairest.

416. What some see to be no fault in one, they will have criminal in another.

417. Nay, how ugly do our failings look to us in the persons of others; which yet we see not in our selves.

418. And but too common it is, for some people, not to know their own maxims and principles in the mouths of other men, when they give occasion to use them.

419. Partiality corrupts our judgment of persons and things, of our selves and others.

420. It contributes more than any thing to factions in government, and feuds in families.

421. It is a prodigal passion, that seldom returns till it is hunger-bit, and disappointments bring it within bounds.

422. And yet we may be indifferent, to a fault.

423. **Indifferency.** Indifference is good in judgment, but bad in relation, and stark naught in religion.

424. And even in judgment, our indifferency must be to the persons, not causes, for one, to be sure, is right.

425. **Neutrality.** Neutrality is some thing else than indifferency; and yet of kin to it too.

426. A judge ought to be indifferent, and yet he cannot be said to be neutral.

427. The one being to be even in judgment, and the other not to meddle at all.

428. And where it is lawful, to be sure, it is best to be neutral.

429. He that espouses parties can hardly divorce himself from their fate; and more fall with their party than rise with it.

430. A wise neuter joins with neither; but uses both, as his honest interest leads him.

431. A neuter only has room to be a peace-maker: for being of neither side, he has the means of mediating a reconciliation of both:

432. **A Party.** And yet where right or religion gives a call, a neuter must be a coward or an hypocrite.

433. In such cases, we should never be backward; nor yet mistaken.

434. When our right or religion is in question, then is the fittest time to affect it.

435. Nor must we always be neutral, where our neighbour is concerned: for though meddling is a fault, helping is a duty.

436. We have a call to do good, as often as we have the power and occasion.

437. If heathens could say, we are not born for our selves; surely Christians should practice it.

438. They are taught so by his example, as well as doctrine, from whom they have borrowed their name.

439. **Ostentation.** Do what good thou canst unknown; and be not vain of what ought rather to be felt than seen,

440. The humble, in the Parable of the Day of Judgment, forgot their good works, Lord, when did we so and so?

441. He that does good, for good's sake, seeks neither praise nor reward; though sure of both at last.

442. **Complete Virtue.** Content not thy self, that thou art virtuous in the general: for one link being wanting, the chain is defective.

443. Perhaps thou art rather innocent than virtuous, and owest more to thy constitution than thy religion.

444. Innocent, is not to be guilty: but virtuous is to overcome our evil inclinations.

445. If thou hast not conquered thy self in that which is thy own particular weakness, thou hast no title to virtue, though thou art free of other men's.

446. For a covetous man to inveigh against prodigality, an atheist against idolatry, a tyrant against rebellion, or a liar against forgery, and a drunkard against intemperance, is for the pot to call the kettle black.

447. Such reproof would have but little success; because it would carry but little authority with it.

448. If thou wouldst conquer thy weakness, thou must never gratify it.

449. No man is compelled to evil, his consent only makes it his.

450. It is no sin to be tempted, but to be overcome.

451. What man, in his right mind, would conspire his own hurt? Men are beside themselves, when they transgress their convictions.

452. If thou wouldst not sin, don't desire, and if thou wouldst not lust, don't embrace the temptation: no, not look at it, nor think of it.

453. Thou wouldst take much pains to save thy body: take some, prithee, to save thy soul.

454. **Religion.** Religion is the fear of God, and its demonstration good works; and faith is the root of both: for without faith we cannot please God, nor can we fear what we do not believe.

455. The devils also believe and know abundance: but in this is

the difference, their faith works not by love, nor their knowledge by obedience; and therefore they are never the better for them: and if ours be such, we shall be of their church, not of Christ's: for as the head is, so must the body be.

456. He was holy, humble, harmless, meek, merciful, etc. when among us; to teach us what we should be, when He was gone: and yet He is among us still, and in us too, a living and perpetual preacher of the same grace, by His spirit in our consciences.

457. A minister of the Gospel ought to be one of Christ's making, if he would pass for one of Christ's ministers.

458. And if he be one of his making, he knows and does as well as believes.

459. That minister, whose life is not the model of his doctrine, is a babbler rather than a preacher, a quack rather than a physician of value.

460. Of old time they were made ministers of the Holy Ghost. And the more that is an ingredient now, the fitter they are for that work.

461. Running streams are not so apt to corrupt; nor itinerant, as settled preachers: but they are not to run before they are sent.

462. As they freely receive from Christ, so they give.

463. They will not make that a trade, which they know ought not, in conscience, to be one.

464. Yet there is no fear of their living that design not to live by it.

465. The humble and true teacher meets with more than he expects.

466. He accounts content with Godliness great gain, and therefore seeks not to make a gain of Godliness.

467. As the ministers of Christ are made by Him, and are like Him, so they beget people into the same likeness.

468. To be like Christ then, is to be a Christian. And regeneration is the only way to the Kingdom of God, which we pray for.

469. Let us to day, therefore hear His voice, and not harden our hearts; who speaks to us many ways. In the scriptures, in our hearts, by His servants and providences: and the sum of all is holiness and charity.

470. St James gives a short draught of the matter, but very full and reaching, pure religion and undefiled before God and the Father, is this, to visit the fatherless and the widows in their

affliction, and to keep our selves unspotted from the world. Which is comprised in these two words, charity and piety.

471. They that truly make these their aim, will find them their attainment; and with them, the peace that follows so excellent a condition.

472. Amuse not thy self therefore, with the numerous opinions of the world, nor value thy self upon verbal orthodoxy, philosophy, or thy skill in tongues, or knowledge of the Fathers; (too much the business and vanity of the world) but in this rejoice, that thou knowest God, that is the Lord, who exerciseth loving kindness, and judgment, and righteousness in the earth.

473. Public worship is very commendable, if well performed. We owe it to God and good example. But we must know that God is not tied to time or place, who is every where at the same time: and this we shall know, as far as we are capable, if where-ever we are, our desires are to be with him.

474. Serving God, people generally confine to the acts of public and private worship: and those, the more zealous do often repeat, in hopes of acceptance.

475. But if we consider that God is an infinite spirit, and, as such, everywhere; and that our Saviour has taught us, that He will be worshipped in spirit and in truth; we shall see the shortness of such a notion.

476. For serving God concerns the frame of our spirits, in the whole course of our lives; in every occasion we have, in which we may show our love to His law.

477. For as men in battle are continually in the way of shot, so we, in this world, are ever within the reach of temptation: and herein do we serve God, if we avoid what we are forbid, as well as do what he commands.

478. God is better served in resisting a temptation to evil, than in many formal prayers.

479. This is but twice or thrice a day: but that every hour and moment of the day. So much more is our continual watch, than our evening and morning devotion.

480. Wouldst thou then serve God? Do not that alone, which thou wouldst not that another should see thee do.

481. Don't take God's name in vain, or disobey thy parents, or wrong thy neighbour, or commit adultery, even in thine heart.

482. Neither be vain, lascivious, proud, drunken, revengeful or angry: nor lie, detract, backbite, overreach, oppress, deceive, or

betray: but watch vigorously against all temptations to these things; as knowing that God is present, the overseer of all thy ways and most inward thoughts, and the avenger of His own law upon the disobedient, and thou wilt acceptably serve God.

483. Is it not reason, if we expect the acknowledgments of those to whom we are bountiful, that we should reverently pay ours to God, our most magnificent and constant benefactor?

484. The world represents a rare and sumptuous palace, mankind the great family in it, and God the mighty Lord and Master of it.

485. We are all sensible what a stately seat it is; the heavens adorned with so many glorious luminaries; and the earth with groves, plains, valleys, hills, fountains, ponds, lakes and rivers; and variety of fruits, and creatures for food, pleasure and profit. In short, how noble an house He keeps, and the plenty and variety and excellency of His table; His orders, seasons, and suitableness of every time and thing. But we must be as sensible, or at least ought to be, what careless and idle servants we are, and how short and disproportionable our behaviour is to His bounty and goodness: how long He bears, and often He reprieves and forgives us: who, notwithstanding our breach of promises, and repeated neglects, has not yet been provoked to break up house, and send us to shift for our selves. Should not this great goodness raise a due sense in us of our undutifulness, and a resolution to alter our course and mend our manners; that we may be for the future more worthy communicants at our Master's good and great table? Especially since it is not more certain that we deserve His displeasure, than that we shall feel it, if we continue to be unprofitable servants.

486. But though God has replenished this world with abundance of good things for man's life and comfort, yet they are all but imperfect goods. He only is the perfect good to whom they point. But, alas! Men cannot see Him for them; though they should always see Him in them.

487. I have often wondered at the unaccountableness of man in this; among other things; that though he loves changes so well, he should care so little to hear or think of his last, great, and best change too, if he pleases.

488. Being, as to our bodies, composed of changeable elements, we, with the world, are made up of and subsist by revolution: but our souls being of another and nobler nature, we should seek our rest in a more enduring habitation.

489. The truest end of life is to know the life that never ends.

490. He that makes this his care will find it his crown at last.

491. Life else were a misery rather than a pleasure, a judgment, not a blessing.

492. For to know, regret, and resent; to desire, hope and fear more than a beast, and not live beyond him, is to make a man less than a beast.

493. It is the amends of a short and troublesome life, that doing well, and suffering ill, entitles man to one longer and better.

494. This ever raises the good man's hope, and gives him tastes beyond the other world.

495. As it is his aim, so none else can hit the mark.

496. Many make it their speculation, but it is the good man's practice.

497. His work keeps pace with his life, and so leaves nothing to be done when he dies.

498. And he that lives to live ever, never fears dying.

499. Nor can the means be terrible to him that heartily believes the end.

500. For though death be a dark passage, it leads to immortality, and that is recompense enough for suffering of it.

501. And yet faith lights us, even through the grave, being the evidence of things not seen.

502. And this is the comfort of the good, that the grave cannot hold them, and that they live as soon as they die.

503. For death is no more than a turning of us over from time to eternity.

504. Nor can there be a revolution without it; for it supposes the dissolution of one form, in order to the succession of another.

505. Death then, being the way and condition of life, we cannot love to live if we cannot bear to die.

506. Let us then not cozen our selves with the shells and husks of things; nor prefer form to power, nor shadows to substance; pictures of bread will not satisfy hunger, nor those of devotion please God.

507. This world is a form: our bodies are forms; and no visible acts of devotion can be without forms. But yet the less form in religion the better, since God is a spirit: for the more mental our worship, the more adequate to the nature of God; the more silent, the more suitable to the language of a spirit.

508. Words are for others, not for our selves: nor for God, who hears not as bodies do; but as spirits should.

509. If we would know this dialect, we must learn of the divine principle in us. As we hear the dictates of that, so God hears us.

510. There we may see him too in all His attributes; though but in little, yet as much as we can apprehend or bear: for as He is in Himself, He is incomprehensible, and dwelleth in that light which no eye can approach. But in His image we may behold His glory; enough to exalt our apprehensions of God, and to instruct us in that worship which pleaseth Him.

511. Men may tire themselves in a labyrinth of search, and talk of God: but if we would know Him indeed, it must be from the impressions we receive of Him; and the softer our hearts are, the deeper and livelier those will be upon us.

512. If He has made us sensible of His justice, by His reproof; of His patience, by His forbearance; of His mercy, by His forgiveness; of His holiness, by the sanctification of our hearts through His spirit; we have a grounded knowledge of God. This is experience, that speculation; this enjoyment, that report. In short, this is undeniable evidence, with the realities of religion, and will stand all winds and weathers.

513. As our faith, so our devotion should be lively. Cold meat won't serve at those repasts.

514. It is a coal from God's altar must kindle our fire: and without fire, true fire, no acceptable sacrifice.

515. Open thou my lips and then, said the Royal Prophet, my mouth shall praise God. But not until then.

516. The preparation of the heart, as well as answer of the tongue, is of the Lord: And to have it, our prayers must be powerful, and our worship grateful.

517. Let us choose, therefore, to commune where there is the warmest sense of religion; where devotion exceeds formality, and practise most corresponds with profession; and where there is at least as much charity as zeal: for where this society is to be found, there shall we find the church of God.

518. As good, so ill men are all of a church; and every body knows who must be head of it.

519. The humble, meek, merciful, just, pious and devout souls are every where of one religion; and when death has taken off the mask, they will know one another, though the diverse liveries they wear here, make them strangers.

520. Great allowances are to be made for education and personal weaknesses: but it is a rule with me, that man is truly religious, that loves the persuasion he is of, for the piety rather than ceremony of it.

521. They that have one end, can hardly disagree when they meet. At least their concern in the greater, moderates their value and difference about the lesser things.

522. It is a sad reflection that many men hardly have any religion at all; and most men have none of their own: for that which is the religion of their education, and not of their judgment, is the religion of another, and not theirs.

523. To have religion upon authority, and not upon conviction, is like a finger watch, to be set forwards or backwards, as he pleases that has it in keeping.

524. It is a preposterous thing, that men can venture their souls where they will not venture their money; for they will take their religion upon trust, but not trust a synod about the goodness of half a crown.

525. They will follow their own judgment when their money is concerned, whatever they do for their souls.

526. But to be sure, that religion cannot be right, that a man is the worse for having.

527. No religion is better than an unnatural one.

528. Grace perfects, but never sours or spoils nature.

529. To be unnatural in defence of grace is a contradiction.

530. Hardly any thing looks worse, than to defend religion by ways that show it has no credit with us.

531. A devout man is one thing, a stickler is quite another.

532. When our minds exceed their just bounds, we must needs discredit what we would recommend.

533. To be furious in religion, is to be irreligiously religious.

534. If he that is without bowels is not a man; how then can he be a Christian?

535. It were better to be of no church than to be bitter for any.

536. Bitterness comes very near to enmity, and that is Beelzebub; because the perfection of wickedness.

537. A good end cannot sanctify evil means; nor must we ever do evil, that good may come of it.

538. Some folk think they may scold, rail, hate, rob and kill too; so it be but for God's sake.

539. But nothing in us, unlike Him, can please Him.

540. It is as great presumption to send our passions upon God's errands, as it is to palliate them with God's name.

541. Zeal dropt in charity is good; without it, good for nothing: for it devours all it comes near.

542. They must first judge themselves that presume to censure others: and such will not be apt to over-shoot the mark.

543. We are too ready to retaliate rather than forgive, or gain by love and information.

544. And yet we could hurt no man that we believe loves us.

545. Let us then try what love will do: for if men do once see we love them, we should soon find they would not harm us.

546. Force may subdue, but love gains: and he that forgives first, wins the laurel.

547. If I am even with my enemy, the debt is paid; but if I forgive it, I oblige him for ever.

548. Love is the hardest lesson in Christianity; but, for that reason, it should be most our care to learn it. *Difficilia quæ Pulchra.*

549. It is a severe rebuke upon us, that God makes us so many allowances, and we make so few to our neighbour: As if charity had nothing to do with religion; or love with faith, that ought to work by it.

550. I find all sorts of people agree, whatsoever were their animosities, when humbled by the approaches of death: then they forgive, then they pray for, and love one another: which shows us that it is not our reason, but our passion, that makes and holds up the feuds that reign among men in their health and fulness. They, therefore, that live nearest to that which they should die, must certainly live best.

551. Did we believe a final reckoning and judgment, or did we think enough of what we do believe, we would allow more love in religion than we do: since religion it self is nothing else but love to God and man.

552. He that lives in love lives in God, says the beloved disciple: and to be sure a man can live no where better.

553. It is most reasonable men should value that benefit, which is most durable. Now tongues shall cease, and prophecy fail, and faith shall be consummated in sight, and hope in enjoyment; but love remains.

554. Love is indeed heaven upon earth; since heaven above would not be heaven without it: for where there is not love, there

is fear: but perfect love casts out fear. And yet we naturally fear most to offend what we most love.

555. What we love, we'll hear; what we love, we'll trust; and what we love, we'll serve, ay, and suffer for too. If you love me, (says our Blessed Redeemer) keep My commandments. Why? Why then He'll love us; then we shall be His friends; then He'll send us the comforter; then whatever we ask, we shall receive; and then where He is, we shall be also, and that for ever. Behold the fruits of love; the power, virtue, benefit and beauty of love!

556. Love is above all; and when it prevails in us all, we shall all be lovely, and in love with God and one with another.

More Fruits of S O L I T U D E,

BEING THE

SECOND PART

O F

Reflections and Maxims. relating
to the Conduct of Human Life.

THE INTRODUCTION TO THE READER

The title of this treatise shows there was a former of the same nature; and the author hopes he runs no hazard in recommending both to his reader's perusal. He is well aware of the low reckoning, the labours of indifferent authors are under, at a time when hardly any thing passes for current, that is not calculated to flatter the sharpness of contending parties. He is also sensible that books grow a very drug where they cannot raise and support their credit, by their own usefulness; and how far this will be able to do it, he knows not; yet he thinks himself tolerably safe in making it public in three respects.

First, *that the purchase is small, and the time but little, that is requisite to read it.*

Next, *though some men should not find it relished* high enough for their finer wits, or warmer palates, it may not perhaps be useless to those of lower flights, and who are less engaged in public heats.

Lastly, *the author honestly aims at as general a benefit as the thing will bear;* to youth *especially, whether he hits the mark or not: and that without the least ostentation, or any private regards.*

Let not envy misinterpret his intention, and he will be accountable for all other faults.

Vale.

REFLECTIONS AND MAXIMS, ETC.

1. **The Right Moralist.** A right moralist is a great and good man, but for that reason he is rarely to be found.

2. There are a sort of people that are fond of the character, who, in my opinion, have but little title to it.

3. They think it enough, not to defraud a man of his pay, or betray his friend; but never consider, that the law forbids the one at his peril, and that virtue is seldom the reason of the other.

4. But certainly he that covets, can no more be a moral man, than he that steals; since he does so in his mind. Nor can he be one that robs his neighbour of his credit, or that craftily undermines him of his trade or office.

5. If a man pays his tailor, but debauches his wife, is he a current moralist?

6. But what shall we say of the man that rebels against his father, is an ill husband, or an abusive neighbour; one that's lavish of his time, of his health, and of his estate, in which his family is so nearly concerned? Must he go for a right moralist, because he pays his rent well?

7. I would ask some of those men of morals, whether he that robs God and himself too, though he should not defraud his neighbour, be the moral man?

8. Do I owe my self nothing? And do I not owe all to God? And if paying what we owe makes the moral man, is it not fit we should begin to render our dues, where we owe our very beginning; ay, our all?

9. The complete moralist begins with God; he gives him his due, his heart, his love, his service; the bountiful giver of his well-being, as well as being.

10. He that lives without a sense of this dependency and obligation cannot be a moral man, because he does not know his returns of love and obedience as becomes an honest and a sensible creature: which very term implies he is not his own; and it cannot be very honest to mis-employ another's goods.

11. But how can there be no debt, but to a fellow creature? Or, will our exactness in paying those dribbling ones, while we neglect our weightier obligations, cancel the bonds we lie under, and render us right and thorough moralists?

12. As judgments are paid before bonds, and bonds before bills

or book debts, so the moralist considers his obligations according to their several dignities.

In the first place, him to whom he owes himself. Next himself in his health and livelihood. Lastly, his other obligations, whether rational or pecuniary; doing to others, to the extent of his ability, as he would have them do unto him.

13. In short, the moral man is he that loves God above all, and his neighbour as himself, which fulfils both tables at once.

14. **The World's Able Man.** It is by some thought the character of an able man, to be dark and not understood. But I am sure that is not fair play.

15. If he be so by silence, it is better; but if by disguises, it is insincere and hateful.

16. Secrecy is one thing, false lights are another.

17. The honest man that is rather free than open, is ever to be preferred; especially when sense is at helm.

18. The glorying of the other humour is in a vice: for it is not humane to be cold, dark, and unconversable. I was going to say they are like pickpockets in a crowd, where a man must ever have his hand on his purse; or as spies in a garrison, that if not prevented betray it.

19. They are the reverse of humane nature, and yet this is the present world's wise man and politician: excellent qualities for Lapland, where, they say, witches, though not many conjurors, dwell.

20. Like highway men, that rarely rob without vizards, or in the same wigs and clothes, but have a dress for every enterprise.

21. At best, he may be a cunning man, which is a sort of lurcher in politics.

22. He is never too hard for the wise man upon the square, for that is out of his element, and puts him quite by his skill. Nor are wise men ever caught by him, but when they trust him.

23. But as cold and close as he seems, he can and will please all, if he gets by it, though it should neither please God nor himself at bottom.

24. He is for every cause that brings him gain, but implacable if disappointed of success.

25. And what he cannot hinder, he will be sure to spoil, by over-doing it.

26. None so zealous then as he, for that which he cannot abide.

27. What is it he will not, or cannot do, to hide his true sentiments.

28. For his interest, he refuses no side or party; and will take the wrong by the hand, when the other won't do, with as good a grace as the right.

29. Nay, he commonly chooses the worst, because that brings the best bribe: his cause being ever money.

30. He fails with all winds, and is never out of his way, where any thing is to be had.

31. A privateer indeed, and every where a bird of prey.

32. True to nothing but himself, and false to all persons and parties, to serve his own turn.

33. Talk with him as often as you please, he will never pay you in good coin; for it is either false or clipt.

34. But to give a false reason for any thing, let my reader never learn of him, no more than to give a brass half crown for a good one: not only because it is not true, but because it deceives the person to whom it is given; which I take to be an immorality.

35. Silence is much more preferable, for it saves the secret, well as the person's honour.

36. Such as give themselves the latitude of saying what they do not mean come to be errant jockeys at more things than one; but in religion and politics it is pernicious.

37. To hear two men talk the reverse of their own sentiments, with all the good breeding and appearance of friendship imaginable, on purpose to cozen or pump each other, is to a man of virtue and honour, one of the melancholiest, as well as most nauseous things in the world.

38. But that it should be the character of an able man, is to disinherit wisdom, and paint out our degeneracy to the life by setting up fraud, an errant impostor, in her room.

39. The trial of skill between these two is who shall believe least of what the other says; and he that has the weakness, or good nature, to give out first, viz. to believe any thing the other says is looked upon to be tricked.

40. I cannot see the policy, any more than the necessity, of a man's mind always giving the lie to his mouth; or his mouth ever giving false alarms of his mind: for no man can be long believed that teaches all men to distrust him; and since the ablest have sometimes need of credit, where lies the advantage of their politic cant or banter upon mankind.

41. I remember a passage of one of Queen Elizabeth's great men; as advice to his friend; the advantage, says he, I had upon others at court, was that I always spoke as I thought, which being not believed by them I both preserved a good conscience, and suffered no damage from that freedom: which, as it shows the vice to be older than our times, so that gallant man's integrity, to be the best way of avoiding it.

42. To be sure it is wise, as well as honest, neither to flatter other men's sentiments, nor dissemble and less contradict our own.

43. To hold one's tongue, or speak truth, or talk only of indifferent things, is the fairest conversation.

44. Women that rarely go abroad without vizard-masks, have none of the best reputation. But when we consider what all this art and disguise are for, it equally heightens the wise man's wonder and aversion: perhaps it is to betray a father, a brother, a master, a friend, a neighbour, or one's own party.

45. A fine conquest! What noble Grecians and Romans abhorred: as if government could not subsist without knavery, and that knaves were the usefullest props to it; though the basest, as well as greatest, perversions of the ends of it.

46. But that it should become a maxim shows but too grossly the corruption of the times.

47. I confess I have heard the style of an useful knave, but ever took it to be a silly or a knavish saying; at least an excuse for knavery.

48. It is as reasonable to think a whore makes the best wife as a knave the best officer.

49. Besides, employing knaves encourages knavery instead of punishing it; and alienates the reward of virtue. Or, at least, must make the world believe the country yields not honest men enough able to serve her.

50. Art thou a magistrate? Prefer such as have clean characters, where they live, and of estates, to secure a just discharge of their trusts; that are under no temptation to strain points, for a fortune: for sometimes such may be found, sooner than they are employed.

51. Art thou a private man? Contract thy acquaintance in a narrow compass, and choose those for the subjects of it, that are men of principles; such as will make full stops, where honour will not lead them on; and that had rather bear the disgrace of not being thorough paced men, that forfeit their peace and reputation by a base compliance.

52. **The Wise Man.** The wise man governs himself by the reason of his case, and because what he does is best; best, in a moral and prudent, not a sinister sense.

53. He proposes just ends, and employs the fairest and probablest means and methods to attain them.

54. Though you cannot always penetrate his design, or his reasons for it, yet you shall ever see his actions of a piece, and his performances like a workman: they will bear the touch of wisdom and honour, as often as they are tried.

55. He scorns to serve himself by indirect means, or be an interloper in government, since just enterprises never want any just ways to succeed them.

56. To do evil, that good may come of it, is for bunglers in politics as well as morals.

57. Like those surgeons that will cut off an arm they can't cure to hide their ignorance and save their credit.

58. The wise man is cautious, but not cunning; judicious, but not crafty; making virtue the measure of using his excellent understanding in the conduct of his life.

59. The wise man is equal, ready, but not officious, has in every thing an eye to sure-footing: he offends no body, nor easily is offended, and always willing to compound for wrongs, if not forgive them.

60. He is never captious nor critical; hates banter and jests. He may be pleasant, but not light; he never deals but in substantial ware and leaves the rest for the toy pates (or shops) of the world; which are so far from being his business, that they are not so much as his diversion.

61. He is always for some solid good, civil or moral; as to make his country more virtuous, preserve her peace and liberty, employ her poor, improve land, advance trade, suppress vice, encourage industry, and all mechanical knowledge; and that they should be the care of the government, and the blessing and praise of the people.

62. To conclude, he is just, and fears God, hates covetousness, and eschews evil, and loves his neighbour as himself.

63. **Of the Government of Thoughts.** Man being made a reasonable and so a thinking creature; there is nothing more worthy of his being than the right direction and employment of his thoughts; since upon this depends both his usefulness to the public, and his own present and future benefit in all respects.

64. The consideration of this has often obliged me to lament the unhappiness of mankind, that through too great a mixture and confusion of thoughts, have been hardly able to make a right or mature judgment of things.

65. To this is owing the various uncertainty and confusion we see in the world, and the intemperate zeal that occasions them.

66. To this also is to be attributed the imperfect knowledge we have of things, and the slow progress we make in attaining to a better; like the children or Israel that were forty years upon their journey, from Egypt to Canaan, which might have been performed in less than one.

67. In fine, it is to this that we ought to ascribe, if not all, at least most of the infelicities we labour under.

68. Clear therefore thy head, and rally and manage thy thoughts rightly, and thou wilt save time, and see and do thy business well; for thy judgment will be distinct, thy mind free, and thy faculties strong and regular.

69. Always remember to bound thy thoughts to the present occasion.

70. If it be thy religious duty, suffer nothing else to share in them and if any civil or temporal affair, observe the same caution, and thou wilt be a whole man to every thing, and do twice the business in the same time.

71. If any point over-labours thy mind, divert and relieve it by some other subject of a more sensible, or manual nature, rather than what may affect the understanding; for this were to write one thing upon another, which blots out our former impressions, or renders them illegible.

72. They that are least divided in their care, always give the best account of their business.

73. As therefore thou art always to pursue the present subject, till thou hast mastered it, so if it fall out, that thou hast more affairs than one upon thy hand, be sure to prefer that which is of most moment, and will least wait thy leisure.

74. He that judges not well of the importance of his affairs, though he may be always busy, he must make but a small progress.

75. But make not more business necessary than is so; and rather lessen than augment work for thy self.

76. Nor yet be over eager in pursuit of any thing; for the mercurial too often happen to leave judgment behind them, and sometimes make work for repentance.

77. He that over-runs his business, leave it for him that follows more leisurely to take it up; which has often proved a profitable harvest to them that never sowed.

78. It is the advantage that slower tempers have upon the men of lively parts, that though they don't lead, they will follow well, and glean clean.

79. Upon the whole matter, employ thy thoughts as thy business requires, and let that have place according to merit and urgency; giving every thing a review and due digestion, and thou wilt prevent many errors and vexations, as well as save much time to thy self in the course of thy life.

80. **Of Envy.** It is the mark of an ill nature to lessen good actions, and aggravate ill ones.

81. Some men do as much begrudge others a good name, as they want one themselves; and perhaps that is the reason of it.

82. But certainly they are in the wrong, that can think they are lessened, because others have their due.

83. Such people generally have less merit than ambition, that covet the reward of other men's; and to be sure a very ill nature, that will rather rob others of their due, than allow them their praise.

84. It is more an error of our will than our judgment: for we know it to be an effect of our passion, not our reason; and therefore we are the more culpable in our partial estimates.

85. It is as envious as unjust, to underrate another's actions, where their intrinsic worth recommends them to disengaged minds.

86. Nothing shows more the folly, as well as fraud of man, than clipping of merit and reputation.

87. And as some men think it an allay to themselves, that others have their right; so they know no end of pilfering to raise their own credit.

88. This envy is the child of pride, and misgives, rather than mistakes.

89. It will have charity, to be obstentation; sobriety, covetousness; humility, craft, bounty, popularity. In short, virtue must be design, and religion, only interest. Nay, the best of qualities must not pass without a but to allay their merit and abate their praise. Basest of tempers! and they that have it, the worst of men!

90. But just and noble minds rejoice in other men's success, and help to augment their praise.

91. And indeed they are not without a love to virtue, that take a

satisfaction in seeing her rewarded, and such deserve to share her character that do abhor to lessen it.

92. **Of Man's Life.** Why is man less durable than the works of his hands, but because this is not the place of his rest?

93. And it is a great and just reproach upon him that he should fix his mind where he cannot stay himself.

94. Were it not more his wisdom to be concerned about those works that will go with him, and erect a mansion for him where time has power neither over him nor it?

95. It is a sad thing for man so often to miss his way to his best, as well as most lasting home.

96. **Of Ambition.** They that soar too high, often fall hard; which makes a low and level dwelling preferable.

97. The tallest trees are most in the power of the winds, and ambitious men of the blasts of fortune.

98. They are most seen and observed, and most envied: least quiet, but most talked of, and not often to their advantage.

99. Those builders had need of a good foundation, that lie so much exposed to weather.

100. Good works are a rock that will support their credit; but ill ones a sandy foundation that yields to calamities.

101. And truly they ought to expect no pity in their fall, that when, in power, had no bowels for the unhappy.

102. The worst of distempers; always craving and thirsty, restless and hated: a perfect delirium in the mind: insufferable in success, and in disappointments most revengeful.

103. **Of Praise or Applause.** We are too apt to love praise, but not to deserve it.

104. But if we would deserve it, we must love virtue more than that.

105. As there is no passion in us sooner moved, or more deceivable, so for that reason there is none over which we ought to be more watchful, whether we give or receive it: for if we give it, we must be sure to mean it, and measure it too.

106. If we are penurious, it shows emulation; if we exceed, flattery.

107. Good measure belongs to good actions; more looks nauseous, as well as insincere, besides, it is persecuting of the meritorious, who are out of countenance to hear what they deserve.

108. It is much easier for him to merit applause than hear of it:

and he never doubts himself more, or the person that gives it, than when he hears so much of it.

109. But to say true, there needs not many cautions on this hand, since the world is rarely just enough to the deserving.

110. However, we cannot be too circumspect how we receive praise: for if we contemplate our selves in a false glass, we are sure to be mistaken about our dues; and because we are too apt to believe what is pleasing, rather than what is true, we may be too easily swelled beyond our just proportion, by the windy complements of men.

111. Make ever therefore allowances for what is said on such occasions, or thou exposest, as well as deceivest thy self.

112. For an over-value of our selves, gives us but a dangerous security in many respects.

113. We expect more than belongs to us; take all that's given us though never meant us; and fall out with those that are not as full of us as we are of our selves.

114. In short, it is a passion that abuses our judgment, and makes us both unsafe and ridiculous.

115. Be not fond therefore of praise, but seek virtue that leads to it.

116. And yet no more lessen or dissemble thy merit, than over-rate it: for though humility be a virtue, an affected one is none.

117. **Of Conduct in Speech.** Enquire often, but judge rarely, and thou wilt not often be mistaken.

118. It is safer to learn than teach; and who conceals his opinion has nothing to answer for.

119. Vanity or resentment often engage us, and it is two to one but we come off losers; for one shows a want of judgment and humility, as the other does of temper and discretion.

120. Not that I admire the reserved; for they are next to unnatural that are not communicable. But if reservedness be at any time a virtue, it is in throngs or ill company.

121. Beware also of affectation in speech; it often wrongs matter, and ever shows a blind side.

122. Speak properly, and in as few words as you can, but always plainly; for the end of speech is not ostentation but to be understood.

123. They that affect words more than matter will dry up that little they have.

124. Sense never fails to give them that have it words enough to make them understood.

125. But it too often happens in some conversations, as in apothecary shops, that those pots that are empty, or have things of small value in them, are as gaudily dressed and flourished, as those that are full of precious drugs.

126. This labouring of slight matter flourished turns of expression, is fulsome, and worse than the modern imitation of tapestry, and East-India goods, in stuffs and linens. In short, it is but tawdry talk, and next to very trash.

127. **Union of Friends.** They that love beyond the world cannot be separated by it.

128. Death cannot kill what never dies.

129. Nor can spirits ever be divided that love and live in the same divine principle; the root and record of their friendship.

130. If absence be not death, neither is theirs.

131. Death is but crossing the world, as friends do the seas; they live in one another still.

132. For they must needs be present that love and live in that which is omnipresent.

133. In this divine glass, they see face to face; and their converse is free, as well as pure.

134. This is the comfort of friends, that though they may be said to die, yet their friendship and society are, in the best sense, ever present, because immortal.

135. **Of being Easy in Living.** It is an happiness to be delivered from a curious mind, as well as from a dainty palate.

136. For it is not only a troublesome but slavish thing to be nice.

137. They narrow their own freedom and comforts, that make so much requisite to enjoy them.

138. To be easy in living is much of the pleasure of life: but difficult tempers will always want it.

139. A careless and homely breeding is therefore perferable to one nice and delicate.

140. And he that is taught to live upon little, owes more to his father's wisdom, than he that has a great deal left him, does to his father's care.

141. Children can't well be too hardly bred: for besides that it fits them bear the roughest providences, it is more masculine, active and healthy.

142. Nay, it is certain, that the liberty of the mind is mightily

preserved by it : for so it is served, instead of being a servant, indeed a slave, to sensual delicacies.

143. As nature is soon answered, so are such satisfied.

144. The memory of the ancients is hardly in any thing more to be celebrated ; than in a strict and useful institution of youth.

145. By labour they prevented luxury in their young people, till wisdom and philosophy had taught them to resist and despise it.

146. It must be therefore a gross fault, to strive so hard for the pleasure of our bodies, and be so sensible and careless of the freedom of our souls.

147. **Of Man's Inconsiderateness and Partiality.** It is very obserable, if our civil rights are invaded or encroached upon, we are mightily touched, and fill every place with our resentment and complaint; while we suffer our selves, our better and nobler selves, to be the property and vassals of sin, the worst of invaders.

148. In vain do we expect to be delivered from such troubles, till we are delivered from the cause of them, our disobedience to God.

149. When he has his dues from us, it will be time enough for him to give us ours out of one another.

150. It is our great happiness, if we could understand it, that we meet with such checks in the career of our worldly enjoyments, lest we should forget the giver, adore the gift, and terminate our felicity here, which is not man's ultimate bliss.

151. Our losses are often made judgments by our guilt, and mercies by our repentance.

152. Besides, it argues great folly in men, to let their satisfaction exceed the true value of any temporal matter ; for disappointments are not always to be measured by the loss of the thing, but the over-value we put upon it.

153. And thus men improve their own miseries, for want of an equal and just estimate of what they enjoy or lose.

154. There lies a proviso upon every thing in this world, and we must observe it at our own peril, viz. to love God above all, and act for judgment, the last I mean.

155. **Of the Rule of Judging.** In all things reason should prevail : it is quite another thing to be stiff than steady in an opinion.

156. This may be reasonable, but that is ever wilful.

157. In such cases it always happens, that the clearer the argument, the greater the obstinacy, where the design is not to be convinced.

158. This is to value humour more than truth, and prefer a sullen pride to a reasonable submission.

159. It is the glory of a man to veil to truth; as it is the mark of a good nature to be easily entreated.

160. Beasts act by sense, man should by reason; else he is a greater beast than ever God made: and the proverb is verified, the corruption of the best things is the worst and most offensive.

161. A reasonable opinion must ever be in danger, where reason is not judge.

162. Though there is a regard due to education, and the tradition of our fathers, truth will ever deserve as well as claim the preference.

163. If like Theophilus and Timothy, we have been brought up in the knowledge of the best things, it is our advantage: but neither they nor we lose by trying the truth; for so we learn their, as well as its intrinsic worth.

164. Truth never lost ground by enquiry, because she is most of all reasonable.

165. Nor can that need another authority, that is self-evident.

166. If my own reason be on the side of a principle, with what can I dispute or withstand it?

167. And if men would once consider one another reasonably, they would either reconcile their differences, or more amicably maintain them.

168. Let that therefore be the standard, that has most to say for it self; though of that let every man be judge for himself.

169. Reason, like the sun, is common to all; and it its for want of examining all by the same light and measure, that we are not all of the same mind: for all have it to that end, though all do not use it so.

170. **Of Formality.** Form is good, but not formality.

171. In the use of the best of forms, there is too much of that I fear.

172. It is absolutely necessary that this distinction should go along with people in their devotion; for too many are apter to rest upon what they do, than how they do their duty.

173. If it were considered, that it is the frame of the mind that gives our performances acceptance, we would lay more stress on our inward preparation than our outward action.

174. **Of the Mean Notion we Have of God.** Nothing more shows the low condition man is fallen into, than the unsuitable notion we must have of God, by the ways we take to please Him.

175. As if it availed any thing to him that we performed so many ceremonies and external forms of devotion, who never meant more by them than to try our obedience, and, through them, to show us something more excellent and durable beyond them.

176. Doing, while we are undoing, is good for nothing.

177. Of what benefit is it to say our prayers regularly, go to church, receive the sacraments, and may be go to confessions too ; ay, feast the priest, and give alms to the poor, and yet lie, swear, curse, be drunk, covetous, unclean, proud, revengeful, vain and idle at the same time ?

178. Can one excuse or balance the other ? Or will God think Himself well served, where His law is violated ? Or well used, where there is so much more show than substance ?

179. It is a most dangerous error for a man to think to excuse himself in the breach of a moral duty, by a formal performance of positive worship ; and less when of human invention.

180. Our blessed Saviour most rightly and clearly distinguished and determined this case, when He told the Jews that they were his mother, His brethren and sisters, who did the will of His father.

181. **Of the Benefit of Justice.** Justice is a great support of society, because an insurance to all men of their property : this violated, there's no security, which throws all into confusion to recover it.

182. An honest man is a fast pledge in dealing. A man is sure to have it if it be to be had.

183. Many are so, merely of necessity : others not so only for the same reason : but such an honest man is not to be thanked, and such a dishonest man is to be pitied.

184. But he that is dishonest for gain is next to a robber, and to be punished for example.

185. And indeed there are few dealers, but what are faulty, which makes trade difficult, and a great temptation to men of virtue.

186. It is not what they should, but what they can get : faults or decays must be concealed : big words given, where they are not deserved, and the ignorance of necessity of the buyer imposed upon for unjust profit.

187. These are the men that keep their words for their own ends, and are only just for fear of the magistrate.

188. A politic rather than a moral honesty ; a constrained, not a chosen justice : according to the proverb, patience per force, and thank you for nothing.

189. But of all injustice, that is the greatest that passes under the name of law. A cut-purse in Westminster Hall exceeds; for that advances injustice to oppression, where law is alleged for that which it should punish.

190. **Of Jealousy.** The jealous are troublesome to others, but a torment to themselves.

191. Jealousy is a kind of civil war in the soul, where judgment and imagination are at perpetual jars.

192. This civil dissension in the mind, like that of the body politic, commits great disorders, and lays all waste.

193. Nothing stands safe in its way: nature, interest, religion, must yield to its fury.

194. It violates contracts, dissolves society, breaks wedlock, betrays friends and neighbours. No body is good, and every one is either doing or designing them a mischief.

195. It has a venom that more or less rankles wherever it bites: and as it reports fancies for facts, so it disturbs its own house as often as other folks.

196. Its rise is guilt or ill-nature, and by reflection it thinks its own faults to be other men's; as he that's over-run with the jaundice takes others to be yellow.

197. A jealous man only sees his own spectrum, when he looks upon other men, and gives his character in theirs.

198. **Of State.** I love service, but not state; one is useful, the other superfluous.

199. The trouble of this, as well as charge, is real; but the advantage only imaginary.

200. Besides, it helps to set us up above our selves, and augments our temptation to disorder.

201. The least thing out of joint, or omitted, makes us uneasy; and we are ready to think our selves ill served, about that which is of no real service at all: or so much better than other men, as we have the means of greater state.

202. But this is all for want of wisdom, which carries the truest and most forceable state along with it.

203. He that makes not himself cheap by indiscreet conversation, puts value enough upon himself every where.

204. The other is rather pageantry than state.

205. **Of a Good Servant.** A true, and a good servant, are the same thing.

206. But no servant is true to his master that defrauds him.

207. Now there are many ways of defrauding a master, as of time, care, pains, respect and reputation, as well as money.

208. He that neglects his work, robs his master, since he is fed and paid as if he did his best; and he that is not as diligent in the absence, as in the presence of his master, cannot be a true servant.

209. Nor is he a true servant that buys dear to share in the profit with the seller.

210. Nor yet he that tells tales without doors; or deals basely in his master's name with other people; or connives at other's loiterings, wastings, or dishonourable reflections.

211. So that a true servant is diligent, secret, and respectful: more tender of his master's honour and interest than of his own profit.

212. Such a servant deserves well, and if modest under his merit, should liberally feel it at his master's hand.

213. **Of an Immoderate Pursuit of the World.** It shows a depraved state of mind, to cark and care for that which one does not need.

214. Some are as eager to be rich, as ever they were to live: for superfluity, as for subsistence.

215. But that plenty should augment covetousness is a perversion of providence; and yet the generality are the worse for their riches.

216. But it is strange, that old men should excel: for generally money lies nearest them that are nearest their graves: as if they would augment their love in proportion to the little time they have left to enjoy it: and yet their pleasure is without enjoyment, since none enjoy what they do not use.

217. So that instead of learning to leave their great wealth easily, they hold the faster, because they must leave it: so sordid is the temper of some men.

218. Where charity keeps pace with gain, industry is blessed: but to slave to get, and keep it sordidly, is a sin against providence, a vice in government, and an injury to their neighbours.

219. Such are they as spend not one fifth of their income, and, it may be, give not one tenth of what they spend to the needy.

220. This is the worst sort of idolatry, because there can be no religion in it, nor ignorance pleaded in excuse of it; and that it wrongs other folks that ought to have a share therein.

221. **Of the Interest of the Public in our Estates.** Hardly any thing is given us for our selves, but the public may claim a share

with us. But of all we call ours, we are most accountable to God and the public for our estates: in this we are but stewards, and to hoard up all to our selves is great injustice as well as ingratitude.

222. If all men were so far tenants to the public, that the superfluities of gain and expense were applied to the exigencies thereof, it would put an end to taxes, leave never a begger, and make the greatest bank for national trade in Europe.

223. It is a judgment upon us, as well as weakness, though we won't see it, to begin at the wrong end.

224. If the taxes we give are not to maintain pride, I am sure there would be less, if pride were made a tax to the government.

225. I confess I have wondered that so many lawful and useful things are excised by laws, and pride left to reign free over them and the public.

226. But since people are more afraid of the laws of man than of God, because their punishment seems to be nearest: I know not how magistrates can be excused in their suffering such excess with impunity.

227. Our noble English patriarchs as well as patriots, were so sensible of this evil, that they made several excellent laws, commonly called sumptuary, to forbid, at least limit the pride of the people; which because the execution of them would be our interest and honour, their neglect must be our just reproach and loss.

228. It is but reasonable that the punishment of pride and excess should help to support the Government, since it must otherwise inevitably be ruined by them.

229. But some say, it ruins trade, and will make the poor burdensome to the public: But if such trade in consequence ruins the kingdom, is it not time to ruin that trade? Is moderation no part of our duty, and temperance an enemy to government?

230. He is a Judas that will get money by any thing.

231. To wink at a trade that effeminates the people, and invades the ancient discipline of the kingdom, is a crime capital, and to be severely punished instead of being excused by the magistrate.

232. Is there no better employment for the poor than luxury? Miserable nation!

233. What did they before they fell into these forbidden methods. Is there not land enough in England to cultivate, and more and better manufactures to be made?

234. Have we no room for them in our plantations, about things that may augment trade, without luxury?

235. In short, let pride pay, and excess be well excised: and if that will not cure the people, it will help to keep the kingdom.

236. **The Vain Man.** But a vain man is a nauseous creature: he is so full of himself, that he has no room for any thing else, be it never so good or deserving.

237. It is I at every turn that does this, or can do that. And as he abounds in his comparisons, so he is sure to give himself the better of every body else; according to the proverb, all his geese are swans.

238. They are certainly to be pitied, that can be so much mistaken at home.

239. And yet I have sometimes thought that such people are in a sort happy, that nothing can put out of countenance with themselves, though they neither have nor merit other people's.

240. But at the same time, one would wonder they should not feel the blows they give themselves, or get from others, for this intolerable and ridiculous temper; nor show any concern at that which makes others blush for, as well as at them (viz.) their unreasonable assurance.

241. To be a man's own fool is bad enough, but the vain man is every body's.

242. This silly disposition comes of a mixture of ignorance, confidence and pride, and as there is more or less of the last, so it is more or less offensive or entertaining.

243. And yet perhaps the worst part of this vanity is its unteach-ableness. Tell it any thing, and it has known it long ago; and out-runs information and instruction, or else proudly puffs at it.

244. Whereas the greatest understandings doubt most, are readiest to learn, and least pleased with themselves; this, with no body else.

245. For though they stand on higher ground, and so see farther than their neighbours, they are yet humbled by their prospect, since it shows them something so much higher, and above their reach.

246. And truly then it is that sense shines with the greatest beauty when it is set in humility.

247. An humble able man is a jewel worth a kingdom: it is often saved by him, as Solomon's poor wise man did the city.

248. May we have more of them, or less need of them.

249. **The Conformist.** It is reasonable to concur where conscience does not forbid a compliance; for conformity is at least a civil virtue.

250. But we should only press it in necessaries, the rest may prove a snare or temptation to break society.

251. But above all, it is a weakness in religion and government, where it is carried to things of an indifferent nature, since besides that it makes way for scruples, libery is always the price of it.

252. Such conformists have little to boast of, and therefore the less reason to reproach others that have more latitude.

253. And yet the latitudinarian that I love, is one that is only so in charity, for the freedom is recommand is no scepticism in judgment, and much less so in practice.

254. **The Obligation of Great Men to Almighty God.** It seems but reasonable that those whom God has distinguished from others, by His goodness, should distinguish themselves to Him by their gratitude.

255. For though He has made of one blood, all nations, He has not ranged or dignified them upon the level, but in a sort of subordination and dependency.

256. If we look upwards, we find it in the heavens, where the planets have their several degrees of glory, and so the other stars of magnitude and lustre.

257. If we look upon the earth, we see it among the trees of the wood, from the cedar to the bramble; among the fishes, from the leviathan to the sprat; in the air among the birds, from the eagle to the sparrow; among the beasts, from the lion to the cat; and among mankind, from the king to the scavenger.

258. Our great men, doubtless, were designed by the wise framer of the world, for our religious, moral and politic planets, for lights and directions to the lower ranks of the numerous company of their own kind, both in precepts and examples; and they are well paid for their pains too, who have the honour and service of their fellow-creatures, and the marrow and fat of the earth, for their share.

259. But is it not a most unaccountable folly that men should be proud of the providences that should humble them? Or think the better of themselves, instead of Him that raised them so much above the level; or of being so in their lives, in return of His extraordinary favours?

260. But it is but too near a-kin to us, to think no farther than our selves, either in the acquisition, or use of our wealth and greatness; when, alas! they are the preferments of heaven, to try our wisdom, bounty and gratitude.

261. It is a dangerous perversion of the end of providence, to

consume the time, power, and wealth He has given us above other men, to gratify our sordid passions, instead of playing the good stewards, to the honour of our great benefactor, and the good of our fellow-creatures.

262. But it is an injustice too; since those higher ranks of men are but the trustees of heaven, for the benefit of lesser mortals who, as minors, are entitled to all their care and provision.

263. For though God has dignified some men above their breathren, it never was to serve their pleasures, but that they might take pleasure to serve the public.

264. For this cause, doubtless, it was that they were raised above necessity, or any trouble to live, that they might have more time and ability to care for others: and it is certain, where that use is not made of the bounties of providence, they are embezzelled and wasted.

295. It has often struck me with a serious reflection, when I have observed the great inequality of the world; that one man should have such numbers of his fellow creatures to wait upon him, who have souls to be saved as well as he; and this not for business, but state. Certainly a poor employment of his money, and a worse of their time.

266. But that any one man should make work for so many; or rather keep them from work, to make up a train, has a levity or luxury in it very reprovable, both in religion and government.

267. But even in allowable services, it has an humbling consideration, and what should raise the thankfulness of the great men to him, that has so much bettered their circumstances, and moderated the use of their dominion over those of their own kind.

268. When the poor Indians hear us call any of our family by the name of servants, they cry out, What, call brethren servants! We call our dogs servants, but never men. The moral certainly can do us no harm, but may instruct us to abate our height, and narrow our state and attendance.

269. And what has been said of their excess, may in some measure be applied to other branches of luxury, that set ill examples to the lesser world, and rob the needy of their pensions.

270. God Almighty touch the hearts of our grandees with a sense of His distinguished goodness, and the true end of it; that they may better distinguish themselves in their conduct, to the glory of Him that has thus liberally preferred them, and to the benefit of their fellow-creatures:

271. **Of Refining upon Other Men's Actions or Interests.** This seems to be the masterpiece of our politicians: but no body shoots more at random than those refiners.

272. A perfect lottery, and mere haphazard. Since the true spring of the actions of men is as invisible as their hearts: and so are their thoughts too of their several interests.

273. He that judges of other men by himself does not always hit the mark, because all men have not the same capacity, nor passions in interest.

274. If an able man refines upon the proceedings of an ordinary capacity, according to his own, he must ever miss it: but much more the ordinary man when he shall pretend to speculate the motives of the able man's actions: for the able man deceives himself by making the other wiser than he is in the reason of his conduct; and the ordinary man makes himself so, in presuming to judge of the reasons of the abler man's actions.

275. It is in short, a wood, a maze, and of nothing are we more uncertain, nor in any thing do we oftener befool our selves.

276. The mischiefs are many that follow this humour, and dangerous: for men misguide themselves, act upon false measures, and meet frequently with mischievous disappointments.

277. It excludes all confidence in commerce; allows of no such thing as a principle in practice: supposes every man to act upon other reasons then what appear, and that there is no such thing as uprightness or sincerity among mankind: a trick instead of truth.

278. Neither allowing nature or religion; but from worldly fetch or advantage: the true, the hidden motive to all men to act or do.

279. It is hard to express its uncharitableness, as well as uncertainty; and has more of vanity than benefit in it.

280. This foolish quality gives a large field, but let what I have said serve for this time.

281. **Of Charity.** Charity has various senses, but is excellent in all of them.

282. It imports, first, the commiseration of the poor and unhappy of mankind, and extends a helping hand to mend their condition.

283. They that feel nothing of this, are at best not above half of kin to human race; since they must have no bowels, which makes such an essential part thereof, who have no more nature.

284. A man, and yet not have the feeling of the wants or needs

of his own flesh and blood! A monster rather! And may he never be suffered to propagate such an unnatural stock in the world.

285. Such an uncharitableness spoils the best gains, and two to one but it entails a curse upon the possessors.

286. Nor can we expect to be heard of God in our prayers, that turn the deaf ear to the petitions of the distressed amongst our fellow-creatures.

287. God sends the poor to try us, as well as He tries them by being such: and he that refuses them a little out of the great deal that God has given him lays up poverty in store for his own posterity.

288. I will not say these works are meritorious, but dare say they are acceptable, and go not without their reward: Though to humble us in our fulness and liberality too, we only give but what is given us to give as well as use; for if we are not our own, less is that so which God has intrusted us with.

289. Next, charity makes the best construction of things and persons, and is so far from being an evil spy, a backbiter, or a detractor, that it excuses weakness, extenuates miscarriages, makes the best of every thing, forgives every body, serves all, and hopes to the end.

290. It moderates extremes, is always for expedients, labours to accommodate differences, and had rather suffer than revenge: and is so far from exacting the utmost farthing, that it had rather lose, than seek her own violently.

291. As it acts freely, so zealously too; but it is always to do good, for it hurts no body.

292. A universal remedy against discord, and an holy cement for mankind.

293. And lastly, it is love to God and the brethren which raises the soul above all worldly considerations; and, as it gives a taste of heaven upon earth, so it is heaven in the fulness of it, to the truly charitable here.

294. This is the noblest sense charity has, after which all should press, as that more excellent way.

295. Nay, most excellent; for as faith, hope and charity were the more excellent way that great apostle discovered to the Christians (too apt to stick in outward gifts and church performances) so of that better way he preferred charity as the best part, because it would out-last the rest, and abide for ever.

296. Wherefore a man can never be a true and good Christian

without charity, even in the lowest sense of it; and yet he may have that part thereof, and still be none of the apostle's true Christian, since He tells us, that though we should give all our goods to the poor, and want charity (in her other and higher senses) it would profit us nothing.

297. Nay, though we had all tongues, all knowledge, and even gifts of prophesy, and were preachers to others, ay, and had zeal enough to give our bodies to be burned, yet if we wanted charity, it would not avail us for salvation.

298. It seems it was his (and indeed ought to be our) unum necessarium, or the one thing needful, which our saviour attributed to Mary, in preference to her sister Martha, that seems not to have wanted the lesser parts of charity.

299. Would God this divine virtue were more implanted and diffused among mankind, the pretenders to Christianity, especially, and we should certainly mind piety more than controversy, and exercise love and compassion instead of censuring and persecuting one another in any manner whatsoever.

THE
ADVICE
OF
William Penn *to his CHILDREN,*
Relating to their
CIVIL and RELIGIOUS CONDUCT.

CHAPTER I

My Dear Children,

§1. Not knowing how long it may please God to continue me amongst you, I am willing to embrace this opportunity of leaving you my advice and counsel, with respect to your Christian and civil capacity and duty in this world: and I both beseech you and charge you, by the relation you have to me, and the affection I have always shown to you, and indeed received from you, that you lay up the same in your hearts, as well as your heads, with a wise and religious care.

§2. I will begin with that which is the beginning of all true wisdom and happiness, the holy fear of God.

Children, fear God; that is to say, have an holy awe upon your minds to avoid that which is evil, and a strict care to embrace and do that which is good. The measure and standard of which knowledge and duty is the light of Christ in your consciences, by which, as in John 3. 20, 21. you may clearly see if your deeds, ay and your words and thoughts too, are wrought in God or not: (for they are the deeds of the mind, and for which you must be judged) I say, with this divine light of Christ in your consciences, you may bring your thoughts, words and works to judgment in yourselves, and have a right true sound and unerring sense of your duty towards God and man. And as you come to obey this blessed light

in its holy convictions, it will lead you out of the world's dark and
degenerate ways and works, and bring you unto Christ's way and
life, and to be of the number of His true self-denying followers, to
take up your cross for His sake, that bore His for yours; and to
become the children of the light, putting it on, as your holy armour;
by which you may see and resist the fiery darts of Satan's temptations, and overcome him in all his assaults.

§3. I would a little explain this principle to you. It is called light,
John, 1. 9, c. 3. 19, 20, 21, and c. 8. 12, Eph. 5. 8, 13, 14. 1 Thes.
5. 5. 1 Ep of John 1. 5, 6, 7. Rev. 21. 23. because it gives man a
sight of his sin. And it is also called the quickening spirit; for so he
is called; and the Lord from heaven, as 1 Cor. 15. 45, 57, who is
called and calls himself the Light of the World, John 8. 12, and why
is he called the spirit? Because he gives man spiritual life. And John
16. 8. Christ promised to send his spirit to convince the world of
their sins: wherefore that which convinces you and all people of
their sins is the spirit of Christ: this is highly prized, Rom. 8. as you
may read in that great and sweet chapter, for the children of God
are led by it. This reveals the things of God, that appertain to man's
salvation and happiness, as 1 Cor. 2. 10, 11, 12. It is the earnest
God gives his people, 2 Cor. 5. 5, It is the great end and benefit and
blessing of the coming of Christ, viz. the shining forth of this light
and pouring forth of this spirit. Yea, Christ is not received by them,
that resist his light and spirit in their hearts; nor can they have the
benefit of his birth, life, death, resurrection, intercession, etc. who
rebel against the light. God sent his son to bless us, in turning of us
from the evil of our ways: therefore have a care of evil, for that
turns you away from God; and wherein you have done evil, do so
no more: but be ye turned, my dear children, from that evil, in
thought as well as in word or deed, or that will turn you from God,
your Creator, and Christ whom He has given you for your
redeemer; who redeems and saves his people from their sins. Tit. 2.
14. not in their sins, read Acts 2. and Heb. 8. and the Christian
dispensation will appear to be that of the Spirit, which sin quen-
cheth, hardens the heart against, and bolts the door upon. This holy
divine principle is called grace too, 1 Tim. 2. 11, 12, there you will
see the nature and office of it, and its blessed effects upon those that
were taught of it in the primitive days. And why grace? Because it
is God's love and not our desert, his good-will, his kindness. He so
loved the world, that he gave his only begotten Son into the world,
that whosoever believeth in him should not perish, but have

everlasting life, John 3. 16, and it is this Holy Son, that in John 1. 14, 16, is declared to be full of grace and truth, and that of his grace we receive grace for grace, that is, we receive of him, the fulness, what measure of grace we need. And the Lord told Paul in his great trials, when ready to stagger about the sufficiency of the grace he had received, to deliver him, my grace is sufficient for thee, 2 Cor. 12. 9. O children, love the grace, hearken to this grace, it will teach you, it will sanctify you, it will lead you to the rest and kingdom of God; as it taught the saints of old, first, what to deny, viz. to deny ungodliness and worldly lusts; and then what to do, viz. to live soberly, righteously and godly in this present world, Tit. 2. 11, 12. And he that is full of grace is full of light, and he that is full of light is the quickening spirit, that gives a manifestation of his spirit to every one to profit with, 1 Cor. 12. 7. And he that is the quickening spirit is the truth. I am the way, the truth and the life, said He, to his poor followers, John 14. 6. And if the truth make you free; said he, to the Jews, then are you free indeed John 8. 32, 36. And this truth sheds abroad it self in man and begets truth in the inward parts, and makes false, rebellious hypocritical man, a true man to God again. Truth in the inward parts is of great price with the Lord. And why called truth? Because it tells man the truth of his spiritual state; it shows him his state, deals plainly with him, and sets his sins in order before him. So that, my dear children, the light, spirit, grace, and truth are not divers principles, but divers words or denominations given to one eternal power and heavenly principle in you, though, not of you, but of God, according to the manifestation or operation thereof in the servants of God of old time: light, to discover and give discerning: spirit, to quicken and enliven: grace, to wit, the love of God: truth, because it tells man the truth of his condition, and redeems him from the errors of his ways; that as darkness, death, sin, and error are the same, so light, spirit, grace and truth, are the same.

§4. This is that which is come by Christ, and a measure of this light, spirit, grace and truth, is given to every man and woman to see their way to go by. This is that, which distinguishes friends from all other societies, as they are found walking in the same, which leads out of vain honours, compliments, lusts and pleasures of the world.

O my dear children, this is the pearl of price, part with all for it, but never part with it for all the world. This is the gospel leaven, to leaven you, that is, sanctify and season you in body, soul, and spirit, to God, your heavenly Father's use and service, and your own lasting comfort. Yea, this is the divine and incorruptible seed of the kingdom; of which all truly regenerate men and women, Christians of Christ's making, are born. Receive it into your hearts, give it room there, let it take deep root in you, and you will be fruitful unto God in every good word and work. As you take heed to it and the holy enlightenings and motions of it, you will have a perfect discerning of the spirit of this world in all its appearances in your selves and others; the motions, temptations and workings of it, as to pride, vanity, covetousness, revenge, uncleanness, hypocrisy and every evil way; you will see the world in all its shapes and features, and you will be able to judge the world by it, and the spirit of the world in all its appearances: you will see as I have done that there is much to deny, much to suffer and much to do: and you will see that there is no power or virtue, but in the light, spirit, grace and truth of Christ, to carry you through the world to God's glory and your everlasting peace. Yea, you will see what religion is from above, and what is from below; what is of God's working, and of man's making and forcing; also what ministry is of his spirit and giving, and what of man's studying, framing, and imposing. You will, I say, discern the rise, nature, tokens and fruits of the true from the false ministry, and what worship is spiritual, and what carnal; and what honour is of God, and what that honour is, which is from below, of men, yea, fallen men, that the Jews and the world so generally love, and which, is spoken against in John 5. 44. you will see the vain and evil communication, that corrupts good manners; the snares of much company and business, and especially the danger of the friendship of this present evil world. And you will also see that the testimony the eternal God hath brought our poor friends unto, as to religion, worship, truth-speaking, ministry, plainness, simplicity, and moderation in apparel, furniture, food, salutation, as you may read in their writings, from the very beginning, is a true and heavenly testimony of His mind, will, work and dispensation in this last age of the world to mankind, being the revival of true primitive Christianity: where your most tender father prays that you may be kept, and charges you to watch that you may be preserved in the faith and practise of that blessed testimony; and count it no small mercy from God, nor honour to you, that you come of parents that counted nothing too dear or near to part with, nor too great to do or suffer, that they might approve themselves to God, and testify their love to his most precious truth in the inward parts, in their generation. And I do also charge you, my dear children, to retain in your remembrance those worthy ancients in the work of Christ, which remained alive to your day and memory, and yet remain to your knowledge; more especially that man of God and prince in Israel, the first born and begotten of our day and age of truth, and the first and the great early instrument of God amongst us, George Fox. And what you have heard, seen and observed, of those heavenly worthies, their holy wisdom, zeal, love, labours and sufferings, and particular tenderness to you, treasure up for your children after you, and tell them what you have heard, seen and known, of the servants and work of God, and progress thereof, as an holy, exemplary, and edifying tradition unto them. And be sure, that you forsake not the assembling your selves with God's people, as the manner of some was Heb. 10. 25. and is at this day, especially among young people, the children of some friends, whom the love of this present evil world hath hurt and cooled in their love to God and his truth. But do you keep close to meetings, both of worship and business of the church, when of an age and capacity proper for it; and that not out of novelty, formality, or to be seen of men, but in pure fear, love and conscience to God your creator, as the public, just and avowed testimony of your duty and homage to him. In which be exemplary both by timely coming, and a reverent and serious deportment during the assembly; in which be not weary or think the time long till it be over, as some did of the Sabbaths of old time; but let your eye be to him you come to wait upon and serve, and do what you do as to him, and he will be your refreshment and reward; for you shall return with the seals and pledges of his love, mercy and blessings.

§5. Above all things, my dear children, as to your communion and fellowship with friends, be careful to keep the unity of the faith in the bond of peace. Have a care of reflectors, detractors, backbiters, that undervalue and undermine brethren behind their backs, or slight the good and wholesome order of truth, for the preserving things quiet, sweet and honourable in the church. Have a care of novelties, and airy changeable people, the conceited, censorious and puffed up; who at last have always shown themselves to be clouds without rain, and wells without water, that will rather disturb and break the peace and fellowship of the church, where they dwell, than not have their wills and ways take place, I charge you in the fear of the living God, that you carefully beware of all such: mark them as the apostle says, Rom. 16. 17, and have no fellowship with them; but to advise, exhort, intreat, and finally reprove them, Eph. 5. 11. For God is and will be with his people in this holy dispensation we are now under, and which is now amongst us, unto the end of days: It shall grow and increase in gifts, graces, power and lustre, for it is the last and unchangeable one: and blessed are your eyes, if they see it, and your ears if they hear it, and your hearts if they understand it; which I pray that you may to God's glory and your eternal comfort.

§6. Having thus expressed my self to you, my dear children, as to the things of God, his truth and kingdom, I refer you to His light, grace, spirit and truth within you, and the holy scriptures of truth without you, which from my youth I loved to read, and were ever blessed to me; and which I charge you to read daily: the Old Testament for history chiefly, the Psalms for meditation and devotion, the prophets for comfort and hope, but especially the New Testament for doctrine, faith and worship: for they were given forth by holy men of God in divers ages, as they were moved of the Holy Spirit; and are the declared and revealed mind and will of the Holy God to mankind under divers dispensations, and they are certainly able to make the man of God perfect, through faith unto salvation; being such a true and clear testimony to the salvation that is of God, through Christ the second Adam, the Light of the World, the quickening Spirit, who is full of grace and truth, whose light, grace, spirit and truth bear witness to them in every sensible soul, as they frequently plainly and solemnly bear testimony to the light, spirit, grace, and truth, both in himself and in and to his people, to their sanctification, justification, redemption and consolation, and in all men to their visitation, reproof and conviction in their evil ways. I say having thus expressed my self in general, I refer you, my dear children, to the light and spirit of Jesus, that is within you, and to the scriptures of truth without you, and such other testimonies to the one same eternal truth as have been born in our day; and shall now descend to particulars that you may more directly apply what I have said in general both as to your religious and civil direction in your pilgrimage upon earth.

CHAPTER II

§2. I will begin here also, with the beginning of time, the morning; so soon as you wake, retire your mind into a pure silence, from all thoughts and ideas of worldly things, and in that frame, wait upon God, to feel his good presence, to lift up your hearts to him, and commit your whole self, into his blessed care and protection. Then rise, if well, immediately; being dressed, read a chapter or more in the scriptures, and afterwards dispose your selves for the business of the day; ever remembring that God is present, the overseer of all your thoughts, words, and actions; and demean your selves, my dear children, accordingly; and do not you dare to do that in His holy all-seeing presence, which you would be ashamed, a man, yea a child, should see you do. And as you have intervals, from your lawful occasions, delight to step home, within your selves, I mean, and commune with your own hearts, and be still; and (as Nebuchadnezzar said on another occasion) One like the Son of God, you shall find and enjoy with you and in you; a treasure the world knows not of, but is the aim, end and diadem of the children of God. This will bear you up against all temptations, and carry you sweetly and evenly through your day's business, supporting you under disappointments, and moderating your satisfaction in success and prosperity. The evening come, read again the holy scripture, and have your times of retirement, before you close your eyes, as in the morning; that so the Lord may be the alpha and omega of every day of your lives. And if God bless you with families, remember good Joshua's Resolution, Josh. 24. 15. But as for me and my house, we will serve the Lord.

§2. Fear God, shew it in desire, refraining and doing: keep the inward watch, keep a clear soul and a light heart. Mind an inward sense, upon doing any thing; when you read the scripture, remark the notablest places, as your spirits are most touched and affected, in a common-place book, with that sense or opening which you receive; for they come not by study or in the will of man, no more than the scripture did; and they may be lost by carelessness, and over-growing thoughts and business of this life; so in pursuing any other good or profitable book; yet rather meditate than read much. For the spirit of a man knows the things of a man, and with that spirit, by observation of the tempers and actions of men you see in the world, and looking into your own spirit, and meditating thereupon, you will have a deep and strong judgment of men and things. For from what may be, what should be, and what is most probable or likely to be, you can hardly miss in your judgement of humane affairs; and you have a better spirit than your own, in reserve for a time of need, to pass the final judgment in important matters.

§3. In conversation, mark well what others say or do, and hide your own mind, at least till last; and then open it as sparingly as the matter will let you. A just observance and reflection upon men and things, give wisdom, those are the great books of learning, seldom read. The laborious bee draws honey from every flower. Be always on your watch, but chiefly in company, then be sure to have your wits about you, and your armour on; speak last and little, but to the point. Interrupt none, anticipate none, read Prov. 10. 8. 13. be quick to hear, slow to speak, Prov. 17. 27. It gives time to understand, and ripens an answer. Affect not words, but matter, and chiefly to be pertinent and plain: truest eloquence is plainest, and brief speaking, I mean, brevity and clearness, to make your selves easily understood by everybody, and in as few words as the matter will admit of, is the best.

§4. Prefer the aged, the virtuous and the knowing; and choose those that excel for your company and friendship, but despise not others.

§5. Return no answer to anger, unless with much meekness, which often turns it away: but rarely make replies, less rejoinders; for that adds fuel to the fire. It is a wrong time to vindicate your selves, the true ear being then never open to hear it. Men are not themselves, and know not well what spirits they are of: silence to passion, prejudice and mockery, is the best answer, and often conquers what resistance inflames.

§6. Learn and teach your children fair writing, and the most useful parts of mathematics, and some business when young; whatever else they are taught.

§7. Cast up your income and live on half, if you can one third, reserving the rest for casualties, charities, portions.

§8. Be plain in clothes, furniture and food, but clean, and then the coarser the better, the rest is folly and a snare. Therefore next to sin, avoid daintiness and choiceness about your person and houses. For if it be not an evil in it self, it is a temptation to it: and may be accounted a nest for sin to brood in.

§9. Avoid differences; what are not avoidable refer, and keep awards strictly, and without grudgings, read Prov. 18. 17, 18. C. 25. 88. Mat. 5. 38, to 41. 1 Cor. 1. 10 to 13. It is good counsel.

§10. Be sure draw your affairs into as narrow a compass as you can, and in method and proportion, time and other requisites proper for them.

§11. Have very few acquaintance, and fewer intimates, but of the best in their kind.

§12. Keep your own secrets, and do not covet others, but if trusted, never reveal them, unless mischievous to somebody; nor then, before warning to the party, to desist and repent. Prov. 11. 13. C. 2. 23. C. 25. 9, 10.

§13. Trust no man with the main chance, and avoid to be trusted.

§14. Make few resolutions, but keep them strictly.

§15. Prefer elders and strangers on all occasions, be rather last than first in conveniency and respect; but first in all virtues.

§16. Have a care of trusting to after games, for then there is but one throw for all; and precipices are ill places to build upon. Wisdom gains time, is before hand, and teaches to choose seasonably and pertinently; therefore ever strike while the iron is hot. But if you lose an opportunity, it differs, in this, from a relapse: less caution and more resolution and industry must recover it.

§17. Above all, remember your creator: remember yourselves and your families, when you have them, in the youthful time, and forepart of your life; for good methods and habits obtained then will make you easy and happy the rest of your days. Every estate has its snare: youth and middle-age, pleasure and ambition; old age, avarice; remember, I tell you, that man is a slave where either prevails. Beware of the pernicious lusts of the eye and the flesh, and the pride of life, 1 John 2. 15, 16, 17. which are not of the Father, but of the world. Get higher and nobler objects, for your immortal part, O my dear children, and be not tied to things without you, for then you can never have the true and free enjoyment of yourselves, to better things; no more than a slave in Algiers has of his house or family in London. Be free, live at home, in yourselves I mean, where lie greater treasures hid, than in the Indies. The pomp, honour, and luxury of the world are the cheats, and the unthinking and inconsiderate are taken by them. But the retired man is upon higher ground, he sees and is aware of the trick, condemns the folly, and bemoans the deluded. This very consideration, doubtless, produced those two passions, in the two greatest Gentiles of their time, Democritus and Heraclitus, the one laughing, the other weeping, for the madness of the world, to see so excellent and reasonable a creature, as man, so meanly trifling and slavishly employed.

§18. Choose God's trades before men's, Adam was a gardener, Cain a plowman, and Abel a grazier or shepherd: these began with the world, and have least of snare, and most of use. When Cain became murderer, as a witty man said,* he turned a builder of cities, and quitted his husbandry: Mechanics, as handicrafts, are also commendable, but they are but a second brood, and younger brothers. If grace employ you not, let nature and useful arts, but avoid curiosity these also, for it devours much time to no profit. I have seen a ceiling of a room, that cost half as much as the house; a folly and sin too.

§19. Have but few books, but let them be well chosen and well read, whether of religious or civil subjects. Shun fantastic opinions: measure both religion and learning by practice; reduce all to that, for that brings a real benefit to you, the rest is a thief and a snare. And indeed reading many books is but a taking off the mind too much from meditation. Reading yourselves and nature in the dealings and conduct of men, is the truest human wisdom. The spirit of a man knows the things of man, and more true knowledge comes by meditation and just reflection than by reading; for much reading is an oppression of the mind, and extinguishes the natural candle; which is the reason of so many senseless scholars in the world.

§20. Do not that which you blame in another. Do not that to another which you would not another should do to you. But above all, do not that in God's sight, you would not man should see you do.

§21. And that you may order all things profitably, divide your day, such a share of time for your retirement and worship of God: such a proportion for your business; in which remember to ply that first which is first to be done; so much time for yourselves, be it for study, walking, visit, etc. In this be first, and let your friends know it, and you will cut off many impertinencies and interruptions, and save a treasure of time to yourselves, which people most unaccountably lavish away. And to be more exact, (for much lies in this) keep a short journal of your time, though a day require but a line; many advantages flow from it.

§22. Keep close to the meetings of God's people, wait diligently

---

* Cowley in his Works, on Agriculture.

at them, to feel the heavenly life in your hearts. Look for that more than words in ministry, and you will profit most. Above all look to the Lord, but despise not instruments, man or woman, young or old, rich or poor, learned or unlearned.

§23. Avoid discontented persons, unless to inform or reprove them. Abhor detraction, the sin of fallen angels, and the worst of fallen men.

§24. Excuse faults in others, own them in yourselves, and forgive them against yourselves, as you would have your Heavenly Father and judge forgive you. Read Prov. 17. 9. and Matt. 6. 14, 15. Christ returns and dwells upon that passage of his prayer, above all the rest, forgiveness, the hardest lesson to man, that of all other creatures most needs it.

§25. Be natural; love one another; and remember, that to be void of natural affection is a mark of apostasy set by the apostle, 2 Tim. 3. 3. Let not time, I charge you, wear out nature; it may kindred according to custom, but it is an ill one, therefore follow it not. It is a great fault in families at this day: have a care of it, and shun that unnatural carelessness. Live as near as you can, visit often, correspond oftener, and communicate with kind hearts to one another, in proportion to what the Lord gives you; and don't be close, nor hoard up from one another as if you had no right or claim in one another, and did not descend of one most tender father and mother.

§26. What I write is to yours, as well as you, if God gives you children. And in case a prodigal should ever appear among them, make not his folly an excuse to be strange or close, and so to expose such an one to more evil; but show bowels, as* John did to the young man that fell into ill company whom with love he reclaimed, after his example that sends his sun and rain upon all.

§27. Love silence, even in the mind; for thoughts are to that, as words to the body, troublesome; much speaking, as much thinking spends, and in many thoughts, as well as words, there is sin. True silence is the rest of the mind, and is to the spirit, what sleep is to the body, nourishment and refreshment. It is a great virtue; it covers folly, keeps secrets, avoids disputes, and prevents sin. See Job 13. 5. Prov. 10. 19. c. 12. 13. 3. c. 18. 6, 7. c. 17. 28.

§28. The wisdom of nations lies in their proverbs, which are brief and pithy; collect and learn them, they are notable measures

---

* Euseb. *Ecc. Hist.* lib. 3. cap. xxiii.

and directions for human life; you have much in little; they save time and speaking; and, upon occasion, may be the fullest and fastest answers.

§29. Never meddle with other folks' business, and less with the public, unless called to the one by the parties concerned, (in which move cautiously and uprightly) and required to the other by the Lord in a testimony for his name and truth; remembering that old, but most true and excellent proverb, *bene qui latuit, bene vixit*, He lives happily that lives hiddenly or privately, for he lives quietly. It is a treasure to them that have it: study it, get it, keep it; too many miss it that might have it: the world knows not the value of it. It doubles man's life by giving him twice the time to himself, that a large acquaintance or much business will allow him.

§30. Have a care of resentment or taking things amiss, a natural, ready and most dangerous passion; but be apter to remit than resent, it is more Christian and wise. For as softness often conquers, where rough opposition fortifies, so resentment, seldom knowing any bounds, makes many times greater faults than it finds; for some people have out-resented their wrong so far, that they made themselves faultier by it, by which they cancel the debt through a boundless passion, overthrow their interest and advantage, and become debtor to the offender.

§31. Rejoice not at the calamity of any, though they be your enemies, Prov. 17. 5. c. 24. 17.

§32. Envy none; it is God that maketh rich and poor, great and small, high and low. Psal. 37. 1. Prov. 3. 31. c. 23. 17. c. 24. 1. 1 Chron. 22. 11, 12. Ps, 107. 40. 41.

§33. Be intreatable. Never aggravate. Never revile or give ill names: it is unmannerly as well as unchristian. Remember Matt. 5. 22. who it was said, He that calls his brother fool, is in danger of hell fire.

§34. Be not morose or conceited; one is rude, the other troublesome and nauseous.

§35. Avoid questions and strife; it shows a busy and contentious disposition.

§36. Add no credit to a report upon conjecture, nor report to the hurt of any. See Exod. 23. 1. Psal. 15. 3.

§37. Beware of jealousy, except it be godly, for it devours love and friendship; it breaks fellowship, and destroys the peace of the mind. It is a groundless and evil surmise.

§38. Be not too credulous; read Prov. 14. 14. Caution is a medium, I recommend it.

§39. Speak not of religion, neither use the name of God in a familiar manner.

§40. Meddle not with government; never speak of it; let others say or do as they please. But read such books of law as relate to the office of a justice, a coroner, sheriff and constable; also the doctor and student; some book of clerkship, and a treatise of wills, to enable you about your own private business only, or a poor neighbour's. For it is a charge I leave with you and yours, meddle not with the public, neither business nor money; but understand how to avoid it, and defend yourselves, upon occasion, against it. For much knowledge brings sorrow, and much doings more. Therefore know God, know yourselves; love home, know your own business and mind it, and you have more time and peace than your neighbours.

§41. If you incline to marry, then marry your inclination rather than your interest: I mean what you love, rather than what is rich. But love for virtue, temper, education, and person, before wealth or quality, and be sure you are beloved again. In all which be not hasty, but serious; lay it before the Lord, proceed in his fear, and be you well advised. And when married, according to the way of God's people, used amongst friends, out of whom only choose, strictly keep covenant; avoid occasion of misunderstanding, allow for weaknesses, and variety of constitution and disposition, and take care of showing the least disgust or misunderstanding to others especially your children. Never lie down with any displeasure in your minds, but avoid occasion of dispute and offence; overlook and cover failings. Seek the Lord for one another; wait upon him together, morning and evening, in His holy fear, which will renew and confirm your love and covenant: give way to nothing that would in the least violate it: use all means of true endearment, that you may recommend and please one another; remembering your relation and union is the figure of Christ's to his church; therefore let the authority of love only bear sway your whole life.

§42. If God give you children, love them with wisdom, correct them with affection: never strike in passion, and suit the correction to their age as well as fault. Convince them of their error before you chastise them, and try them, if they show remorse before severity, never use that but in case of obstinacy or impenitency. Punish them more by their understandings than the rod, and show them the folly, shame and undutifulness of their faults rather with a grieved than an angry countenance, and you will sooner affect their natures, and with a nobler sense, than a servile and rude chastisement can produce. I know the methods of some are severe corrections for faults, and artificial praises when they do well, and sometimes rewards: but this course awakens passions worse than their faults; for one begets base fear, if not hatred; the other pride and vain glory, both which should be avoided in a religious education of youth, for they equally vary from it and deprave nature. There should be the greatest care imaginable, what impressions are given to children; that method which earliest awakens their understandings to love, duty, sobriety, just and honourable things, is to be preferred. Education is the stamp parents give their children; they pass for that they breed them, or less value perhaps, all their days. The world is in nothing more wanting and reprovable, both in precept and example; they do with their children as with their souls, put them out at livery for so much a year. They will trust their estates or shops with none but themselves, but for their souls and posterity they have less solicitude. But do you breed your children yourselves, I mean as to their morals, and be their bishops and teachers in the principles of conversation: as they are instructed, so they are likely to be qualified, and your posterity by their precepts and examples which they receive from yours. And were mankind herein more cautious they would better discharge their duty to God and posterity; and their children would owe them more for their education than for their inheritances. Be not unequal in your love to your children, at least in the appearances of it: it is both unjust and indiscreet: it lessens love to parents, and provokes envy amongst children. Let them wear the same clothes, eat of the same dish, have the same allowance as to time and expense. Breed them to some employment, and give all equal but the eldest: and to the eldest a double portion is very well. Teach them also frugality, and they will not want substance for their posterity. A little beginning with industry and thrift will make an estate; but there is great difference between saving and sordid. Be not scanty any more than superfluous; but rather make bold with yourselves, than be straight to others; therefore let your charity temper your frugality and theirs.

What I have written to you, I have written to your children, and theirs.

§43. Servants you will have, but remember, the fewer the better, and those rather aged than young; you must make them such, or dispose of them often. change is not good, therefore choose well, and the rather because of your children; for children, thinking they can take more liberty with servants than with their parents, often choose the servants' company, and if they are idle, wanton, ill examples, children are in great danger of being perverted. Let them therefore be friends, and such as are well recommended: let them know their business as well as their wages; and as they do the one, pay them honestly the other. Though servants yet remember they are brethren in Christ, and that you also are but stewards and must account to God. Wherefore let your moderation appear unto them, and that will provoke them to diligence for love rather than fear, which is the truest and best motive to service. In short, as you find them, so keep, use and reward them, or dismiss them.

§44. Distrust is of the nature of jealousy, and must be warily entertained upon good grounds, or it is injurious to others, and instead of safe, troublesome to you. If you trust little, you will have but little cause to distrust. Yet I have often been whispered in my self of persons and things at first sight and motion, that hardly ever failed to be true; though by neglecting the sense, or suffering myself to be argued or importuned from it, I have more than once failed of my expectation. Have therefore a most tender and nice regard to those first sudden and unpremeditated sensations.

§45. For your conduct in your business and in the whole course of your life, though what I have said to you, and recommend you to, might be sufficient; yet I will be more particular as to those good and gracious qualifications, I pray God Almighty to season and accomplish you with, to his glory and your temporal and eternal felicity.

CHAPTER III

§1. Be humble. It becomes a creature, a depending and borrowed being, that lives not of itself, but breathes in another's air, with another's breath, and is accountable for every moment of time, and can call nothing its own, but is absolutely a tenant at will of the great Lord of heaven and earth. And of this excellent quality you cannot be wanting, if you dwell in the holy fear of the omnipresent and all-seeing God; for that will show you your vileness and His excellency, your meanness and His majesty, and withal, the sense of His love to such poor worms, in the testimonies He gives of His daily care, and mercy and goodness; that you cannot but be abased, laid low and humble. I say, the fear and love of God begets humility, and humility fits you for God and men. You cannot step well amiss if this virtue dwell but richly in you; for then God will teach you. The humble He teacheth his Ways, and they are all pleasant and peaceable to His children: yea, He giveth grace to the humble but resisteth the proud Jam. 4. 6. 1 Pet, 5. 5. He regardeth the proud afar off. Psal. 138. 6. They shall not come near Him, nor will He hear them in the day of their distress. Read Prov. 11. 2, c. 15. 33. c. 16. 18, 19. Humility seeks not the last word, nor first place; she offends none, but prefers others, and thinks lowly of herself; is not rough or self-conceited, high, loud, or domineering; blessed are they that enjoy her. Learn of me, said Christ, for I am meek and lowly in heart. He washed His disciples' feet, John 13, indeed himself was the greatest pattern of it. Humility goes before honour. Prov. 18. 12. There is nothing shines more clearly through Christianity than humility; of this the Holy Author of it is the greatest instance. He was humble in His incarnation; for He that thought it no robbery to be equal with God, humbled Himself to become a man; and many ways made Himself of no reputation. As first in His birth or descent, it was not of the princes of Judah but a virgin of low degree, the espoused of a carpenter; and so she acknowledges in her heavenly anthem, or ejaculation, Luke 1, 47, 48, 52. speaking of the great honour God had done her: And my spirit hath rejoiced in God my Saviour, for He hath regarded the low estate of his hand-maiden; He has put down the mighty from their seats, and exalted them of low degree. Secondly, He was humble in His life: He kept no court but in deserts and mountains and in solitary places; neither was He served in state, His attendants being of the mechanic size. By the miracles He wrought we may understand the food He ate, viz. barley-bread and fish; and it is not to be thought there was any curiosity in dressing them. And we have reason to believe His apparel was as moderate as His table. Thirdly, He was humble in His sufferings and death: He took all affronts patiently, and in our nature triumphed over revenge: He was despised, spit upon, buffeted, whipped, and finally crucified between thieves, as the greatest malefactor; yet He never reviled them, but answered all in silence and submission, pitying, loving and dying for those by whom He was ignominiously put to death. O mirror of humility! Let your eyes be continually upon it, that you may see your selves by it. Indeed His whole life was one continued great act of self-denial : and because He needed it not for Himself, He must needs do it for us ; thereby leaving us an example that we should follow His steps, 1 Pet. 2. 21. And as He was we should be in this world according to the beloved disciple 1 John 2. 6. So what He did for us was not to excuse but excite our humility. For as He is like God, we must be like Him, and that the froward, the contentious, the revengeful, the striker, the dueller, etc. cannot be said to be of that number, is very evident. And the more to illustrate this virtue, I would have you consider the folly and danger of pride its opposite : for this it was that threw the angels out of heaven, man out of paradise, destroyed cities and nations, was one of the sins of Sodom, Ezek. 16. 49. the destruction of Assyria and Israel, Isa. 3. 16. and the reason given by God for His great vengeance upon Moab and Ammon, Zeph. 2. 9, 10. Besides, pride is the vainest passion that can rule in man, because he has nothing of his own to be proud of, and to be proud of another's shows want of wit and honesty too. He did not only not make himself, but is born the nakedest and most helpless of almost all creatures. Nor can he add to his days or stature, or so much as make one hair of his head white or black. He is so absolutely in the power of another, that as I have often said, he is at best but a tenant at will of the great Lord of all, holding life, health, substance, and every thing at his sovereign disposal ; and the more man enjoys the less reason he has to be proud, because he is the more indebted and engaged to thankfulness and humility.

Wherefore avoid pride as you would avoid the devil ; remembering you must die, and consequently those things must die with you, that could be any temptation to pride ; and that there is a judgment follows, at which you must give an account both for what you have enjoyed and done.

§2. From humility springs meekness. Of all the rare qualities, of wisdom, learning, valour, etc. with which Moses was endowed, he was denominated by his meekness : this gave the rest a lustre they must otherwise have wanted. The difference is not great between these excellent graces ; yet the scripture observes some. God will teach the humble his way, and guide the meek in judgment. It seems to be humility perfectly digested, and from a virtue become a nature. A meek man is one that is not easily provoked, yet easily grieved ; not peevish or testy, but soft, gentle, and inoffensive. O blessed will you be, my dear children, if this grace adorn you ! There are divers great and precious promises to the meek in scripture. That God will clothe the meek with salvation; and blessed are they for they shall inherit the earth. Psal. 37. 11. Mat. 5. 5. Christ presses it in his own example, Learn of me for I am meek, etc, Mat. 11. 29. And requires his to become as little children in order to salvation, Mat. 18. 3. and a meek and quiet spirit is of great price with the Lord 1, Pet. 3. 4. It is a fruit of the spirit, Gal: 5. 22, 23, exhorted to Eph: 4. 2. Col. 3. 12. Tit. 3. 2. and many places more to the same effect.

§3. Patience is an effect of a meek spirit and flows from it: it is a bearing and suffering disposition; not choleric or soon moved to wrath, or vindictive; but ready to hear and endure too, rather than be swift and hasty in judgment or action. Job is as much famed for this, as was Moses for the other virtue: without it there is no running the Christian race, or obtaining the heavenly crown; without it there can be no experience of the work of God, Rom. 5. 3, 4, 5. For patience worketh, saith the apostle, experience; nor hope of an eternal recompense, for experience worketh that hope. Therefore, says James, let patience have its perfect work, Jam. 1. 4. It is made the saints excellency; here is the patience of the saints, Rev. 13. 10. It is joined with the kingdom of Christ, Rev. 1. 9. read Luke 21. 19. In patience possess your souls. Rom. 12. 12. ch. 15. 4. 2 Cor. 6, 4. 1 Thes. 5. 14. Be patient towards all men, Tit, 2. 2. Heb. 6. 12. ch. 10. 36. which shows the excellency and necessity of patience, as that does the true dignity of a man. It is wise and will give you great advantage over those you converse with on all accounts. For passion blinds men's eyes, and betrays men's weakness; patience sees the advantage and improves it. Patience enquires, deliberates and brings to a mature judgment; though your civil as well as Christian course you cannot act wisely and safely without it; therefore I recommend this blessed virtue to you.

§4. Show mercy, whenever it is in your power, that is forgive, pity and help, for so it signifies. Mercy is one of the attributes of God, Gen: 19. 19. Exod. 20. 6. Psal. 86. 15. Jer. 3. 12. It is exalted in scripture above all His works, and is a noble part of His image in man. God hath recommended it Hos. 12. 6. Keep mercy and judgment and wait on the Lord. God hath shown it to man, and made it his duty, Mic. 6. 8. He hath showed thee O man what is good, and what doth the Lord require of thee, but to do justly, and to love mercy and to walk humbly, or to humble thy self to walk with thy God: a short but ample expression of God's love, and man's duty; happy are you if you mind it. In which you see mercy is one of the noblest virtues. Christ has a blessing for them that have it, blessed are the merciful, (Mat. 5.) for they shall find mercy; a strong motive indeed. In Luke, 6. 35, 36. he commands it. Be you merciful as your Father is merciful. He bid the Jews that were so over-righteous, but so very unmerciful, learn what this meaneth: I will have mercy and not sacrifice, Matt. 9. 13: He hit them in the eye. And in his parable of the Lord and his servants, he shows what will be the end of the unmerciful steward, Mat. 18. 34, 35, that having been forgiven much by his master, would not forgive a little to his fellow-servant. Mercy is a great part of God's law, Exod. 23. 4, 5. It is a material part of God's true fast. Isa. 58. 6, 7. It is a main part of God's covenant, Jer. 31. 34. Heb. 8. 12. And the reason and rule of the last judgment, Mat. 25. 31, to the End: pray read it. It is a part of the undefiled religion, Jam. 1. 27. c. 3. 17. Read Prov. 14. 21, 22. But the merciful man's mercy reaches farther, even to his beast; then surely to man, his fellow-creature, he shall not want it. Wherefore, I charge you, oppress no body, man nor beast. Take no advantage upon the unhappy, pity the afflicted, make their case your own, and that of their wives and poor innocent children the condition of yours, and you cannot want sympathy, bowels, forgiveness, nor a disposition to help and succour them to your ability. Remember, it is the way for you to be forgiven, and helped in time of trial. Read the Lord's Prayer, Luke 11. Remember the nature and goodness of Joseph to his brethren; follow the example of the Good Samaritan, and let Edom's unkindness to Jacob's stock, Obad. 10–16. And the heathen's to Israel, Zach. 1. 21. c. 2. 8. 9, be a warning to you. Read also, Prov. 25. 21, 22. Rom. 12. 19, 20.

§5. Charity is a near neighbour to mercy: it is generally taken to consist in this, not to be censorious, and to relieve the poor. For the first, remember you must be judged. Mat. 7. 1. And for the last, remember you are but stewards. Judge not, therefore, lest you be judged. Be clear yourselves before you fling the stone. Get the beam out of your own eye; it is humbling doctrine, but safe. Judge, therefore, at your own peril: see it be righteous judgment, as you will answer it to the Great Judge. This part of charity also excludes whisperings, backbiting, talebearing, evil-surmising, most pernicious follies and evils, of which beware. Read 1. Cor. 13. For the other part of charity, relieving the poor, it is a debt you owe to God: you have all you have or may enjoy, with the rent-charge upon it. The saying is, that he who gives to the poor, lends to the Lord: but it may be said, not improperly, the Lord lends to us to give to the poor: they are at least partners by providence with you, and have a right you must not defraud them of. You have this privilege, indeed, when, what, and to whom; and yet, if you heed your guide, and observe the object, you will have a rule for that too.

I recommend little children, widows, infirm and aged persons, chiefly to you: spare something out of your own belly rather than let theirs go pinched. Avoid that great sin of needless expense on your persons and on your houses, while the poor are hungry and naked. My bowels have often been moved, to see very aged and infirm people, but especially poor helpless children, lie all night in bitter weather at the thresholds of doors, in the open streets, for want of better lodging. I have made this reflection, if you were so exposed, how hard would it be to endure? The difference between our condition and theirs has drawn from me humble thanks to God, and great compassion and some supply to those poor creatures. Once more be good to the poor: what do I say? be just to them, and you will be good to yourselves: think it your duty, and do it religiously. Let the moving passage, Mat. 25. 35. to the end, live in your minds: I was hungry, and thirsty, and naked, sick, and in prison, and you administered unto me, and the blessing that followed: also what he said to another sort, I was an hungry, and thirsty, and naked, and sick, and in prison, and you administered not unto me; for a dreadful sentence follows to the hard-hearted world. Woe be to them that take the poor's pledge, Ezek. 18. 12, 13. or eat up the poor's right. O devour not their part! Less lay it out in vanity, or lay it up in bags, for it will curse the rest. Hear what the Psalmist says, Psal. 41. Blessed is he that considereth the poor, the Lord will deliver him in time of trouble: the Lord will preserve and keep him alive, and he shall be blessed upon the earth: and thou wilt not deliver him into the will of his enemies. The Lord will strengthen him upon the bed of languishing: thou wilt make all his bed in his sickness. This is the reward of being faithful stewards and treasurers for the poor of the earth. Have a care of excuses, they are, I know, ready at hand: but read Prov. 3. 27, 28. Withhold not good from them, to whom it is due, when it is in the power of thine hand to do it. Say not unto thy neighbour go, and come again, and to morrow I will give, when thou hast it by thee. Also bear in mind Christ's doctrine, Mat. 5. 42. Give to him that asketh thee, and from him that would borrow of thee, turn not thou away. But above all, remember the poor woman, that gave her mite; which Christ preferred above all, because she gave all, but it was to God's treasury, Mark 12. 42, 43, 44.

§6. Liberality or bounty is a noble quality in man, entertained of few, yet praised of all, but the covetous dislike it, because it reproaches their sordidness. In this she differs from charity, that she has sometimes other objects, and exceeds in proportion. For she will cast her eye on those that do not absolutely want, as well as those that do; and always outdoes necessities and services. She finds out virtue in a low degree, and exalts it. She eases their burden that labour hard to live: many kind and generous spells such find at her hand, that don't quite want, whom she thinks worthy. The decayed are sure to hear of her: she takes one child, and puts out another, to lighten the loads of over-charged parents, more to the fatherless. She shows the value of services in her rewards, and is never debtor to kindness; but will be creditor on all accounts. Where another give six pence, the liberal man gives his shilling; and returns double the tokens he receives. But liberality keeps temper too; she is not extravagant any more than she is sordid; for she hates niggard's feasts as much as niggard's fasts; and as she is free, and not starched, so she is plentiful, but not superfluous and extravagant. You will hear of her in all histories, especially in scripture, the wisest as well as best of books: her excellency and her reward are there. She is commanded and commended, Deut. 15. 3, 4, 7, 8, and Psal. 37. 21. 26. The righteous showeth mercy and giveth, and the good man is merciful and ever lendeth. He shows favour and lendeth, and disperseth abroad. Psal. 112. 5. There is that scattereth, and yet encreaseth; and there is that withholdeth more than is meet, but it tendeth to poverty; the liberal soul shall be fat. Prov. 11. 24, 25. The bountiful eye shall be blessed, Prov. 22. 9. The churl and liberal man are described, and a promise to the latter, that his liberality shall uphold him, Isa. 32. 78. Christ makes it a part of his religion and the way to be the children of the highest (Read Luke 6. 34, 35.) to lend and not receive again, and this to enemies as well as friends; yea to the unthankful and to the evil; no exception made, no excuse admitted. The apostle Paul, 2 Cor. 9. 5–10, enjoins it, threatens the strait-handed, and promises the open-hearted a liberal reward.

Wheresoever therefore, my dear children, liberality is required of you, God enabling of you, sow not sparingly not grudgingly, but with a cheerful mind, and you shall not go without your reward; though that ought not to be your motive. But avoid ostentation, for that is using virtue to vanity, which will run you to profuseness, and that to want; which begets greediness, and that avarice, the contrary extreme. As men may go westward until they come east, and travel until they and those they left behind them, stand antipodes, up and down.

§7. Jutice or righteousness, is another attribute of God, Deut. 32. 4. Psal. 9. 7. 8. 5. 8. Dan. 9. 7. Of large extent in the life and duty of man. Be just therefore in all things, to all; to God as your Creator; render to Him that which is His, your hearts, for that acknowledgement He has reserved to Himself, by which only, you are entitled to the comforts of this and a better life. And if He has your hearts, you have Him for your treasure, and with Him all things requite to your felicity. Render also to Cæsar that which is his, lawful subjection; not for fear only, but conscience sake. To parents, a filial love and obedience. To one another, natural affection. To all people in doing as you would be done by hurt no man's name or person. Covet no man's property in any sort. Consider well of David's tenderness to Saul, when he sought his life, to excite your duty; and Ahab's unjust covetousness and murder of Nabath, to provoke your abhorrence of injustice. David, though anointed King, took no advantages, he believed, and therefore did not make haste, but left it to God to conclude Saul's reign, for he would not hasten it. A right method and a good end, my dear children, God has shown it you, and requires it of you.

Remember the tenth commandment, it was God gave it, and that will judge you by it. It comprehends restitution as well as acquisition, and especially the poor man's wages, Lev. 19. 13. Deut. 24. 14, 15. Jer. 22. 13. Amos. 5. 11. Mal. 3. 5. Samuel is a great and good example of righteousness, 1 Sam. 12. 3. He challenged the whole house of Israel, whom he had oppressed or defrauded. The like did the apostle to the Corinthians, 2 Cor. 7. 2. He exhorted that Christians to be careful that they did not defraud, 1 Thes. 4. 6, for this reason, that God was the avenger of the injured. But as bad as it was, there must be no going to law amongst Christians, 1 Cor. 6. 7. To your utmost power, therefore, owe no one any thing but love, and that in prudence as well as righteousness; for justice gives you reputation, and adds a blessing to your substance; it is the best security you can have for it.

I will close this head, with a few scriptures to each branch. To your superiors: submit to every ordinance of man, for the Lord's sake! Pet. 2. 12. Obey those that have rule over you. Heb. 13. 17.

Speak not evil of dignities. Jude 8. Pet. 2. 10. My Son fear thou the Lord and the King, and meddle not with them; that are given to change. P10. 24. 21. To your parents; Honour your father and your mother, that the days may be long in the land, which the Lord your God shall give you. Exod. 20. 12. Children obey your parents, it is the first command with promise. Ephef. 6. 1, 2. Great judgments follow those that disobey this law, and defraud their parents of their due. Whose robbeth his father or his mother, and saith, it is no transgression, the same is the companion of a destroyer. Prov. 28. 24: Or such would destroy their parents if they could. It is charged by the prophet Ezekiel upon Jerusalem, as a mark of her wicked state: in thee have thy princes set lightly by father or mother, oppressed strangers, and vexed fatherless and widows. Ezek. 22. 6, 7. To thy neighbour, hear what God's servants taught. To do justice and judgment is more acceptable to the Lord than sacrifice. Prov. 21. 3. Divers weights and measures are alike abomination unto the Lord. Levit. 19. 36. Deut. 25. 13. to 16. inclusive. Prov. 11. 1. c. 20. 10, 23. Read Prov. 22. 16, 22, 23, c. 23. 10, 11. Peruse the 6th of Micah, also Zech. 8. 16, 17. And especially the 15. Psal. As a short but full measure of life, to give acceptance with God.

I have said but little to you of distributing justice, or being just in power or government; for I should desire you may never be concerned therein, unless it were upon your own principles, and then the less the better, unless God require it from you. But if it ever be your lot; know no man after the flesh; know neither rich nor poor, great nor small, nor kindred, nor stranger, but the cause according to your understanding and conscience, and that upon deliberate enquiry and information. Read Exod. 23. from 1. to 10. Deut. 1. 16, 17. c. 16. 19, 20. c. 24. 17. 2 Sam. 23. 3. Jer. 22. 3, 4. Prov. 24, 23. Lam. 3. 35, 36. Hos. 12. 6. Amos 8. 4, 5, 6, 7, 8. Zeph. 2. 3. c. 3. 1. 3. Zech. 7. 9, 10. Jer. 5. 4, 5, 6. c. 8. 6, 7. Which show both God's commands and complaints, and man's duty in authority; which as I said before, wave industriusly at all times, for privacy is freed from the clamour, danger, incumbrance and temptation that attend stations in government: never meddle with it, but for God's sake.

§8. Integrity is a great and commendable virtue. A man of integrity, is a true man, a bold man and a steady man; he is to be trusted and relied upon. No bribes can corrupt him, no fear daunt him; his word is slow in coming but sure. He shines brightest in the fire, and his friend hears of him most, when he most needs him. His courage grows with danger, and conquers opposition by constancy. As he cannot be flattered or frightened into that he dislikes, so he hates flattery and temporizing in others. He runs with truth, and not with the times; with right and not with might. His rule is straight; soon seen but seldom followed: It has done great things. It was integrity preferred Abel's offering, translated Enoch, saved Noah, raised Abraham to be God's friend, and father of a great nation, rescued Lot out of Sodom, blessed and encreased Jacob, kept and exalted Joseph, upheld and restored Job, honoured Samuel before Israel, crowned David over all difficulties, and gave Solomon peace and glory, while he kept it; it was this preserved Mordecai and his people, and signally defended Daniel among the lions, and the children in the flames, that it drew from the greatest king upon earth, and an heathen too, a most pathetical confession, to the power and wisdom of the God that saved them, and which they served. Thus is the scripture fulfilled, the integrity of the upright shall guide them. Prov. 11. 3. O my dear children! fear love and obey this great holy and unchangeable God, and you shall be happily guided, and preserved through your pilgrimage to eternal glory.

§9. Gratitude or thankfulness is another virtue of great lustre, and so esteemed with God and all good men. It is an owning of benefits received, to their honour and service that confer them. It is indeed a noble sort of justice, and might in a sense be referred as a branch to that head; with this difference, though, that since benefits exceed justice, the tie is greater to be grateful, than to be just; and consequently there is something baser, and more reproachful in ingratitude than injustice. So that though you are not obliged by legal bonds or judgments, to restitution with due interest, your virtue, honour and humanity, are naturally pledges for your thankfulness: and by how much the less you are under external ties, esteem your inward ties so much the stronger. Those that can break them, would know no bounds: for make it a rule to you, the ungrateful would be unjust too, but for fear of the law. Always own therefore the benefits you receive, and then to choose, when they may most honour or serve those that conferred them. Some have lived to need the favours they have done, and should they be put to ask, where they ought to be invited? No matter if they have nothing to show for it, they show enough when they show themselves to those they have obliged: and such see enough to induce their gratitude, when they see their benefactors in adversity; the less law, the more grace and the stronger tie. It is an evangelical virtue, and works as faith does, only by love: in this it exactly resembles a Christian state, we are not under the law, but under grace, and it is by grace, and not by merit that we are saved. But are our obligations the less to God, that He heaps His favours so undeservedly upon us? Surely no. It is the like here, that which we receive is not owned or compelled, but freely given so no tie; but choice, a voluntary goodness without bargain or condition, but has this therefore no security? Yes certainly, the greatest; a judgment writ, and acknowledged in the mind; He is His to the altar with a good conscience: but how long? as long as He lives. The characters of gratitude, like those of friendship, are only defaced by death, else indelible. A friend loveth at all times, says Solomon, Prov. 17. 17. c. 27. 10. And thine own friend and thy father's friend forsake not. It is injustice, which makes gratitude a precept. There are three sorts of men that can hardly be grateful, the fearful man, for in danger he loses his heart, with which he should help his friend: the proud man, for he takes that virtue for a reproach: he that unwillingly remembers he owes any thing to God, will not readily remember he is beholden to man. History lays it to the charge of some, of this sort of great men, that uneasy to see the authors of their greatness, have not been quiet, till they have accomplished the ruin of those that raised them. Lastly, the covetous man, is as ill at it as the other two; his gold has spoiled his memory, and won't let him dare be grateful, though perhaps he owes the best part, at least the beginning of it, to another's favour. As there is nothing more unworthy of a man, so nothing in man, so frequently reproached in scripture. How often does God put the Jews in mind, for their forgetfulness and unthankfulness, for the mercies and favours they received from him, Read Deut. 32. 15. Jesurun waxed fat, and kicked against God, grew unmindful, forgot and forsook his rock that had done mighty things for him. Thus Moses, Deut. 31. 16, 17. Also Judg. 10. 11, 12, 13. and I Sam. 8. 8. David likewise in his 78. 105, 106. Psalms, gives an history of God's love to Israel, and their ingratitude. So Isa. 17. 1 to 11. Likewise Jer. 2. 31. 32. c. 5. 7. to 20. c. 15. 6. c. 16. 10, 11, 12, 20, 21. c. 18. 15. Hos. 8: 9. It is a mark of apostasy, from Christianity, by the apostle. 2 Tim. 3. 2.

§10. Diligence is another virtue useful and laudable among men: it is a discreet and understanding application of one's self to business; and avoids the extremes of idleness and drudgery. It gives great advantages to men: it loses no time, it conquers difficulties, recovers disappointments, gives dispatch, supplies want of parts; and is that to them, which a pond is to a spring; though it has no water of it self, it will keep what it gets, and is never dry. Though that has the heels, this has the wind; and often wins the prize. Nor does it only concern handicrafts and bodily affairs, the mind is also engaged, and grows foul, rusty and distempered without it. It belongs to you, throughout your whole man; be no more santering in your minds than in your bodies. And if you would have the full benefit of this virtue, don't baulk it by a confused mind. Shun diversions; think only of the present business, till that be done. Be busie to purpose; for a busy man, and a man of business, are two different things. Lay your matters right, and diligence succeeds them, else pain is lost. How laborious are some to no purpose? Consider your end well, suit your means to it, and then diligently employ them, and you arrive where you would be, with God's blessing. Solomon praises diligence very highly. First, it is the way to wealth: the diligent hand makes rich, Prov. 10. 4. The soul of the diligent shall be made fat, c. 13. 4. There is a promise to it, and one of another sort to the sluggard, c. 23, 21. Secondly, it prefers men, ver. 29. seest thou a man diligent in his business he shall stand before kings. Thirdly, it preserves an estate: be thou diligent to know the state of thy flocks, and look well to thy herd; for riches are not for ever, ch. 27. 23. 24. There is no living upon the principal, you must be diligent to preserve what you have, whether it be acquisition or inheritance, else it will consume. In short the wise man advises, whatsoever thy hand finds to do, do it with thy might. Eccl. 9. 10. As it mends temporal state, no spiritual one can be got or kept without it. Moses earnestly presses it upon the Israelites, Deut. 4. 9. and 6. 7. The Apostle Paul commends it in the Corinthians, and Titus to them for that reason 2 Cor. 8, 7. 22. So he does Timothy to the Philippians on the same account, and urges them to work out their salvation, Phil. 2. 12. 20, 21. Peter also exhorts the churches to that purpose: wherefore the rather brethren, says he, give diligence to make your calling and election sure: for if you do these things you shall never fail, 2 Pet. 1. 10. and in ch. 3. 13. 14. Wherefore beloved, seeing that you look for such things; (the end of the world and last judgment) be diligent that you may be found of him in peace, without spot and blameless. Thus diligence is an approved virtue: but remember that is a reasonable pursuit or execution of honest purposes, and not an overcharging or oppressive prosecution, to mind or body, or most lawful enterprises. Abuse it not therefore to ambition or avarice. Let necessity, charity, and conveniency govern it, and it will be well employed and you may expect prosperous returns.

§11. Frugality is a virtue too, and not of little use in life, the better way to be rich, for it has less toil and temptation. It is proverbial, a penny saved is a penny got; it has a significant moral; for this way of getting is more in your own power and less subject to hazard, as well as snares, free of envy, void of suits, and is beforehand with calamities. For many get that cannot keep and for want of frugality spend what they get, and so come to want what they have spent. But have a care of the extreme: want not with abundance, for that is avarice, even to sordidness; it is fit you consider children, age and casualties, but never pretend those things to palliate and gratify covetousness. As I would have your liberal but not prodigal; and diligent but not drudging; so I would have you frugal but not sordid. If you can, lay up one half of your income for those uses, in which let charity have at least the second consideration; but not Judas's, for that was in the wrong place.

§12. Temperance I must earnestly recommend to you, throughout the whole course of your life: it is numbered amongst the fruits of the spirit, Gal. 22, 23, and is a great and requisite virtue. Properly and strictly speaking, it refers to diet; but in general may be considered as having relation to all the affections and practices of men. I will therefore begin with it in regard to food, the sense in which it is customarily taken. Eat to live, and not live to eat, for that's below a beast. Avoid curiosities and provocations; let your chiefest sauce be a good stomach, which temperance will help to get you. You cannot be too plain in your diet, so you are clean; nor too sparing, so you have enough for nature. For that which keeps the body low, makes the spirit clear, as silence makes it strong. It conduces to good digestion, that to good rest, and that to a firm constitution. Much less feast any, except the poor; as Christ taught, Luke 14. 12, 13. For entertainments are rarely without sin; but receive strangers readily. As in diet so in apparel, observe I charge you an exemplary plainness. Choose your clothes for their usefulness not the fashion, and for covering and not finery, or to please a vain mind in yourselves or others: they are fallen souls that think clothes can give beauty to man. The life is more than raiment, Mat. 6. 25. Man cannot mend God's work, who can give neither life nor parts. They show little esteem for the wisdom and power of their creator, that underrate His workmanship (I was a going to say His image) to a tailor's invention: gross folly and profanity! But do you, my dear children, call to mind who they were of old, that Jesus said, took so much care about what they should eat, drink and put on. Were they not gentiles, heathens, a people without God in the world? Read Mat. 6, and when you have done that, peruse those excellent passages of the apostle Paul and Peter, 1 Tim. 2. 9, 10, and 1 Pet. 3. 3. 5, where, if you find the exhortation to women only, conclude it was effeminate, and a shame then for men to use such arts and cost upon their person. Follow you the example of those primitive Christians, and not voluptuous Gentiles, that perverted the very order of things: for they felt lust above nature, and the means above the end, and preferred vanity to conveniency: a wanton excess that has no sense of God's mercies, and therefore cannot make a right use of them, and less yield the returns they deserve. In short, these intemperances are great enemies to health and to posterity; for they disease the body, rob children, and disappoint charity, and are of evil example; very catching, as well as pernicious evils. Nor do they end there: they are succeeded by other vices, which made the apostle put them together in his epistle to the Galatians, Ch. 5. 20. 21. The evil fruits of this part of intemperance, are so many and great, that upon a serious reflection, I believe there is not a country, town, or family, almost, that does not labour under the mischief of it. I recommend to your perusal the first part of, *No Cross No Crown*, and of the *Address to Protestants*, in which I am more particular in my censure of it: as are the authorities I bring in favour of moderation. But the virtue of temperance does not only regard eating, drinking, and apparel: but furniture, attendance, expens–ce, gain, parsimony, business, diversion, company, speech, sleeping, watchings, and every passion of the mind, love, anger, pleasure, joy, sorrow, resentment, are all concerned in it: therefore bound your desires, learn your will's subjection, take Christ for your example, as well as guide. It was he that led and taught a life of faith in providence, and told his disciples the danger of the cares and pleasures of this world; they choked the seed of the kingdom, stifled and extinguished virtue in the soul, and rendered man barren of good fruit. His sermon upon the Mount is one continued divine authority in favour of an universal temperance. The apostle, well aware of the necessity of this virtue, gave the Corinthians a seasonable caution. Know ye not, says he, that they which run in a race, run all, but one receiveth the prize? So run that ye may obtain. And every man that striveth for mastery, (or seeketh victory) is temperate in all things: (he acts discreetly and with a right judgment) Now, they do it to obtain a corruptible crown, but we an incorruptible. I therefore so run as not uncertainly; so fight I, not as one that beateth the air: but I keep under my body, and bring it into subjection; left that by any means, when I have preached to others, I my self should become a castaway, 1 Cor. 9. 25. 27. In another chapter he presses the temperance almost to indifferency: but this I say, brethren, the time is short: it remaineth then, that both they that have wives, be as though they had none; and those that weep as though they wept not; and they that rejoice, as though they rejoiced not; and they that use this world as not abusing it. And all this is not without reason: he gives a very good one for it. For, sayeth he, the fashion of the world passeth away: but I would have you without carefulness, 1 Cor. 7. 29–32. It was for this cause he presided it so hard upon Titus to warn the elders of that time to be sober, grave, temperate, Tit. 2. 2. not eager, violent, obstinate, tenacious, or inordinate in any sort. He makes it an indispensible duty in pastors of churches, that they be not self-willed, soon angry, given to wine or filthy lucre, but lovers of hospitality, of good men, sober, just, holy, temperate, Tit. 1. 7, 8. And who so? Because against these excellent virtues there is no law., Gal. 5. 23.

I will shut up this head (being touched upon in divers places of this advice) with this one most comprehensive passage of the apostle, Philip. 4. 5. Let your moderation be known unto all men, for the Lord is at hand. As if He had said, Take heed! Look to your ways! Have a care what ye do! For the Lord is near you, even at the door; He sees you, He marks your steps, tells your wanderings, and He will judge you. Let this excellent, this home and close sentence live in your minds: let it ever dwell upon your spirits, my beloved children, and influence all your actions, ay, your affections and thoughts. It is a noble measure, sufficient to regulate the whole; they that have it are easy as well as safe. No extreme prevails; the world is kept at arm's end; and such have power over their own spirits, which gives them the truest enjoyment of themselves and what they have: a dominion greater than that of empires. O may this virtue be yours! You have grace from God for that end, and it is sufficient: employ it, and you cannot miss of temperance, nor therein of the truest happiness in all your conduct.

§13. I have chosen to speak in the language of the scripture;

which is that of the Holy Ghost, the spirit of truth and wisdom, that wanted no art or direction of man to speak by; and express itself fitly to man's understanding. But yet that blessed principle, the eternal word I begun with to you, and which is that light, spirit, grace and truth, I have exhorted you to in all its holy appearances of manifestations in your selves, by which all things were at first made, and man enlightened to salvation, is Pythagoras's great light and salt of ages, Anaxagoras's divine mind, Socrates's good spirit, Timæus's unbegotten principle, and author of all light, Hieron's God in man, Plato's eternal, ineffable and perfect principle of truth, Zeno's maker and father of all, and Plotin's root of the soul: who as they thus styled the eternal word, so the appearance of it in man, wanted not very significant words. A domestic God, or God within says Hieron, Pythagoras, Epictetus and Seneca; genius, angel or guide says Socrates and Timæus; the light and spirit of God says Plato; the divine principle in man says Plotin; the divine power and reason, the infallible immortal law in the minds of men, says Philo; and the law and living rule of the mind, the interior guide of the soul, and everlasting foundation of virtue, says Plutarch. Of which you may read more in the first part of the Christian Quaker, and in the Confutation of Atheism, by Dr Cudworth. These were some of those virtuous gentiles commended by the Apostle, Rom. 2. 13, 14, 15. that though they had not the law given to them, as the Jews had, with those instrumental helps and advantages, yet, doing by nature the things contained in the law, they became a law unto themselves.

WILLIAM PENN

A L E T T E R *from* WILLIAM PENN, *Proprietary and Governour of* Pennſylvania *in* America, *to the* Committee *of the* Free Society *of* Traders *of that* Province, *Reſiding in* London. *Containing a General Deſcription of the ſaid* Province, *it's* Soil, Air, Water, Seaſons *and* Produce, *both Natural and Artificial, and the* Good Increaſe *thereof.* *With an Account of the* Natives, *or* Aborigines.

My Kind Friends:

The kindness of yours by the ship *Thomas* and *Anne*, doth much oblige me; for by it I perceive the interest you take in my health and reputation, and the prosperous beginning of this province, which you are so kind as to think may much depend upon them. In return of which, I have sent you a long letter, and yet containing as brief an account of myself, and the affairs of this province, as I have been able to make.

In the first place, I take notice of the news you sent me, whereby I find some persons have had so little wit, and so much malice, as to report my death, and to mend the matter, dead a Jesuit too. One might have reasonably hoped, that this distance, like death, would have been a protection against spite and envy; and indeed, absence being a kind of death, ought alike to secure the name of the absent as the dead; because they are equally unable, as such, to defend themselves: But they that intend mischief, do not use to follow good rules to effect it. However, to the great sorrow and shame of the inventors, I am still alive, and no Jesuit, and I thank God, very well. And without injustice to the authors of this, I may venture to infer that they that wilfully and falsely report, would have been glad it had been so. But I perceive many frivolous and idle stories have been invented since my departure from England, which, perhaps, at this time, are no more alive than I am dead.

But if I have been unkindly used by some I left behind me, I found love and respect enough where I came: an universal kind welcome, every sort in their way. For here are some of several nations, as well as divers judgments: nor were the natives wanting in this, for their kings, queens, and great men, both visited and presented me; to whom I made suitable returns, etc.

For the PROVINCE, the General Condition of it take as followeth.

1. The country itself in its soil, air, water, seasons and produce, both natural and artificial, is not to be despised. The land containeth

divers sorts of earth, and sand yellow and black, poor and rich:
also gravel both loomy and dusty; and in some places, a fast fat
earth, like to our best vales in England, especially by inland brooks
and rivers, God in His wisdom having ordered it so, that the
advantages of the country are divided, the backlands being generally
three to one richer than those that lie by navigable waters. We have
much of another soil, and that is a black hasel-mould, upon a stony
or rocky bottom.

2. The air is sweet and clear, the heavens serene, like the south
parts of France, rarely overcast; and as the woods come by numbers
of people to be more cleared, that it self will refine.

3. The waters are generally good, for the rivers and brooks have
mostly gravel and stony bottoms, and in number hardly credible.
We have also mineral waters, that operate in the same manner with
Barnet and North Hall, not two miles from Philadelphia.

4. For the seasons of the year, having by God's goodness now
lived over the coldest and hottest that the oldest liver in the province
can remember, I can say something to an English understanding.

First, of the fall, for then I came in: I found it from the 24th of
October, to the beginning of December, as we have it usually in
England in September, or rather like an English mild spring. From
December to the beginning of the month called March, we had
sharp frosty weather; not foul, thick, black weather, as our North-
east winds bring with them in England; but a sky as clear as in
summer, and the air dry, cold, piercing and hungry; yet I remember
not, that I wore more clothes than in England. The reason of this
cold is given, from the great lakes that are fed by the fountains of
Canada. The winter before was as mild, scarce any ice at all; while
this, for a few days, froze up our great River Delaware. From that
month, to the month called June, we enjoyed a sweet spring, no
gusts, but gentle showers, and a fine sky. Yet this I observe, that the
winds here, as there, are more inconstant spring and fall, upon that
turn of nature, than in summer or winter. From thence, to this
present month, which endeth the summer, (commonly speaking) we
have had extraordinary heats, yet mitigated sometimes by cool
breezes. The wind that ruleth the summer season, is the south-west;
but spring, fall and winter, it is rare to want the wholesome north-
western seven days together: and whatever mists, fogs or vapours,
foul the heavens by easterly or southerly winds in two hours time
are blown away; the one is followed by the other: a remedy that
seems to have a peculiar providence in it to the inhabitants; the

multitude of trees yet standing being liable to retain mists and vapours, and yet not one quarter so thick as I expected.

5. The natural produce of the country, of vegetables, is trees, fruits, plants, flowers. The trees of most note are the black walnut, cedar, cyprus, chestnut, poplar, gumwood, hickory, sassafras, ash, beech and oak of divers sorts, as red, white and black; Spanish chesnut and swamp, the most durable of all: of all which there is plenty for the use of man.

The fruits that I find in the woods, are the white and black mulberry, chestnut, walnut, plums, strawberries, cranberries, hurtleberries, and grapes of divers sorts. The great red grape (now ripe) called by ignorance, the fox-grape, (because of the relish it hath with unskilled palates) is in it self an extraordinary grape, and by art, doubtless, may be cultivated to an excellent wine, if not so sweet, yet little inferior to the frontiniack, as it is not much unlike in taste, ruddiness set aside, which in such things, as well as mankind, differs the case much. There is a white kind of muskatel, and a little black grape, like the cluster-grape of England, not yet so ripe as the other; but they tell me, when ripe, sweeter, and that they only want skilful vinerons to make good use of them: I intend to venture on it with my Frenchman this season who shows some knowledge in those things. Here are also peaches, and very good, and in great quantities, not an Indian plantation without them; but whether naturally here at first, I know not, however one may have them by bushels for little; they make a pleasant drink, and I think not inferior to any peach you have in England, except the true Newington. It is disputable with me, whether it be best to fall to fining the fruits of stems and sets, already good and aproved. It seems most reasonable to believe, that not only a thing groweth best, where it naturally grows; but will hardly be equalled by another species of the same kind, that doth not naturally grow there. But to solve the doubt I intend, if God give me life, to try both, and hope the consequence will be as good wine, as any European countries, of the same latitude, do yield.

6. The artificial produce of the country is wheat, barley, oats, rye, peas, beans, squashes, pumpkins, water-melons, musk-melons, and all herbs and roots that our gardens in England usually bring forth.*

* Note, that Edward Jones, son-in-law to Thomas Wynn, living on the Schulkil, had with ordinary cultivation, for one grain of *English* barley, seventy stalks and ears of barley: And it is common in this country, from one bushel sown, to reap forty, often fifty, and sometimes sixty: and three pecks of wheat sows an acre here.

7. Of living creatures: fish, fowl, and the beasts of the woods, here are divers sorts, some for food and profit, and some for profit only: for food, as well as profit, the elk, as big as a small ox, deer bigger than ours, beaver, racoon, rabbits, squirrels, and some eat young bear, and commend it. Of fowl of the land, there is the turkey, (forty and fifty pound weight) which is very great; pheasants, heath-birds, pigeons, and partridges in abundance. Of the water, the swan, goose, white and gray; brands, ducks, teal, also the snipe and curlew, and that in great numbers; but the duck and teal excel, nor so good have I ever eaten in other countries. Of fish, there is the sturgeon, herring, rock, shad, catshead, sheepshead, eel, smelt, perch, roach; and in inland rivers, trout, some say, salmon, above the falls. Of shell-fish, we have oysters, crabs, cockles, conchs, and muscles; some oysters six inches long; and one sort of cockles as big as the stewing-oysters, they make a rich broth. The creatures for profit only, by skin or fur, and that are natural to these parts, are the wild cat, panther, otter, wolf, fox, fisher, minx, muskrat: And, of the water, the whale for oil, of which we have good store, and two companies of whalers, whose boats are built, will soon begin their work, which hath the appearance of a considerable improvement. To say nothing of our reasonable hopes of good cod in the bay.

8. We have no want of horses, and some are very good and shapely enough; two ships have been freighted to Barbados, with horses and pipe-staves, since my coming in. Here is also plenty of cow-cattle, and some sheep; the people plow mostly with oxen.

9. There are divers plants, that not only the Indians tell us, but we have had occasion to prove by swellings, burnings, cuts, etc. that they are of great virtue, suddenly curing the patient: and for smell, I have observed several, especially one, the wild myrtle; the other I know not what to call, but are most fragrant.

10. The woods are adorned with lovely flowers, for colour, greatness, figure and variety: I have seen the gardens of London best stored with that sort of beauty, but think they may be improved by our woods: I have sent a few to a person of quality this year for a trial.

Thus much of the country, next of the natives, or aborigines.

11. The natives I shall consider in their persons, language, manners, religion and government, with my sense of their original. For their persons, they are generally tall, straight, well-built, and of singular

proportion; they tread strong and clever, and mostly walk with a lofty chin: of complexion, black, but by design, as the gypsies in England. They grease themselves with bears' fat clarified, and using no defence against sun or weather, their skins must needs be swarthy. Their eye is little and black, not unlike a straight-looked Jew. The thick lip and flat nose, so frequent with the East Indians and blacks, are not common to them; for I have seen as comely European-like faces among them of both, as on your side the sea; and truly an Italian complexion hath not much more of the white, and the noses of several of them have as much of the Roman.

12. Their language is lofty, yet narrow, but like the Hebrew, in signification full, like short-hand in writing; one word serveth in the place of three, and the rest are supplied by the understanding of the hearer: imperfect in their tenses, wanting in their moods, participles, adverbs, conjunctions, interjections: I have made it my business to understand it; that I might not want an interpreter on any occasion: and I must say, that I know not a language spoken in Europe that hath words of more sweetness or greatness, in accent and emphasis, than theirs. For instance, Octocockon, Rancocas, Oricton, Shak, Marian, Poquesien, all which are names of places, and have grandeur in them. Of words of sweetness, anna, is mother, issimus, a brother, netcap, friend, usque oret, very good, pane, bread, metse, eat, matta, no, hatta, to have, payo, to come; sepassen, passion, the names of places; Tamane, Secane, Menanse, Secatereus, are the names of persons. If one ask them for any thing they have not, they will answer, *Mattá ne hattá*, which to translate is, not I have, instead of I have not.

13. Of their customs and manners, there is much to be said. I will begin with children. So soon as they are born, they wash them in water, and while very young and in cold weather to choose, they plunge them in the rivers, to harden and embolden them. Having wrappped them in a clout, they lay them on a straight thin board, a little more than the length and breadth of the child, and swadle it fast upon the board to make it straight; wherefore all Indians have flat heads; and thus they carry them at their backs. The children will go very young, at nine months commonly; they wear only a small clout round their waist till they are big; if boys, they go fishing till ripe for the woods, which is about fifteen; then they hunt, and after having given some proofs of their manhood, by a good return of skins, they may marry, else it is a shame to think of a wife. The girls stay with their mothers, and help to hoe the

ground, plant corn, and carry burdens; and they do well to use them to that young, they must do when they are old; for the wives are the true servants of the husbands; otherwise the men are very affectionate to them.

14. When the young women are fit for marriage, they wear something upon their heads for an advertisement, but so as their faces are hardly to be seen, but when they please: the age they marry at, if women, is about thirteen and fourteen, if men, seventeen and eighteen; they are rarely older.

15. Their houses are mats, or barks or trees, set on poles, in the fashion of an English barn, but out of the power of the winds, for they are hardly higher than a man; they lie on reeds or grass. In travel, they lodge in the woods about a great fire, with the mantle of duffills they wear by day wrapt about them, and a few boughs stuck round them.

16. Their diet is maize, or Indian corn, divers ways prepared; sometimes roasted in the ashes, sometimes beaten and boiled with water, which they call hominy; they also make cakes, not unpleasant to eat: they have likewise several sorts of beans and peas, that are good nourishment; and the woods and rivers are their larder.

17. If an European comes to see them, or calls for lodging at their house, or wigwam, they give him the best place, and first cut. If they come to visit us, they salute us with an itah, which is as much as to say, good be to you, and set them down, which is mostly on the ground, close to their heels, their legs upright; it may be they speak not a word, but observe all passages: if you give them anything to eat or drink, well, for they will not ask; and be it little or much, if it be with kindness, they are well-pleased, else they go away sullen, but say nothing.

18. They are great concealers of their own resentments, brought to it, I believe, by the revenge that hath been practised among them; in either of these, they are not exceeded by the Italians. A tragical instance fell out since I came into the country: a king's daughter thinking herself slighted by her husband, in suffering another woman to lie down between them, rose up, went out, plucked a root out of the ground, and ate it, upon which she immediately died; and for which, last week, he made an offering to her husband for atonement, and liberty of marriage; as two others did to the kindred of their wives that died a natural death: for till widowers have done so, they must not marry again. Some of the young

women are said to take undue liberty before marriage, for a portion; but when married, chaste; when with child, they know their husbands no more till delivered, and during their month, they touch no meat they eat, but with a stick, lest they should defile it; nor do their husbands frequent them, till that time be expired.

19. But in liberality they excel, nothing is too good for their friend; give them a fine gun, coat, or other thing, it may pass twenty hands before it sticks; light of heart, strong affections, but soon spent; the most merry creatures that live, feast and dance perpetually, they never have much, nor want much: wealth circulateth like the blood, all parts partake; and though none shall want what another hath, yet exact observers of property. Some kings have sold, others presented me with several parcels of land; the pay, or presents I made them were not hoarded by the particular owners, but the neighbouring kings and their clans being present when the goods were brought out, the parties chiefly concerned, consulted what, and to whom they should give them. To every king then, by the hands of a person for that work appointed, is a proportion sent, so sorted and folded, and with that gravity that is admirable. Then that king sub-divideth it in like manner among his dependents, they hardly leaving themselves an equal share with one of their subjects: and be it on such occasions as festivals, or at their common meals, the kings distribute, and to themselves last. They care for little, because they want but little, and the reason is, a little contents them in this they are sufficiently revenged on us; if they are ignorant of our pleasures, they are also free from our pains. They are not disquieted with bills of lading and exchange, nor perplexed with Chancery suits and Exchequer-reckonings. We sweat and toil to live; their pleasure feeds them; I mean, their hunting, fishing and fowling, and this table is spread every where: they eat twice a day, morning and evening; their seats and table are the ground. Since the Europeans came into these parts, they are grown great lovers of strong liquors, rum especially; and for it exchange the richest of their skins and furs. If they are heated with liquors, they are restless till they have enough to sleep; that is they cry some more, and I will go to sleep, but, when drunk, one of the most wretchedest spectacles in the world.

20. In sickness, impatient to be cured, and for it give anything, especially for their children, to whom they are extremely natural: they drink at those times, a teran, or decoction of some roots in spring water; and if they eat any flesh, it must be of the female of

any creature. If they die, they bury them with their apparel, be they man or woman, and the nearest of kin fling in something precious with them, as a token of their love: Their mourning is blacking of their faces, which they continue for a year: They are choice of the graves of their dead; for lest they should be lost by time, and fall to common use, they pick off the grass that grows upon them, and heap up the fallen earth with great care and exactness.

21. These poor people are under a dark night in things relating to religion, to be sure, the tradition of it; yet they believe in God and immortality, without the help of metaphysics; for they say, there is a great king that made them, who dwells in a glorious country to the southward of them, and that the souls of the good shall go thither, where they shall live again. Their worship consists of two parts, sacrifice and cantico: their sacrifice is their first fruits; the first and fattest buck they kill, goeth to the fire, where he is all burnt, with a mournful ditty of him that performeth the ceremony, but with such marvellous fervency, and labour of body, that he will even sweat to a foam. The other part is their cantico, performed by round-dances, sometimes words, sometimes songs, then shouts, two being in the middle that begin and by singing and drumming on a board, direct the chorus. Their postures in the dance are very antic, and differing, but all keep measure. This is done with equal earnestness and labour, but great appearance of joy. In the fall, when the corn cometh in, they begin to feast one another; there have been two great festivals already, to which all come that will: I was at one my self; their entertainment was a great seat by a spring, under some shady trees, and twenty bucks, with hot cakes of new corn, both wheat and beans, which they make up in a square form, in the leaves of the stem, and bake them in the ashes; and after that they fall to dance. But they that go must carry a small present in their money, it may be six pence, which is made of the bone of a fish; the black is with them as gold, the white, silver; they call it all wampum.

22. Their government is by kings, which they call Sachema, and those by succession, but always of the mother's side: for instance, the children of him that is now king will not succeed, but his brother by the mother or the children of his sister, whose sons, (and after them the children of her daughters) will reign; for no woman inherits, the reason they render for this way of descent is that their issue may not be spurious.

23. Every king hath his council, and that consists of all the old

and wise men of his nation, which perhaps is two hundred people : nothing of moment is undertaken, be it war, peace, selling of land or traffic, without advising with them ; and which is more, with the young men too. It is admirable to consider how powerful the kings are, and yet how they move by the breath of their people. I have had occasion to be in council with them upon treaties for land, and to adjust the terms of trade ; their order is thus : The king sits in the middle of an half moon, and hath his council, the old and wise on each hand ; behind them or at a little distance sit the younger fry, in the same figure. Having consulted and resolved their business, the king ordered one of them to speak to me ; he stood up, came to me, and in the name of his king saluted me, then took me by the hand, and told me he was ordered by his king to speak to me, and that now it was not he, but the king that spoke, because what he should say was the king's mind. He first prayed me to excuse them that they had not complied with me the last time ; he feared, there might be some fault in the interpreter, being neither Indian nor English ; besides, it was the Indian custom to deliberate and take up much time in council, before they resolve ; and that if the young people and owners of the land had been as ready as he, I had not met with so much delay. Having thus introduced his matter, he fell to the bounds of the land they had agreed to dispose of, and the price, (which now is little and dear, that which would have bought twenty miles not buying now two) during the time that this person spoke, not a man of them was observed to whisper or smile ; the old grave, the young reverent in their deportment ; they do speak little, but fervently, and with elegancy : I have never seen more natural sagacity, considering them without the help (I was going to say, the spoil) of tradition ; and he will deserve the name of wise, that outwits them in any treaty about a thing they understand. When the purchase was agreed, great promises passed between us of kindness and good neighbourhood, and that the Indians and English must live in love, as long as the sun gave light. Which done, another made a speech to the Indians, in the name of all the sachamakers or kings, first to tell them what was done ; next, to charge and command them to love the Christians, and particularly live in peace with me, and the people under my government : that many governors had been in the river, but that no governor had come himself to live and stay here before ; and having now such an one that had treated them well, they should never do him or his any wrong. At every sentence of which they shouted, and said amen, in their way.

24. The justice they have is pecuniary. In case of any wrong or evil fact, be it murder itself, they atone by feasts and presents of their wampum, which is proportioned to the quality of the offence or person injured, or of the sex they are of: for in case they kill a woman, they pay double, and the reason they render, is, that she breedeth children, which men cannot do. It is rare that they fall out if sober; and if drunk, they forgive it, saying, it was the drink, and not the man, that abused them.

25. We have agreed that in all differences between us, six of each side shall end the matter: don't abuse them, but let them have justice, and you win them: the worst is, that they are the worse for the Christians who have propagated their vices, and yielded them tradition for ill, and not for good things. But as low an ebb as these people are at, and as glorious as their own condition looks, the Christians have not out-lived their sight with all their pretensions to an higher manifestation: what good then might not a good people graft, where there is so distinct a knowledge left between good and evil? I beseech God to incline the hearts of all that come into these parts, to out-live the knowledge of the natives, by a fixed obedience to their greater knowledge of the will of God; for it were miserable indeed for us to fall under the just censure of the poor Indian conscience, while we make profession of things so far transcending.

26. For their original, I am ready to believe them of the Jewish race, I mean, of the stock of the ten tribes, and that for the following reasons; first they were to go to a land not planted or known, which to be sure Asia and Africa were, if not Europe; and he that intended that extraordinary judgment upon them, might make the passage not uneasy to them, as it is not impossible in it self, from the eastern-most parts of Asia, to the western-most of America. In the next place, I find them of like countenance, and their children of so lively resemblance, that a man would think himself in Dukes Place or Berry Street in London, when he seeth them. But this is not all; they agree in rites, they reckon by moons, they offer their first fruits, they have a kind of feast of tabernacles, they are said to lay their altar upon twelve stones; their mourning a year, customs of women, with many things that do not now occur.

So much for the natives, next the old planters will be considered in this relation, before I come to our colony, and the concerns of it.

27. The first planters in these parts were the Dutch, and soon after them the Swedes and Finns. The Dutch applied themselves to

traffic, the Swedes and Finns to husbandry. There were some disputes between them some years, the Dutch looking upon them as intruders upon their purchase and possession, which was finally ended in the surrender made by John Rizeing, the Swedish governor, to Peter Styvesant, governor for the states of Holland, Anno 1655.

28. The Dutch inhabit mostly those parts of the province that lie upon or near to the bay, and the Swedes the freshes of the River Delaware. There is no need of giving any description of them, who are better known there than here; but they are a plain, strong, industrious people, yet have made no great progress in culture or propagation of fruit trees, as if they desired rather to have enough, than plenty or traffic. But I presume the Indians made them the more careless, by furnishing them with the means of profit, to wit, skins and furs, for rum, and such strong liquors. They kindly received me, as well as the English, who were few, before the people concerned with me came among them: I must needs commend their respect to authority and kind behaviour to the English; they do not degenerate from the old friendship between both kingdoms. As they are people proper and strong of body, so they have fine children, and almost every house full; rare to find one of them without three or four boys and as many girls; some six, seven and eight sons: and I must do them that right, I see few young men more sober and laborious.

29. The Dutch have a meeting-place for religious worship at Newcastle, and the Swedes, three, one at Chrislina, one at Tenecum, and one at Wicoco, within half a mile of this town.

30. There rests, that I speak of the condition we are in, and what settlement we have made, in which I will be as short as I can; for I fear, and not without reason, that I have tried your patience with this long story. The country lieth bounded on the east by the river and bay of Delaware, and Eastern Sea; it hath the advantage of many creeks, or rivers rather, that run into the main river or bay; some navigable for great ships, some for small craft: those of most eminency are Christina, Brandywine, Skilpot and Skulkill; any one of which have room to lay up the royal navy of England, there being from four to eight fathom water.

31. The lesser creeks or rivers, yet convenient for sloops and ketches of good burden, are Lewis, Mespilion, Cedar, Dover, Cranbrook, Feversham, and Georges below, and Chichester, Chester, Toacawny, Pemmapecka, Portquessin, Neshimenck and Pennberry in the freshes; many lesser that admit boats and shallops. Our

people are mostly fettled upon the upper rivers, which are pleasant and sweet, and generally bounded with good land. The planted part of the province and territories is cast into six counties, Philadelphia, Buckingham, Chester, Newcastle, Kent and Sussex, containing about four thusand souls. Two general assemblies have been held, and with such concord and dispatch that they sat but three weeks, and at least seventy laws, were passed without one different in any material thing. But of this more hereafter, being yet raw and new in our gear. However, I cannot forget their singular respect to me in this infancy of things, who by their own private expenses so early considered mine for the public, as to present me with an impost upon certain goods imported and exported: which after my acknowledgements of their affection, I did as freely remit to the province and the traders to it. And for the well government of the said counties, courts of justice are established in every county, with proper officers, as justices, sheriffs, clerks, constables, etc. which courts are held every two months. But to prevent law-suits, there are three peace-makers chosen by every county-court, in the nature of common arbitrators, to heat and end differences betwixt man and man; and spring and fall there is an orphan's court in each county, to inspect and regulate the affairs of orphans and widows.

32. Philadelphia, the expectation of those that are concerned in this province, is at last laid out, to the great content of those here, that are any way interested therein: the situation is a neck of land, and lieth between two navigable rivers, Delaware and Skulkill, whereby it hath two fronts upon the water, each a mile, and two from river to river. Delaware is a glorious river, but the Skulkill being an hundred miles boatable above the falls, and its course north-east toward the fountain of Susquahannah (that tends to the heart of the province, and both sides our own) it is like to be a great part of the settlement of this age. I say little of the town itself, because a platform will be shown you by my agent, in which those who are purchasers of me will find their names and interests: but this I will say for the good providence of God, that of all the many places I have seen in the world, I remember not one better seated; so that it seems to me to have been appointed for a town, whether we regard the rivers, or the conveniency of the coves, docks, springs, the loftiness and soundness of the land and the air, held by the people of these parts to be very good. It is advanced within less than a year to about four-score houses and cottages, such as they are, where merchants and handicrafts are following their vocations

as fast as they can, while the country-men are close at their farms:
some of them got a little winter-corn in the ground last season, and
the generality have had an handsome summer-crop, and are preparing for their winter-corn. They reaped their barley this year in
the month called May; the wheat in the month following; so that
there is time in these parts for another crop of diverse things before
the winter season. We are daily in hopes of shipping to add to our
number; for blessed be God, here is both room and accommodation
for them; the stories of our necessity being either the fear of our
friends, or the scarecrows of our enemies; for the greatest hardship
we have suffered hath been salt-meat, which by fowl in winter, and
fish in summer, together with some poultry, lamb, mutton, veal,
and plenty of venison the best part of the year, hath been made very
passable. I bless God, I am fully satisfied with the country and
entertainment I can get in it; for I find that particular content which
hath always attended me, where God in His providence hath made
it my place and service to reside. You cannot imagine, my station
can be at present free of more than ordinary business, and as such,
I may say, it is a troublesome work, but the method things are
putting in will facilitate the charge, and give an easier motion to the
administration of affairs. However, as it is some men's duty to
plow, some to sow, some to water, and some to reap; so it is the
wisdom as well as duty of a man, to yield to the mind of providence,
and cheerfully, as well as carefully, embrace and follow the guidance
of it.

33. For your particular concern, I might entirely refer you to the
letters of the president of the society; but this I will venture to say,
your provincial settlements both within and without the town, for
situation and soil, are without exception: your city-lot is a whole
street, and one side of a street, from river to river, containing near
one hundred acres, not easily valued, which is besides your four
hundred acres in the city-liberties, part of your twenty thousand
acres in the country. Your tannery hath such plenty of bark; the
saw-mill for timber, and the place of the glasshouse are so con-
veniently posted for water-carriage, the city-lot for a dock, and the
whalery for a sound and fruitful bank, and the town Lewis by it to
help your people, that by God's blessing the affairs of the society
will naturally grow in their reputation and profit. I am sure I have
not turned my back upon any offer that tended to its prosperity;
and though I am ill at projects, I have sometimes put in for a share
with her officers, to countenance and advance her interest. You are

already informed what is fit for you farther to do, whatsoever tends to the promotion of wine, and to the manufacture of linen in these parts, I cannot but wish you to promote it; and the French people are most likely in both respects to answer that design: to that end, I would advise you to send for some thousands of plants out of France with some able vinerons, and people of the other vocation. But because I believe you have been entertained with this and some other profitable subjects by your president, I shall add no more, but to assure you, that I am heartily inclined to advance your just interest, and that you will always find me,

Your kind cordial friend,
W. PENN

Philadelphia, the 16th of the 6th Month, called August, 1683.

Part II
Writings on Religious Liberty

The People's Ancient and Juſt LIBERTIES Aſſerted,
in the Trial of *William Penn* and *William Mead*, at the Seſſions held
at the *Old-Baily* in *London*, the Firſt, Third, Fourth and Fifth of
September, 1670, againſt the moſt Arbitrary Procedure of that
COURT.

TO THE ENGLISH READER

If ever it were time to speak, or write, it is now, so many strange
occurrences requiring both.

How much thou art concerned in this ensuing trial where not
only the prisoners, but the fundamental laws of *England* have been
most arbitrarily arraigned, read, and thou mayest plainly judge.

Liberty of conscience, is counted a pretence for rebellion, and
religious assemblies, routs and riots; and the defenders of both, are
by them reputed factious, and disaffected.

Magna Charta, is Magna Far – with the recorder of London;
and to demand right, an afront to the court.

Will and power are their Great Charter, but to call for England's,
is a crime; incurring the penalty of their bale-dock and nasty hole;
nay, the menace of a gag, and iron shackles too.

The jury (though proper Judges of Law and fact) they would
have over-ruled in both, as if their verdict signified no more, than
to echo back the illegal charge of the bench; and because their
courage and honesty, did more than hold pace with the threat and
abuse of those who sat as judges (after two days and two nights
restraint for a verdict) in the end were fined and imprisoned for
giving it.

Oh! What monstrous and illegal proceedings are these? Who
reasonably can call his coat his own? When property is made
subservient to the will and interest of his judges; or, who can truly
esteem himself a free man? When all pleas for liberty are esteemed
sedition, and the laws that give and maintain them, so many
insignificant pieces of formality.

And what do they less than plainly tell us so, who at will and
pleasure, break open our locks, rob our houses, raze our foundations, imprison our persons, and finally, deny us justice to our

relief; as if they then acted most like Christian men, when they were most barbarous, in ruining such as are really so; and that no sacrifice could be so acceptable to God, as the destruction of those that most fear him.

In short, that the conscientious should only be obnoxious, and the just demand of our religious liberty, the reason why we should be denied our civil freedom (as if to be a Christian and an Englishman were inconsistent) and that so much solicitude and deep contrivance should be employed ony to ensnare and ruin so many ten thousand conscientious families (so eminently industrious, serviceable and exemplary; whilst murders can so easily obtain pardon, rapes be remitted, public uncleanness pass unpunished, and all manner of levity, prodigality, excess, prophaneness and atheism, universally connived at, if not in some respect manifestly encouraged) cannot but be detestably abhorrent to every serious and honest mind.

Yet that this lamentable state is true, and the present project in hand, let London's recorder, and Canterbury's chaplain be heard.

The first in his public panegyrick upon the Spanish Inquisition, highly admiring the prudence of the Romish church in the erection of it, as an excellent way to prevent schism, which unhappy expression at once passeth sentence; both against our fundamental laws, and protestant reformation.

The second in his printed mercenary discourse against toleration, asserting for a main principle that it would be less injurious to the government, to dispense with profane and loose persons, than to allow a toleration to religious dissenters: It were to over-do the business to say any more, where there is so much said already.

And therefore to conclude, we cannot choose but admonish all, as well persecutors, to relinquish their heady, partial, and inhumane persecutions (as what will certainly issue in disgrace here, and inevitable condign punishment hereafter) as those who yet dare express their moderation (however out of fashion, or made the brand of fanaticism) not to be hushed, or menaced out of that excellent temper, to make their parts and persons subservient to the base humors, and sinister designs of the biggest mortal upon earth; but reverence and obey the eternal just God, before whose great tribunal all must render their accounts, and where he will recompence to every person according to his works.

THE TRIAL ETC.

As there can be no observation, where there is no action; so it's impossible there shall be a judicious intelligence without due observation.

And since there can be nothing more reasonable than a right information, especially of Public Acts; and well knowing, how industrious some will be to misrepresent this trial, to the disadvantage of the cause and prisoners, it was thought requisite, in defence of both, and for the satisfaction of the people, to make it more public; nor can there be any business wherein the people of England are more concerned than in that which relates to their civil and religious liberties, questioned in the persons before named at the Old Bailey, the first, third, fourth and fifth of Sept. 1670.

There being present on the Bench, as Justices,

Sam. Starling, Mayor,	*John Robinson*, Alderm.
John Howel, Recorder,	*Joseph Shelden*, Alderm.
Tho. Bludworth, Alderm.	*Richard Brown*,
William Peak, Alderm.	*John Smith*, } Sheriffs.
Richard Ford, Alderm.	*James Edwards*,

The citizens of London that were summoned for jurors, appearing, were impanelled, viz.

CLE. Call over the Jury.

CRY. O yes, Thomas Veer, Ed Bushel, John Hammond, Charles Milson, Gregory Walklet, John Brightman, Wil. Plumstead, Henry Henley, James Damask, Henry Michel, Wil. Lever, John Baily.

The Form of the Oath.

You shall well and truly try, and true deliverance make betwixt our Sovereign Lord the King and the prisoners at the Bar, according to your evidence: so help you God.

THE INDICTMENT.

That William Penn, Gent. and William Mead, late of London, Linen-Draper, with divers other persons, to the jurors unknown, to the number of three hundred, the 15th Day of August, in the 22nd year of the king, about eleven of the clock in the forenoon the same day, with force and arms, etc. in the parish of St. Bennet Grace-Church, in Bridge Ward, London, in the street called Grace-Church-Street, unlawfully and tumultuously did assemble and congregate themselves together, to the disturbance of the peace of the said Lord the King: and the aforesaid William Penn and William Mead, together with other persons, to the jurors aforesaid unknown, then and there so assembled and congregated together; the aforesaid William Penn, by agreement between him and William Mead, before made, and by abetment of the aforesaid William Mead, then and there in the open street, did take upon himself to preach and speak, and then and there, did preach and speak unto the aforesaid William Mead, and other persons there, in the street aforesaid, being assembled and congregated together, by reason whereof a great concourse and tumult of people in the street aforesaid, then and there, a long time did remain and continue in contempt of the said Lord the King, and of his law; to the great disturbance of his peace, to the great terror and disturbance of many of his liege people and subjects, to the ill example of all others in the like case offenders, and against the peace of the said Lord the King, his crown and dignity.

What say you William Penn, and William Mead, are you guilty, as you stand indicted, in manner and form as aforesaid, or not guilty?

PENN. It is impossible that we should be able to remember the indictment verbatim, and therefore we desire a copy of it, as is customary on the like occasions.

REC. You must first plead to the indictment before you can have a copy of it.

PENN. I am unacquainted with the formality of the law, and therefore before I shall answer directly, I request two things of the court. *First*, that no advantage may be taken against me, nor I deprived of any benefit which I might otherwise have received. Secondly, that you will promise me a fair hearing and liberty of making my defence.

COURT. No advantage shall be taken against you: you shall have liberty; you shall be heard.

PENN. Then I plead not guilty in manner and form.

CLE. What sayest thou, William Mead: Art thou guilty in manner and form, as thou standest indicted, or not guilty?

MEAD. I shall desire the same liberty as is promised to William Penn.

COURT. You shall have it.

MEAD. Then I plead not guilty in manner and form.

The court adjourned until the afternoon.

CRY. O yes, etc.

CLE. Bring William Penn and William Mead to the bar.

OBSER. The said prisoners were brought, but were set aside, and other business prosecuted: where we cannot choose but observe that it was the constant and unkind practice of the court to the prisoners to make them wait upon the trials of felons and murderers, thereby designing in all probability, both to affront and tire them.

After five hours attendance, the court broke up, and ajourned to the third instant.

The Third of September, 1670, the Court Sat.

CRY. O yes, etc.

MAYOR. Sirrah, who bid you put off their hats ? Put on their hats again.

OBSER. Whereupon one of the officers putting the prisoners hats upon their heads (pursuant to the order of the court) brought them to the Bar.

RECORD. Do you know where you are ?

PENN. Yes.

REC. Do you know it is the King's court ?

PENN. I know it to be a court, and I suppose it to be the King's court.

REC. Do you know there is respect due to the court ?

PENN. Yes.

REC. Why do you not pay it then ?

PENN. I do so.

REC. Why do you not put off your hat then ?

PENN. Because I do not believe that to be any respect.

REC. Well, the court sets forty marks a-piece upon your heads, as a fine, for your contempt of the court.

PENN. I desire it may be observed that we came into the court with our hats off, (that is, taken off) and if they have been put on since, it was by order from the bench ; and therefore not we, but the bench should be fined.

MEAD. I have a question to ask the Recorder : am I fined also ?

REC. Yes.

MEAD. I desire the Jury, and all people to take notice of this injustice of the Recorder, who spake not to me to pull off my hat, and yet hath he put a fine upon my head. O fear the Lord, and dread his power, and yield to the guidance of His Holy Spirit ; for He is not far from every one of you.

The Jury sworn again.

OBSER. J. Robinson, Lieutenant of the Tower, disingenuously objected against Edw. Bustel, as if he had not kissed the Book, and therefore would have him sworn again ; though indeed it was on purpose, to have made use of his tenderness of conscience, in avoiding reiterated oaths, to have put him by his being a juryman, apprehending him to be a person not fit to answer their arbitrary ends.

The Clerk read the indictment, as aforesaid.

CLE. Cryer, Call James Cook into the court, give him his oath.

CLE. James Cook, lay your hand upon the Book, 'The evidence you shall give to the Court, betwixt our Sovereign the King, and the prisoners at the Bar, shall be the truth, and the whole truth, and nothing but the truth: So help you God,' etc.

COOK. I was sent for from the Exchange to go and disperse a meeting in Gracious Street, where I saw Mr Penn speaking to the people, but I could not hear what he said, because of the noise; I endeavoured to make way to take him, but I could not get to him for the crowd of people; upon which Captain Mead came to me about the kennel of the street, and desired me to let him go on; for when he had done, he would bring Mr Penn to me.

COURT. What number do you think might be there?

COOK. About three or four hundred people.

COURT. Call Richard Read, give him his oath.

Read being sworn, was asked, What do you know concerning the prisoners at the Bar?

READ. My Lord, I went to Gracious Street, where I found a great crowd of people, and I heard Mr Penn preach to them, and I saw Captain Mead speaking to Lieutenant Cook, but what he said I could not tell.

MEAD. What did William Penn say?

READ. There was such a great noise, that I could not tell what he said.

MEAD. Jury, observe this evidence, he saith, he heard him preach, and yet sayeth, he doth not know what he said.

JURY. Take notice, he swears now a clean contrary thing, to what he swore before the Mayor, when we were committed: for now he swears that he saw me in Gracious Street and yet swore before the Mayor, when I was committed, that he did not see me there. I appeal to the Mayor himself if this be not true; but no answer was given.

COURT. What number do you think might be there?

Read. *About four or five hundred.*

PENN. I desire to know of him what day it was?

READ. The 14th day of August.

PENN. Did he speak to me, or let me know he was there; for I am very sure I never saw him.

CLE. Cryer, call __ into the court.

COURT. Give him his oath.

__ My Lord, I saw a great number of people, and Mr Penn I suppose was speaking; I saw him make a motion with his hands, and heard some noise, but could not understand what he said; but for Captain Mead, I did not see him there.

REC. What say you Mr Mead? Were you there?

MEAD. It is a maxim in your own law, *Nemo tenetur accusare seipsum*, which if it be not true Latin, I am sure that it is true English, that no man is bound to accuse himself: and why dost thou offer to ensnare me with such a question? Doth not this show thy malice? Is this like unto a judge that ought to be council for the prisoner at the bar?

REC. Sir, hold your tongue, I did not go about to ensnare you.

PENN. I desire we may come more close to the point, and that silence be commanded in the court.

CRY. O yes, all manner of persons keep silence upon pain of imprisonment. __ Silence in the court.

PENN. We confess ourselves to be so far from recanting, or declining to vindicate the assembling of our selves, to preach, pray, or worship the eternal, holy, just God, that we declare to all the world, that we do believe it to be our indispensable duty, to meet incessantly upon so good an account; nor shall all the powers upon earth be able to divert us from reverencing and adoring our God, who made us.

BROWN. You are not here for worshipping God, but for breaking the law: You do yourselves a great deal of wrong in going on in that discourse.

PENN. I affirm I have broken no law, nor am I guilty of the indictment that is laid to my charge: and to the end, the Bench, the Jury, and my self, with those that hear us, may have a more direct understanding of this procedure, I desire you would let me know by what law it is you prosecute me, and upon what law you ground my indictment.

REC. Upon the Common Law.

PENN. Where is that Common Law?

REC. You must not think that I am able to run up so many years, and over so many adjudged cases, which we call Common Law, to answer your curiosity.

PENN. This answer I am sure is very short of my question; for if it be common, it should not be so hard to produce.

REC. Sir, Will you plead to your indictment?

PENN. Shall I plead to an indictment that hath no foundation in law? If it contain that law you say I have broken, why should you decline to produce that law, since it will be impossible for the Jury to determine, or agree to bring in their verdict, who have not the law produced, by which they should measure the truth of this indictment, and the guilt, or contrary of my fact.

REC. You are a saucy fellow; speak to the indictment.

PENN. I say, it is my place to speak to matter of law; I am arraigned a prisoner; my liberty, which is next to life itself, is now concerned; you are many mouths and ears against me, and if I must not be allowed to make the best of my case, it is hard: I say again, unless you show me, and the people, the law you ground your indictment upon, I shall take it for granted, your proceedings are meerly arbitrary.

OBSER. [At this time several upon the Bench urged hard upon the prisoner to bear him down.]

REC. The question is, whether you are guilty of this indictment?

PENN. The question is not whether I am guilty of this indictment, but whether this indictment be legal: it is too general and imperfect an answer, to say it is the Common Law, unless we knew both where, and what it is; for where there is no law, there is no transgression; and that law which is not in being, is so far from being common, that it is no law at all.

REC. You are an impertinent fellow; will you teach the court what law is? It's *Lex non scripta*, that which many have studied thirty or forty years to know, and would you have me tell you in a moment?

PENN. Certainly, if the Common Law be so hard to be understood, it's far from being very common; but if the Lord Cook in his institutes, be of any consideration, he tells us, that Common Law is Common Right; and that Common Right is the Great Charter privileges, confirmed 9 Hen. 3. 29. 25 Edw. 1. 1. 2 Edw. 3. 8. Cook Inst. 2. p. 56.

REC. Sir, you are a troublesome fellow, and it is not for the honour of the court to suffer you to go on.

PENN. I have asked but one question and you have not answered me; though the rights and privileges of every Englishman be concerned in it.

REC. If I should suffer you to ask questions till to morrow-morning, you would be never the wiser.

PENN. That's according as the answers are.

REC. Sir, we must not stand to hear you talk all night.

PENN. I design no affront to the court, but to be heard in my just plea; and I must plainly tell you that if you will deny me the Oyer of that law, which you suggest I have broken, you do at once deny me an acknowledged right, and evidence to the whole world your resolution to sacrifice the privileges of Englishmen, to your sinister and arbitrary designs.

REC. Take him away: My Lord, if you take not some course with this pestilent fellow to stop his mouth, we shall not be able to do anything tonight.

MAYOR. Take him away, take him away; turn him into the bail dock.

PENN. These are but so many vain exclamations: is this justice, or true judgment? Must I therefore be taken away because I plead for the fundamental laws of England? However, this I leave upon your consciences, who are of the Jury, (and my sole judges) that if these ancient fundamental laws, which relate to liberty and property, (and are not limited to particular persuasions in matters of religion) must not be indispensably maintained and observed, Who can say he hath right to the coat upon his back? Certainly our liberties are openly to be invaded; our wives to be ravished; our children slaved; our families ruined; and our estates led away in triumph, by every sturdy beggar, and malicious informer, as their trophies, but our (pretended) forfeits for conscience sake: the Lord of heaven and earth will be judge between us in this matter.

REC. Be silent there.

PENN. I am not to be silent in a case wherein I am so much concerned; and not only myself, but many ten thousand families besides.

OBSER. They having rudely haled him into the bail dock, William Mead they left in court, who spake as followeth.

MEAD. You men of the Jury, here I do now stand to answer to an indictment against me, which is a bundle of stuff full of lies and falsehoods; for therein I am accused that I met Vi & Armis, Illicité & Tumultuosè: time was, when I had freedom to use a carnal weapon, and then I thought I feared no man; but now I fear the living God, and dare not make use thereof, nor hurt any man; nor do I know I demeaned myself as a tumultuous person. I say, I am a peaceable man, therefore it is a very proper question what William

Penn demanded in this case, an Oyer of the Law, on which our indictment is grounded.

REC. I have made answer to that already.

MEAD. Turning his face to the Jury, said, you men of the Jury, who are my judges, if the Recorder will not tell you what makes a riot, a rout, or an unlawful assembly. Cook, he that once they called the Lord Cook, tells us what makes a riot, a rout, and an unlawful assembly, – a riot is when three or more, are met together to beat a man, or to enter forcibly into another man's land, to cut down his grass, his wood, or break down his pales.

OBSER. Here the Recorder interrupted him, and said, I thank you sir, that you will tell me what the law is, scornfully pulling off his hat.

MEAD. Thou mayest put on thy hat, I have never a fee for thee now.

Brown. He talks at random, one while an independent, another while some other religion, and now a Quaker, and next a Papist.

MEAD. *Turpe est doctori cum culpa redarguit ipsum.*

MAYOR. You deserve to have your tongue cut out.

REC. If you discourse in this manner, I shall take occasion against you.

MEAD. Thou didst promise me I should have fair liberty to be heard. Why may I not have the privilege of an Englishman? I am an Englishman, and you might be ashamed of this dealing.

REC. I look upon you to be an enemy to the laws of England, which ought to be observed and kept, nor are you worthy of such privileges as others have.

MEAD. The Lord is judge between me and thee in this matter.

OBSER. Upon which they took him away into the bail dock, and the Recorder proceeded to give the Jury their charge, as followeth.

REC. You have heard what the indictment is; it is for preaching to the people, and drawing a tumultuous company after them; and Mr Penn was speaking: if they should not be disturbed, you see they will go on; there are three or four witnesses that have proved this, that he did preach there, that Mr Mead did allow of it; after this, you have heard by substantial witnesses what is said against them: now we are upon the matter of fact, which you are to keep to and observe, as what hath been fully sworn, at your peril.

OBSER. The prisoners were put out of the court, into the bail dock, and the charge given to the Jury in their absence, at which

W.P. with a very raised voice, it being a considerable distance from the bench, spoke.

PENN. I appeal to the Jury, who are my judges, and this great assembly, whether the proceedings of the court are not most arbitrary, and void of all law in offering to give the Jury their charge in the absence of the prisoners: I say, it is directly opposite to, and destructive of the undoubted right of every English prisoner, as Cook in the 2 Inst. 29. on the chapter of Magna Charta speaks.

OBSER. The Recorder being thus unexpectedly lasht for his extra-judicial procedure, said, with an enraged smile,

REC. Why ye are present, you do hear: Do you not?

PENN. No thanks to the court that commanded me into the bail dock; and you of the Jury take notice that I have not been heard, neither can you legally depart the court, before I have been fully heard, having at least ten or twelve material points to offer, in order to invalidate their indictment.

REC. Pull that fellow down; pull him down.

MEAD. Are these according to the rights and privileges of Englishmen, that we should not be heard, but turned into the bail dock for making our defence, and the Jury to have their charge given them in our absence? I say, these are barbarous and unjust proceedings.

REC. Take them away into the hole; to hear them talk all night, as they would, that I think doth not become the honour of the court; and I think you (i.e. the Jury) yourselves would be tired out, and not have patience to hear them.

OBSER. The Jury were commanded up to agree upon their verdict, the prisoners remaining in the stinking hole; after an hour and half's time, eight came down agreed, but four remained above; the Court sent an officer for them, and they accordingly came down: the bench used many unworthy threats to the four that dissented; and the Recorder addressing himself to Bushel, said, Sir, you are the cause of this disturbance, and manifestly show yourself an abettor of faction; I shall set a mark upon you, sir.

J. ROBINSON. Mr Bushel, I have known you near this fourteen years; you have thrust your self upon this jury, because you think there is some service for you; I tell you, you deserve to be indicted more than any man that hath been brought to the Bar this day.

BUSHEL. No, Sir John, there were threescore before me, and I would willingly have got off, but could not.

BLUDW. I said when I saw Mr Bushel, what I see is come to pass;

for I knew he would never yield. Mr Bushel, we know what you are.

Mayor. Sirrah, you are an impudent fellow, I will put a mark upon you.

OBSER. They used much menacing language, and behaved themselves very imperiously to the Jury, as persons not more void of justice, than sober education. After this barbarous usage, they sent them to consider of bringing in their verdict, and after some considerable time they returned to the court. Silence was called for, and the Jury called by their names.

CLE. Are you agreed upon your verdict?

JURY. Yes.

CLE. Who shall speak for you?

JURY. Our foreman.

CLE. Look upon the prisoners at the Bar: How say you? Is William Penn guilty of the matter wherof he stands indicted in manner and form, or not guilty?

FOREMAN. Guilty of speaking in Gracious Street.

COURT. Is that all?

FOREMAN. That is all I have in commission.

REC. You had as good say nothing.

MAYOR. Was it not an unlawful assembly? You mean he was speaking to a tumult of people there?

FOREMAN. My Lord, this was all I had in commission.

OBSER. Here some of the Jury seemed to buckle to the questions of the court, upon which Bushel, Hammond, and some others opposed themselves, and said they allowed of no such word as an unlawful assembly in their verdict; at which the Recorder, Mayor, Robinson, and Bludworth, took great occasion to vilify them with most opprobrious language; and this verdict not serving their turns, the Recorder expressed himself thus:

REC. The Law of England will not allow you to depart, till you have given in your verdict.

JURY. We have given in our verdict, and we can give in no other.

REC. Gentlemen, you have not given in your verdict, and you had as good say nothing; therefore go and consider it once more, that we may make an end of this troublesome business.

JURY. We desire we may have pen, ink, and paper.

OBSER. The court adjourns for half an hour; which being expired, the court returns, and the Jury not long after.

The prisoners were brought to the Bar, and the jurors' names called over.

CLE. Are you agreed of your verdict?

JURY. Yes.

CLE. Who shall speak for you?

JURY. Our Foreman.

CLE. What say you? Look upon the prisoners: Is William Penn guilty in manner and form as he stands indicted, or not guilty?

FOREMAN. Here is our verdict; holding forth a piece of paper to the Clerk of the Peace, which follows:

We the jurors, hereafter named, do find William Penn to be guilty of speaking or preaching to an assembly, met together in Gracious Street, the 14th of August last, 1670, and that William Mead is not guilty of the said indictment.

Foreman,	Thomas Veer,	Henry Michel,	John Baily,
	Edward Bushel,	John Brightman,	William Lever,
	John Hammond,	Charles Milson,	James Damask,
	Henry Henly,	Gregory Walklet,	William Plumstead.

OBSER. This both Mayor and Recorder resented at so high a rate, that they exceeded the bounds of all reason and civility.

MAYOR. What will you be led by such a silly fellow as Bushel; an impudent canting fellow? I warrant you, you shall come no more upon juries in haste; you are a Foreman indeed (addressing himself to the Foreman). I thought you had understood your place better.

REC. Gentlemen, you shall not be dismissed, till we have a verdict that the court will accept; and you shall be locked up, without meat, drink, fire, and tobacco: you shall not think thus to abuse the court; we will have a verdict by the help of God, or you shall starve for it.

PENN. My Jury, who are my judges, ought not to be thus menaced; their verdict should be free, and not compelled; the bench ought to wait upon them, but not forestall them: I do desire that justice may be done me, and that the arbitrary resolves of the bench may not be made the measure of my Jury's verdict.

REC. Stop that prating fellow's mouth, or put him out of the court.

MAYOR. You have heard that he preached; that he gathered a company of tumultuous people; and that they do not only disobey the martial power, but the civil also.

PENN. It is a great mistake; we did not make the tumult, but they that interrupted us. The Jury cannot be so ignorant as to think that we met there with a design to disturb the civil peace, since (1st) we were by force of arms kept out of our lawful house, and met as near it in the street, as the soldiers would give us leave: and (2nd) because it was no new thing, (nor with the circumstances expressed in the indictment, but what was usual and customary with us;) it is very well known that we are a peaceable people, and cannot offer violence to any man.

OBSER. The Court being ready to break up, and willing to huddle the prisoners to their jail, and the Jury to their chamber, Penn spoke as follows:

PENN. The agreement of twelve men is a verdict in law, and such a one being given by the Jury, I require the Clerk of the Peace to record it, as he will answer it at his peril: And if the Jury bring in another verdict contrary to this, I affirm they are perjured men in law. (And looking upon the Jury, said), You are Englishmen, mind your privilege, give not away your right.

BUSHEL, etc. Nor will we ever do it.

OBSER. One of the Jurymen pleaded indisposition of body, and therefore desired to be dismissed.

MAYOR. You are as strong as any of them; starve then, and hold your principles.

REC. Gentlemen, you must be content with your hard fate; let your patience overcome it; for the court is resolved to have a verdict, and that before you can be dismissed.

JURY. We are agreed, we are agreed, we are agreed.

OBSER. The court swore several persons to keep the Jury all night, without meat, drink, fire, or any other accommodation; they had not so much as a chamberpot, though desired.

CRY. O yes, etc.

OBSER. The court adjourned till seven of the clock next morning, (being the fourth instant, vulgarly called Sunday at which time the prisoners were brought to the bar, the court sat, and the Jury called in, to bring in their verdict.

CRY. O yes, etc. – Silence in the court upon pain of imprisonment. The Jury's names called over.

CLE. Are you agreed upon your verdict?

JURY. Yes.

CLE. Who shall speak for you.

JURY. Our foreman.

CLE. What say you? Look upon the prisoners at the bar: Is William Penn guilty of the matter whereof he stands indicted, in manner and form as aforesaid, or not guilty?

FOREMAN. William Penn is guilty of speaking in Gracious Street.

MAYOR. To an unlawful assembly.

BUSHEL. No, my Lord, we give no other verdict than what we gave last night; we have no other verdict to give.

MAYOR. You are a factious fellow; I'll take a course with you.

BLUDW. I knew Mr Bushel would not yield.

BUSHEL. Sir Thomas, I have done according to my conscience.

MAYOR. That conscience of yours would cut my throat.

BUSHEL. No, my lord, it never shall.

MAYOR. But I will cut yours so soon as I can.

REC. He has inspired the Jury; he has the spirit of divination; methinks I feel him; I will have a positive verdict, or you shall starve for it.

PENN. I desire to ask the Recorder one question: Do you allow of the verdict given of William Mead?

REC. It cannot be a verdict because you are indicted for a conspiracy; and one being found not guilty, and not the other, it could not be a verdict.

PENN. If not guilty be not a verdict, then you make of the Jury, and Magna Charta, but a mere nose of wax.

MEAD. How! Is not guilty no verdict?

REC. No, 'tis no verdict.

PENN. I affirm, That the consent of a Jury is a verdict in law; and if William Mead be not guilty, it consequently follows that I am clear, since you have indicted us of a conspiracy, and I could not possibly conspire alone.

OBSER. There were many passages that could not be taken, which passed between the Jury and the court. The Jury went up again, having received a fresh charge from the Bench, if possible to extort an unjust verdict.

CRY. O yes, etc. – Silence in the court.

COURT. Call over the Jury __ which was done.

CLE. What say you? Is William Penn guilty of the matter wherof he stands indicted, in manner and form aforesaid, or not guilty?

FOREMAN. Guilty of speaking in Gracious Street.

REC. What is this to the purpose? I say I will have a verdict. And speaking to E. Bushel, said, you are a factious fellow; I will set a mark upon you; and whilst I have any thing to do in the city, I will have an eye upon you.

MAYOR. Have you no more wit than to be led by such a pitiful fellow? I will cut his nose.

PENN. It is intolerable that my Jury should be thus menaced; is this according to the fundamental law? Are not they my proper judges by the Great Charter of England? What hope is there of ever having justice done, when juries are threatened, and their verdicts rejected? I am concerned to speak, and grieved to see such arbitrary proceedings. Did not the Lieutenant of the Tower render one of them worse than a felon? And do you not plainly seem to condemn such for factious fellows, who answer not your ends? Unhappy are those juries, who are threatened to be fined, and starved, and ruined, if they give not in their verdicts contrary to their consciences.

REC. My Lord, you must take a course with that same fellow.

MAYOR. Stop his mouth; jailer, bring fetters, and stake him to the ground.

PENN. Do your pleasure, I matter not your fetters.

REC. Till now I never understood the reason of the policy and prudence of the Spaniards in suffering the Inquisition among them: and certainly it will never be well with us till something like the Spanish Inquisition be in England.

OBSER. The Jury being required to go together to find another verdict, and steadfastly refusing it (saying they could give no other verdict than what was already given) the Recorder in great passion was running off the bench, with these words in his mouth, I protest I will sit here no longer to hear these things. At which the Mayor calling, stay, stay, he returned, and directed himself unto the Jury, and spake as followeth.

REC. Gentlemen, we shall not be at this pass always with you; you will find the next sessions of Parliament there will be a law made, that those that will not conform shall not have the protection of the law. Mr Lee, draw up another verdict, that they may bring it in special.

LEE. I cannot tell how to do it.

JURY. We ought not to be returned, having all agreed, and set our hands to the verdict.

REC. Your verdict is nothing, you play upon the court; I say, you shall go together, and bring in another verdict, or you shall starve; and I will have you carted about the city, as in Edward the Third's time.

FOREMAN. We have given in our verdict, and all agreed to it, and if we give in another, it will be a force upon us to save our lives.

MAYOR. Take them up.

OFFICER. My Lord they will not go up.

OBSER. The Mayor spoke to the sheriff, and he came off his seat, and said:

SHER. Come gentlemen, you must go up; you see I am commanded to make you go.

OBSER. Upon which the Jury went up; and several sworn to keep them without any accommodation as aforesaid, till they brought in their verdict.

CRY. O yes, etc. The court adjourns till tomorrow morning at seven of the clock.

OBSER. The prisoners were remanded to Newgate, where they remained till next morning, and then were brought into the court, which being sat, they proceeded as followeth.

CRY. O yes, etc. – Silence in the court upon pain of imprisonment.

CLERK. Set William Penn and William Mead to the Bar. Gentlemen of the Jury, answer to your names, Thomas Veer, Edward Bushel, John Hammond, Henry Henley, Henry Michel, John Brightman, Charles Milson, Gregory Walklet, John Bailey, William Lever, James Damask, William Plumstead, are you all agreed of your verdict?

JURY. Yes.

CLERK. Who shall speak for you?

JURY. Our Foreman.

CLERK. Look upon the prisoners. What say you; is William Penn guilty of the matter whereof he stands indicted, in manner and form, etc. or not guilty?

FOREMAN. You have there read in writing already our verdict, and our hands subscribed.

OBSER. The Clerk had the paper, but was stoped by the Recorder from reading of it; and he commanded to ask for a positive verdict.

FOREMAN. If you will not accept it; I desire to have it back again.

COURT. That paper was no verdict, and there shall be no advantage taken against you by it.

CLERK. How say you? Is William Penn guilty, etc. or not guilty?
FOREMAN. Not guilty.

CLERK. How say you? Is William Mead guilty, etc. or not guilty?
FOREMAN. Not guilty.

CLERK. Then hearken to your verdict, yon say, that William Penn is not guilty in manner and form, as he stands indicted; you say, that William Mead is not guilty in manner and form, as he stands indicted, and so you say all.

JURY. Yes, we do so.

OBSER. The Bench being unsatisfied with the verdict, commanded that every person should distinctly answer to their names, and give in their verdict, which they unanimously did, in saying not guilty, to the great satisfaction of the assembly.

RECORD. I am sorry, gentlemen you have followed your own judgments and opinions, rather than the good and wholesome advice, which was given you; God keep my life out of your hands; but for this the court fines you forty marks a man, and imprisonment until paid: at which Penn stepped up towards the Bench, and said,

PENN. I demand my liberty, being freed by the Jury.

MAYOR. No, you are in for your fines.

PENN. Fines, for what?

MAYOR. For contempt of the court.

PENN. I ask if it be according to the fundamental laws of England that any Englishman should be fined, or amerced, but by the judgment of his peers, or jury? Since it expressly contradicts the fourteenth and twenty-ninth chapter of the Great Charter of England, which says, no freeman ought to be amerced, but by the oath of good and lawful men of the vicinity.

REC. Take him away, take him away, take him out of the court.

PENN. I can never urge the fundamental laws of England, but you cry, take him away, take him away; but it is no wonder, since the Spanish Inquisition hath so great a place in the Recorder's heart; God Almighty who is just, will judge you all for these things.

OBSER. They haled the prisoners to the bail dock, and from thence sent them to Newgate, for non-payment of their fines; and so were their Jury.

THE
Great CASE of Liberty of Conscience.

Once more briefly Debated aud Defended, by the Authority of REASON, SCRIPTURE, and ANTIQUITY: Which may serve the Place of a General Reply to such late Discourses; as have Oppos'd a *Toleration*.

The Author *W. P.*

Whatsoever ye would that Men should do to you, do ye even so to them:
Mat. 7. 12.
Render unto Cæsar, *the Things that are* Cæsar's; *and to* God, *the Things that are* God's. Mark 12. 17.

TO THE SUPREAM AUTHORITY OF ENGLAND

Toleration (for these ten years past) has not been more the cry of some, than PERSECUTION has been the practice of others, though not on grounds equally rational.

The present cause of this address is to solicit a conversion of that power to our relief, which hitherto has been employed to our depression; that after this large experience of our innocency, and long since expired apprenticeship of cruel sufferings, you will be pleased to cancel all our bonds, and give us a possession of those freedoms, to which we are entitled by English birthright.

This has been often promised to us, and we as earnestly have expected the performance; but to this time we labour under the unspeakable pressure of nasty prisons, and daily confiscation of our goods, to the apparent ruin of entire families.

We would not attribute the whole of this severity to malice, since not a little share may justly be ascribed to mis-intelligence.

For it is the infelicity of governors to see and hear by the eyes and ears of other men; which is equally unhappy for the people.

And we are bold to say, that supposition and mere conjectures have been the best measures that most have taken of us, and of our principles; for whilst there have been none more inoffensive, we have been marked for capital offenders.

It is hard that we should always lie under this undeserved imputation; and which is worse be persecuted as such, without the liberty of a just defence.

In short, if you are apprehensive, that our principles are inconsistent with the civil government, grant us a free conference about the points in question, and let us know, what are those laws essential to preservation, that our opinions carry an opposition to? And if upon a due enquiry we are found so heterodox as represented, it will be then but time enough to inflict these heavy penalities upon us.

And as this medium seems the fairest, and most reasonable; so can you never do your selves greater justice, either in the vindication of your proceedings against us, if we be criminal; or if innocent, in disengaging your service of such, as have been authors of so much misinformation.

But could we once obtain the favour of such debate we doubt not to evince a clear consistency of our life and doctrine with the English government; and that an indulging of dissenters in the sense defended, is not only most Christian and rational, but prudent also. And the contrary (how plausibly soever insinuated) the most injurious to the peace, and destructive of that discreet balance, which the best and wisest states, have ever carefully observed.

But if this fair and equal offer, find not a place with you, on which to rest its foot; much less that it should bring us back the olive branch of toleration; we heartily embrace and bless the providence of God; and in his strength resolve, by patience, to outweary persecution, and by our constant sufferings, seek to obtain a victory, more glorious, than any our adversaries can achieve by all their cruelties.

> *Vincit qui patitur.*
> From a prisoner for conscience-sake,
> W. P.

Newgate, the 7th of the 12th
Month, called February, 1670 [1671].

THE PREFACE

Were some as Christian, as they boast themselves to be, it would save us all the labour we bestow in rendering persecution so unchristian, as it most truly is: nay were they those men of reason they character themselves, and what the civil law styles good citizens, it had been needless for us to tell them, that neither can any external coercive power convince the understanding of the poorest idiot, nor fines and prisons be judged fit and adequate penalties for faults purely intellectual; as well as that they are destructive of all civil government.

But we need not run so far as beyond the seas, to fetch the sense of the codes, institutes, and digests, out of the *Corpus Civile*, to adjudge such practices incongruous with the good of civil society; since our own good, old, admirable laws of England have made such excellent provision for its inhabitants, that if they were but thought as fit to be executed by this present age, as they were rightly judged necessary to be made by our careful ancestors: we know how great a stroke they would give such as venture to lead away our property in triumph (as our just forfeiture) for only worshipping our God in a differing way, from that which is more generally professed and established.

And indeed it is most truly lamentable, that above others (who have been found in so unnatural and antichristian an employment) those, that by their own frequent practices and voluminous apologies, have defended a separation (from the Papacy) should now become such earnest persecutors for it, not considering that the enaction of such laws, as restrain persons from the free exercise of their consciences, in matters of religion, is but a knotting whip-cord to lash their own posterity; whom they can never promise to be conformed to a national religion. Nay, since mankind is subject to such mutability, they can't ensure themselves from being taken by some persuasions that are esteemed heterodox, and consequently catch themselves in snares of their own providing. And for men thus liable to change, (and no ways certain of their own belief to be the most infallible,) as by their multiplied concessions may appear, to enact any religion, or prohibit persons from the free exercise of theirs, sounds harsh in the ears of all modest and unbiased men. We are bold to say our Protestant ancestors thought of nothing less than to be succeeded by persons vain glorious of their reformation, and yet adversaries to liberty of conscience; for to people in their wits, it seems a paradox.

Not that we are so ignorant as to think it is within the reach of humane power to fetter conscience, or to restrain its liberty strictly taken: But that plain English, of liberty of conscience, we would be understood to mean, is this; namely, the free and uninterrupted exercise of our consciences, in that way of worship, we are most clearly persuaded, God requires us to serve Him in (without endangering our undoubted birthright of English freedoms) which being matter of faith, we sin if we omit, and they can't do less, that shall endeavour it.

To tell us we are obstinate and enemies to government, are but those groundless phrases, the first reformers were not a little pestered with; but as they said, so say we, the being called this or that, does not conclude us so; and hitherto we have not been detected of that fact, which only justifies such criminations.

But however free we can approve our selves of actions prejudicial to the civil government; is most certain we have not suffered a little, as criminals, and therefore have been far from being free from sufferings; indeed, in some respect, horrid plunders: Widows have lost their cows, orphans their beds, and labourers their tools. A tragedy so sad, that methinks it should oblige them to do in England as they did at Athens; when they had sacrificed their divine Socrates to the sottish fury of their lewd and comical multitude, they so regretted their hasty murder, that not only the memorial of Socrates was most venerable with them, but his enemies they esteemed so much theirs, that none would trade or hold the least commerce with them; for which some turned their own executioners, and without any other warrant than their own guilt, hanged themselves. How near akin the wretched mercenary informers of our age are to those, the great resemblance that is betwixt their actions manifestly shows.

And we are bold to say, the grand fomenters of persecution, are no better friends to the English state, than were Anytus and Aristophanes of old to that of Athens, the case being so nearly the same, as that they did not more bitterly envy the reputation of Socrates amongst the Athenians for his grave and religious lectures (thereby giving the youth a diversion from frequenting their plays) than some now emulate the true dissenter, for his pious life and great industry.

And as that famous common-wealth was noted to decline, and the most observing persons of it dated its decay from that illegal and ingrateful carriage towards Socrates (witness their dreadful plagues, with other multiplied disasters) So it is not less worthy observation, that heaven hath not been wholly wanting to scourge this land, for, as well their cruelty to the conscientious, as their other multiplied provocations.

And when we seriously consider the dreadful judgments that now impend the nation (by reason of the robbery, violence, unwonted oppression, that almost every where, have not only been committed upon the poor, the widow, and the fatherless; but most tenaciously justified, and the actors manifestly encouraged) in mere pity, and concern, for the everlasting welfare of such as have not quite sinned away their visitation (for some have) we once more bring to public view our reasons against persecution, back with the plainest instances, both of scripture and antiquity. If but one may be persuaded, to desist from making any farther progress in such an anti-protestant, and truly anti-christian path, as that of persecuting honest and virtuous Englishmen, for only worshipping the God that made them, in the way they judge most acceptable with him.

But if those who ought to think themselves obliged to weigh these affairs with the greatest deliberation, will obstinately close their eyes to these last remonstrances; and slightly overlook the pinching case of so many thousand families, that are by these severities exposed for prey to the unsatiable appetites of a villanous crew of broken informers (daubing themselves with that deluding apprehension of pleasing God, or at least of profiting the country; (whilst they greatly displease the one, and evidently ruin the other as certain as ever the Lord God Almighty destroyed Sodom and laid waste Gomorrah, by the consuming flames of His just indignations; will He hasten to make desolate this wanton land, and not leave an hiding place for the oppressor.

Let no man therefore think himself too big to be admonished, nor put too slight a value upon the lives, liberties and properties, of so many thousand free-born English families, embarked in that one concern of liberty of conscience. It will become him better to reflect upon his own mortality, and not forget his breath is in his nostrils, and that every action of his life the everlasting God will bring to judgment, and him for them.

CHAPTER I

That imposition, restraint, and persecution for conscience sake, highly invade the Divine Prerogative, and divest the Almighty of a right, due to none beside Himself, and that in five eminent particulars.

The great case of liberty of conscience so often debated and defended (however dissatisfactorily to such as have so little conscience as to persecute for it) is once more brought to public view, by a late act against dissenters, and bill, or an additional one, that we all hoped the wisdom of our rulers had long since laid aside, as what was fitter to be passed into an act of perpetual oblivion. The kingdoms are alarmed at this procedure, and thousands greatly at a stand, wondering what should be the meaning of such hasty resolutions that seem as fatal as they were unexpected: some ask what wrong they have done; others, what peace they have broken; and all, what plots they have formed to prejudice the present government, or occasions given, to hatch new jealousies of them and their proceedings, being not conscious to themselves of guilt in any such respect.

For mine own part, I publicly confess myself to be a very hearty dissenter from the established worship of these nations, as believing protestants to have much degenerated from their first principles, and as owning the poor despised Quakers, in life and doctrine, to have espoused the cause of God, and to be the undoubted followers of Jesus Christ, in his most holy, straight and narrow way that leads to the eternal rest. In all which I know no treason, nor any principle that would urge me to a thought injurious to the civil peace. If any be defective in this particular, it is equal, both individuals and whole societies should answer for their own defaults, but we are clear.

However, all conclude that union very ominous, and unhappy, which makes the first discovery of it self, by a John Baptist's head in a charger, They mean that feast some are designed to make upon the liberties and properties of free-born Englishmen, since to have the entail of those undoubted hereditary rights cut off (for matters purely relative of another world) is a severe beheading in the law; which must be obvious to all, but such as measure the justice of things only by the proportion they bear with their own interest.

A sort of men that seek themselves, though at the apparent loss of whole societies, like to that barbarous fancy of old, which had rather that Rome should burn, than it be without the satisfaction of a bonfire: And sad it is, when men have so far stupified their understandings with the strong doses of their private interest, as to become insensible of the public's. Certainly such an over-fondness for self, or that strong inclination, to raise themselves in the ruin of what does not so much oppose them, as that they will believe so, because they would be persecuting, is a malignant enemy to that tranquillity, which, all dissenting parties seem to believe, would be the consequence of a toleration.

In short we say there can be but two ends in persecution, the one to satisfy (which none can ever do) the insatiable appetites of a decimating clergy (whose best arguments are fines and imprisonments) and the other, as thinking therein they do God good service; but it is so hateful a thing upon any account, that we shall make it appear by this ensuing discourse to be a declared enemy to God, religion, and the good of humane society.

The whole will be small, since it is but an epitome of no larger a tract than fourteen sheets; yet divides it self into the same particulars, everyone of which we shall defend against imposition, restraint, and persecution, though not with the scope of reason (nor consequently pleasure to the readers) being by other contingent disappointments, limited to a narrow stint.

The terms explained, and the question stated

First, by liberty of conscience, we understand not only a mere liberty of the mind, in believing or disbelieving this or that principle or doctrine, but the exercise of our selves in a visible way of worship, upon our believing it to be indispensibly required at our hands, that if we neglect it for fear or favour of any mortal man, we sin, and incur divine wrath: Yet we would be so understood to extend and justify the lawfulness of our so meeting to worship God, as not to contrive, or abet any contrivance destructive of the government and laws of the land, tending to matters of an external nature, directly, or indirectly; but so far only, as it may refer to religious matters, and a life to come, and consequently wholly independent of the secular affairs of this, wherein we are supposed to transgress.

Secondly, by imposition, restraint, and persecution, we don't only mean the strict requiring of us to believe this to be true, or that to be false; and upon refusal, to incur the penalties enacted in such cases; but by those terms we mean thus much, any coercive or hindrance to us from meeting together to perform those religious exercises which are according to our faith and persuasion.

The question stated

For proof of the aforesaid terms thus given, we singly state the question thus,

Whether imposition, restraint, and persecution, upon persons for exercising such a liberty of conscience, as is before expressed, and so circumstantiated, be not to impeach the honour of God, the meekness of the Christian religion, the authority of scripture, the privilege of nature, the principles of common reason, the well-being of government, and apprehensions of the greatest personages of former and latter ages.

First, then we say that imposition, restraint, and persecution for matters relating to conscience, directly invade the divine prerogative, and divest the Almighty of a due, proper to none besides himself. And this we prove by these five particulars.

1. First, if we do allow the honour of our creation, due to God only, and that no other besides himself has endowed us with those excellent gifts of understanding, reason, judgment and faith, and consequently that He only is the Object as well as Author, both of our faith, worship, and service, then whosoever shall interpose their authority to enact faith and worship, in a way that seems not to us congruous with what he has discovered to us to be faith and worship (whose alone property it is to do it) or to restrain us from what we are persuaded is our indispensible duty, they evidently usurp this authority and invade his incommunicable right of government over conscience: For the inspiration of the Almighty gives understanding: and faith is the gift of God, says the divine writ.

Secondly. Such magisterial determinations carry an evident claim to that infallibility, which Protestants have been hitherto so jealous of owning, that to avoid the Papists, they have denied it to all, but God himself.

Either they have forsook their old plea, or if not, we desire to know when, and where, they were invested with that divine excellency, and whether imposition, restraint, and persecution were deemed by God ever the fruits of his spirit: however, that it self was not sufficient; for unless it appear as well to us, that they have it, as to them who have it, we cannot believe it upon any convincing evidence, but by tradition only; an anti-Protestant way of believing.

Thirdly, it enthrones man as king over conscience, the alone just claim and privilege of his Creator, whose thoughts are not as men's thoughts but has reserved to himself, that empire from all the Cæsars on earth; for if men in reference to souls and bodies, things appertaining to this and the other world shall be subject to their fellow creatures, what follows? but that Cæsar (however he got it) has all, God's share, and his own too ; and being Lord of both, both are Cæsar's and not God's.

Fourthly, it defeats God's work of grace, and the invisible operation of his eternal spirit which can alone beget faith, and is only to be obeyed in and about religion and worship, and attributes men's conformity to outward force and corporal punishments, a faith subject to as many revolutions as the powers that enact it.

Fifthly and lastly, such persons assume the judgment of the great tribunal unto themselves ; for to whomsoever men are imposedly or restrictively subject and accountable in matters of faith, worship and conscience ; in them alone must the power of judgment reside ; but it is equally true that God shall judge all by Jesus Christ, and that no man is so accountable to his fellow creatures, as to be imposed upon, restrained, or persecuted for any matter of conscience whatever.

Thus and in many more particulars are men accustomed to entrench upon divine property, to gratify particular interests in the world (and at best) through a misguided apprehension to imagine they do God good service, that where they cannot give faith, they will use force, which kind of sacrifice is nothing less unreasonable than the other is abominable : God will not give His honour to another, and to Him only that searches the heart and tries the reins, it is our duty to ascribe the gifts of understanding and faith, without which none can please God.

CHAPTER II

They overturn the Christian religion; 1. In the nature of it, which is meekness; 2. In the practice of it, which is suffering; 3. In the promotion of it, since all further discoveries are prohibited; 4. In the rewards of it, which are eternal.

The next great evil which attends external force in matters of faith and worship is no less than the overthrow of the whole Christian religion, and this we will briefly evidence in these four particulars 1. That there can be nothing more remote from the nature. 2. The practice. 3. The promotion. 4. The rewards of it.

1. First, it is the privilege of the Christian faith above the dark suggestions of ancient and modern superstitious traditions to carry with it a most self-evidencing verity, which ever was sufficient to proselyte believers, without the weak auxiliaries of external power ;

The Son of God, and great example of the world, was so far from calling his Father's omnipotency in legions of angels to His defence, that He at once repealed all acts of force, and defined to us the nature of his religion in this one great saying of His, my kingdom is not of this world. It was spiritual, not carnal, accompanied with weapons, as heavenly as its own nature, and designed for the good and salvation of the soul, and not the injury and destruction of the body: no goals, fines, exiles, etc. but sound reason, clear truth and a strict life. In short, the Christian religion entreats all, but compels none.

Secondly, that restraint and persecution overturn the practise of it; I need go no farther than the allowed martyrologies of several ages, of which the scriptures claim a share; begin with Abel, go down to Moses, so to the prophets, and then to the meek example of Jesus Christ himself; how patiently devoted was he to undergo the contradictions of men and so far from persecuting any, that he would not so much as revile his persecutors, but prayed for them; thus lived his apostles and the true Christians, of the first three hundred years: nor are the famous stories of our first reformers silent in the matter; witness the Christian practices of the Waldenses, Lollards, Hussites, Lutherans, and our noble martyrs, who as became the true followers of Jesus Christ, enacted and confirmed their religion, with their own blood, and not with the blood of their opposers.

Thirdly, restraint and persecution obstruct the promotion of the Christian religion, for if such as restrain, confess themselves miserable sinners, and altogether imperfect, it either follows that they never desire to be better, or that they should encourage such as may be capable of farther informing and reforming them; they condemn the Papists for encoffining the scriptures and their worship in an unknown tongue, and yet are guilty themselves of the same kind of fact.

Fourthly; they prevent many of eternal rewards, for where any are religious for fear, and that of men, it is slavish, and the recompence of such religion is condemnation, not peace: besides it is man that is served, who having no power but what is temporary, his reward must needs be so too; he that imposes a duty, or restrains from one, must reward; but because no man can reward for such duties, no man can or ought to impose them, or restrain from them, so that we conclude imposition, restraint and persecution are destructive of the Christian religion, in the nature, practice, promotion and rewards of it, which are eternal.

CHAPTER III

They oppose the plainest testimonies of divine writ that can be, which condemn all force upon conscience.

We farther say, that imposition, restraint and persecution are repugnant to the plain testimonies and precepts of the scriptures.

1. The inspiration of the Almighty gives understanding, Job 32. 8. If no man can believe before he understands, and no man can understand before he is inspired of God, then are the impositions of men excluded as unreasonable, and their persecutions for non-obedience as inhuman.

2. Woe unto them that take counsel, but not of me, Isa. 3. 1.

3. Woe unto them that make a man an offender for a word, and lay a snare for him that reproves in the gate, and turn aside the just for a thing of nought, Isa. 29. 15. 21.

4. Let the wheat and the tares grow together, until the time of the harvest, or end of the world. Mat. 13. 27, 28, 29.

5. And Jesus called them unto him, and said ye know that the princes of the Gentiles, exercise dominion over them, and they that are great exercise authority upon them, but it shall not be so amongst you. Mat. 20. 25, 26,

6. And Jesus said unto them, render unto Cæsar the things that are Cæsar's, and unto God the things that are God's. Luke, 20. 25.

7. When his disciples saw this (that there were non-conformists then as well as now) they said, wilt thou that we command fire to come down from heaven and consume them. as Elias did; but he turned, and rebuked them, and said, Ye know not what Spirit ye are of; for the Son of Man is not come to destroy men's lives but to save them, Luke 9. 54, 55, 56.

8. Howbeit, when the Spirit of Truth is come, He shall lead you into all truth, John 16. 8. 13.

9. But now the anointing which ye have received of Him, abides in you, and you need not that any man teach you, (much less impose upon any, or restrain them from what any are persuaded it leads to) but as the same anointing teaches you of all things, and is truth and is no lie, 1 John 2. 27.

10. Dearly beloved, avenge not your selves, but rather give place

unto wrath (much less should any be wrathful that are called Christians, where no occasion is given) therefore if thine enemy hunger, feed him, and if he thirst, give him drink; recompence no man evil for evil, Rom. 12. 19, 20. 21.

11. For though we walk in the flesh (that is in the body or visible world) we do not war after the flesh, for the weapons of our warfare are not carnal. 2 Cor. 10. 3. (but fines and imprisonments are, and such use not the apostle's weapons that employ those) for a bishop, 1 Tim. 3. 3. (faith Paul) must be of good behaviour, apt to teach, no striker, but be gentle unto all men, patient, in meekness instructing, (not persecuting) those that oppose themselves, if God peradventure will give them repentance to the acknowledging of the truth, 2 Tim. 2. 24, 25.

12. Lastly, we shall subjoin one passage more, and then no more of this particular; whatsoever ye would that men should do you, do ye even so to them. Mat. 7. 12. Luke 6. 31.

Now upon the whole we seriously ask whether any should be imposed upon, or restrained, in matters of faith and worship? Whether such practices become the Gospel, or are suitable to Christ's meek precepts and suffering doctrine? And lastly, whether those, who are herein guilty, do to us, as they would be done unto by others.

What if any were once severe to you; many are unconcerned in that, who are yet liable to the last, as if they were not. But if you once thought the imposition of a directory unreasonable, and a restraint from your way of worship, unchristian, can you believe that liberty of conscience is changed, because the parties, in point of power, are? or that the same reasons do not yet remain in vindication of an indulgence for others, that were once employed by you, for yourselves? Surely such conjectures would argue gross weakness.

To conclude, whether persecutors at any time read the scriptures, we know not; but certain we are, such practise, as little of them as may be, who with so much delight reject them, and think it no small accession to the discovery of their loyalty, to lead us and our properties in triumph after them.

CHAPTER IV

They are enemies to the privilege of nature; 1. as rendering some more, and others less than men; 2. As subverting the universal good that is God's gift to men; 3. As destroying all natural affection. Next, they are enemies to the noble principle of reason, as appears in eight great instances.

We farther say, that imposition, restraint, and persecution, are also destructive of the great privilege of nature and principle of reason: of nature in three instances:

First, If God Almighty has made of one blood all nations, as Himself has declared, and that He has given them both senses corporal and intellectual, to discern things and their differences, so as to assert or deny from evidences and reasons proper to each; then where any enacts the belief or disbelief of anything upon the rest, or restrains any from the exercise of their faith to them indispensible, such exalts himself beyond his bounds; enslaves his fellow creatures, invades their right of liberty, and so perverts the whole order of nature.

Secondly, mankind is hereby robbed of the use and benefit of that instinct of a deity which is so natural to him that he can be no more without it, and be, than he can be without the most essential part of himself. For to what serves that divine principle in the universality of mankind, if men be restricted by the prescriptions of some individuals? But if the excellent nature of it inclines men to God, not Man; if the power of accusing and excusing be committed to it; if the troubled thoughts and sad reflections of forlorn and dying men make their tendency that way only, (as being hopeless of all other relief and succour from any external power or command) what shall we say, but that such as invalidate the authority of this heavenly instinct, (as imposition and restraint evidently do) destroy nature, or that privilege which men are born with, and to.

Thirdly, all natural affection is destroyed; for those who have so little tenderness as to persecute men, that cannot for conscience sake yield them compliance, manifestly act injuriously to their fellow creatures, and consequently are enemies to nature; for nature being one in all, such as ruin those who are equally entitled with themselves to nature, ruin it in them, as in liberty, property, etc. And so bring the state of nature to the state of war, the great Leviathan of the times, as ignorantly, as boldly, does assert.

But secondly, we also prove them destructive of the noble principle of reason, and that in these eight particulars.

1. In that those who impose, or restrain are uncertain of the truth, and justifiableness of their actions in either of these, their

own discourses and confessions are pregnant instances, where they tell us, that they do not pretend to be infallible, only they humbly conceive it is thus, or it is not. Since then they are uncertain and fallible, how can they impose upon, or restrain others whom they are so far from assuring, as they are not able to do so much for themselves? what is this, but to impose an uncertain faith, upon certain penalties?

3. As he that acts doubtfully is damned, so faith in all acts of religion is necessary: now in order to believe, we must first will; to will, we must judge; to judge anything, we must first understand; if then we cannot be said to understand anything against our understanding; no more can we judge, will, or believe against our understanding: and if the doubter be damned, what must he be that conforms directly against his judgment and belief, and they likewise that require it from him? In short, that man cannot be said to have any religion, that takes it by another man's choice, not his own.

4. Where men are limited in matters of religion, there the rewards which are entailed on the free acts of men, are quite overthrown; and such as supersede that Grand Charter of liberty of conscience, frustrate all hopes of recompence by rendering the actions of men unavoidable: but those think perhaps, they do not destroy all freedom, because they use so much of their own.

5. Fifthly; they subvert all true religion; for where men believe not because it is true, but because they are required to do so, there they will unbelieve, not because it is false, but so commanded by their superiors, whose authority their interest and security oblige them rather to obey, than dispute.

6. Sixthly, they delude, or rather compel people out of their eternal rewards; for where men are commanded to act in reference to religion, and can neither be secured of their religion, not yet saved harmless from punishment, that so acting and believing, disprivileges them for ever of that recompense which is provided for the faithful.

7. Seventhly, men have their liberty and choice in external matters; they are not compelled to marry this person, to converse with that, to buy here, to eat there, nor to sleep yonder; yet if men had power to impose or restrain in anything, one would think it should be in such exterior matters; but that this liberty should be unquestioned, and that of the mind destroyed, issues here, that it does not unbrute us; but unman us; for, take away understanding,

reason, judgment, and faith, and like Nebuchadnezzar, let us go graze with the beasts of the field.

8. Eighthly and lastly, that which most of all blackens the business, is persecution; for though it is very unreasonable to require faith, where men cannot choose but doubt, yet after all, to punish them for disobedience, is cruelty in the abstract, for we demand, shall men suffer for not doing what they cannot do? Must they be persecuted here if they do not go against their consciences, and punished hereafter if they do? But neither is this all; for that part that is yet most unreasonable, and that gives the clearest sight of persecution, is still behind, namely, the monstrous arguments they have to convince an heretic with: not those of old, as spiritual as the Christian religion, which were to admonish, warn, and finally to reject; but such as were employed by the persecuting Jews and heathens against the great example of the world, and such as followed him, and by the inhuman Papists against our first reformers, as clubs, staves, stocks, pillories, prisons, dungeons, exiles, etc. In a word, ruin to whole familes, as if it were not so much their design to convince the soul, as to destroy the body.

To conclude: there ought to be an adequation and resemblance betwixt all ends, and the means to them, but in this case there can be none imaginable: the end is the conformity of our judgments and understandings to the acts of such as require it, the means are fines and imprisonments (and bloody knocks to boot.)

Now, what proportion or assimulation these bear, let the sober judge: The understanding can never be convinced, nor properly submit, but by such arguments, as are rational, persuasive, and suitable to its own nature; something that can resolve its doubts, answer its objections, enervate its proposition, but to imagine those barbarous Newgate instruments of clubs, fines, prisons, etc. with that whole troop of external and dumb materials of force, should be fit arguments to convince the understanding, scatter it's scuples, and finally, convert it to their religion, is altogether irrational, cruel, and impossible. Force may make an hypocrite; it is faith grounded upon knowledge, and consent that makes a Christian. And to conclude, as we can never betray the honour of our conformity (only due to truth) by a base and timorous hypocrisy to any external violence under heaven, so must we needs say, unreasonable are those imposers, who secure not the imposed or restrained from what may occur to them upon their account; and most inhuman are those persecutors that punish men for not obeying them, though to their utter ruin.

CHAPTER V

They carry a contradiction to government: 1. In the nature of it, which is justice. 2. In the execution of it, which is prudence. 3. In the end of it, which is fidelity. Seven common but grand objections, fairly stated, and briefly answered.

We next urge, that force in matters relating to conscience, carries a plain contradiction to government in the nature, execution and end of it.

By government we understand an external order of justice, or the right and prudent disciplining of any society, by just laws, either in the relaxation, or execution of them.

First, it carried a contradiction to government in the nature of it, which is justice, and that in three respects.

1. It is the first lesson, that great synteresis so much renowned by philosophers and civilians learns mankind to do as they would be done to; since he that gives what he would not take, or takes what he would not give, only shows care for himself, but neither kindness nor justice for another.

2. The just nature of government lies in a fair and equal retribution; but what can be more unequal, than that men should be rated more than their proportion to answer the necessities of government, and yet that they should not only receive no protection from it, but by it be disseized of their dear liberty and properties; we say to be compelled to pay that power, that exerts it self to ruin those that pay it, or that any should be required to enrich those that ruin them is hard, and unequal, and therefore contrary to the just nature of government. If we must be contributaries to the maintenance of it, we are entitled to a protection from it.

3. It is the justice of government to proportion penalties to the crime committed. Now granting our dissent to be a fault, yet the infliction of a corporal or external punishment, for a mere mental error (and that not voluntary) is unreasonable and inadequate, as well as against particular directions of the Scriptures, Tit. iii. 9, 10, 11. For as corporal penalties cannot convince the understanding; so neither can they be commensurate punishments for faults purely intellectual: And for the government of this world to intermeddle

with what belongs to the government of another, and which can have no ill aspect or influence upon it, shows more of invasion than right and justice.

Secondly, it carries a contradiction to government in the execution of it, which is prudence, and that in these instances.

1. The state of the case is this, that there is no republic so great, no empire so vast, but the laws of them are resolvable into these two series or heads of laws fundamental, which are indispensible and immutable, and laws superficial, which are temporary and alterable: and as it is justice and prudence to be punctual in the execution of the former, so by circumstances it may be neither, to execute the latter, they being suited to the present conveniency and emergency of state; as the prohibiting of cattle out of Ireland was judged of advantage to the farmers of England, yet a Murrain would make it the good of the whole, that the law should be broke, or at least the execution of it suspended. That the law of restraint in point of conscience is of this number, we may farther manifest, and the imprudence of thinking otherwise: for first, if the saying were as true as it is false, no bishop, no king, (which admits of various readings; as no decimating clergy, or no persecution, no king,) we should be as silent, as some would have us; but the confidence of their assertion, and the impolicy of such as believe it, makes us to say that a greater injury cannot be done to the present government. For if such laws and establishments are fundamental, they are as immutable as mankind itself; but that they are as alterable, as the conjectures and opinions of governors have been is evident; since the same fundamental indispensible laws and policy of these kingdoms have still remained, through all variety of opposite ruling opinions and judgments, and disjoined from them all. Therefore to admit such a fixation to temporary laws must needs be highly imprudent, and destructive of the essential parts of the government of these countries.

2. That since there has been a time of connivance, and that with no ill success to public affairs, it cannot be prudence to discontinue it, unless it was imprudence before to give it, and such little deserve it that think so.

3. Dissenters not being conscious to themselves of any just forefeiture of that favour, are as well grieved in their resentments of this alteration, as the contrary did oblige them to very grateful acknowledgments.

4. This must be done to gratify all, or the greatest part, or but

some few only; it is a demonstration all are not pleased with it; that the greatest number is not, the empty public auditories will speak: in short, how should either be when six parties are sacrificed to the seventh; that this cannot be prudence, common maxims and observations prove.

5. It strikes fatally at Protestant sincerity for will the Papists say, did Protestants exclaim against us for persecutors, and are they now the men themselves? Was it an instance of weakness in our religion, and is it become a demonstration of strength in theirs? Have they transmuted it from anti-christian in us, to Christian in themselves? Let persecutors answer.

6. It is not only an example, but an incentive to the Romanists, to persecute the reformed religion abroad; for when they see their actions (once void of all excuse) now defended by the example of Protestants that once accused them, (but now themselves) doubtless they will revive their cruelty.

7. It overturns the very ground of the Protestants retreat from Rome; for if men must be restrained upon pretended prudential considerations, from the exercise of their conscience in England; why not the same in France, Holland, Germany, Constantinople, etc. where matters of state may equally be pleaded? This makes religion, state policy; and faith and worship, subservient to the humours and interests of superiors: such doctrine would have prevented our ancestors' retreat; and we wish it be not the beginning of a back-march; for some think it shrewdly to be suspected, where religion is suited to the government, and conscience to its conveniency.

8. Vice is encouraged; for if licentious persons see men of virtue molested for assembling with a religious purpose to reverence and worship God, and that are otherwise most serviceable to the commonwealth, they may and will infer, it is better for them to be as they are, since not to be demure, as they call it, is half way to that kind of accomplishment which procures preferment.

9. For such persons as are so poor spirited as to truckle under such restraints; what conquest is there over them? that before were conscientious men, and now hypocrites; who so forward to be avenged of them that brought this guilt upon them, as they themselves? And how can the imposers be secure of their friendship, whom they have taught to change with the times?

10. Such laws are so far from benefitting the country, that the execution of them will be the assured ruin of it, in the revenues, and

consequently in the power of it; for where there is a decay of families, there will be of trade; so of wealth, and in the end of strength and power; and if both kinds of relief fail, men, the prop of republics; money, the stay of monarchies; this, as requiring mercenaries; that, as needing freemen; farewell the interest of England; it is true, the priests get (though that's but for a time) but the king and people lose; as the event will show.

11. It ever was the prudence of wise magistrates to oblige their people; but what comes shorter of it than persecution? What's dearer to them than the liberty of their conscience? What cannot they better spare than it? Their peace consists in the enjoyment of it: and he that by compliance has lost it, carries his penalty with him, and is his own prison. Surely such practices must render the government uneasy, and beget a great disrespect to the governors, in the hearts of the people.

12. But that which concludes our prudential part shall be this, that after all their pains and good will to stretch men to their measure, they never will be able to accomplish their end: And if he be an unwise man that provides means where he designs no end, how near is he kin to him that proposes an end inobtainable. Experience has told us, 1. How invective it has made the imposed on. 2. What distractions have ensued such attempts. 3. What reproach has followed to the Christian religion, when the professors of it have used a coercive power upon conscience. And lastly, that force never yet made either a good Christian, or a good subject.

Thirdly and lastly, since the proceedings we argue against are proved so destructive to the justice and prudence of government, we ought the less to wonder that they should hold the same malignity against the end of it, which is felicity, since the wonder would be to find it otherwise; and this is evident from these three considerations.

1. Peace (the end of war and government, and its great happiness too) has been, is, and yet will be broken by the frequent tumultuary disturbances that ensue the disquieting our meetings, and the estreating fines upon our goods and estates. And what these things may issue in concerneth the civil magistrate to consider.

2. Plenty, (another great end of government) will be converted into poverty by the destruction of so many thousand families as refuse compliance and conformity, and that not only to the sufferers, but influentially to all the rest; a demonstration of which we have in all those places where the late act has been anything

considerably put in execution. Besides, how great provocation such incharity and cruel usage, as stripping widows, fatherless, and poor of their very necessaries for human life, merely upon an account of faith or worship, must needs be to the just and righteous Lord of Heaven and Earth; scriptures, and plenty of other histories plainly show us.

3. Unity, (not the least, but greatest end of government is lost) for by seeking an unity of opinion (by the ways intended) the unity requisite to uphold us, as a civil society, will be quite destroyed. And such as relinquish that, to get the other (besides that they are unwise) will infallibly lose both in the end.

In short, we say that it is unreasonable we should not be entertained as men, because some think we are not as good Christians as they pretend to wish us; or that we should be deprived of our liberties and properties, who never broke the laws that gave them to us: what can be harder than to take that from us by a law, which the great indulgence and solicitude of our ancestors took so much pains to entail upon us by law; An. 18 Ed. 3. Stat. 3. also Stat. 20 Ed. 3. Cap. 1. again Petition of Right, An. 3. Car. and more fully in Magna Charta; further peruse 37 Ed. 5. Cap. 8. 28. 42 Ed. 3. Cap. 3. 28 Hen. Cap. 7.

And we are persuaded that no temporary subsequential law whatever to our fundamental rights, (as this of force on conscience is) can invalid so essential a part of the government, as English liberty and property: nor that it's in the power of any on earth, to deprive us of them, till we have first done it ourselves, by such enormous facts, as those very laws prohibit, and make our forfeiture of that benefit we should otherwise receive by them; for these being such cardinal and fundamental points of English law doctrine, individually, and by the collective body of the people agreed to; and on which as the most solid basis, our secondary legislative power, as well as executive is built; it seems most rational that the superstructure cannot quarrel or invalidate its own foundation, without manifestly endangering its own security, the effect is ever less noble than the cause, the gift than the giver, and the superstructure than the foundation.

The single question to be resolved in the case, briefly will be this, whether any visible authority (being founded in its primitive institution upon those fundamental laws that inviolably preserve the people in all their just rights and privileges) may invalidate all, or any of the said laws, without an implicit shaking of its own foundation, and a clear overthrow of its own constitution of government, and so reduce them to their *Statu quo prius*, or first principles: the resolution is every man's, at his own pleasure. Read Hen. 3. 9. 14. 29. 25 Ed. 3. Cook's Instit. 2. 19. 50, 51.

Those who intend us no share or interest in the laws of England, as they relate to civil matters, unless we correspond with them in points of faith and worship, must do two things: first, it will lie heavy on their parts to prove that the ancient compact and original of our laws carries that proviso with it; else we are manifestly dispossessed of our free customs.

Secondly, they are to prove the reasonableness of such proceedings to our understandings that we may not be concluded by a law, we know not how to understand; for it I take the matter rightly (as I think I do) we must not buy or sell unless of this or that persuasion in religion; not considering civil society was in the world before the Protestant profession; men, as such, and in affairs peculiarly relative of them, in an external and civil capacity, have subsisted many ages under great variety of religious apprehensions, and therefore not so dependent on them as to receive any variation or revolution with them. What shall we say then? but that some will not that we should live, breathe, and commerce as men, because we are not such modelled Christians as they coercively would have us; they might with as much justice and reputation to themselves forbid us to look or see unless our eyes were grey, black, brown, blue, or some one colour best suiting theirs: for not to be able to give us faith, or save our consciences harmless, and yet to persecute us for refusing conformity, is intolerable hard measure.

In short, that coercive way of bringing all men to their height of persuasion, must either arise from exorbitant zeal and superstition; or from a consciousness of error and defect, which is unwilling anything more sincere and reformed should take place; being of that cardinal's mind, who therefore would not hearken to a reformation, at the sitting of the counsel of Trent; because he would not so far approve the reformers' judgment (for having once condescended to their apprehensions, he thought it would forever enslave them to their sense) though otherwise he saw as much as any man, the grand necessity of a reformation, both of the Roman doctrine and conversation.

Some grand objections in the way must be considered

Objection 1. *But you are a people that meet with designs to disaffect the people, and to ruin the government.*

Answer. A surmise is no certainty, neither is a maybe or conjecture any proof: that from the first we have behaved ourselves inoffensively, is a demonstration; that our meetings are open, where all may hear our matter, and have liberty to object or discuss any point, is notorious. Ignorant calumnies are sandy foundations to build so high a charge upon. Let us fairly be heard in a public conference how far we can justify our principles from being deservedly suspected of sedition or disloyalty, and not overrun us with mere suppositions. We declare our readiness to obey the ordinance of man, which is only relative of human or civil matters, and not points of faith, or practice in worship: but if accusations must stand for proofs, we shall take it for granted that we must stand for criminals; but our satisfaction will be that we shall not deserve it otherwise than as prejudice seeks to traduce us.

Object. 2. *But you strike at the doctrine, at least the discipline of the church, and consequently are heretics.*

Answ. This story is as old as the reformation; if we must be objected against out of pure reputation, let it be in some other matter than what the Papists objected against the first Protestants; otherwise you do but hit yourselves in aiming at us? To say you were in the right, but we are in the wrong, is but a mere begging of the question; for doubtless the Papists said the same to you, and all that you can say to us: your best plea was, conscience upon principles, the most evident and rational to you: do not we the like? What if you think our reasons thick, and our ground of separation mistaken? Did not the Papists harbour the same thoughts of you? You persuaded as few of them as we of you: were you therefore in the wrong? No more are we: it was not what they thought of you, or enacted against you, that concluded you: and why should your apprehensions conclude us? If you have the way of giving faith beyond what they had, and have the faculty of persuasion, evidence as much; but if you are as destitute of both, as they were to you; why should fines and prisons, once used by them against you, and by you exclaimed against, as un-christian ways of reclaiming heretics (supposing yourselves to be such) be employed by you as rational, Christian, and convincing upon us? To say we deserve them more is to suppose yourselves in the right, and us in the wrong, which proves nothing. Besides, the question is not barely this, whether heretics or no heretics; but whether an heretic should be persecuted into a disclaiming of his error; your old arguments run thus, as I well remember.

1. Error is a mistake in the understanding.

2. This is for want of a better illumination.

3. This error can never be dislodged but by reason and persuasion, as what are most suitable to the intellect of man.

4. Fines, goals, exiles, gibbets, etc. are no convincing arguments to the most erring understandng in the world, being slavish and brutish.

5. This way of force makes, instead of an honest dissenter, but an hypocritical conformist; than whom nothing is more detestable to God and man.

This being the Protestants' plea, we are not to be disliked by Protestants, for following their own avowed maxims and axioms of conscience in defence of its own liberty.

In short, either allow separation upon the single principle of my conscience owns this, or disowns that; or never dwell in that building, which knew no better foundation, (indeed good enough) but, accusing your forefathers of schism, and heresy, return to the Romish church. What short of this can any say to an anti-liberty-of-conscience-Protestant.

Object. 3. *But at this rate ye may pretend to cut our throats, and do all manner of savage acts.*

Ans. Though the objection be frequent, yet it is as foully ridiculous. We are pleading only for such a liberty of conscience, as preserves the nation in peace, trade, and commerce; and would not exempt any man, or party of men, from not keeping those excellent laws, that tend to sober, just, and industrious living. It is a Jesuitical moral, to kill a man before he is born: first, to suspect him of an evil design, and then kill him to prevent it.

Object. 4. *But do not you see what has been the end of this separation? Wars and revolutions, and danger to government; witness our late troubles.*

Ans. We see none of all this, but are able to make it appear, that the true cause of all that perplexed disturbance, which was amongst the Homoousians and Arrians of old, and among us of latter years (as well as what has modernly attended our neighbouring countries) took its first rise from a narrowness of spirit, in not tolerating others to live the freemen God made them, in external matters upon the earth, merely upon some difference in religion.

And were there once but an hearty toleration established, it would be a demonstration of the truth of this assertion. On this ground, empire stands safe; on the other, it seems more uncertain.

But these are only the popular devices of some to traduce honest men and their principles; whose lazy life, and intolerable advice become questioned by a toleration of people better inclined.

Object. 5. *But what need you take this pains to prove liberty of conscience reasonable and necessary, when none questions it; all that is required is, that you meet but four more than your own families; and can you not be contented with that? Your disobedience to a law, so favourable, brings suffering upon you.*

Ans. Here is no need of answering the former part of the objection; it is too apparent throughout the land, that liberty of conscience, as we have stated it, has been severely prosecuted, and therefore not so frankly enjoined: the latter part, I answer thus, if the words lawful or unlawful may bear their signification from the nature of the things they stand for, then we conceive that a meeting of four thousand is no more unlawful than a meeting of four; for number singly considered criminates no assembly: but the reason of their assembling; the posture in which; and the matter transacted, with the consequences thereof.

Now if those things are taken for granted, to be things dispensible (as appears by the allowance of four besides every family) certainly the number can never render it unlawful; so that the question will be this, whether if four met to worship God be an allowable meeting, four thousand met with the same design be not an allowable meeting?

It is so plain a case, that the matter in question resolves it.

Object. 6. *But the Law forbids it.*

Answ. If the enacting anything can make it lawful, we have done; but if an Act so made by the Papists against Protestants was never esteemed so by a true Protestant; and if the nature of the matter will not bear it; and lastly, that we are as much commanded by God to meet four thousand, as four; we must desire to be excused, if we forbear not the assembling of ourselves together, as the manner of some is.

Object. 7. *But the reason of the prohibition of the number is (for you see they allow all that can be said to four thousand to be said to the family and four) that tumults may arise, and plots may be made, and the like inconveniencies happen to the government.*

Ans. Great assemblies are so far from being injurious that they are the most inoffensive; for, first, they are open, exposed to the view of all, which of all things plotters are the shyest of; but how fair an opportunity it were, for men so principled, to do it in those allowed meetings of but four besides the family, is easy to guess, when we consider that few make the best and closest council; and next, that such an assembly is the most private and clandestine, and so fitted for mischief and surprise.

Secondly, such assemblies are not only public and large, but they are frequented, as well by those that are not of their way, as by their own; from whence it follows that we have the greatest reason to be cautious and wise in our behaviour, since the more there be at our meetings, the more witnesses are against us, if we should say or act anything that may be prejudicial to the government.

Lastly, for these several years none could ever observe such an ill use made of that freedom, or such wicked designs to follow such assemblies; and therefor it is high uncharity to proceed so severely upon mere suppositions.

To this we shall add several authorities and testimonies for farther confirmation of our sense of the matter, and to let imposers see that we are not the only persons who have impleaded persecution, and justified liberty of conscience, as Christian and rational.

CHAPTER VI

They reflect upon the sense and practice of the wisest, greatest, and best states, and persons of ancient and modern times; as of the Jews, Romans, Egyptians, Germans, French, Hollanders, nay Turks and Persians too. And Cato, Livy, Tacitus, Justin Martyr, Tertullian, Jovianus, Chaucer, Dominicus Soto, Malvetzey, Grotius, Rawleigh, Doctor and Student, French and Dutch Protestants in England, Dr Hammond, Dr Taylor, a nameless but great person, Lactantius, Hilary, Jerom, Chrysostom, Polish and Bohemian Kings, King James, and King Charles the First.

A brief collection of the sense and practice of the greatest, wisest, and most learned commonwealths, kingdoms, and particular persons of their times, concerning force upon conscience.

First, though the Jews above all people had the most to say for imposition and restraint within their own dominions, having their religion instituted by so many signal proofs of divine original, it being delivered to them by the hand of God himself, yet such was their indulgence to dissenters, that if they held the common received Noachical principles tending to the acknowledgment of one God, and a just life, they had the free exercise of their distinct modes of ways of worship, which were numerous. Of this their own rabbis are witnesses, and Grotius out of them.

2. The Romans themselves, as strict as they were, not only had thirty thousand Gods (if Varro may be credited) but almost every family of any note had its distinct sacra, or peculiar way of worship.

3. It was the sense of that grave, exemplary commonwealthsman, Cato, in Salast, that among other things which ruin any government want of freedom of speech, or men's being obliged to humour times, is a great one; which we find made good by the Florentine republic, as Guiccardine relates.

4. Livy tells us it was a wonder that Hannibal's army, consisting of divers nations, divers humours, differing habits, contrary religions, various languages, should live thirteen years from their own country under his command without so much as once mutining, either against their general, or among themselves. But what Livy relates for a wonder, that ingenious marquess, Virgilio Malvetzy gives the reason of, namely, that the difference of their opinion, tongues, and customs was the reason of their preservation and conquest; for, said he, it was impossible so many contrary spirits should combine, and if any should have done it, it was the general's power to make the greater party by his equal hand; they owing him more of reverence, than they did of affection to one another: this, says he, some impute to Hannibal, but howsoever great he was, I give it to the variety of humours in the army. For (adds he) Rome's army was ever less given to mutiny when joined with the provincial auxiliaries, than when entirely Roman; thus much and more, in his public discourses upon Cornelius Tacitus.

5. The same, best statist of his time, C. Tacitus, tells us in the case of Cremtius, that it had been the interest of Tiberius not to have punished him, in as much as curiosity is begotten by restriction of liberty to write or speak, which never missed of proselytes.

6. Just. Martyr. I will forbear to quote, in less than this, two whole apologies, dedicated to Adrian and Antoninus Pius, as I take it.

7. Tertullian ad Scapulam, that learned and judicious apologist, plainly tells us that it is not the property of religion to compel or persecute for religion, he should be accepted for herself, not for force; that being a poor and beggarly one, that has no better arguments to convince; and a manifest evidence of her superstition and falshood.

8. Of this we take the nine-month reign of the Emperor Jovianus to be an excellent demonstration, whose great wisdom and admirable prudence in granting toleration (expresly saying, he would have none molested for the exercise of their religion) calmed the impetuous storms of dissention betwixt the Homoousians and Arrians; and reduced the whole empire before agitated with all kind of commotions during the reigns of Constantine, Constantius, and Julian, to a wonderful serenity and peace, as Socrates Scholasticus affirms.

9. That little kingdom of Egypt had no less than forty thousand persons retired to their private and separate ways of worship, as Eusebius out of Philo Judeus and Josephus relates.

10. And here let me bring honest Chaucer, whose matter (and not his poetry) heartily affects me: it was in a time when priests were as rich and lofty as they are now, and causes of evil alike.

> (a) The time was once, and may return again,
>   (for oft may happen that hath been beforn)
>   when shepherds had none inheritance,
>   ne of land, nor fee in sufferance,
>   But what might arise of the bare sheep,
>   (were it more or less) which they did keep,
>   well ywis was it with shepherds tho':
>   nought having, nought fear'd they to forgo,
>   For Pan (God) himself was their inheritance,
>   and little them serv'd for their maintenance,
>   The shepherd's God so well them guided,
>   that of nought were they unprovided;
>
> (b) Butter enough, honey, milk, and whay,
>   and their flock fleeces them to array.

But tract of time and long prosperity,
   (that nurse of vice, this of insolency)
Lulled the shepherds in such security,
   that not content with loyal obeysance,
Some gan to gap for greedy governance,
   and match themselves with mighty potentates.

(c) Lovers of lordships and troublers of states;
      then gan shepherds swains to look aloft,
And leave to live hard, and learn to lig soft,
      though under colour of shepherds same while
There crept in wolves full of fraud and guile,
      that often devour'd their own sheep,
And often the shepherd that did them keep,

(d) This was the first source of the shepherds sorrow.
      that nor will be quit, with bale, nor borrow.

11. Who knows not that our first reformers were great champions for liberty of conscience, as Wickliff in his remonstrance to the parliament. The Albigenses to Lewis the 11th and 12th of France. Luther to the several diets under Frederick and Charles the Fifth; Calvin to Francis the First, and many of our English martyrs, as the poor Plowman's Famous Complaint, in Fox's Martyrology, etc.

12. The present affairs of Germany plainly tell us that toleration is the preservation of their states; the contrary having formerly, almost quite wasted them.

13. The same in France: who can be so ignorant of their story, as not to know that the timely indulgence of Henry the Fourth; and the discreet toleration of Richlieu and Mazarin, saved that kingdom from being ruined both by the Spaniards, and one another.

14. Holland, than which, what place is there so improved in wealth, trade and power, chiefly owes it to her indulgence, in matters of faith and worship.

15. Among the very Mahumetans of Turkey, and Persia, what

(a) The primitive state of things observed by a poet, more than 300 years old; by which the clergy may read their own apostacy and character.

(b) Time and prosperity corrupted them, and then they grew statesmen.

(c) It was now they began to persecute; they hated any that were more devout than themselves: devotion was counted disaffection; religious assemblies, conventicles; primitive-spirited Christians, upstart heretics; thus the tragedy began, Cain flaying Abel about religion.

(d) He truly maketh their avarice the cause of their degeneration; for it is the root of all evil.

variety of opinions, yet what unity and concord is there? We mean in maters of a civil importance.

16. It was the opinion of that great master of the sentences, Dominicus a Soto, that every man had a natural right, to instruct others in things that are good: and he may teach the gospel truths also, but cannot compel any to believe them, he may explain them, and to this, (says he) every man has a right, as in his 4 Sent. Dist. 5. Art. 10. Pag. 115. 7.

17. Strifes about religion, said Judicious and learned Grotius, are the most pernicious and destructive, where provision is not made for dissenters: the contrary most happy; as in Muscovy; he farther says upon the occasion of Campanella, that not a rigid but easy government suits best with the northern people; he often pleads the relaxation of temporary laws to be reasonable and necessary. As in the case of the Curatij and Horatij, and Fabius Vitulanus; and others stinted to time and place, as the Jewish laws, etc. Polit. Maxims, P. 12, 18. 78, 98.

18. The famous Rawleigh tell us that the way for magistrates to govern well and gain the esteem of their people is to govern by piety, justice, wisdom and a gentle and moderate carriage towards them; and that disturbance attends those states where men are raised or depressed by parties. See his observations and maxims of state.

19. If I mistake not, the French and Dutch Protestants enjoy their separate ways of worship in London, if not in other parts of these lands without molestation; we do the like in remote countries, but not in our own.

20. This must needs be the meaning of the learned doctor, to his inquisitive student in their judicious dialogue, about the fundamental laws of the kingdoms, when he says that such laws as have not their foundation in nature justice and reason, are void *ipso facto*. And whether persecution or restraint upon conscience, be congruous with either, let the impartial judge. Lib. 1. chap. 6.

21. Doctor Hammond himself, and the grand patron of the English Church, was so far from urging the legality of restriction in matters relating to conscience, that he writ, argued, and left upon his dying-bed his sense to the contrary: As the author of his life might have been pleased to observe, but that interest stood in the way, the doctor exhorting his party not to seek to displace those, then in the university; or to persecute them for any matter of religious difference.

22. That a person of no less ability, in the Irish Protestant church did the same. I mean D. Jer. Taylor, his whole discourse of liberty of prophecy is a most pregnant demonstration.

23. It was the saying of a person once, too great to be named now, that liberty of conscience is every man's natural right, and he who is deprived of it is a slave in the midst of the greatest liberty: and since every man should do as he would be done to, such only don't deserve to have it that won't give it.

24. Lactantius reflects upon persecutors thus, if you will with Blood, with evil, and with torments defend your worship, it shall not thereby be defended but polluted, Lib. 5. cap. 20.

25. Hilary against Auxentius, faith the Christian Church does not persecute, but is persecuted.

26. Jerom, thus, heresy must be cut off, with the sword of the spirit, Proæm. Lib. 4.

27. Chrysostom faith, that is not the manner of the children of God, to persecute about their religion, but an evident token of antichrist, — Relig. Uris. Pag. 192.

28. Stephen, king of Poland, declared his mind in the point controverted, thus, *I am king of men, not of conscience; a commander of bodies, not of souls.*

29. The king of Bohemia was of opinion that men's consciences ought in no sort to be violated, urged, or constrained.

30. And lastly, let me add (as what is, or should be now of more force) the sense of King James and Charles the First, men famed for their great natural abilities and acquired learning; that no man ought to be punished for his religion, nor disturbed for his conscience; in that it is the duty of every man to give what he would receive. 'It is a sure rule in divinity, said King James, that God never loves to plant his church by violence and bloodshed. And in his Exposition on Revel. 20. he saith, That persecution is the note of a false church. And in the last king's advice to the present king, he says, Take heed of abetting any factions; your partial adhering to any one side gains you not so great advantages in some men's hearts, (who are prone to be of their king's religion) as it loseth you in others, who think themselves, and their profession, first despised, then persecuted by you.

Again, 'Beware of exasperating any factions, by the crossness, and asperity of some men's passions, humors, or private opinions employed by you grounded only upon their difference, in lesser matters, which are but the skirts and suburbs of religion. Wherein a charitable connivence and Christian toleration often dissipates their strength, whom rougher opposition fortifies; and puts the despised and oppressed party into such combinations; as may most enable them to get a full revenge on those they count their persecutors who are commonly assisted by that vulgar commiseration, which attends all that are said to suffer under the notion of religion.

Always keep up solid piety, and those fundamental truths (which mend both hearts and lives of men) with impartial favour and justice. Your prerogative is best shown and exercised in remitting, rather than exacting the rigour of laws; there being nothing worse than legal tyranny.'

Now upon the whole, we ask what can be more equal, what more reasonable than liberty of conscience; so correspondent with the reverence due to God, and respect to the nature, practice, promotion, and rewards of the Christian religion; the sense of divine writ; the great privilege of nature, and noble principle of reason; the justice, prudence, and felicity of government; and lastly, to the judgment and authority of a whole cloud of famous witnesses, whose harmony in opinion, as much detects the unreasonableness, and uncharity of persecutors, as their savage cruelties imply an high contempt of so solid determinations; of which number I cannot forbear the mention of two, whose actions are so near of kin to one another, and both to inhumanity, as the same thing can be to it self.

The first is a great lord of Buckinghamshire, but so hearty a persecutor of the poor Quakers that rather than they should peaceably enjoy the liberty of worshipping God, (and to supply the county defect of informers) he has encouraged a pair of such wretches that it had been a disgrace for the meanest farmer to converse with; one having been prisoner in Ailsbury, for theft, and said to have been burnt in the hand; and the other of a complexion not much less scandalous and immoral.

To give an undeniable testimony of their merit, once for all, I shall briefly relate a most notorious piece of perjury. They suspecting a religious assembly to be at a certain place in the same county, came; and finding one in reality, repaired to one they call, Sir Tho. Clayton, and a justice, where they deposed, that not only a meeting was at such an house, but one Tho. Zachery and his wife were there, who at the same time, as at the trial upon indictment for perjury at Aylsbury, was proved by sufficient witnesses from London, were then at that city, yet fined not only for being there, but for the speaker also, though none spoke that day.

Upon the prosecution of these men, as perjured men, and by the law disprivileged of all employ, and never to be credited more in evidence; several delays were made, much time spent, and not a little pains bestowed, all in hopes of an exemplary success, which proved so, but the wrong way, for the very last sessions, when the matter should have received an absolute decision, and the attendants have been dismissed (especially on the score of the witnesses that came from London the second time, upon no other account) a letter was reported to have been writ from the aforesaid lord, in favour of these informers, to this purpose, that since Sir Tho. Clayton was not present, the business could not well be determined, but if the court would undertake the ending of it, he besought them to be favourable to those honest men, if this be true as said, it is a most aggravated shame to nobility: what! to protect them from the lash of the law, who went about to destroy truth the life of it: it is a dishonour to the government, a scandal to the county, and a manifest injury to an inoffensive and useful inhabitant.

The other is as well known by his cruelty as by his name, and he scarce deserves another; however, he is understood by that of the reading knight errant, and always in armour for the Devil; a man whose life seems to be whole Bonner revived: Hogestrant, the Popish inquisitor, could not hate Martin Luther more than he does a poor dissenter; and wants but as much power as he has will, to hang more than he has imprisoned. The laws made against Papists, he inflicts upon the Quakers; and makes it crime enough for a præmunire, to have an estate to lose.

The single question is not, were you at such a meeting? which the act intends, but will you swear, which it intends not, and women escape him as little for this as those of his own tribe do for some things else: but what of all things most aggravates the man's impiety, is the making a devilish snare of a Christian duty; since such as have come to visit the imprisoned have been imprisoned themselves for their charity; so that with him it seems a current maxim that those must not come to see prisoners, and not be such themselves, who will not take the oath of allegiance to do it.

To relate the whole tragedy would render him as bad as the discourse big; and the latter not less voluminous, than the former odious. But three things I shall observe.

First, that he has crowded seventy-two persons (of those called Quakers) men and women, immodestly into jail, not suffering them to enjoy common conveniences. And for his diversion, and the punishment of little children, he pours cold water down their necks.

Secondly, his imprisonments are almost perpetual. First he præmunires them without any just cause of suspicion, then imprisons them, and lastly plunders them, and that by a law enacted against Romanists; which, if all be true that is said, is more his concern than theirs, if without offence, it may be supposed he has any religion at all.

Thirdly, some have been there about eight years, and should be eighteen more, were he as sure to live (being more than 70) and enjoy his power, as doubtless he hopes to die before those good laws overtake him, that would make an example of such an oppressor; in short, wives, widows, poor and fatherless, are all fish for his net; and whether over or under age; he casts none away, but seems to make it his privilege to correct law, by out-doing it. When we have said all we can (and we can never say too much, (if enough) he is still his own best character.

Such are the passions, follies, and prejudices, men devoted to a spirit of imposition, and persecution, are attended with.

Non enim possumus que vidimus, et audivimus non loqui.

In short, what religious, what wise, what prudent, what good natured person would be a persecutor; certainly it's an office only fit for those who being void of all reason, to evidence the verity of their own religion, fancy it to be true, from that strong propensity and greedy inclination they find in themselves to persecute the contrary; a weakness of so ill a consequence to all civil societies, that the admission of it ever was, and ever will prove their utter ruin, as well as their great infelicity who pursue it.

And though we could not more effectually express our revenge than by leaving such persons to the scope of their own humours; yet being taught to love and pray for our persecutors, we heartily wish their better information, that (if it be possible) they may act more suitably to the good pleasure of the eternal just God, and beneficially to these nations.

To conclude, liberty of conscience (as thus stated and defended) we ask as our undoubted right by the law of God, of nature, and of our own country: it has been often promised, we have long waited for it, we have writ much, and suffered in its defence, and have made many true complaints, but found little or no redress.

However, we take the righteous Holy God to record, against all objections, that are ignorantly or designedly raised against us. That:

1st. We hold no principle destructive of the English government.

2d. That we plead for no such dissenter (if such an one there be.)

3d. That we desire the temporal and eternal happiness of all persons (in submission to the divine will of God) heartily forgiving our cruel persecutors:

4thly, and lastly, we shall engage, by God's assistance, to lead peaceable, just and industrious lives amongst men, to the good and example of all. But if after all we have said, this short discourse should not be credited, not answered in any of its sober reasons, and requests; but sufferings should be the present lot of our inheritance from this generation, be it known to them all that meet we must, and meet we cannot but encourage all to do (whatever hardship we sustain) in God's name and authority, who is Lord of Hosts and King of Kings; at the revelation of whose righteous judgments and glorious tribunal, mortal men shall render an account of the deeds done in the body; and whatever the apprehensions of such may be, concerning this discourse, it was writ in love and from a true sense of the present state of things: and time and the event will vindicate it from untruth. In the mean while, it is matter of great satisfaction to the author, that he has so plainly cleared his conscience, in pleading for the liberty of other men's, and publicly born his honest testimony for God, not out of season to his poor country.

A PERSWASIVE to Moderation to Church-Dissenters, in Prudence and Conscience: Humbly submitted to the KING and His Great Council.

THE EPISTLE

Having of late time observed the heat, aversion and scorn with which some men have treated all thoughts of ease to church dissenters, I confess I had a more than ordinary curiosity to examine the grounds those gentlemen went upon: for I could not tell how to think moderation should be a vice, where Christianity was a virtue, when the great doctor of that religion commands, that our moderation be known unto all men; and why? For the Lord is at hand: And what to do? but to judge our rancour, and retaliate and punish our bitterness of spirit. and, to say true, it is a severe reflection we draw upon ourselves, that though Pagan emperors could endure the addresses of primitive Christians, and Christian Caesars receive the apologies of infidels, for indulgence, yet it should be thought of some men, an offence to seek it, or have it of a Christian prince, whose interest I dare say it is, and who himself so lately wanted it: but the consideration of the reason of this offence will increase our admiration; for they tell us it is dangerous to the prince to suffer it, while the prince is himself a dissenter: this difficulty is beyond all skill to remove that it should be against the interest of a dissenting prince to indulge dissent. For though it will be granted there are dissenters on differing principles from those of the prince, yet they are still dissenters, and dissent being the prince's interest, it will naturally follow that those dissenters are in the interest of the prince, whether they think on it or no.

Interest will not lie: men embarked in the same vessel, seek the safety of the whole in their own, whatever other differences they may have. And self-safety is the highest worldly security a prince can have; for though all parties would rejoice their own principles prevailed, yet every one is more solicitous about its own safety, than the other's verity. Wherefore it cannot be unwise, by the security of all, to make it the interest as well as duty of all, to advance that of the public.

Angry things, then, set aside, as matters now are, what is best to be done? This I take to be the wise man's question, as to consider and answer it, will be his business. Moderation is a Christian duty, and it has ever been the prudent man's practice. For those governments that have used it in their conduct, have succeeded best in all ages.

I remember it is made in Livy the wisdom of the Romans, that they relaxed their hand to the Privernates, and thereby made them most faithful to their interest. And it prevailed so much with the Petilians, that they would endure any extremity from Hannibal, rather than desert their friendship, even then, when the Romans discharged their fidelity, and sent them the despair of knowing they could not relieve them. So did one act of humanity overcome the Falisci above arms, which confirms that noble saying of Seneca, *Mitius imperanti Melius paretur*, the mildest conduct is best obeyed. A truth celebrated by Grotius and Campanella, practised, doubtless, by the bravest princes; for Cyrus exceeded when he built the Jews a temple, and himself no Jew; Alexander astonished the princes of his train with the profound veneration he paid the high priest of that people; and Augustus was so far from suppressing the Jewish worship that he sent Hecatombs to Jerusalem to increase their devotion. Moderation filled the reigns of the most renowned Caesars: and story says they were Neros and Caligulas that loved cruelty.

But others tell us that dissenters are mostly antimonarchical, and so not to be indulged, and that the agreement of the Church of England and Rome in monarchy and hierarchy, with their nearness in other things should oblige her to grant the Roman Catholics a special ease, exclusive of the other dissenters. But with the leave of those worthy gentlemen, I would say, nobody is against that which is for him: and that the aversion apprehended to be in some against the monarchy, rather comes from interest than principle: for governments were never destroyed by the interests they preserve.

In the next place, it is as plain that there is a fundamental difference between those churches in religion and interest. In religion, it appears by a comparison of the thirty-nine articles with the doctrine of the Council of Trent. In interest, they differ; fundamentally, because our church is in the actual possession of the churches and livings that the other church claims. What better mixture then can these two churches make than that of iron and clay ? Nor do I think it well-judged, or wise, in any that pretend to be sons of the Church of England, to seek an accommodation from the topic of affinity, since it is that some of her dissenters have always objected, and she as constantly denied to be true.

I say, this way of reconciling or indulging Roman Catholics stumbles far greater numbers of people of nearer creeds, and gives the Church of England the lie. But suppose the trick took, and they only of all dissenters had indulgence, yet their paucity considered, I am sure, a pair of Sir Kenelm Digby's breeches would set with as good a grace upon the late Lord Rochester's dwarf. Upon the whole matter, let men have ease, and they will keep it ; for those that might plot to get it, would not plot to lose it. Men love the bridge they need and pass : and that prince who has his people fast by interest, holds them by the strongest human tie ; for other courses have failed as often as they have been tried. Let us then once try a true liberty : never did the circumstances of any kingdom lie more open and fair to so blessed an accommodation than we do at this time.

But we are told the King has promised to maintain the Church of England ; I grant it ; but if the Church of England claims the King's promise of protection, her dissenters cannot forget that of his clemency ; and as they were both great, and admirably distinguished, so by no means are they inconsistent or impracticable.

Will not his justice let him be wanting in the one ? And can his greatness of mind let him leave the other behind him in the storm, unpitied and unhelped ? Pardon me, we have not to do with an insensible prince, but one that has been touched with our infirmities ; more than any body fit to judge our cause, by the share he once had in it. Who should give ease like the prince that has wanted it ? To suffer for his own conscience looked great ; but to deliver other men's were glorious. It is a sort of paying the vows of his adversity, and it cannot therefore be done by anyone else, with so much justice and example.

Far be it from me to solicit anything in diminution of the just rights of the Church of England : Let her rest protected where she is. But I hope none will be thought to intend her wrong, for refusing to understand the King's promise to her, in a ruinous sense to all others ; and I am sure she would understand her own interest better, if she were of the same mind. For it is morally impossible that a conscientious prince can be thought to have tied himself to compel others to a communion, that himself cannot tell how to be of; or that anything can oblige him to shake the firmness of those he has confirmed by his own royal example.

Having then so illustrious an instance of integrity, as the hazard of the loss of three crowns for conscience. Let it at least excuse dissenters constancy, and provoke the friends of the succession to moderation, that no man may lose his birth-right for his persuasion, and us to live dutifully, and so peaceably under our own vine, and under our own fig-tree, with glory to God on high, to the king honour, and good-will to all men.

A PERSWASIVE TO MODERATION, ETC.

Moderation, the subject of this discourse, is in plainer English liberty of conscience to church dissenters: a cause I have, with all humility, undertaken to plead against the prejudices of the times.

That there is such a thing as conscience, and the liberty of it, in reference to faith and worship towards God, must not be denied, even by those that are most scandalised at the ill use some seem to have made of such pretences. But to settle the terms: by conscience, I understand the apprehension and persuasion a man has of his duty to god: by liberty of conscience, I mean, a free and open profession and exercise of that duty; especially in worship: but I always premise this conscience to keep within the bounds of morality, and that it be neither frantic nor mischievous, but a good subject, a good child, a good servant, in all the affairs of life: as exact to yield to Caesar the things that are Caesar's, as jealous of withholding from God the thing that is God's.

In brief, he that acknowledges the civil government under which he lives, and that maintains no principle hurtful to his neighbour in his civil property.

For he that in anything violates his duty to these relations cannot be said to observe it to God who ought to have his tribute out of it. Such do not reject their prince, parent, master or neighbour, but God who enjoins that duty to them. Those pathetic words of Christ will naturally enough reach the case, in that ye did it not to them, ye did it not to me, for duty to such relations hath a divine stamp: and divine right runs through more things of the world, and acts of our lives than we are aware of: and sacrilege may be committed against more than the church. Nor will a dedication to God, of the robbery from man, expiate the guilt of disobedience; for though zeal could turn gossip to theft, his altars would renounce the sacrifice.

The conscience then that I state, and the liberty I pray, carrying so great a salvo and deference to public and private relations, no ill design can, with any justice, be fixed upon the author, or reflection upon the subject, which by this time, I think, I may venture to call a toleration.

But to this so much craved, as well as needed, toleration, I meet with two objections of weight, the solving of which will make way for it in this kingdom. And the first is a disbelief of the possibility of the thing. Toleration of dissenting worships from that established, is not practicable (say some) without danger to the state, with which it is interwoven. This is political. The other objection is that admitting dissenters to be in the wrong, (which is always premised by the national church) such latitude were the way to keep up the disunion, and instead of compelling them into a better way, leave them in the possession and pursuit of their old errors, this is religious. I think I have given the objections fairly; it will be my next business to answer them as fully.

The strength of the first objection against this liberty is the danger suggested to the state; the reason is, the national form being interwoven with the frame of the government. But this seems to me only said, and not only (with submission) not proved, but not true: for the established religion and worship are no other ways interwoven with the government than that the government makes profession of them, and by divers laws has made them the current religion, and required all the members of the state to conform to it.

This is nothing but what may as well be done by the government, for any other persuasion, as that. It is true, it is not easy to change an established religion, nor is that the question we are upon; but state religions have been changed without the change of states. We see this in the governments of Germany and Denmark upon the Reformation: But more clearly and near ourselves, in the case of Henry the Eighth, Edward the Sixth, Queen Mary and Elizabeth; for the monarchy stood, the family remained and succeeded under all the revolutions of state religion, which could not have been, had the proposition been generally true.

The change of religion then, does not necessarily change the government, or alter the state; and if so, *a fortiori*, indulgence of church dissenters, does not necessarily hazard a change of the state, where the present state religion or church remains the same; for that I premise.

So me may say that it were more facile to change from one national religion to another, than to maintain the monarchy and church against the ambition and faction of divers dissenting parties. But this is improbable at least. For it were to say, that it is an easier thing to change a whole kingdom, than with the sovereign power, followed with armies, navies, judges, clergy, and all the conformists of the kingdom, to secure the government from the ambition and faction of diffenters, as differing in their interests within themselves, as in their persuasions; and were they united, have neither power to awe, nor rewards to allure to their party. They can only be formidable when headed by the sovereign. They may stop a gap, or make, by his accession a balance: otherwise, until it is harder to fight broken and divided troops than an entire body of an army, it will be always easier to maintain the government under a toleration of dissenters, than in a total change of religion, and even then itself has not failed to have been preserved. But whether it be more or less easy, is not our point; if they are many, the danger is of exasperating, not of making them easy; for the force of our question is whether such indulgence be safe to the state? And here we have the first and last, the best and greatest evidence for us, which is fact and experience, the journal and resolves of time, and treasure of the sage.

For first, the Jews, that had most to say for their religion, and whose religion was twin to their state, (both being joined, and sent with wonders from heaven) indulged strangers in their religious dissents. They required but the belief of the Noachical principles, which were common to the world: no idolater, and but a moral man, and he had his liberty, aye, and some privileges too, for he had an apartment in the temple, and this without danger to the government. Thus Maimonides, and others of their own rabbis, and Grotius out of them.

The wisdom of the Gentiles was very admirable in this, that though they had many sects of philosophers among them, each dissenting from the other in their principles, as well as discipline, and that not only in physical things, but points metaphysical, in which some of the fathers were not free, the school-men deeply engaged, and our present academies but too much perplexed; yet they indulged them and the best livers with singular kindness: the greatest statesmen and captains often becoming patrons of the sects they best affected, honouring their readings with their presence and applause. So far were those ages, which we have made as the original of wisdom and politeness, from thinking toleration an error of state, or dangerous to the government. Thus Plutarch, Strabo, Laertius, and others.

To these instances I may add the latitude of old Rome, that had almost as many deities as houses: for Varro tells us of no less than thirty thousand several sacra, or religious rites among her people, and yet without a quarrel: unhappy fate of Christianity! the best of religions, and yet her professors maintain less charity than idolaters, while it should be peculiar to them. I fear, it shows us to have but little of it at heart.

But nearer home, and in our own time, we see the effects of a discreet indulgence, even to emulation. Holland, that bog of the world, neither sea nor dry land, now the rival of tallest monarchs; not by conquests, marriages, or accession of royal blood, the usual ways to empire, but by her own superlative clemency and industry; for the one was the effect of the other: she cherished her people, whatsoever were their opinions, as the reasonable stock of the country, the heads and hands of her trade and wealth; and making them easy in the main point, their conscience, she became great by them; this made her fill with people, and they filled her with riches and strength.

And if it should be said, she is upon her declension for all that. I answer, all states must know it, nothing is here immortal. Where are the Babylonian, Persian, and Grecian empires? And are not Lacedæmon, Athens, Rome and Carthage gone before her? Kingdoms and commonwealths have their births and growths, their declensions and deaths, as well as private families and persons. but it is owing neither to the armies of France, nor navies of England, but her own domestic troubles.

Seventy-two sticks in the bones yet: the growing power of the Prince of Orange, must, in some degree, be an ebb to that state's strength; for they are not so unanimous and vigorous in their interest as formerly: but were they secure against the danger of their own ambition and jealousy, anybody might insure their glory at five per cent. But some of their greatest men apprehending they are in their climacterical juncture, give up the ghost, and care not, if they must fall, by what hand it is.

Others choose a stranger, and think one afar off will give the best terms, and least annoy them: whilst a considerable party have chosen a domestic prince, kin to their early successes by the fore-father's side (the gallantry of his ancestors) And that his own greatness and security are wrapped up in theirs, and therefore modestly hope to find their account in his prosperity. But this is a kind of digression, only before I leave it, I dare venture to add, that if the Prince of Orange changes not the policies of that state, he will not change her fortune, and he will mightily add to his own.

But perhaps I shall be told that nobody doubts that toleration is an agreeable thing to a commonwealth, where every one thinks he has a share in the government; aye, that the one is the consequence of the other, and therefore most carefully to be avoided by all monarchical states. This indeed were shrewdly to the purpose, in England, if it were but true. But I don't see how there can be one true reason advanced in favour of this objection: monarchies, as well as commonwealths, subsisting by the preservation of the people under them.

But, first, if this were true, it would follow, by the rule of contraries, that a republic could not subsist with unity and hier-archy, which is monarchy in the church; but it must, from such monarchy in church, come to monarchy in state too. But Venice, Genoa, Lucca, seven of the cantons of Switzerland, (and Rome herself, for she is an aristocracy) all under the loftiest hierarchy in church, and where is no toleration, show in fact, that the contrary is true.

But, secondly, this objection makes a commonwealth the better government of the two, and so overthrows the thing it would establish. This is effectually done, if I know anything, since a commonwealth is hereby rendered a more copious, powerful and beneficial government to mankind, and is made better to answer contingencies and emergencies of state, because this subsists either way, but monarchy not, if the objection be true. The one prospers by union in worship and discipline, and by toleration of dissenting churches from the national. The other only by an universal con-formity to a national church. I say, this makes monarchy (in itself, doubtless, an admirable government) less powerful, less extended, less propitious, and finally less safe to the people under it, than a commonwealth; In that no security is left to monarchy under diversity of worships, which yet no man can defend or forbid, but may often arrive, as it hath in England, more than five times, in the two last ages. And truly it is natural for men to choose to settle where they may be safest from the power and mischief of such accidents of state.

Upon the whole matter, it is to reflect the last mischief upon monarchy, the worst enemies it has could hope to disgrace, or endanger it by; since it is to tell the people under it, that they must either conform or be destroyed, or to save themselves, turn hypocrites, or change the frame of the government they live under. A perplexity both to monarch and people, that nothing can be greater, but the comfort of knowing the objection is false. And that which ought to make every reasonable man of this opinion, is the cloud of witnesses that almost every age of monarchy affords us.

I will begin with that of Israel, the most exact and sacred pattern of monarchy, begun by a valiant man, translated to the best, and improved by the wisest of kings, whose ministers were neither fools, nor fanatics: here we shall find provision for dissenters: their *proselyti domicilii* were so far from being compelled to their national rites, that they were expressly forbid to observe them. Such were the Egyptians that came with them out of Egypt, the Gibeonites and Canaanites, a great people, that after their several forms worshipped in an apartment of the same temple. The Jews with a liturgy, they without one: The Jews had priests, but these none: the Jews had variety of oblations, these people burnt offerings only. All that was required of them was the natural religion of Noah, in which the acknowledgment and worship of the true God, was, and it still ought to be, the main point; nay, so far were they from coercive conformity, that they did not so much as oblige them to observe their sabbath, though one of the Ten Commandments: Grotius and Selden say more. Certainly this was great indulgence, since so unsuitable an usage looked like prophaning their devotion, and a common nuisance to their national religion. One would think by this, that their care lay on the side of preserving their cult from the touch of accession of dissenters, and not of forcing them, by undoing penalties, to conform. This must needs be evident: for if God's religion and monarchy (for so we are taught to believe it) did not, and would not, at a time when religion lay less in the mind, and more in ceremony, compel conformity from dissenters, we hope we have got the best presidents on our side.

But if this instance be of most authority, we have another very exemplary, and to our point pertinent, for it shows what monarchy may do: it is yielded us from the famous story of Mordecai. He, with his Jews, were in a bad plight with the King Ahasuerus, by the

ill offices Hamon did them: the arguments he used were drawn
from the common topics of faction and sedition, that they were an
odd and dangerous people, under differing laws of their own, and
refused obedience to his; so denying his supremacy. Dissenters with
a witness: things most tender to any government.

The King thus incensed, commands the laws to be put in
execution, and decrees the ruin of Mordecai with all the Jews: but
the King is timely entreated, his heart softens, the decree is revoked,
and Mordecai and his friends saved. The consequence was, as
extreme joy to the Jews, so peace and blessings to the King. And
that which heightens the example is the greatness and infidelity of
the prince: had the instance been in a Jew, it might have been
placed to his greater light, or piety: in a petty prince, to the paucity
or entireness of his territories: But that an heathen, and King of
one hundred and seven and twenty provinces should throughout his
vast dominions not fear, but practise toleration with good success,
has something admirable in it.

If we please to remember the tranquility and success of those
heathen Roman emperors that allowed indulgence; that Augustus
sent Hecatombs to Jerusalem, and the wisest honoured the Jews,
and at least spared the divers sects of Christians, it will certainly
oblige us to think that princes, whose religions are nearer of kin, to
those of the dissenters of our times, may not unreasonably hope for
quiet from a discreet toleration, especially when there is nothing
peculiar in Christianty to render princes unsafe in such an indulgence. The admirable prudence of the Emperor Jovianus, in a quite
contrary method to those of the reigns of his predecessors, settled
the most embroiled time of the Christian world, almost to a
miracle; for though he found the heats of the Arrians and Orthodox
carried to a barbarous height, (to say nothing of the Novatians, and
other dissenting interests) the Emperor esteeming those calamities
the effect of coercing conformity to the prince's or state's religion,
and that this course did not only waste Christians, but expose
Christians to the scorn of heathens, and so scandal those whom
they should convert, he resolutely declared that he would have none
molested for the different exercise of their religious worship; which
(and that in a trice (for he reigned but seven months) calmed the
impetuous storms of dissention, and reduced the empire, before
agitated with the most uncharitable contents) to a wonderful
security and peace; thus a kindly amity brought a civil unity to the
state; which endeavours for a forced unity never did to the church,

but had formerly filled the government with incomparable miseries, as well as the church with uncharity : and which is sad, I must needs say, that those leaders of the church that should have been the teachers and examples of peace, in so singular a juncture of the churches ferment, did, more than any, blow the trumpet, and kindle the fire of division. So dangerous is it to super-fine upon the text, and then impose it upon penalty, for faith.

Valentinian the Emperor (we are told by Socrates Scholasticus) was a great honourer of those that favoured his own faith ; but so, as he molested not the Arrians at all. And Marcellinus farther adds in his honour, that he was much renowed for his moderate carriage during his reign ; insomuch, that amongst sundry sects of religion, he troubled no man for his conscience, imposing neither this nor that to be observed ; much less, with menacing edicts and injunctions, did he compel others, his subjects, to bow the neck, or conform to that which himself worshipped, but left such points as clear and untouched as be found them.

Gratianus, and Theodosius the Great indulged divers sorts of Christians ; but the Novatians of all the dissenters were preferred : which was so far from insecuring, that it preserved the tranquility of the empire. Nor till the time of Celestine Bishop of Rome, were the Novatians disturbed ; and the persecution of them, and the assumption of the secular power, began much at the same time. But the Novatians at Constantinople were not dealt withal ; for the Greek bishops continued to permit them the quiet enjoyment of their dissenting assemblies ; as Socrates tells us in his fifth and seventh books of Ecclesiastical story.

I shall descend nearer our own times ; for notwithstanding no age has been more furiously moved, than that which Jovianus found, and therefore the experiment of indulgence was never better made, yet to speak more in view of this time of day, we find our contemporaries, of remoter judgments in religion, under no manner of difficulty in this point. The Grand Seignior, Great Mogul, Czars of Muscovia, King of Persia ; the Great Monarchs of the East have long allowed and prospered with a toleration : and who does not know that this gave great Tamerlane his mighty victories ? In these western countries we see the same thing.

Cardinal d'Ossat in his 92d letter to Villeroy, secretary to Henry the Fourth of France, gives us docrine and example for the subject in hand ; 'Besides (says he) that necessity has no law, be it in what case it will ; our Lord Jesus Christ instructs us by his gospel, to let the tares alone, lest removing them may endanger the wheat. That other Catholic princes have allowed it without rebuke. That particularly the Duke of Savoy, who (as great a zealot as he would be thought for the Catholic religion) tolerates the heretics in three of his provinces, namely, Angroyne, Lucerne and Perone. That the King of Poland does as much, not only in Sweedland, but in Poland itself. That all the Princes of the Austrian family, that are celebrated as pillars of the Catholic church do the like, not only in the towns of the empire, but in their proper territories, as in Austria itself, from whence they take the name of their honour. In Hungary, Bohemia, Moravia, Lusatia, Stirria, Camiolia and Croatia the like. That Charles the Fifth, father of the King of Spain, was the person that taught the King of France and other princes, how to yield to such emergencies. That his son, the present King of Spain, who is esteemed Arch Catholic, and that is, as the Atlas of the Catholic church, tolerates notwithstanding, at this day, in his kingdoms of Valentia and Granada, the Moors themselves in their Mahometism, and has offered to those of Zealand, Holland, and other heretics of the Low Countries the free exercise of their pretended religion, so that they will but acknowledge and obey him in civil matters.' It was of those letters of this extraordinary man, for so he was (whether we regard him in his ecclesiastical dignity, or his greater Christian and civil prudence) that the great Lord Fulkland said, a Minister of State should no more be without Cardinal d'Ossat's letters, than a parson without his bible. And indeed, if we look into France, we shall find the indulgence of those Protestants, hath been a flourishing to that kingdom, as their arms a succour to their King. It is true, that since they helped the ministers of his greatness to success, that haughty monarch has changed his measures, and resolves their conformity to his own religion, or their ruin; but no man can give another reason for it, than that he thinks it for his turn to please that part of his own church, which are the present necessary and unwearied instruments of his absolute glory. But let us see the end of this conduct, it will require more time to approve the experiment.

As it was the royal saying of Stephen, King of Poland, that he was a king of men, and not of conscience; a commander of bodies, and not of souls. So we see a toleration has been practised in that country of a long time, with no ill success to the state the cities of Cracovia Racovia and many other towns of note, almost wholly dissenting from the common religion of the kingdom, which is

Roman Catholic, as the others are Socinian and Calvinist, mighty opposite to that, as well as to themselves.

The King of Denmark, in his large town of Altona, but about a mile from Hamburg, and therefore called so, that is, all-to-near, is a pregnant proof to our point. For though his seat be so remote from the place, another strong and insinuating state so near, yet under his indulgence of divers persuasions, they enjoy their peace, and he that security, that he is not upon better terms in any of his more immediate and uniform dominions. I leave it to the thinking reader, if it be not much owing to this freedom, and if a contrary course were not the way for him to furnish his neighbours with means to depopulate the place, or make it uneasy and chargeable to him to keep?

If we look into other parts of Germany, where we find a stout and warlike people, fierce for the thing they opine, or believe, we shall find the Prince Palatine of the Rhine has been safe, and more potent by his indulgence, witness his improvements at Manheim: and as (believe me) he acted the Prince to his people in other things, so in this to the empire; for he made bold with the constitution of it in the latitude he gave his subjects in this affair.

The Elector of Brandenburg is himself a Calvinist, his people mostly Lutheran, yet in part of his dominions, the Roman Catholics enjoy their churches quietly.

The Duke of Newburg, and a strict Roman Catholic, brother-in law to the present emperor, in his province of Juliers, has, not only at Dewsburg, Mulheim, and other places, but in Duseldorp itself, where the court resides, Lutheran, and Calvinist, as well as Roman Catholic, assemblies.

The Elector of Saxony, by religion a Lutheran, in his city of Budissin, has both Lutherans and Roman Catholics in the same church, parted only by a grate.

In Ausburg, they have two chief magistrates, as their Duumvirat, one must always be a Roman Catholic, and the other a Lutheran.

The Bishop of Osnaburg is himself a Lutheran, and in the town of his title, the Roman Catholics, as well as Lutherans, have their churches: and which is more, the next Bishop must be a Catholic too: for like the buckets in the well, they take turns: one way to be sure, so that one be but in the right.

From hence we will go to Sultzbach, a small territory, but has a great prince, I mean, in his own extraordinary qualities; for, among other things, we shall find him act the moderator among his people.

By profession he is a Roman Catholic, but has *Simultaneum Religionis Exercitium*, not only Lutherans and Roman Catholics enjoy their different worships, but alternatively in one and the same place, the same day ; so balancing his affection by his wisdom, that there appears neither partiality in him, nor envy in them, though of such opposite persuasions.

I will end these foreign instances with a prince and bishop, all in one, and he a Roman Catholic too, and that is the Bishop of Mentz ; who admits, with a very peaceable success such Lutherans, with his Catholics, to enjoy their churches, as live in his town of Erford. Thus doth practice tell us, that neither monarchy nor hierarchy are in danger from a toleration. On the contrary, the laws of the empire, which are the acts of the emperor, and the soverign princes of it, have tolerated these three religious persuasions, viz., the Roman Catholic, Lutheran and Calvinist, and they may as well tolerate three more, for the same reasons, and with the same success. For it is not their greater nearness or consistency in doctrine, or in worship on the contrary, they differ much, and by that, and other circumstances, are sometimes engaged in great controversies, yet is a toleration practicable, and the way of peace with them.

And which is closest to our point, at home itself, we see that a toleration of the Jews, French and Dutch in England, all dissenters from the national way ; and the connivance that has been in Ireland : and the downright toleration in most of the King's plantations abroad, prove the assertion that toleration is not dangerous to monarchy. For experience tells us, where it is in any degree admitted, the King's Affairs prosper most ; people, wealth and strength being sure to follow such indulgence.

But after all that I have said in reason and fact, why toleration is safe to monarchy, story tells us that worse things have befallen princes in countries under ecclesiastical union than in places under divided forms of worship ; and so tolerating countries stand to the Prince, upon more than equal terms with conforming ones. And where princes have been exposed to hardship in tolerating countries, they have as often come from the conforming, as non-conforming party ; and so the dissenter is upon equal terms to the prince or state, with the conformist.

The first is evident in the Jews, under the conduct of Moses ; their dissention came from the men of their own tribes, such as Corah, Dathan and Abiram, with their partakers. To say nothing of the Gentiles.

The miseries and slaughters of Mauritius the Emperor prove my point; who be the greatest church-men of his time was withstood, and his servant that perpetrated the wickedness, by them, substituted in his room, because more officious to their grandure. What power but that of the church, dethroned Childerick, King of France, and set Pepin in his place? The miseries of the emperors, Henry the Fourth and Fifth, father and son, from their rebellious subjects raised and animated by the power of conformists, dethroning both, as much as they could, are notorious. It is alleged that Sigismund King of Sweedland, was rejected by that Lutheran country, because he was a Roman Catholic.

If we come nearer home, which is most suitable to the reasons of the discourse, we find the churchmen take part with William Rufus and Henry the First, against Robert their elder brother; and after that, we see some of the greatest of them made head against their King, namely Anselm, Archbishop of Canterbury, and his party, as did his successor Thomas of Becket to the second Henry. Stephen usurped the crown when there was a church union. And King John lived miserable for all that, and at last died by one of his own religion too. The dissentions that agitated the reign of his son Henry the third, and the Barons' war, with Bishop Grosteeds blessing to Mumford their general: the deposition and murder of the second Edward, and Richard, and sixth Henry, and his son the prince, the usurpation of Richard the Third, and the murder of the sons of Edward the Fourth, in the Tower of London. The civil war that followed between him and the Earl of Richmond, afterwards our wise Henry the Seventh, were all perpetrated in a country of one religion, and by the hands of conformists. In short, if we will but look upon the civil war that so long raged in this kingdom between the Houses of York and Lancaster, and consider that they professed but one and the same religion, and both backed with numbers of churchmen too (to say nothing of the miserable end of many of our King's princely ancestors in Scotland, especially the first and third James we shall find cause to say, that church uniformity is not a security for princes to depend upon.

If we will look next into countries where dissenters from the national church are tolerated, we shall find the conformist not less culpable than the dissenter.

The disorders among the Jews, after they were settled in the land that God had given them, came not from those they tolerated, but themselves. They cast off Samuel, and the government of the judges.

It was the children of the national church that fell in with the ambition of Absolom, and animated the rebellion against their father David. They were the same that revolted from Solomon's son, and cried in behalf of Jeroboam, to your tents, O Israel!

Not two ages ago, the church of France, too generally fell in with the family of Guise, against their lawful soverign, Henry the Fourth: nor were they without countenance of the greatest of their belief, who styled it an Holy War: At that time, fearing (not without cause) the defection of that kingdom from the Roman See. In this conjuncture, the dissenters made up the best part of that King's armies, and by their loyalty and blood, preserved the blood royal of France, and set the crown on the head of the prince. That king was twice assassinated, and the last time murdered, as was Henry the Third, his predecessor; but they fell, one by the hand of a churchman, the other, at least by a conformist.

It is true that the next civil war was between the Catholics and the Huguenots, under the conduct of Cardinal Richlieu and the Duke of Rohan; but as I will not justfy the action, so their liberties and cautions so solemnly settled by Henry the Fourth, as the reward of their singular merit, being by the ministry of that Cardinal invaded, they say they did but defend their security, and that rather against the Cardinal, than the King, whose softness suffered him to become a property to the great wit and ambition of that person: and there is this reason to believe them, that if it had been otherwise, we are sure that King Charles the First would not in the least have countenanced the quarrel.

However, the Cardinal, like himself, wisely knew when to stop: for though he thought it the interest of the Crown to moderate their greatness and check their growth, yet having fresh in memory the story of the foregoing age; he saw it was wise to have a balance upon occasion. But this was more than recompensed in their fixed adhesion to the crown of France, under the ministry and direction of the succeeding Cardinal, when their persuasion had not only number, and many good officers to value itself upon, but yielded their King the ablest captain of the age, namely, Turene: it was an Huguenot then, at the head of almost an Huguenot army, that fell in with a Cardinal himself (see the union interest makes) to maintain the Imperial Crown of France, and that on a Roman Catholic's head: And together with their own indulgence, that religion, as national too, against the pretences of a Roman Catholc army, headed by a prince brave and learned of the same religion.

I mention not this to prefer one party to another; for contrary instances may be given elsewhere, as interests have varied. In Sweedland a prince was rejected by Protestants; and in England and Holland, and many of the principalities of Germany, Roman Catholics have approved themselves loyal to their kings, princes and states. But this suffices to us that we gain the point; for it is evident in countries where dissenters are tolerated, the insecurity of the prince and government may as well come from the conforming, as dissenting party, and that it comes not from dissenters, because such.

But how happy and admirable was this civil union between the Cardinal and Turene? Two most opposite religions, both followed by people of their own persuasion: one says his mass, the other his directory: both invoke one diety, by several ways, for one success, and it followed with glory, and a peace to this day. O why should it be otherwise now! What has been may be: methinks wisdom and charity are on that side still.

It will doubtless be objected that the dissenting party of England, fell in with the state-dissenter in our late civil, but unnatural war: and this seems to be against us, yet three things must be confessed: first, that the war rather made the dissenters than the dissenters made the war. Secondly, that those that were then in being were not tolerated, as in France, but prosecuted. And, lastly, that they did not lead, but follow great numbers of church-goers of all qualities, in that unhappy controversy; and which began upon other topics than liberty for church-dissenters. And though they were herein blameable, reason is reason, in all climates and latitudes. This does not affect the question: such calamities are no necessary consequences of church dissent, because they would then follow in all places where dissenters are tolerated, which we see they do not: but these may sometimes indeed be the effects of a violent endeavour of uniformity, and that under all forms of government, as I fear they were partly here under our monarchy. But then, this teaches us to conclude that a toleration of those, that a contrary course makes uneasy and desperate, may prevent or cure intestine troubles; as anno forty eight; it ended the strife, and settled the peace of Germany. For it is not now the question, how far men may be provoked, or ought to resent it; but, whether government is safe in a toleration, especially monarchy: and to this issue we come in fact, that it is safe, and that conformists (generally speaking) have, for their interests, as rarely known their duty to their prince, as dissenters for their consciences. So that the danger seems to lie on this side, of forcing uniformity against faith, upon severe penalties, rather than of a discreet toleration.

In the next place, I shall endeavour to show the prudence and reasonableness of a toleration, by the great benefits that follow it.

Toleration, which is an admission of dissenting worships, with impunity to the dissenters, secures property, which is civil right, and that eminently the line and power of the monarchy: for if no man suffer in his civil right for the sake of such dissent, the point of succession is settled without a civil war, or a recantation; since it were an absurd thing to imagine, that a man born to five pounds a year, should not be liable to forfeit his inheritance for non-conformity, and yet a prince of the blood, and an heir to the imperial crown, should be made incapable of inheritance for his church dissent.

The security then of property, or civil right, from being forfeitable for religious dissent, becomes a security to the Royal Family, against the difficulties lately laboured under in the business of the succession. And though I have no commission for it, besides the great reason and equity of the thing itself, I dare say, there can hardly be a dissenter at this time of day so void of sense and justice, as well as duty and loyalty, as not to be of the same mind. Else it were to deny that to the prince, which he needs, and prays for from him. Let us not forget the story of Sigismund of Sweedland, of Henry the Fourth of France, and especially of our own Queen Mary. Had property been fixed, the line of those Royal Families could not have met with any let or interruption. It was this consideration that prevailed with Judge Hales, though a strong Protestant, after King Edward's death, to give his opinion for Queen Mary's succession against that of all the rest of the judges to the contrary; which noble president was recompense in the loyalty of Archbishop Heath, a Roman Catholic, in favour of the succession of Queen Elizabeth: and the same thing would be done again, in the like case, by men of the same integrity.

I know it may be said that there is little reason now for the prince to regard this argument in favour of dissenters, when it was so little heeded in the case of the presumptive heir to the crown. But as this was the act and heat of conforming men within doors, so if it were, in counsel or desire, the folly and injustice of any dissenters without doors, shall many entire parties pay the reckoning of the few busy offenders? they would humbly hope, that the

singular mildness and clemency, which make up a great a part of
the King's public assurances, will not leave him in his reflection
here.

It is the mercies of princes, that above all their works, give them
the nearest resemblance to divinity in their admininstration. Besides,
it is their glory to measure their actions by the reason and
consequence of things, and not by the passions the possess and
animate private breasts: for it were fatal to the interest of a prince,
that the folly or undutifulness of any of his subjects should put him
out of the way, or tempt him to be unsteady to his principle and
interest: And yet, with submission, I must say, it would be the
consequence of coercion: for, by exposing property for opinion,
the prince exposes the consciences and property of his own family,
and plainly disarms them of all defence, upon any alteration of
judgment. Let us remember that several of the same gentlemen, who
at first sacrificed civil rights for non-conformity in common dissenters, fell at last to make the succession of the crown the price of
dissent in the next heir of the royal blood. So dangerous a thing it
is to hazard property to serve a turn for any party, or suffer such
examples in the case of the meanest person in a kingdom.

Nor is this all the benefit that attends the Crown by the
preservation of civil rights; for the power of the monarchy is kept
more entire by it. The King has the benefit of his whole people, and
the reason of their safety is owing to their civil, and not ecclesiastical
obedience: their loyalty to Cæsar, and not conformity to the
church. Whereas the other opinion would have it that no conformity
to the church, no property in the state, which is to clog and narrow
the civil power, for at this rate, no churchman, no English-man;
and no conformist, no subject. A way to alien the King's people,
and practise an exclusion upon him, from, it may be, a fourth part
of his dominions. Thus it may happen that the ablest statesman, the
bravest captain, and the best citizen may be disabled, and the prince
forbid their employment to his service.

Some instances of this we have had since the late King's restoration: for upon the first Dutch war, Sir William Penn being
commanded to give in a list of the ablest sea officers in the kingdom,
to serve in that expedition, I do very well remember he presented
our present King with a catalogue of the knowingest and bravest
officers the age had bred, with this subscribed, These men, if his
Majesty will please to admit of their persuasions, I will answer for
their skill, courage and integrity. He picked them by their ability,

not their opinions; and he was in the right; for that was the best way of doing the King's business. And of my own knowledge, conformity robbed the King at the time of ten men, whose greater knowledge and valour, than any one ten of that fleet, had in their room, been able to have saved a battle or perfected a victory. I will name three of them: The first was old Vice Admiral Goodson, than whom nobody was more stout, or a seaman. The second, Captain Hill, that in the Saphire, beat Admiral Everson hand to hand, that came to the relief of Old Trump. The third was Captain Potter, that in the Constant Warwick, took Captain Beach, after eight hours smart dispute. And as evident it is, that if a war had proceeded between this kingdom and France seven years ago, the business of conformity had deprived the King of many land officers, whose share in the late wars of Europe, had made knowing and able.

But which is worst of all, such are not safe with their dissent, under their own extraordinary prince. For, though a man were a great honourer of his King, a lover of his country, an admirer of the government: in the course of his life, sober, wise, industrious and useful, if a dissenter from the established form of worship, in that condition there is no liberty for his person, nor security to his estate: As useless to the public, so ruined in himself. For this net catches the best. Men true to their conscience, and who indulged, are most like to be so to their prince; whilst the rest are left to cozen him by their change; for that is the unhappy end of forced conformity in the poor spirited compliers. And this must always be the consequence of necessitating the prince to put more and other tests upon his people, than are requisite to secure him of their loyalty.

And when we shall be so happy in our measures, as to consider this mischief to the monarchy, it is to be hoped it will be thought expedient to disintangle property from opinion, and cut the untoward knot some men have tied, that hath so long hampered and gauled the prince as well as people. It will be then, when civil punishments shall no more follow church faults, that the civil tenure will be recovered to the government, and the natures of acts, rewards and punishments, so distinguished, as loyalty shall be the safety of dissent, and the whole people made useful to the government.

It will, perhaps, be objected, that dissenters can hardly be obliged to be true to the Crown, and so the Crown unsafe in their very services; for they may easily turn the power given them to serve it, against it, to greaten themselves. I am willing to obviate everything, that may with any pretence be offered against our entreated indulgence. I say no, and appeal to the King himself (against whom the prejudices of our late times ran highest, and who therefore has most reason to resent) If ever he was better loved or served than by the old round-headed seaman, the Earl of Sandwich, Sir William Penn, Sir J. Lawson, Sir G. Ascue, Sir R. Stanier, Sir J. Smith, Sir J. Jordan, Sir J. Harmon, Sir Christopher Minns, Captain Sansum, Curtins, Clark, Robinson, Molton, Wager, Tern, Parker, Haward, Hubbard, Fen, Langborn, Daws, Earl, White; to say nothing of many yet living, of real merit, and many inferior officers, expert and brave. And to do our prince justice, he deserved it from them, by his humility, plainness and courage, and the care and affection that he always showed them.

If any say, that most of these men were conformists, I presume to tell them, I know as well as any man, they served the King never the better for that: on the contrary, it was all the strife that some of them had in themselves, in the doing that service, that they must not serve the King without it; and if in that they could have been indulged, they had performed it with the greatest alacrity. Interest will not lie. Where people find their reckoning, they are sure to be true. For it is want of wit that makes any man false to himself. It was he that knew all men's hearts, that said, where the treasure is, there will the heart be also. Let men be easy, safe, and upon their preferment with the prince, and they will be dutiful, loyal, and most affectionate.

Mankind by nature fears power, and melts at goodness. Pardon my zeal, I would not be thought to plead for dissenters' preferment; it is enough they keep what they have, and may live at their own charges. Only I am for having the prince have room for his choice, and not be cramped and stinted by opinion; but employ those who are best able to serve him: And, I think out of six parties, it is better picking, than out of one, and therefore the prince's interest is to be head of all of them, which a toleration effects in a moment, since those six (divided interests, within themselves) having but one civil head, become one entire civil body to the prince. And I am sure, I have monarchy on my side, if Solomon and his wisdom may stand for it, who tell us that the glory of a king is in the multitude of his people.

Nor is this all, for the consequences of such an universal content, would be of infinite moment to the security of the monarchy, both at home and abroad. At home, for it would behead the factions without blood, and banish the ringleaders without going abroad. When the great bodies of dissenters see the care of the government for their safety, they have no need of their captains, nor these any ground for their pretences: for as they used the people to value themselves and raise their fortunes with the prince, so the people followed their leaders to get that ease, they see their heads promised, but could not, and the government can, and does give them.

Multitudes cannot plot, they are too many, and have not conduct for it, they move by another spring. Safety is the pretence of their leaders: If once they see they enjoy it, they have yet wit enough not to hazard it for any body: for the endeavours of busy men are then discernable; but a state of severity gives them a pretence, by which the multitude is easily taken. Men may indiscreetly plot to get what they would never plot to lose. So that ease is not only their content, but the prince's security.

This I say, upon a supposition, that the dissenters could agree against the government; which is a begging of the question: for it is improbable (if not impossible without conformists since, besides the distance they are at in their persuasions and affections, they dare not hope for so good terms from one another, as the government gives: and that fear, with emulation, would draw them into that duty, that they must all fall into a natural dependence, which I call, holding of the prince, as the great head of the state.

From abroad, we are as safe as from within ourselves: for if leading men at home are thus disappointed of their interest in the people, foreigners will find here no interpreters of their dividing language, nor matter (if they could) to work upon for the point is gained, the people they would deal in are at their ease, and cannot be bribed; and those that would, can't deserve it.

It is this that makes princes live independent of their neighbours: and, to be loved at home is to be feared abroad: one follows necessarily the other. Where princes are driven to seek a foreign assistance, the issue either must be the ruin of the prince, or the absolute subjection of the people; not without the hazard of becoming a province to the power of the neighbour that turns the scale. These consequences have on either hand an ill look, and should rebate extremes.

The greatness of France carries those threats to all her neighbours, that, politically speaking, it is the melancholiest prospect England has had to make since eighty eight: the Spaniard at the time, being shorter in all things but his pride and hope, than the French King is now, of the same universal monarchy. This greatness, begun with the eleventh Louis, some will have it, has not been so much advanced by the wisdom of Richlieu, and craft of Mazarene, no, nor the arms of the present monarch, as by the assistance or connivance of England, that has most to lose by him.

O. Cromwell began, and gave him the scale against the Spaniard. The reason of state he went upon was the support of usurped dominion: and he was not out in it; for the exile of the Royal Family was a great patt of the price of that aid, in which we see how much interest prevails above nature. It was not royal kindred could shelter a King against the solicitation of an usurper with the son of his mother's brother.

But it will be told us by some people we have not degenerated, but exactly followed the same steps ever since, which has given such an increase to those beginnings that the French monarchy is almost above our reach. But suppose it were true, what's the cause of it? It has not been old friendship or nearness of blood, or neighbourhood. Nor could it be from an inclination in our ministers to bring things here to a like issue, as some have suggested; for then we should have clogged his successes, instead of helping them in any kind, lest in so doing, we should have put it into his power to hinder our own.

But perhaps our cross accidents of state may sometimes have compelled us into his friendship, and his councils have carefully improved the one, and husbanded the other to great advantages, and that this was more than made for our English interest: And yet it is but too true, that the extreme heats of some men, that most inveighed against it, went too far to strengthen that understanding, by not taking what would have been granted, and creating an interest at home that might naturally have dissolved that correspondence abroad.

I love not to revive things that are uneasily remembered, but in points most tender to the late King, he thought himself sometimes too closely pressed, and hardly held; and we are all wise enough now to say, a milder conduct had succeeded better: for if reasonable things may be reasonably pressed, and with such private intentions, as induce a denial, heats about things doubtful, unwise or unjust must needs harden and prejudice.

Let us then create an interest for the prince at home, and foreign friendships (at best, uncertain and dangerous) will fall of course;

for if it be allowed to private men, shall it be forbid to princes only, to know and to be true to their own support?

It is no more than what every age makes us to see in all parties of men. The parliaments of England, since the Reformation, giving no quarter to Roman Catholics, have forced them to the crown for shelter. And to induce the monarchy to yield them the protection they have needed they have with mighty address and skill recommended themselves as the great friends of the prerogative, and so successfully too, that it were not below the wisdom of that constitution to reflect what they have lost by that costiveness of theirs to Catholics. On the other hand, the Crown having treated the Protestant dissenters with the severity of the laws that affected them, suffering the sharpest of them to fall upon their persons and estates, they have been driven successively to parliaments for succour, whose privileges, with equal skill and zeal, they have abetted, and our late unhappy wars are too plain a proof how much their accession gave the scale against the power and courage of both conformists and Catholics that adhered to the Crown.

Nor must this contrary adhesion be imputed to love or hatred, but necessary interest: refusal in one place makes way for address in another. If the scene be changed, the parts must follow; for as well before, as after Cromwell's usurpation, the Roman Catholics did not only promise the most ready obedience to that government in their printed apologies for liberty of conscience; but actually treated by some of their greatest men with the ministers of those times, for indulgence, upon the assurances they offered to give of their good behaviour to the government, as then established.

On the other hand, we see the Presbyterians, that in Scotland began the war, and in England promoted and upheld it to forty seven, when ready to be supplanted by the Independents, wheel to the King. In Scotland they crown him, and come into England with an army to restore him, where their brethren join them; but being defeated, they help, by private collections, to support him abroad; and after the overthrow of Sir George Booth's attempt, to almost a miracle, restore him. And which is more, a great part of that army too, whose victories came from the ruin of the prince they restored.

But to give the last proofs our age has of the power of interest, against the notion opposed by this discourse. First, the Independents themselves held the greatest republicans of all parties, were the most lavish and superstitious adorers of monarchy in Oliver Cromwell, because of the regard he had to them; allowing him, and his son after him, to be *Custos Utriusq*; tabulae, over all causes, as well ecclesiastical as civil supreme governor. And next, the conformists in parliament reputed the most loyal and monarchical men, did more than any body question and oppose the late King's declaration of indulgence; even they themselves would not allow so much prerogative to the Crown, but pleased and opposed his political capacity.

This proves the power of interest, and that all persuasions center with it: and when they see the government engaging them with a fixed liberty of conscience, they must for their own sakes seek the support of it, by which it is maintained. This union, directed under the prince's conduct, would awe the greatness of our neighbours, and soon restore Europe to its ancient balance, and that into his hand too: so that he may be the great arbiter of the Christian world. But if the policy of the government places the security of its interest in the destruction of the civil interest of the dissenters, it is not to be wondered at, if they are less found in the praises of its conduct than others to whom they are offered up a sacrifice by it.

I know it will be insinuated that there is danger in building upon the union of divers interests; and this will be aggravated to the prince, by such as would engross his bounty and intercept his grace from a great part of his people. But I will only oppose to that mere suggestion three examples to the contrary, with this challenge, that if after rummaging the records of all time, they find one instance to contradict me, I shall submit the question to their authority.

The first is given by those Christian emperors, who admitted all sorts of dissenters into their armies, courts and senates. This, the ecclesiastical story of those times, assures us, and particularly Socrates, Evagrius, and Onuphrius.

The next instance is that of Prince William of Orange, who by a timely indulgence united the scattered strength of Holland, and all animated by the clemency as well as valour of their captain, crowned his attempts with an extraordinary glory; and, what makes, continues great.

The last is given us by Livy, in his account of Hannibal's army; 'That they consisted of divers nations, languages, customs and religions: that under all their successes of war and peace, for thirteen years together, they never mutinied against their general, nor fell out among themselves.' What Livy relates for a wonder, the Marquis Virgilio Malvetzy gives the reason of, to wit, their variety and difference, well-managed by their general; for, said he, 'It was impossible for so many nations, customs and religions to combine, especially when the general's equal hand gave him more reverence with them than they had of affection for one another.' This (says he) some would wholly impute to Hannibal; but however great he was, I attribute it to the variety of people in the army, 'For (adds he) Rome's army was ever less given to mutiny, when balanced with auxiliary legions, than when entirely Roman.' Thus much in his discourse upon Cornelius Tacitus.

And they are neither few, nor of the weakest sort of men, that have thought the concord of discords a firm basis for government to be built upon. The business is to tune them well, and that must be the skill of the musician.

In nature we see all heat consumes, all cold kills: that three degrees of cold to two of heat allays the heat, but introduces the contrary quality, and over-cools by a degree; but two degrees of cold to two of heat, makes a poise in elements, and a balance in nature. And in those families where the evenest hand is carried, the work is best done, and the master is most reverenced.

This brings me to another benefit, which accrues to the monarchy by a toleration, and that is a balance at home: for though it be improbable, it may so happen, that either the conforming or non-conforming party may be undutiful; the one is then a balance of the other. This might have prevented much mischief to our second and third Henry, King John, the Second Edward, and Richard, and unhappy Henry the Sixth, as it undeniably saved the Royal Family of France and secured Holland, and kept it from truckling under the Spanish monarchy. While all hold of the government, it is that which gives the scale to the most dutiful; but still, no farther than to show its power, and awe the disorderly into obedience, not to destroy the balance, lest it should afterwards want the means of over-poising faction.

That this is more than fancy, plain it is, that the dissenter must firmly adhere to the government for his being, while the churchman is provided for. The one subsists by its mercy, the other by it's bounty. This is tied by plenty, but that by necessity, which being the last of ties, and strongest obligation, the security is greatest from him, that it is fancied most unsafe to tolerate.

But besides this, the tranquility which it gives at home will both oblige those that are upon the wing for foreign parts, to pitch here again; and at a time when our neighbouring monarch is wasting his people, excite those sufferers into the King's dominions, whose number will encrease that of his subjects, and their labour and consumption, the trade and wealth of his territories.

For what are all conquests, but of people ? And if the government may by indulgence add the inhabitants of ten cities to those of its own, it obtains a victory without charge. The ancient persecution of France and the Low Countries, has furnished us with an invincible instance; for of those that came hither on that account, we were instructed in most useful manufactures, as by courses of the like nature, we lost a great part of our woollen trade. And as men in times of danger, draw in their stock, and either transmit it to other banks, or bury their talent at home for security (that being out of sight, it may be, out of reach too (and either is fatal to a kingdom) so this mildness obtained, setting every man's heart at rest, every man will be at work, and the stock of the kingdom employed, which, like the blood, that hath its due passage, will give life and vigour to every member in the public body.

And here give me leave to mention the experiment made at home by the late King, in his declaration of indulgence. No matter how well or ill built that act of state was, it is no part of the business in hand, but what effect the liberty of it had upon the peace and wealth of the kingdom, may have instruction in it to our present condition. It was evident, that all men laboured cheerfully, and traded boldly, when they had the royal word to keep what they got, and the King himself became the universal insurer of dissenters' estates. Whitehall, then, and St James's, were as much visited and courted by their respective agents as if they had been of the family : for that which eclipsed the royal goodness, being by his own hand thus removed, his benign influences drew the returns of sweetness and duty from that part of his subjects, that the want of those influences had made barren before. Then it was that we looked like the members of one family, and children of one parent. Nor did we envy our eldest brother, episcopacy, his inheritance, so that we had but a child's portion : for not only discontents vanished, but no matter was left for ill spirits, foreign or domestic, to brood upon, or hatch to mischief. Which was a plain proof that it is the union of interests, and not of opinions, that gives peace to kingdoms.

And with all deference to authority, I would speak it, the liberty of the declaration seems to be our English amomum at last, the sovereign remedy to our English constitution. And, to say true, we shifted luck (as they call it) as soon as we had lost it; like those that lose their royal gold, their evil returns. For all dissenters seemed then united in their affection to the government, and followed their affairs without fear or distraction. Projects, then, were stale and unmerchantable, and nobody cared for them, because no body wanted any: that gentle opiate, at the prince's hand, laid the most busy and turbulent to sleep, but when the loss of that indulgnece made them uncertain, and that uneasy; their persons and estates being again exposed to pay the reckoning of their dissent, no doubt but every party shifted then as they could: most grew selfish, at least, jealous, fearing one should make bargains apart, or exclusive of the other. This was the fatal part dissenters acted to their common ruin, and I take this partiality to have had too great a share in our late animosities; which, by fresh accidents falling in, have swelled to a mighty deluge, such an one as hath overwhelmed our former civil concord and serenity. And pardon me if I say, I cannot see that those waters are like to assuage, until this olive-branch of indulgence be some way or other restored; the waves will still cover our earth, and a spot of ground will hardly be found in this glorious isle, for a great number of useful people to set a quiet foot upon. And, to pursue the allegory, what was the ark itself, but the most apt and lively emblem of toleration? A kind of natural temple of indulgence in which we find two of every living creature dwelling together, of both sexes too, that they might propagate; and that as well of the unclean as clean kind: so that the baser and less useful sort were saved. Creatures never like to change their nature, and so far from being whipped and punished to the altar, that they were expressly forbid. These were saved, these were fed and restored to their ancient pastures. Shall we be so mannerly as to complement the conformists with the style of clean, and so humble as to take the unclean kind, to ourselves, who are the less noble, and more clownish sort of people? I think verily we may do it, if we may but be saved too by the commander of our English ark. And this the peaceable and virtuous dissenter has the less reason to fear, since sacred text tell us, it was vice, and not opinion, that brought the deluge upon the rest. And here (to drop our allegory) I must take leave to hope, that though the declaration be gone, if the reason of it remain, I mean the interest of the monarchy, the King and his great council will graciously please to think a toleration no dangerous nor obsolete thing.

But as it has many arguments for it that are drawn from the advantages that have and would come to the public by it, so there are divers mischiefs and must unavoidably follow the persecution of dissenters, that may reasonably dissuade from such severity. For they must either be ruined, fly, or conform; and perhaps the last is not the safest. If they are ruined in their estates, and their persons imprisoned, modestly computing, a fourth of the trade and manufactury of the kingdom sinks; and those that have helped to maintain the poor must come upon the poor's book for maintenance. This seems to be an impoverishing of the public. But if to avoid this, they transport themselves, with their estates, into other governments; nay, though it were to any of the King's plantations, the number were far too great to be spared from home. So much principal stock wanting to turn the yearly traffic, and so many people too, to consume our yearly growth, must issue fatally to the trade one way, and to the lands and rents of the kingdom the other way.

And lastly, if they should resolve, neither to suffer nor fly, but conform to prevent both. It is to be enquired, if this cure of church division be safe to the state; or not rather, a raking up coals under ashes, for a future mischief? He whom fear or policy hath made treacherous to his own conscience ought not to be held true to anything but his own safety and revenge. His conformity gives him the first, and his resentment of the force that compels it will on no occasion let him want the last. So that conformity cozens nobody but the government; for the state fanatic (which is the unsafe thing to the state) being christened by conformity, he is eligible everywhere, with persons the most devoted to the prince: and all men will hold themselves protected in their votes by it.

A receipt to make faction, keep and preserve disloyalty against all weathers. For whereas the nature of tests is to discover, this is the way to conceal the inclinations of men from the government. Plain dissent is the prince with a candle in his hand: He sees the where and what of persons and things; He discriminates, and makes that a rule of conduct, but forced conformity is the prince in the dark: It blows out his candle, and leaves him without distinction. Such subjects are like figures in sand, when water is slapped upon them, they run together, and are indiscernible, or written tradition, made illegible by writing the oaths and canons upon it: the safest way of blotting out danger.

I know not how to forbear saying that this necessary conformity makes the church dangerous to the state: for even the hypocrisy that follows makes the church both conceal and protect the hypocrites, which, together with their liberality to the parson, charity to the poor, and hospitality to their neighbours, recommends them to the first favour they have to bestow. That fort is unsafe, where a party of the garrison consists of disguised enemies; for when they take their turns at the watch, the danger is hardly evitable. It would then certainly be for the safety of the fort, that such friends in masquerade were industriously kept out, instead of being whipped in.

And it was something of this, I remember, that was made an argument for the declaration of indulence, in the preamble, to wit, the greater safety of the government, from open and public, than private, dissenting meetings of worship; as indeed the rest bear the same resemblance. For these were the topics quieting the people, encouraging strangers to come and live among us, and trade by it; and lastly, preventing the danger that might arise to the government by private meetings, of greater reason then from private men, not less discontended, but more concealed and secure by the great brake of church conformity. It is this will make a comprehension of the next dissenters to the church dangerous, though it were practicable, of whichever side it be. For in an age, the present frame of government shall feel the art and industry of the comprehended. So that a toleration is in reason of state to be preferred. And if the reasons of the declaration were ever good, they are so still, because the emergencies of state that made them so remain; and our neighbours are not less powerful to improve them to our detriment.

But it will be now said, though the government should find its account in what has been last alleged, this were the way to overthrow the church, and encourage dissenters to continue in their errors. Which is that second main objection I proposed at first, to answer in its proper place, and that I think is this:

I humbly say, if it prove the interest of the three considerable church interests in this kingdom, a relaxation, at least, can hardly fail us. The three church interests are, that of the Church of England; that of the Roman Catholic dissenter; and that of the Protestant dissenter.

That the Church of England ought in conscience and prudence to consent to the ease desired.

I pray, first, that it be considered, how great a reflection it will be upon her honour, that from persecuted, she should be accounted a persecuting church: An overthrow none of the enemies have been able to give to her many excellent apologies. Nor will it be excused, by her saying, she is in the right, which her persecutors were not; since this is a confidence not wanting in any of them, or her dissenters: and the truth is, it is but the begging of a question, that will by no means be granted.

Nobody ought to know more than churchmen that conscience cannot be forced, that offerings against conscience are as odious to God, as uneasy to them that make them. That God loves a free sacrifice. That Christ forbade fire, though from heaven (itself) to punish dissenters; and commanded that the tares should grow with the wheat till the harvest. In fine, that we should love enemies themselves: and to exclude worldly strife for religion; that His kingdom is not of this world. This was the doctrine of the blessed Saviour of the world.

Saint Paul purifies the same course: is glad Christ is preached, be it of envy; the worst ground for dissent that can be. It was he that asked that hard but just question, who art thou that judgest another man's servant? To his own lord he standeth or falleth. He allows the church a warfare, and weapons to perform it, but they are not carnal, but spiritual. Therefore it was so advised, that every man in matters of religion should be fully persuaded in his own mind, and if any were short or mistaken, God would, in his time, inform them better.

He tells us of schismatics and heretics too, and their punishment, which is to the point in hand: He directs to a first and second admonition, and if that prevail not, reject them. That is, refuse them church fellowship, disown their relation, and deny them Communion. But in all this there is not a word of fines or imprisonments, nor is it an excuse to any Church, that the civil magistrate executes the severity, while they are members of her communion, that make or execute the laws.

But if the church could gain her point, I mean confirmity, unless she could gain consent too, it were but constraint at last, a rape upon the mind which may increase her number, not her devotion. On the contrary, the rest of her sons are in danger by their hypocrisy, the most close, but watchful and revengeful thing in the world. Besides, the scandal can hardly be removed: to over value coin, and rate brass to silver, beggars any country; and to own them for sons she never begat, debases and destroys any church. It were better to indulge foreign coin of intrinsic value, and let it pass for its weight. It is not number, but quality. Two or three sincere Christians, that form an evangelical church : And though the church were less, more charity on the one hand, and piety on the other, with exact church censure, and less civil coercion, would give her credit with conscience in all sects ; without which, their accession it self would be no benefit, but disgrace, and hazard to the constitution.

And to speak prudently in this affair, it is the interest of the Church of England not to suffer the extinction of dissenters, that she may have a counter-balance to the Roman Catholics, who, though few in number, are great in quality, and greater in their foreign friendships and assistance. On the other hand, it is her interest to indulge the Roman Catholic, that by his accession, she may at all times have the balance in her own hand, against the Protestant dissenter, leaning to either, as she finds her doctrine undermined by the one, or her discipline by the other ; or lastly, her civil interest endangered from either of them.

And it is certainly the interest of both those extremes of dissent, that she, rather than either of them should hold the scale. For as the Protestant dissenter cannot hope for any tenderness, exclusive of Roman Catholics, but almost the same reasons may be advanced against him. So on the other hand, it would look imprudent, as well as unjust, in the Roman Catholics, to solicit any indulgence exclusive of Protestant dissenters. For besides that, it keeps up the animosity, which it is their interest to bury ; the consequence will be to take the advantage of time, to snatch it from one another, when an united request for liberty, once granted, will oblige both parties, in all times, for example's sake, to have it equally preserved. Thus are all church interests of conformists and dissenters rendered consistent and safe in their civil interest one with the other.

But it will last of all, doubtless, be objected, that though a toleration were never so desirable in itself, and in its consequence beneficial to the public, yet the government cannot allow it, without ruin to the Church of England, which it is obliged to maintain.

But I think this will not affect the question at all, unless by maintaining the Church of England, it is understood that he should force whole parties to be of her communion, or knock them on the head : let us call to mind, that the religion that is true allows no man to do wrong, that right may come of it. And that nothing has lessened the credit of any religion more, than declining to support itself by its own charity and piety, and taking sanctuary in the arms, rather than the understandings of men. Violences are ill pillars for truth to rest upon. The Church of England must be maintained: right, but can't that be done without the dissenter be destroyed? In vain then did Christ command Peter to put up his sword, with this rebuke, they that take the sword, shall perish with the sword, if his followers are to draw it again. He makes killing for religion, murder, and deserving death: was he then in the right, not to call legions to his assistance? And are not his followers of these times in the wrong, to seek to uphold their religion by any methods of force. The Church of England must be maintained, therefore the dissenters that hold almost the same doctrine, must be ruined. A consequence most unnatural, as it is almost impossible. For besides that, the drudgery would unbecome the civil magistrate, who is the image of divine justice and clemency, and that it would fasten the character of a false church, upon one that desires to be esteemed a true one; she puts the government upon a task that is hard to be performed. Kings can no more make brick without straw, than slaves. The condition of our affairs is much changed, and the circumstances our government are under differ mightily from those of our ancestors. They had not the same dissents to deal with, nor those dissents the like bodies of people to render them formidable, and their prosecution mischievous to the state. Nor did this come of the prince's neglect or indulgence: there are other reasons to be assigned, of which, the opportunities domestic troubles gave to their increase and power, and the severities used to suppress them, may go for none of the least. So that it was as involuntary in the prince, as to the church anxious. And under this necessity to tie the magistrate to old measures, is to be regardless of time, whose fresh circumstances give aim to the conduct of wise men in their present actions. Governments, as well as courts, change their fashions: The same clothes will not always serve, and Politics made obsolete by new accidents are as unsafe to follow as antiquated dresses are ridiculous to wear.

Thus seamen know, and teach us in their daily practice: they humour the winds, though they will lie as near as they can, and trim their sails by their compass: and by patience under these constrained and uneven courses, they gain their port at last. This justifies the government's change of measures from the change of things; for *res nolunt malè administrari*.

And to be free, it looks more than partial, to elect and reprobate too. That that the Church of England is preferred, and has the fat of the earth, the authority of the magistrate, and the power of the sword in her sons' hands, which comprehend all the honours, places, profits, and powers of the kingdom, must not be repined at: let her have it, and keep it all, and let none dare seek or accept an office that is not of her. But to ruin dissenters to complete her happiness, (pardon the allusion) is Calvinism in the worst Sense; for this is that *horrendum decretum* reduced to practice: and to pursue that ill-natured principle, men are civilly damned for that they cannot help, since faith is not in man's power, though it sometimes exposes one to it.

It is a severe dilemma that a man must either renounce that of which he makes conscience in the sight of God, or be civilly and ecclesiastically reprobated. There was a time when the Church of England herself stood in need of indulgence, and made up a great part of the non-conformists of this kingdom, and what she then wanted, she pleaded for, I mean a toleration, and that in a general style, as diverse of the writings of her doctors tell us: of which let it be enough but to mention that excellent discourse of Dr Taylor, Bishop of Down, entitled *Liberty of Prophecy*.

And that which makes severity look the worse in the members of the Church of England is the modesty she professes about the truth of the things she believes: for though perhaps it were indefensible in any church to compel a man to that which she were infallibly assured to be true, unless she superseded his ignorance by conviction, rather than authority, it must, doubtless, look rude, to punish men into conformity to that, of the truth of which, the church herself pretends no certainty.

Not that I would less believe a church so cautious than one more confident; but I know not how to help thinking persecution harsh, when they ruin people for not believing that which they have not in themselves the power of believing, and which she cannot give them, and of which her self is not infallibly assured. The drift of this is moderation, which well becomes us poor mortals, that for every idle word we speak, must give an account at the day of judgment, if our Saviour's doctrine have any credit with us.

It would much mitigate the severity if the dissent were sullen, or in contempt: But if men can't help or hinder their belief, they are rather unhappy than guilty, and more to be pitied than blamed. However they are of the reasonable stock of the country, and though they were unworthy of favour, they may not be unfit to live. It is capital, at law, to destroy bastards, and by-blows are laid to the parish to keep: they must maintain them at last: and shall not these natural sons, at least, be laid at the door of the kingdom? Unhappy fate of dissenters! to be less heeded, and more destitute than anybody. If this should ever happen to be the effect of their own folly, with submission, it can never be the consequence of the government's engagements.

Election does not necessarily imply a reprobation of the rest. If God hath elected some to salvation, it will not follow of course, that he hath absolutely rejected all the rest. For though he was God of the Jews, he was God of the Gentiles too, and they were his people, though the Jews were his peculiar people. God respects not persons, says St Peter, the good of all nations are accepted. The difference at last, will not be of opinion, but works: sheep or goats, all, of all judgments will be found: And come, well done; or go ye workers of iniquity will conclude, their eternal state: let us be careful therefore of an opinion-reprobation of one another.

We see the God of nature hath taught us softer doctrine in his great Book of the World: His sun shines, and His rain falls upon all. All the productions of nature are by love, and shall it be proper to religion only to propagate by force? The poor hen instructs us in humanity, who, to defend her feeble young, refuses no danger. All the seeds and plants that grow for the use of man are produced by the kind and warm influences of the sun. It is kindness that upholds human race. People don't multiply in spite: and if it be by gentle and friendly ways that nature produces and matures the creatures of the world, certainly religion should teach us to be mild and bearing.

Let your moderation be known to all mean, was the saying of a great doctor of the Christian faith, and his reason for that command Cogeni, for the Lord is at hand. As if he had said, have a care what you do, be not bitter nor violent, for the judge is at the door: do as you would be done to, lest what you deny to others, God should refuse to you.

And after all this, shall the Church of England be less tender of men's consciences, than our common law is of their lives, which had rather a thousand criminals should escape, than that one innocent should perish? Give me leave to say that there are many innocents (conscience excepted) now exposed, men honest, peaceable and useful; free of ill designs; that pray for Cæsar, and pay their tribute to Cæsar.

If any tell us, they have, or may, ill use their toleration. I say, this must be looked to, and not liberty therefore refused; for the English church cannot so much forget her own maxim to dissenters, that *propter abusum non est tollendus usus*. It suffices to our argument, it is no necessary consequence, and that fact and time are for us. And if any misuse such freedom, and entitle conscience to misbehaviour, we have other laws enough to catch and punish the offenders, without treating one party with the spoils of six. And when religion becomes no man's interest, it will hardly ever be any man's hypocrisy. Men will choose by conscience, which at least preserves integrity, though it were mistaken: and if not in the wrong, truth recompences inquiry, and light makes amends for dissent.

And since a plain method offers itself, from the circumstances of our ease, I take the freedom to present it for the model of the entreated toleration.

Much has been desired, said and pressed, in reference to the late King's being head of a Protestant league, which takes in but a part of the Christian world; the Roman and Grecian Christians being excluded. But I most humbly offer that our wise men would please to think of another title for our King, and that is Head of a Christian League, and give the experiment here at home in his own dominions.

The Christian religion is admired of all in the text, and by all acknowledged in the apostle's creed. Here every party of Christians meet, and centre as in a general. The several species of Christians, that this genus divideth it self into, are those divers persuasions we have within this kingdom; the Church of England, Roman-Catholics, Grecians, Lutherans, Presbyterians, Independents, Anabaptists, Quakers, Socinians: these I call so many orders of Christians, that unite in the text, and differ only in the comment; all owning one diety, saviour and judge, good works, rewards and punishments: which bodies once regulated, and holding of the prince as head of the government, maintaining charity, and pressing piety, will be an honour to Christianity, a strength to the prince, and a benefit to the public: for in lieu of an unattainable, (at best an unsincere) uniformity, we shall have in civils unity, and amity in faith.

The Jews before, and in the time of Herod, were divided into divers sects. There were Pharisees, Sadducees, Herodians, and Essenes. They maintained their dissent without ruin to the government: and the magistrates fell under no censure from Christ for that toleration.

The Gentiles, as already has been observed, had their divers orders of philosophers, as disagreeing as ever Christians were, and that without danger to the peace of the state.

The Turks themselves show us that both other religions, and divers sects of their own, are very tolerable, with security to their government.

The Roman church is a considerable instance to our point; for she is made up of divers orders of both sexes, of very differing principles, fomented sometimes to great feuds and controversies; as between Franciscans, Dominicans, Jesuits, and Sorbonists; yet without danger to the political state of the church. On the contrary, she therefore cast herself into that method, that she might safely give vent to opinion and zeal, and suffer both without danger of schism. And these regulars are, by the Pope's grants, privileged with an exemption from episcopal visitation and jurisdiction.

GOD Almighty inspire the King's heart, and the hearts of His great council, to be the glorious instruments of this blessing to the kingdom.

Part III
Writings about Quaker Faith and Practice

Primitive CHRISTIANITY Revived, in the *Faith* and *Practice* of the People called *QUAKERS*. Written in Testimony to the present Dispensation of God *through them*, to the World; *that* Prejudices *may be Removed*, *the* Simple *Informed*, *the* Well-Inclined *Encouraged*, *and the* TRUTH, *and it's* Innocent FRIENDS *Rightly Represented*. *By* W. P.

Reader,

By this short ensuing treatise, thou wilt perceive the subject of it, viz. The light of Christ in man, as the manifestation of God's love for man's happiness. Now, for as much as this is the peculiar testimony and characteristic of the people called Quakers; their great fundamental in religion; that by which they have been distinguished from other professors of Christianity in their time, and to which they refer all people about faith, worship, and practice, both in their ministry and writings; that as the fingers shoot out of the hand, and the branches from the body of the tree; so true religion, in all the parts and articles of it, springs from this divine principle in man. And because the prejudices of some are very great against this people and their way; and that others, who love their seriousness, and commend their good life, are yet, through mistakes, or want of enquiry, under jealousy of their unsoundness in some points of faith; and that there are not a few in all persuasions, which desire earnestly to know and enjoy God in that sensible manner this people speak of, and who seem to long after a state of holiness and acceptance with God; but are under doubts and despondings of their attaining it, from the want they find in themselves of inward power to enable them, and are unacquainted with this efficacious agent, which God hath given and appointed for their supply.

For these reasons and motives, know, Reader, I have taken in hand to write this small tract, *Of the Nature and Virtue of the Light of Christ Within Man*; what, and where it is, and for what end, and therein of the religion of the people called Quakers; that, at the same time, all people may be informed of their true character, and what true religion is, and the way to it, in this age of high pretences, and as deep irreligion. That so the merciful visitation of the God of light and love, (more especially to these nations) both immediately and instrumentally, for the promotion of piety, (which is religion indeed) may no longer be neglected by the inhabitants thereof, but that they may come to see and say, with heart and mouth, this is a dispensation of love and life from God to the world; and this poor people, that we have so much despised, and so often trod upon, and treated as the off-scouring of the earth, are the people of God, and children of the Most High. Bear with me, Reader, I know what I say and am not high-minded, but fear: for I write with humility towards God, though with confidence towards thee. Not that thou shouldst believe upon my authority, nothing less; for that's not to act upon knowledge, but trust; but that thou shouldst try and approve what I write: for that is all I ask, as well as all I need for thy conviction, and my own justification. The whole, indeed, being but a spiritual experiment upon the soul, and therefore seeks for no implicit credit, because it is self-evident to them that will uprightly try it.

And when thou, Reader, shalt come to be acquainted with this principle, and the plain and happy teachings of it, thou wilt, with us, admire thou shouldst live so long a stranger to that which was so near thee, and as much wonder that other folks should be so blind as not to see it, as formerly thou thoughtest us singular for obeying it. The day, I believe, is at hand that will declare this with an uncontroulable authority, because it will be with an unquestionable evidence.

I have done, Reader, with this Preface, when I have told thee, first, that I have stated the principle, and opened, as God has enabled me, the nature and virtue of it in religion; wherein the common doctrines and articles of the Christian religion, are delivered and improved; and above which, I have endeavoured to express my self in plain and proper terms, and not in figurative, allegorical, or doubtful phrases; that so I may leave no room for an equivocal or double sense; but that the truth of the subject I treat upon, may appear easily and evidently to every common understanding. Next, I have confirmed what I have writ, by Scripture, reason, and the effects of it upon so great a people; whose uniform concurrence in the experience and practice thereof; through all times and sufferings, since a people, challenge the notice and regard of every serious Reader. Thirdly, I have written briefly, that so it might be every one's money and reading: and, much in a little is best, when we see daily that the richer people grow, the less money or time they have for God or religion. And perhaps those that would not buy a large book may find in their hearts to give away some of these for their neighbour's good, being little and cheap. Be serious, Reader, be impartial, and then be as inquisitive as thou canst; and that for thine own soul, as well as the credit of this most misunderstood and abused people: And the God and Father of lights and spirits, so bless thine, in the perusal of this short treatise, that thou mayst receive real benefit by it, to His glory, and thine own comfort, which is the desire and end of him that wrote it; who is, in the bonds of Christian charity, very much, and very ardently,

Thy real Friend,
WILLIAM PENN

PRIMITIVE CHRISTIANITY REVIVED, ETC.

Chapter 1. §1. *Their fundamental principle.* §2. *The nature of it.* §3. *Called by several names.* §4. *They refer all to this, as to faith and practice, ministry and worship.*

§1. That which the people called Quakers lay down, as a main fundamental in religion, is this, that God, through Christ, hath placed a principle in every man, to inform him of his duty, and to enable him to do it; and that those that live up to this principle are the people of God, and those that live in disobedience to it, are not God's people, whatever name they may bear, or profession they may make of religion. This is their ancient, first, and standing testimony: with this they began, and this they bore, and do bear to the world.

§2. By this principle they understand something that is divine; and though in man, yet not of man, but of God; and that it came from Him, and leads to Him all those that will be led by it.

§3. There are divers ways of speaking they have been led to use, by which they declare and express what this principle is, about which I think fit to precaution the reader, viz. they call it, the light of Christ within man, or, light within, which is their ancient, and most general and familiar phrase, also the (a) manifestation (b) or appearance of Christ (c), the (d) witness of God, the (e) seed of God, the (f) seed of the kingdom, (g) wisdom the (h) word in the heart, the grace (i) that appears to all men, the (k) spirit given to every man to profit with the (l) truth in the inward parts, the (m) spiritual leaven, that leavens the whole lump of man: which are many of them figurative expressions, but all of them such as the Holy Ghost hath used, and which will be used in this treatise, as they are most frequently in the writings and ministry of this people. But that this variety and manner of expression may not occasion any misapprehension or confusion in the understanding of the reader, I would have him know, that they always mean by these terms, or denominations, not another, but the same principle, before mentioned: which, as I said, though it be in man, is not of man, but of God, and therefore divine: and one in itself, though diversly expressed by the holy men, according to the various manifestations and operations thereof.

§4. It is to this principle of light, life and grace, that this people refer all: For they say it is the great agent in religion; that, without which, there is no conviction, so no conversion, or regeneration; and consequently no entering into the kingdom of God. That is to say, there can be no true sight of sin, nor sorrow for it, and therefore no forsaking or overcoming of it, or remission or justification from it. A necessary and powerful principle indeed, when neither sanctification, nor justification can be had without it. In short, there is no becoming virtuous, holy and good, without this principle; no acceptance with God, nor peace of soul, but through it. But on the contrary, that the reason of so much irreligion among Christians, so much superstition, instead of devotion, and so much profession without enjoyment, and so little heart reformation, is because people in religion overlook this principle, and leave it behind them.

They will be religious without it, and Christians without it, though this be the only means of making them so indeed. So natural is it to man, in his degenerate state, to prefer sacrifice before obedience, and to make prayers go for practice, and so flatter himself to hope, by ceremonial and bodily service, to excuse himself with God from the stricter discipline of this principle in the soul, which leads man to take up the cross, deny self, and do that which God requires of him: and that is every man's true religion, and every such man is truly religious: that is, he is holy, humble, patient, meek, merciful, just, kind, and charitable; which they say, no man can make himself; but that this principle will make them all so, that will embrace the convictions and teachings of it, being the root of all true religion in man, and the good seed from whence all good fruits proceed. To sum up what they say upon the nature and virtue of it, as contents of that which follows, they declare that this principle is, first, divine. Secondly, universal. Thirdly, efficacious: in that it gives man:

First, the knowledge of God, and of himself, and therein a sight of his duty and disobedience to it.

Secondly, it begets a true sense and sorrow for sin in those that seriously regard the convictions of it.

Thirdly, it enables them to forsake sin, and sanctifies from it.

Fourthly, it applies God's mercies in Christ for the forgiveness of sins that are past, unto justification, upon such sincere repentance and obedience.

Fifthly, it gives, to the faithful, perseverance unto a perfect man, and the assurance of blessedness, world without end.

To the truth of all which, they call in a threefold evidence: First, The Scriptures, which give an ample witness, especially those of the New and better Testament. Secondly, The reasonableness of it in itself. And lastly, a general experience, in great measure: but particularly, their own, made credible by the good fruits they have brought forth, and the answer God has given to their ministry: which, to impartial observers, have commended the principle, and gives me occasion to abstract their history, in divers particulars, for a conclusion to this little treatise.

Chapter II. §1. *The evidence of Scripture for this principle*, John 1. 4. 9. §2. *Its divinity*. §3. *All things created by it*. §4. *What it is to man, as to salvation*.

§1. I shall begin with the evidence of the blessed Scriptures of Truth, for this divine principle, and that under the name of light, the first and most common word used by them, to express and denominate this principle by, as well as most apt and proper in this dark state of the world.

John 1. 1. In the Beginning was the Word, and the Word was with God, and the Word was God.

Vers. 3. All things were made by Him.

Vers. 4. In Him was life, and that life was the light of men.

Vers. 9. That was the true light, which lighteth every man that cometh into the world.

§2. I have begun with him, that begun his history with him that was the beginning of the creation of God; the most beloved disciple, and longest liver of all the apostles, and he, that for excellent knowledge and wisdom in heavenly things, is justly entitled John the Divine. He tells us first, what he was in the beginning, viz. the Word. In the beginning was the Word.

And though that shows what the Word must be, yet he adds and explains, that the Word was with God, and the Word was God; lest any should doubt of the divinity of the Word, or have lower thoughts of Him than He deserved. The Word then, is divine, and an apt term it is, that the Evangelist styles Him by, since it is so great an expression of the wisdom and power of God to men.

§3. All things were made by Him. If so, He wants no power. And if we were made by Him, we must be new made by Him too, or we can never enjoy God. His power shows His dignity, and that nothing can be too hard for such a sufficiency as made all things, and without which nothing was made, that was made. As Man's Maker must be his husband, so his Creator must be his Redeemer also.

§4. In him was life, and the life was the light of men. This is our point. The Evangelist first begins with the nature and being of the Word: From thence he descends to the works of the Word: and lastly, then he tells us what the Word is, with respect to man above the rest of the creation, viz. the Word was life, and the life was the light of men. The relation must be very near and intimate, when the very life of the word (that was with God, and was God) is the light of men: as if men were next to the Word, and above all the rest of his works; for it is not said so of any other creature.

Man cannot want light then; no not a divine light: for if this be not divine, that is the life of the Divine Word, there can be no such thing at all as divine or supernatural light and life. And the text does not only prove the divinity of the light, but the universality of it also, because man mentioned in it, is mankind: which is yet more distinctly expressed in His ninth verse, that was the true light, which lighteth every man that cometh into the world. Implying, that he that lighteth not mankind is not that true light; and therefore John was not that light, but bore witness of Him that was, who lighteth every man; to wit, the Word that took flesh: so that both the divine nature, and universality of the light of Christ within are confirmed together.

Chapter III. §1. *How this Scripture is wrested.* §2. *That it is a natural light.* §3. *That it lighteth not all.* §4. *That it is only the doctrine and life of Christ when in the flesh. All answered, and its divinity and universality proved.*

§1. But though there be no passage or proposition to be found in Holy Scripture, in which mankind is more interested, or that is more clearly laid down by the Holy Ghost, than this I have produced, yet hardly hath any place been more industriously wrested from its true and plain sense: especially since this people have laid any stress upon it, in defence of their testimony of the light within. Some will have it to be but a natural light, or a part of man's nature, though it be the very life of the Word by which the world was made; and mentioned within those verses, which only concern His eternal power and Godhead. But because I would be understood, and treat of things with all plainness, I will open the terms of the objection as well as I can, and then give my answer to it.

§2. If by natural be meant a created thing, as man is, or anything that is requisite to the composition of man, I deny it: the text is expressly against it; and says, the light with which man is lighted, is the life of the Word, which was with God, and was God. But if by natural is only intended that the light comes along with us into the world; or that we have it as sure as we are born, or have nature; and is the light of our nature, of our minds and understandings, and is not the result of any revelation from without, as by angels or men; then we mean and intend the same thing. For it is natural to man to have a supernatural light, and for the creature to be lighted by an uncreated light, as is the life of the creating word. And did people but consider the constitution of man, it would conduce much to preserve or deliver them from any dilemma upon this account. For man can be no more a light to his mind, than he is to his body: he has the capacity of seeing objects when he has the help of light, but cannot be a light to himself, by which to see them. Wherefore as the sun in the firmament is the light of the body, and gives us discerning in our temporal affairs; so the life of the Word is the glorious light and sun of the soul: our intellectual luminary, that informs our mind, and give us true judgment and distinction about those things that more immediately concern our betters, inward and eternal man.

§3. But others will have this text read thus, not that the Word enlightens all mankind, but that all who are enlightened are enlightened by him, thereby not only narrowing and abusing the text, but rendering God partial, and so severe to his creatures, as to leave the greatest part of the world in darkness, without the means of opportunity of salvation; though we are assured from the

Scriptures that (a) all have light, that Christ is the (b) light of the world, and that he (c) died for all; yea, the (d) ungodly, and that God desires not the (e) death of any, but rather that all should repent and come to the knowledge of the truth and be saved; and (f) that the grace of God has appeared to all men, etc.

§4. There is a third sort that will needs have it understood, not of any illumination by a divine light or spirit in man, but by the doctrine Christ preached, and the life and example he lived, and led in the world; and which yet neither reached the thousandth part of mankind, nor can consist with what the apostle John intends in the beginning of his history, which wholly relates to what Christ was before He took flesh, or at least, what He is to the soul, by His immediate inshinings and influences. It is most true, Christ was, in a sense, the light of the world, in that very appearance, and shined forth by his heavenly doctrine, many admirable miracles, and His self-denying life and death: but still that hinders not, but that He was and is that spiritual light, which shineth more or less, in the hearts of the sons and daughters of men. For as He was a light in His life and conversation, He was only a light in a more excellent sense than He spoke of to his disciples, when He said, ye are the lights of the world. But Christ the Word enlightened them, and enlightens us, and enlightens all men that come into the world; which He could not be said to do, if we only regard His personal and outward appearance: for in that sense it is long since He was that light, but in this He is continually so. In that respect He is remote, but in this sense He is present and immediate, else we should render the text, that was the true light which did lighten, instead of which lighteth every man that cometh into the world. And that the Evangelist might be so understood, as we speak, he refers to this as an evidence of His being the Messiah, and not John; for whom many people had much reverence, for Vers. 8. He saith of John, he was not that light, but was sent to bear witness of that light: now comes his proof and our testimony, That was the true light which lighteth every man that cometh into the world; which was not John, or any else, but the Word that was with God, and was God. The Evangelist did not describe him by his fasting forty days, preaching so many sermons, working so many miracles, and living so holy a life; and, after all, so patiently suffering death, (which yet Christ did) thereby to prove him the light of the world; but, says the Evangelist, that was the true light, the Word in flesh, the Messiah, and not John, or any else, which lighteth every man that cometh into the world. So that Christ is manifested and distinguished by giving light: and indeed so are all his followers from other people, by receiving and obeying it. There are many other scriptures, of both testaments, that refer to the light within; either expressly, or implicitly; which, for brevity's sake, I shall waive reciting; but the reader will find some directions in the margin, which will guide him to them.

Chapter IV. §1. *The virtue of the light within; It gives* discerning. §2. *It* manifests God. §3. *It gives life to the soul.* §4. *It is the* apostolical *message.* §5. *Objection answered about two lights.* §6. *About natural and spiritual light: Not* two *darknesses within, therefore not* two *lights within.* §7. *The apostle* John *answers the objection fully: The light the same,* 1 John 2. 8, 9.

§1. The third thing is the virtue and efficacy of this light for the end for which God hath given it, viz. to lead and guide the soul of man to blessedness. In order to which, the first thing it does in and for man, is to give him a true sight of discerning of himself: what he is, and what he does; that he may see and know his own condition, and what judgment to make of himself, with respect to religion and a future state: of which, let us hear what the Word Himself saith, that cannot err, as John relates it, Chap. 3. 20, 21. For everyone that doth evil, hateth the light, neither cometh to the light, lest his deeds should be reproved. But he that doth truth cometh to the light, that his deeds may be made manifest, that they are wrought in God. A most pregnant instance of the virtue and authority of the light. First, it is that which men ought to examine themselves by. Secondly, it gives a true discerning betwixt good and bad, what is of God, from what is not of God. And, lastly, It is a judge, and condemneth or acquitteth, reproveth or comforteth the soul of man, as he rejects or obeys it. That must needs be divine and efficacious, which is able to discover to man, what is of God, from what is not of God; and which gives him a distinct knowledge, in himself, of what is wrought in God, from what is not wrought in God. By which it appears that this place does not only regard the discovery of man and his works, but, in some measure, it manifesteth God, and His Works also, which is yet something higher; for as much as it gives the obedient man a discovery of what is wrought or performed by God's power and after His Will, from what is the mere workings of the creature of Himself. If it could not manifest God, it could not tell man what was God's mind, nor give him such a grounded sense and discerning of the rife, nature, and tendency of the workings of his mind or inward man, as is both expressed and abundantly implied in this passage of our Saviour. And if it reveals God, to be sure it manifests Christ, that flows and comes from God. Who then would oppose or slight this blessed light?

§2. But that this light doth manifest God, is yet evident from Rom. 1. 19. Because that which may be known of (God) is manifest in men, for God hath showed it unto them. An universal proposition; and we have the apostle's word for it, who was one of a thousand, and inspired on purpose to tell us the truth: let it then have its due weight with us. If that which may be known of God is manifest in men, the people called Quakers cannot, certainly, be out of the way in preaching up the light within, without which, nothing can be manifested to the mind of man; as saith the same apostle to the Ephesians, Eph. 5. 13. Whatsoever doth make manifest is light. Well then may they call this light within a manifestation or appearance of God, that showeth in and to man, all that may be known of God. A passage much like unto this, is that of the prophet Micah, Chap. 6. 8. God hath showed thee, O man, what is good; and what doth the Lord require of thee, but to do justly, and to love mercy, and to walk humbly with thy God? God hath showed thee. O man! It is very emphatical. But how hath He showed him? Why by his light in the conscience, which the wicked rebel against, Job 24. 13. Who, for that cause, know not the ways, nor abide in the paths thereof: for its way are ways of pleasantness, and all its paths are peace to them that obey it.

§3. But the light giveth the light of life, which is eternal life to them that receive and obey it. Thus, says the blessed Saviour of the world, John 8. 12. I am the light of the world, he that followeth me shall not abide in darkness, but shall have the light of life. Now He is the light of the world, because He lighteth every man that cometh into the world, and they that obey that light obey Him, and therefore have the light of life. That is, the light becomes eternal life to the soul: that as it is the life of the Word, which is the light in man, so it becomes the life in man, through his obedience to it, as his heavenly light.

§4. Furthermore, this light was the very ground of the apostolical message, as the beloved disciple assures us. 1 John 1. 5, 6, 7. This then is the message, which we have heard of Him, and declare unto you, that God is light, and in Him is no darkness at all: if we say we have fellowship with Him, and walk in darkness, we lie, and do not the truth: but if we walk in the light, as He is in the light, we have fellowship one with another, and the blood of Jesus Christ cleanseth us from all sin. Which is so comprehensive of the virtue and excellency of the light, in reference to man, that there is little need that more should be said upon it; for as much as, first, it reveals God, and that God himself is light. Secondly, it discovers darkness from light, and that there is no fellowship between them. Thirdly, that man ought to walk in the light. Fourthly, that it is the way to obtain forgiveness of sin, and sanctification from it. Fifthly, that it is the means to have peace and fellowship with God and his people; His true church, redeemed from the pollutions of the world.

§5. Some, perhaps, may object, as indeed it hath been more than once objected upon us, that this is another light, not that light wherewith every man is enlightened. But the same apostle, in his evangelical history, tells us that in the Word was life, and the life was the light of men, and that that very light, that was the life of the Word, was the true light which lighteth every man that cometh into the world, John 1. 4, 9. Where is there so plain a text to be found against the sufficiency, as well as universality of the light within; or a plainer for any article of faith in the whole book of God? Had the beloved disciple intended two lights in his evangelical history, and his epistles, to be sure he would have noted to us his distinction: but we read of none, and by the properties ascribed in each writing, we have reason to conclude he meant the same.

§6. But if any shall yet object, That this is to be understood a spiritual light, and that ours is to be a natural one, I shall desire them to do two things: First, to prove that a natural light, as they phrase it, doth manifest God, other than as I have before explained and allowed: since whatever is part of man, in his constitution, but especially in his degeneracy from God, is so far from yielding him the knowledge of God, that it cannot rightly reprove or discover that which offends him without the light we speak of: and it is granted, that what we call divine, and some, mistakenly, call natural light, can do both. Secondly, if this light be natural, notwithstanding it doth manifest our duty, and reprove our disobedience to God, they would do well to assign us some certain medium, or way, whereby we may truly discern and distinguish between the manifestations and reproofs of the natural light within, from those of the divine light within, since they allow the manifestation of God, and reproof of evil, as well to the one, as to the other. Let them give us but one Scripture that distinguishes between a natural and a spiritual light within. They may, with as much reason, talk of a natural and spiritual darkness within. It is true, there is a natural proper darkness, to wit, the night of the outward world; and there is a spiritual darkness, viz. the clouded and benighted understandings of men, through disobedience to the light and spirit of God: but let them assign us a third, if they can. People use, indeed, to say, improperly, of blind men, they are dark, we may call a natural or idiot so, if we will: but where is there another darkness of the understanding, in the things of God? If they can, I say, find that, in and about the things of God, they do something.

Christ distinguished not between darkness and darkness, or light and light, in any such sense; nor did any of his disciples: yet both have frequently spoken of darkness and light. What difference, pray, doth the Scripture put between spiritual darkness, and darkness, mentioned in these places, Luke 1. 7, 9. Mat. 4. 16. John 1. 5 and 3. 19. & 8. 12, 31, 46. 1 Thes. 5. 4. 1 John 1. 6. Acts 26. 18. Rom. 13. 12. 2 Cor. 6. 14, 22. Eph. 5. 8. Col. 1. 13. Upon the strictest comparison of them I find none. It is all one spiritual darkness. Neither is there so much as one Scripture that affords us a distinction between light within and light within; or that there are really two lights from God, in man, that regard religion. Peruse Mat. 4. 16. Luke 2. 32 and 15. 8. John 1. 4, 5, 7, 8, 9. and 3. 19, 20, 21. and 8. 12. Acts 26. 18. Rom. 13. 12. 2 Cor. 4. 6. and 6. 14. Eph. 5. 8, 13. Col. 1. 12. 1 Thess. 5. 5. 1 Tim. 6. 16. 1 Pet. 2. 9. 1 John 1. 5, 7. and 2. 8. Rev. 21. 23, 24. and 22. 5. And we believe the greatest opposer, to our assertion, will not be able to sever light from light, or find out two lights within, in the passages here mentioned, or any other, to direct man in his duty to God and his neighbour: And if he cannot, pray let him forbear his mean thoughts and words of the light of Christ within man, as man's guide in duty to God and man. For as he must yield to us, that the light manifesteth evil, and reproveth for it, so doth Christ himself teach us of the light, John 3. 20. For every one that doth evil hateth the light, neither cometh unto the light, lest his deeds should be reproved. And the apostle Paul plainly saith, Eph. 5. 13. But all things that are reproved are made manifest by the light; therefore there are not two distinct lights within, but one and the same manifesting, reproving, and teaching light within. And this the apostle John, in his First epistle, makes plain, beyond all exception, to all considerate people: first, in that he calls God, light, Chap. 1. 5. Secondly, in that he puts no medium or third thing between that light and darkness, Verse 6. If we say we have fellowship with Him, and walk in darkness, we lie, etc. Intimating, that men must walk either in light or darkness, and not in a third, or other state or region. I am sure, that which manifests and reproves darkness, cannot be darkness. This all men must confess.

§7. And, as if the apostle John would have anticipated their objection, viz. it is true, your light within reproves for evil, but it is not therefore the divine light which leads into higher things, and which comes by the gospel; he thus expresseth himself, 1 John 2. 8, 9. The darkness is past, and the true light now shineth. He that saith he is in the light, and hateth his brother, is in darkness even until now; which is not another light than that mentioned before, Chap. 1. For as light is put there, in opposition to darkness, so light here is put in opposition to darkness. And as the darkness is the same, so must the light be the same. Wherefore we may plainly see that it is not another light, than that which reproves a man for hating his brother, which brings a man into fellowship with God, and to the blood of cleansing, as the next verse speaks: therefore that light which reproveth a man for hating his brother, is of a divine and efficacious Nature. In short, that light which is opposite to, and reproves spiritual darkness in a man and woman, is a spiritual light; but such a light is that which we confess, testify to, and maintain: therefore it is a spiritual light. It is also worth our notice, that the apostle useth the same manner of expression here, Chap. 2. 8. The true light shineth, that he doth in his evangelical history, Chap. 1. 9. That was the true light; intimating the same divine Word, or true light now shineth; and that it is the same true light in the account, that reproveth such as hate their brethren: consequently, that light that so reproveth them is the true light. And strange it is, that Christ and His disciples, but especially His beloved one, should so often make that very light, which stoops to the lowest step of immorality, and to the reproof of the grossest evil, to be no other than the same divine light, in a farther degree of manifestation, which brings such as follow it to the light of life, to the blood of cleansing, and to have fellowship with God, and one with another: nay, not only so, but the apostle makes a man's being a child of God, to depend upon his answering of this light in a palpable and common case, viz. not hating of his brother: And that yet any should shut their eyes so fast against beholding the virtue of it, as to conclude it a natural and insufficient light, is both unscriptural and unreasonable. Shall we slight it, because we come so easily by it, and it is so familiar and domestic to us? Or make its being so common an argument to undervalue so inestimable a mercy? What is more common than light and air, and water? And should we therefore condemn them, or prize them? Prize them, certainly, as what we cannot live, nor live comfortably without. The more general the mercy is, the greater, and therefore the greater obligation upon man to live humbly and thankfully for it. And to those alone that do so, are its divine secrets revealed.

Chapter V. §1. *The light the same with the spirit. Is is of God; proved by its properties.* §2. *The properties of the spirit compared with those of the light.* §3. *The light and grace flow from the same principle, proved by their agreeing properties.* §4. *An objection answered.* §5. *Difference in Manifestation, or operation, especially in gospel times, but not in principle, illustrated.*

Obj. But some may say, *We could willingly allow to the spirit and grace of God, which seemed to be the peculiar blessing of the new and second covenant, and the fruit of the coming of Christ, all that which you ascribe to the* light within; *but except it appeared to us that this light were the same in nature with the spirit and grace of God, we cannot easily bring our selves to believe what you say in favour of the light within.*

Answ. This objection, at first look, seems to carry weight with it: but upon a just and serious review, it will appear to have more words than matter, show than substance: yet because it gives occasion to solve scruples, that may be slung in the way of the simple, I shall attend it throughout. I say, then, if it appear that the properties, ascribed to the light within, are the same with those that are given to the Holy Spirit and grace of God; and that those several terms or epithets are only to express the divers manifestations or operations of one and the same principle, then it will not, it cannot be denied, but this light within is divine and efficacious, as we have asserted it. Now, that it is of the same nature with the spirit and grace of God, and tends to the same end, which is to bring people to God, let the properties of the light be compared with those of the spirit and grace of God. I say, they are the same, in that, first, the light proceeds from the one Word, and one life of that one Word, which was with God and was God, John 1. 4. and 1. 9. Secondly it is universal, it lighteth every man. Thirdly, it giveth the knowledge of God, and fellowship with Him. Rom. 1. 19. John 3. 21. 1 John 1. 5, 6. Fourthly, it manifesteth and reproveth evil,

John 3. 20. Eph. 5. 13. Fifthly, it is made the rule and guide of Christian walking, Psalm 43. 3. John 8. 12. Eph. 5. 13, 15. Sixthly, it is the path for God's people to go in, Psalm 119. 105. Prov. 4. 18. Isaiah 2. 5. 1 John 1. 7. Rev. 24. 23. And the nations of them that are saved, shall walk in the light of the (Lamb.) Lastly, it is the armour of the children of God against Satan, Psalm 27. 1. The Lord is my light, whom shall I fear? Rom. 13. 12. Let us put on the armour of light.

§2. Now let all this be compared with the properties of the Holy Spirit, and their agreement will be very manifest. First, it proceedeth from God, because it is the spirit of God, Rom. 6. 11. Secondly, it is universal. It strove with the old world, Gen. 6. 3. Then to be sure with the new one: everyone hath a measure of it given to profit withal, 1 Cor. 12. 7. Thirdly, it revealeth God, Job 32. 8. 1 Cor. 2. 10, 11. Fourthly, it reproveth sin, John 16. 8. Fifthly, it is a rule and guide for the children of God to walk by, Rom. 8. 14. Sixthly, it is also the path they are to walk in, Rom. 8. 1. Gal. 5. 15. Walk in the spirit. Lastly, this is not all; it is likewise the spiritual weapon of a true Christian, Eph. 6. 17. Take the sword of the spirit, which is the Word of God. After this, I hope none will deny that this light and this spirit must be of one and the same nature, that work one and the same effect, and tend evidently to one and the same holy end.

§3. And what is said of the light and spirit, may also very well be said of the light and grace of God; in that, first, the grace floweth from Christ, the Word, that took flesh, as well as the light; for as in Him was life, and that life the light of men, so he was full of grace and truth, and of his fulness have all we received, and grace for grace, John 1. 4, 9, 14, 16. Secondly, it is universal; both from this text, and what the apostle to Titus teacheth; for the grace of God that bringeth salvation, hath appeared to all men, Tit. 2. 11, 12. Thirdly, it manifesteth evil, for if it teaches to deny ungodliness and worldly lusts, it must needs detect them, and so says the text. Fourthly, it revealeth godliness, and consequently it must manifest God. Fifthly, it is an instructor and guide; for, says the apostle, it teaches to deny ungodliness and wordly lusts, and to live soberly, righteously, and godly in this present world, and herein a rule of life, Tit. 2. 11, 12. Sixthly, it is, to all that receive it, all that they can need or desire. 2 Cor. 12. 9. My grace is sufficient for thee. A high testimony from heaven, to the power of this teaching and saving grace, under the strongest temptations.

§4. *Obj. But there is little mention made of the spirit, and none of the grace, before Christ's coming, and therefore the spirit, as spoken of in the writings of the New Testament, and especially the Grace, must be another, and a nobler thing than the light within.*

Answ. By no means another thing, but another name, from another manifestation or operation, of the same principle. It is called light from the distinction and discerning it gives. Let there be light, and there was light, said God in the beginning of the old world; so there is first light in the beginning of the new creation of God in man. It is called spirit, because it giveth life, sense, motion, and vigour: and it is as often mentioned in the writings of the Old as New Testament; which every reader may see, if he will but please to look into his Scripture concordance. Thus God's spirit strove with the old world, Gen. 6. 3. and with Israel in the wilderness, Neh. 9. 30. And David asked, in the agony of his soul, whither shall I go from they spirit? Ps. 139. 7. and the prophets often felt it. It is styled grace, not from its being another principle, but because it was a fuller dispensation of the virtue and power of the same divine principle: and that being purely God's favour and mercy, and not man's merit, is aptly, and deservedly called the grace, favour, or good-will of god, to undeserving man. The wind does not always blow fresh, nor heaven send down its rain freely, nor the sun shine forth clearly; shall we therefore say, it is not of the same kind of wind, rain or light, when it blows, rains, or shines but a little, as when it blows, rains, or shines much? It is certainly the same in nature and kind; and so is this blessed principle, under all its several dispensations, manifestations and operations, for the benefit of man's soul, ever since the world began.

§5. But this is most freely, humbly and thankfully acknowledged by us, that the dispensation of the gospel, was the clearest, fullest, and noblest of all other; both with regard to the coming of Christ in the flesh, and being our one holy offering to God for sin, through the eternal spirit; and the breaking forth of man, in a more excellent manner, after His ascension. For though it was not another light, or spirit, than that which He had given to man in former ages, yet it was another and greater measure; and that is the privilege of the gospel above former dispensations. What before shined but dimly, shines since with great glory. Then it appeared but darkly, but now with open face. Types, figures and shadows veiled its appearances and made them look low and faint; but in the gospel time, the veil is rent, and the hidden glory manifest. It was under the law but as a dew, or small rain, but under the gospel, it may be said to be poured out upon men: according to that gracious and notable promise of God, by the prophet Joel, in the latter days I will pour out of my spirit upon all flesh. Thus we say when it rains plentifully, look how it pours. So God augments His light, grace and spirit to these latter days. They shall not have it sparingly, and by small drops, but fully and freely, and overflowing too. And thus Peter, that deep and excellent apostle, applies that promise in Joel, on the day of Pentecost, as the beginning of the accomplishment of it. This is grace and favour, and goodness indeed. And therefore well may this brighter illumination, and greater effusion of the spirit, be called grace; for as the coming of the Son excelled that of the servant, so did the manifestation of the light and spirit of God, since the coming of Christ, excel that of the foregoing dispensations; yet ever sufficient to salvation, to all those that walked in it. This is our sense of the light, spirit, and grace of God. And by what is said, it is evident they are one and the same principle, and that He that has light, need not want the spirit or grace of God, if he will but receive it, in the love of it: for the very principle, that is light to show him, is also spirit to quicken him, and grace to teach, help, and comfort him. It is sufficient in all circumstances of life, to them that diligently mind and obey it.

Chapter VI. §1. *An objection answered: All are not good, though* all are lighted. §2. *Another objection answered, that gospel truths were known before* Christ's coming. §3. *Another: The Gentiles had the* same light, *though not with those advantages: Proved from Scripture.*

§1. *But some may yet say, if it be as you declare, how comes it, that all who are enlightened, are not so good as they should be; or, as you say, this would make them?*

Answ. Because people don't receive and obey it: all men have reason, but all men are not reasonable. Is it the fault of the grain, in the granary, that it yields no increase, or of the talent in the napkin, that it is not improved? It is plain a talent was given; and as plain that it was improveable; both because the like talents were actually improved by others, and, that the just judge expected his talent with advantage; which else, to be sure, he would never have done. Now when our objectors will tell us, whose fault it was the talent was not improved, we shall be ready to tell them why the unprofitable servant was not so good as he should have been. The blind must not blame the sun, nor sinners tax the grace of insufficiency. It is sin that darkens the eye, and hardens the heart, and that hinders good things from the sons of men. If we do His will, we shall know of His divine doctrine, so Christ tells us. Men not living to what they know, cannot blame God, that they know no more. The unfruitfulness is in us, not in the talent. It were well indeed, that this were laid to heart. But, alas! Men are too apt to follow their sensual appetites, rather than their reasonable mind, which renders them brutal instead of rational. For the reasonable part in man, is his spiritual part, and that guided by the divine λίγος, or word, which Tertullian interprets reason in the most excellent sense, makes man truly reasonable; and then it is that man comes to offer up himself to God a reasonable sacrifice. Then a man indeed; a complete man; such a man as God made, when He made man in His own image, and gave him paradise for his habitation.

§2. Obj. *But some yet object, if mankind had always this principle, how comes it that gospel truths were not so fully known before the coming of Christ, to those that were obedient to it.*

Answ. Because a child is not a grown man, nor the beginning the end; and yet He that is the beginning, is also the end: the principle is the same, though not the manifestation. As the world has many steps and periods of time towards its end, so hath man to his perfection. They that are faithful to what they know of the dispensation of their own day, shall hear the happy welcome, of well done, good and faithful servant. And yet many of God's people in those days had a prospect of the glory of the latter times, the improvement of religion, the happiness of the Church of God.

This we see in the Prophesy of Jacob and Moses, concerning the restoration of Israel by Christ. So David, in many of his excellent Psalms, expressing most sensible and extraordinary enjoyments, as well as Prophesies; particularly his 2, 15, 18, 22, 23, 25, 27, 32, 36, 37, 42, 43, 45, 51, 84, etc. The prophets are full of it, and for that reason have their name; particularly Isaiah, Chap. 2. 9, 11. 25, 28, 32, 35, 42, 49, 50, 51, 52, 53, 54, 59, 60, 61, 63, 65, 66. Jeremiah also, Chap. 23, 30, 31, 33. Ezekiel, Chap. 20, 34, 36, 37. Daniel, Chap. 8, 9, 10, 11, 12. Hosea. Chap. 1, 3. Joel, Chap. 2, 3. Amos, Chap. 9. Micah, Chap. 4, 5. Zachariah, Chap. 6, 8, 9, 11, 13, 14. Malachy, Chap. 3. 4. This was not another principle, though another manifestation of the same principle, nor was it common, but particular and extraordinary in the reason of it.

It was the same spirit that came upon Moses, which came upon John the Baptist, and it was also the same spirit that came upon Gideon and Sampson, that fell upon Peter and Paul; but it was not the same dispensation of that spirit. It hath been the way of God, to visit and appear to men, according to their states and conditions, and as they have been prepared to receive Him, be it more outwardly or inwardly, sensibly or spiritually. There is no capacity too low, or too high, for this divine principle: for as it made and knows all, so it reaches unto all people. It extends to the meanest, and the highest cannot subsist without it. Which made David break forth in his expostulations with God, whither shall I go from thy spirit, or whither shall I flee from thy presence? Psal. 139, 7, 8, 9, 10. Implying it was every where, though not every where, nor at every time alike. If I go to heaven, to hell, or beyond the seas, even there shall thy hand lead me, and thy right hand shall hold me. That is, there will this divine word, this light of men, this spirit of God, fine me, lead me, help me, and comfort me. For it is with me where ever I am, and where ever I go, in one respect or other; Prov. 6. 22. When thou goest, it shall lead thee; when thou sleepest, it shall keep thee; and when thou awakest, it shall talk with thee: And I can no more get rid of it, if I would, than of myself, or my own nature; so present is it with me; and so close it sticks unto me. Isa. 43. 2. When thou passest through the waters, I will be with thee; and through the rivers, they shall not overflow thee; when thou walkest through the fire, thou shalt not be burnt, neither shall the flame kindle upon thee. David knew it, and therefore had a great value for it. In thy light shall we see light, or we shall be enlightened by thy light. Thou wilt light my candle; the Lord my God will lighten my darkness. Again, the Lord is my light, whom shall I fear. It was his armour against all danger. It took fear away from him, and he was undaunted, because he was safe in the way of it. Of the same blessed word he says elsewhere, it is a lamp unto my feet, and a lanthorn to my paths. In short, a light to him in his way to blessedness.

§3. Obj. *But if the* Jews *had this Light, it does not follow that the* Gentiles *had it also; but by your doctrine all have it.*

Answ. Yes, and it is the glory of this doctrine which we profess, that God's love is therein held forth to all. And besides the texts cited in general, and that are as full and positive as can be expressed, the apostle is very particular in the second chapter of His epistle to the Romans, that the Gentiles having not the law, did by nature the things contained in the law, and were a law unto themselves. That is, they had not an outward law, circumstanced as the Jews had; but they had the work of the law written in their hearts, and therefore might well be a law to themselves, that had the law in themselves. And so had the Jews too, but then they had greater outward helps to quicken their obedience to it; such as God afforded not unto any other nation: And therefore the obdience of the Gentiles, or uncircumcision, is said to be by nature, or naturally, because it was without those additional, external, and extraordinary ministries and help, which the Jews had to provoke them to duty. Which is so far from lessening the obedient Gentiles, that it exalts them in the apostle's judgment; because though they had less advantages than the Jews, yet the work of the law written in their hearts was made so much the more evident by the good life they lived in the world. He adds, their consciences bearing witness (or as it may be rendered, witnessing with them) and their thoughts, meanwhile, accusing, or else excusing one another in the day when God shall judge the secrets of all hearts by Jesus Christ, according to my gospel. Which presents us with four things to our point, and worth our serious reflection. First, that the Gentiles had the law written in their hearts. Secondly, that their conscience was an allowed witness of evidence about duty. Thirdly, that the judgment made thereby shall be confirmed by the apostles' gospel at the great day, and therefore valid and irreversible. Fourthly, that this could not be, if the light of this conscience were not a divine and sufficient light: for conscience truly speaking, is no other than the sense a man hath, or judgment he maketh of his duty to God, according to the understanding God gives him of His will. And that no ill, but a true and scriptural use may be made of this word conscience, I limit it to duty, and that to a virtuous and holy life, as the apostle evidently doth, about which we cannot miss, or dispute; Read Verses 7, 8, and 9. It was to that therefore the apostles of our Lord Jesus Christ desired to be made manifest, for they dared to stand the judgment of conscience, in reference to the doctrine they preached and pressed upon men. The beloved disciple also makes it a judge of man's present and future state, under the term heart, for if our heart condemn us, God is greater than our heart, and knoweth all things. Beloved, if our heart condemn us not, then have we confidence towards God. Plain and strong words: and what were they about, but whether we love God, in deed and in truth: and how must that appear? Why, in keeping his commandments, which is living up to what we know. And if any desire to satisfy themselves farther of the divinity of the Gentiles, let them read Plato, Seneca, Plutarch, Epictetus, Marcus Aurelius Antoninus, and the Gentile writers. They will also find many of their sayings, collected in the first part of a book, called, *The Christian Quaker*, and compared with the testimonies of scripture, not for their authority, but agreeableness. In them they may discern many excellent truths and taste great love and devotion to virtue: a fruit that grows upon no tree, but that of life, in no age or nation. Some of the most eminent writers of the first ages, such as Justin Martyr, Origen, Clemens Alexandrinus, etc. bore them great respect, and thought it no lessening to the reputation of Christianity that it was defended in many Gentile authors, as well as that they used and urged them to engage their followers to the faith, as Paul did the Athenians with their own poets.

Chapter VII. §1. *An objection answered about the various dispensations of God: The principle the same.* §2. *God's work of a piece, and* Truth *the same under divers* shapes. §3. *The reason of the prevalency of* idolatry. §4. *The* Quaker's *testimony the best antidote against it, viz. walking by a divine principle in man.* §5. *It was God's end in all His manifestations, that man might be* God's image and delight.

§1. Obj. *But it may be said, if it were one principle, why so many modes and shapes of religion, since the world began? For the Patriarchal, Mosaical, and Christian have their great differences; to say nothing of what has befallen the Christian, since the publication of it to the world.*

Answ. I know not how properly they may be called divers religions, that assert the *true God* for the object of worship; the Lord Jesus Christ, for the only Saviour; and the light, or spirit of Christ, for the great agent and means of man's conversion, and eternal felicity, any more than infancy, youth, and manhood, make three men, instead of three growths or periods of time, of one and the same man. But passing that, the many modes, or ways of God's appearing to men, arise, as hath been said, from the diverse states of men, in all which it seems to have been His main design to prevent idolatry and vice by directing their minds to the true object of worship, and pressing virtue and holiness. So that though mediately he spoke to the patriarchs, mostly by angels, in the fashion of men, and by them to their families, over and above the illumination in themselves; so to the prophets, for the most part, by the revelation of the Holy Ghost in them, and by them to the Jews; And since the gospel dispensation, by His Son, both externally, by His coming in the flesh, and internally, by His spiritual appearance in the soul, as He is the great light of the world: Yet all its flowings mediately through others, have still been from the same principle, co-operating with the manifestation of it immediately in man's own particular.

§2. This is of great weight, for our information and encouragement, that God's work, in reference to man, is all of a piece, and, in itself, lies in a narrow compass, and that His eye has ever been upon the same thing in all His dispensations, viz. to make men truly good, by planting His holy awe and fear in their hearts: though He has condescended, for the hardness and darkness of men's hearts, to approach, and spell out His holy mind, to them, by low and carnal ways, as they may appear to our more enlightened understandings: suffering truth to put on divers sorts of garments, the better to reach to the low state of men, to engage them from false gods, and ill lives; seeing them sunk so much below their nobler part, and what He made them, that, like brute beasts, they knew not their own strength and excellency.

§3. And if we do but well consider the reason of the prevalency of idolatry upon the earlier and darker times of the world of which the Scripture is very particular, we shall find that it ariseth from this; that it is more sensual, and therefore calculated to please the senses of men; being more outward or visible, or more in their own power to perform, than one more spiritual in its object. For as their gods were the workmanship of men's hands, they could not prefer them, that being the argument which did most of all gaul their worshippers, and what of all things, for that reason, they were most willing to forget. But their incidency to idolatry, and the advantages it had upon the true religion with them plainly came from this, that it was more outward and sensual: they could see the object of their devotion, and had it in in their power to address it when they would. It was more fashionable too, as well as better accommodated to their dark, and too brutal, state. And therefore it was that God, by many afflictions, and greater deliverances, brought forth a people, to endear himself to them, that they might remember the hand that saved them, and worship Him, and Him only; in order to root up idolatry, and plant the knowledge, and fear of Him, in their minds, for an example to other nations. Whoever reads Deuteronomy, which is a summary of the other four books of

Moses, will find the frequent and earnest care and concern of that good man for Israel, about this very point; and how often that people slipped and lapsed, notwithstanding God's love, care and patience over them, into the idolatrous customs of the nations about them. Diverse other scriptures inform us also, especially those of the prophets, Isaiah 44. and 45. Psalms 37. and 115. and Jer. 1c. where the Holy Ghost confutes and rebukes the people, and mocks their idols with a sort of holy disdain.

§4. Now that which is farthest from idolatry and the best antidote against it, is the principle we have laid down, and the more people's minds are turned and brought to it, and that they resolve their faith, worship, and obedience into the holy illuminations and power of it, the nearer they grow to the end of their creation, and consequently to their Creator. They are more spiritually qualified, and become better fitted to worship God as He is: who, as we are told, by our Lord Jesus Christ, is a spirit, and will be worshipped in spirit and in truth, and that they are such sort of worshippers which God seeketh to worship Him, in this gospel day. The hour cometh, saith He, and now is. That is, some now do so, but more shall. A plain assertion in present, and a promise and prophesy of the increase of such worshippers in future. Which shows a change intended from a ceremonial worship and state of the Church of God, to a spiritual one. Thus the text; but the time cometh, and now is, when true worshippers shall worship the Father in spirit and in truth. Which is as much as to say, when the worship of God shall be more inward than outward, and so more suitable to the nature of God, and the nobler part of man, his inside, or his inward and better man: for so those blessed words import, in spirit and in truth. In spirit, that is, through the power of the spirit. In truth, that is, in realities, not in shadows, ceremonies, or formalities, but in sincerity, with and in life, being divinely prepared and animated; which brings man not only to offer up right worship, but also into intimate communion and fellowship with God, who is a spirit.

§5. And if it be duly weighed, it will appear, that God, in all His manifestations of Himself, hath still come nearer and nearer to the insides of men, that He might reach to their understandings, and open their hearts, and give them a plainer and nearer acquaintance with Himself in spirit: and then it is that man must seek and find the knowledge of God for his eternal happiness. Indeed, all things, that are made show forth the power and wisdom of God, and his goodness too, to mankind; and therefore many men urge the creation to silence atheistical objections: But though all those things show a God, yet man does it, above all the rest. He is the precious stone of the king, and the most glorious jewel of the globe; to whose reasonable use, service, and satisfaction, the whole seems to be made and dedicated. But God's delight (by whom man was made, we are told by the Holy Ghost) is in the habitable parts of the earth, with the sons of men, Prov. 8. 31. And with those that are contrite in spirit, Isaiah 66. 1. And why is man His delight, but because man only, of all His works, was of His likeness. This is the intimate relation of man to God: somewhat nearer than ordinary; for of all other beings, man only had the honour of being His image; and, by his resemblance to God, as I may say, came his kindred with God and knowledge of Him. So that the nearest and best way for man to know God, and be acquainted with Him, is to seek Him in himself, in his image; and, as he finds that, he comes to find and know God. Now man may be said to be God's image in a double respect. First, as he is of an immortal nature; and, next, as that nature is enbued with those excellencies in small, and proportionable to a creature's capacity, that are by nature infinitely and incomparably in his Creator, for instance, wisdom, justice, mercy, holiness, patience, and the like. As man becomes holy, just, merciful, patient, etc. By the copy He will know the original, and by the workmanship in himself, he will be acquainted with the Holy Workman. This, reader, is the regeneration and new creature we press, (Gal. 6. 15, 16.) and according to this rule, we say, men ought to be religious and walk in this world. Man, as I said just now, is a composition of both worlds; his body is of this, his soul of the other world. The body is as the temple of the soul, the soul the temple of the Word, and the Word the great temple and manifestation of God. By the body the soul looks into and beholds this world, and by the Word it beholds God, and the world that is without end. Much might be said of this order of things, and their respective excellencies, but I must be brief.

Chapter VIII. §1. *The doctrines of* satisfaction *and* justification *owned and worded according to* Scripture. §2. *What constructions we can't believe of them, and which is an abuse of them.* §3. *Christ owned a sacrifice and a mediator.* §4. Justification twofold, *from the guilt of sin, and from the power and pollution of it.* §5. *Exhortation to the reader upon the whole.*

Obj. i. *Though there be many good things said, how Christ appears and works in a soul, to awaken, convince and convert it; yet you seem not particular enough about the death and sufferings of Christ: and it is generally rumoured and charged upon you by your adversaries that you have little reverence to the doctrine of Christ's satisfaction to God for our sins, and that you do not believe that the active and passive obedience of Christ, when he was in the world, is the alone ground of a sinner's justification before God.*

Answ. The doctrines of satisfaction and justification, truly understood are placed in so strict an union, that the one is a necessary consequence of the other, and what we say of them is what agrees with the suffrage of Scripture, and for the most part in the terms of it; always believing, that in points where there arises any difficulty, be it from the obscurity of expression, mistranslation, or the dust raised by the heats of partial writers, or nice critics, it is ever best to keep close to the text, and maintain charity in the rest. I shall first speak negatively, what we do not own, which perhaps hath given occasion to those who have been more hasty than wise, to judge us defective in our belief of the efficacy of the death and sufferings of Christ to justification: as,

§2. First, we cannot believe that Christ is the cause, but the effect of God's love, according to the testimony of the beloved disciple, John, Chap. 3. God so loved the world, that He gave his only begotten Son into the world, that whosoever believeth in him should not perish, but have everlasting life.

Secondly, we cannot say, God could not have taken another way to have saved sinners than by the death and sufferings of his Son, to satisfy His justice, or that Christ's death and sufferings were a strict and rigid satisfaction for that eternal death and misery due to man for sin and transgression: for such a notion were to make God's mercy little concerned in man's salvation; and indeed we are at too great a distance from his infinite wisdom and power to judge of the liberty or necessity of his actings.

Thirdly, we cannot say Jesus Christ was the greatest sinner in the world, (because He bore our sins on His cross, or because He was made sin for us, who knew no sin) an expression of great levity and unsoundness, yet often said by great preachers and professors of religion.

Fourthly, we cannot believe that Christ's death and sufferings so satisfies God, or justifies men, as that they are thereby accepted of God: they are indeed thereby put into a state capable of being

accepted of God, and through the obedience of faith and sanctification of the spirit, are in a state of acceptance: for we can never
think a man justified before God while self-condemned; or that any
man can be in Christ who is not a new creature; or that God looks
upon men otherwise than they are. We think it a state of presumption and not of salvation to call Jesus Lord, and not by the work of
the Holy Ghost. Master, and He not yet master of their affections:
Saviour, and they not saved by Him from their sins: Redeemer, and
yet they not redeemed by Him from their passion, pride, covetousness, wantonness, vanity, vain honours, friendships, and glory of
this world: which were to deceive themselves; for God will not be
mocked, such as men sow, such they must reap. And though Christ
did die for us, yet we must, by the assistance of his grace, work out
our salvation with fear and trembling: as He died for sin, so we
must die to sin, or we cannot be said to be saved by the death
and sufferings of Christ, or throughly justified and accepted with
God. Thus far negatively. Now, positively, what we own as to
justification.

§3. We do believe that Jesus Christ was our holy sacrifice,
atonement, and propitiation; that He bore our iniquities, and that
by His stripes we were healed of the wounds Adam gave us in his
fall; and that God is just in forgiving true penitents upon the credit
of that holy offering Christ made of Himself to God for us; and
that what He did and suffered, satisfied and pleased God, and was
for the sake of fallen man, that had displeased God: and that
through the offering up of Himself once for all, through the eternal
spirit, he hath for ever perfected those (in all times) that were
sanctified, who walked not after the flesh, but after the spirit, Rom.
8. 1. Mark that.

§4. In short, justification consists of two parts, or hath a twofold
consideration, viz. justification from the guilt of sin, and justification from the power and pollution of sin, and in this sense
justification gives a man a full and clear acceptance before God. For
want of this latter part it is, that so many souls, religiously inclined,
are often under doubts, scruples, and despondencies, notwithstanding all that their teachers tell them of the extent and efficacy of the
first part of justification. And it is too general an unhappiness
among the professors of Christianity, that they are apt to cloak
their own active and passive disobedience with the active and
passive obedience of Christ. The first part of justification, we do
reverently and humbly acknowledge, is only for the sake of the

death and sufferings of Christ: nothing we can do, though by the operation of the Holy Spirit, being able to cancel old debts, or wipe out old scores: it is the power and efficacy of that propitiatory offering, upon faith and repentance, that justifies us from the sins that are past; and it is the power of Christ's spirit in our hearts, that purifies and makes us acceptable before God. For until the heart of man is purged from sin, God will never accept of it. He reproves, rebukes and condemns those that entertain sin there, and therefore such cannot be said to be in a justified state; condemnation and justification being contraries: so that they that hold themselves in a justified state by the active and passive obedience of Christ, while they are not actively and passively obedient to the spirit of Christ Jesus, are under a strong and dangerous delusion; and for crying out against this sin-pleasing imagination, not to say doctrine, we are staged and reproached as deniers and despisers of the death and sufferings of our Lord Jesus Christ. But be it known to such, they add to Christ's sufferings, and crucify to themselves afresh the Son of God, and trample the blood of the covenant under their feet, that walk unholily under a profession of justification; for God will not acquit the guilty, nor justify the disobedient and unfaithful. Such deceive themselves, and at the great and final judgment their sentence will not be, come ye blessed, because it cannot be said to them, well done good and faithful, for they cannot be so esteemed that live and die in a reproveable and condemnable state; but, go ye cursed, etc.

§5. Wherefore, O my reader! rest not thyself wholly satisfied with what Christ has done for thee in His blessed person without thee, but press to know His power and kingdom within thee, that the strong man, that has too long kept thy house, may be bound, and his goods spoiled, his works destroyed, and sin ended, according to 1 John 3. 7. For which end, says that beloved disciple, Christ was manifested, that all things may become new: new heavens and new earth, in which righteousness dwells. Thus thou wilt come to glorify God in thy body and in thy spirit, which are His; and live to him and not to thy self. Thy love, joy, worship and obedience; thy life, conversation, and practice; thy study, meditation, and devotion, will be spiritual: for the Father and the Son will make Their abode with thee, and Christ will manifest himself to thee; for the secrets of the Lord are with them that fear him: And an holy unction or anointing have all those which leads them into all truth, and they need not the teachings of men. They are better taught, being instructed by the divine oracle : no bare hearsay, or traditional Christians, but fresh and living witnesses : those that have seen with their own eyes, and heard with their own ears, and have handled with their own hands, the word of life, in the divers operations of it, to their souls salvation. In this they meet, in this they preach, and in this they pray and praise : behold the new covenant fulfilled, the Church and worship of Christ, the great anointed of God, and the great anointing of God, in His holy high priesthood, and offices in his Church !

Chapter IX. §1. *A confession to Christ and his work, both in doing and suffering.* §2. *That ought not to make void our belief and testimony of His inward and spiritual appearance in the soul.* §3. *What our testimony is in the latter respect : That it is impossible to be saved by Christ without us, while we reject His work and power within us.* §4. *The dispensation of grace, in its nature and extent.* §5. *A farther acknowledgment to the death and sufferings of Christ.* §6. *The conclusion, showing our adversary's unreasonableness.*

§1. And lest any should say we are equivocal in our expressions, and allegorize away Christ's appearance in the flesh ; meaning only thereby, our own flesh ; and that as often as we mention Him, we mean only a mystery, or a mystical sense of Him, be it as to His coming, birth, miracles, sufferings, death, resurrection, ascension, mediation and judgment ; I would yet add, to preserve the well-disposed from being staggered by such suggestions, and to inform and reclaim such as are under the power and prejudice of them, that, we do, we bless God, religiously believe and confess, to the glory of God the Father, and the honour of His dear and beloved Son, that, Jesus Christ took our nature upon him, and was like unto us in all things, sin excepted : that He was born of the Virgin Mary, suffered under Pontius Pilate, the Roman governor, was crucified, dead, and buried in the sepulchre of Joseph of Atimathea ; rose again the third day, and ascended into heaven, and sits on the right hand of God, in the power and majesty of his Father ; who will one day judge the world by Him, even that blessed man, Christ Jesus, according to their works.

§2. But because we so believe, must we not believe what Christ said, He that is with you shall be in you, John 14. I in them, and they in me, etc. Chap. 17. When it pleased God to reveal his Son in me, etc. Gal. The mystery hid from ages is Christ in the Gentiles the hope of glory, Col. 1. Unless Christ be in you, ye are reprobates? 2 Cor. 13. Or must we be industriously represented deniers of Christ's coming in the flesh, and the holy ends of it, in all the parts and branches of His doing and suffering, only because we believe and press the necessity of believing, receiving and obeying his inward and spiritual appearance and manifestation of himself, through his light, grace and spirit in the hearts and consciences of men and women, to reprove, convict, convert and change them? This we esteem hard and unrighteous measure; nor would our warm and sharp adversaries be so dealt with by others: but to do as they would be done to, is too often no part of their practice, whatever it be of their profession.

§3. Yet we are very ready to declare to the whole world, that we cannot think men and women can be saved by their belief of the one, without the sense and experience of the other; and that is what we oppose, and not his blessed manifestation in the flesh. We say that He then overcame our common enemy, foiled him in the open field, and in our nature triumphed over him that had overcome and triumphed over it in our forefather Adam and his posterity: and that as truly as Christ overcame him in our nature, in His own person, so, by His divine grace, being received and obeyed by us, He overcomes him in us: that is, He detects the enemy by His light in the conscience, and enables the creature to resist him, and all his fiery darts; and finally, so to fight the good fight of faith, as to overcome him, and lay hold on eternal life.

§4. And this is the dispensation of grace, which we declare has appeared to all, more or less; teaching those that will receive it, to deny ungodliness and worldly lusts, and to live soberly, righteously, and godly in this present world; looking for (which none else can justly do) the blessed hope, and glorious appearing of the great God, and our Saviour Jesus Christ, etc. Tit. 2. 11, 12, 13. And as from the teachings, experience and motion, of this grace we minister to others, so the very drift of our ministry is to turn people's minds to this grace in themselves, that all of them may up and be doing, even the good and acceptable will of God, and work out their salvation with fear and trembling, and make their high and heavenly calling and election sure; which none else can do, whatever be their profession, church and character: for such as men sow they must reap; and His servants we are whom we obey. Regeneration we must know, or we cannot be children of God, and heirs of eternal glory: and to be born again, another spirit and principle must prevail, leaven, season, and govern us, than either the spirit of the world, or our own depraved spirits; and this can be no other spirit than that which dwelt in Christ; for unless that dwell in us, we can be none of his, Rom. 8. 9. And this spirit begins in conviction, and ends in conversion and perseverance; and the one follows the other. Conversion being the consequence of convictions obeyed, and perseverance a natural fruit of conversion, and being born of God; for such sin not, because the seed of God abides in them: John 3. 7, 8. But such, through faithfulness, continue to the end, and obtain the promise, even everlasting life.

§5. But let my reader take this along with him, that we do acknowledge that Christ, through His holy doing and suffering, (for being a Son He learned obedience) has obtained mercy of God His Father for mankind, and that His obedience has an influence to our salvation, in all the parts and branches of it, since thereby he became a conqueror, and led captivity captive, and obtained gifts for men, with divers great and precious promises, that thereby we might be partakers of the divine nature, having (first) escaped the corruption that is in the world, through lust. I say, we do believe and confess that the active and passive obedience of Christ Jesus affects our salvation throughout, as well from the power and pollution of sin, as from the guilt, He being a conqueror as well as a sacrifice, and both through suffering; yet they that reject his divine gift, so obtained, (and which He has given to them, by which to see their sin and the sinfulness of it, and to repent and turn away from it, and do so no more; and to wait upon God for daily strength to resist the fiery darts of the enemy, and to be comforted through the obedience of faith in and to this divine grace of the Son of God) such do not please God, believe truly in God, nor are they in a state of true Christianity and salvation. Woman, said Christ, to the Samaritan at the well, hadst thou known the gift of God, and who it is that speaketh to thee, etc. People know not Christ, and God, whom to know is life eternal, John 17. because they are ignorant of the gift of God, viz. a measure of the spirit of God that is given to every one to profit with, 1 Cor. 12. 7. which reveals Christ and God to the soul, Chap. 2. Flesh and blood cannot do it, Oxford and Cambridge cannot do it, tongues and philosophy cannot do it: for they that by wisdom knew not God, had these things for their wisdom. They were strong, deep and accurate in them; but, alas! they were clouded, puffed up, and set farther off from the inward and saving knowledge of God, because they fought for it in them, and thought to find God there. But the key of David is another thing, which shuts and no man opens, and opens and no man shuts; and this key have all they that receive the gift of God into their hearts, and it opens to them the knowledge of God and themselves, and gives them a quite other sight, taste and judgment of things than their educational or traditional knowledge afforded them. This is the beginning of the new creation of God, and thus it is we come to be new creatures.

And we are bold to declare, there is no other way like this, by which people can come into Christ, or be true Christians, or receive the advantage that comes by the death and sufferings of the Lord Jesus Christ. Wherefore we say, and upon good authority, even that of our own experience, as well as that of the Scriptures of truth, Christ will prove no saving sacrifice for them, that refuse to obey Him for their example. They that reject the gift, deny the giver instead of themselves for the giver's sake, O that people were wise, that they would consider their latter end, and the things that make for the peace thereof! Why should they perish in a vain hope of life, while death reigns? Of living with God, who live not to Him, nor walk with Him? Awake thou that sleepest in thy sin, or at best, in thy self-righteousness! Awake, I say, and Christ shall give thee life! For He is the Lord from heaven, the quickening spirit, that quickens us, by His spirit, if we do not resist it and quench it by our disobedience, but receive, love and obey it, in all the holy leadings and teachings of it. Rom. 8. 14, 15. To which holy spirit I commend my reader, that he may the better see where He is, and also come to the true belief and advantage of the doings and sufferings of our dear and blessed Lord and Saviour Jesus Christ, who saves from the power and pollution, as well as guilt of sin, all those that hear His knocks, and open the door of their hearts to Him, that he may come in and work a real and thorough reformation in and for them; and so the benefit, virtue and efficacy of His doings and sufferings without us, will come to be livingly and effectually applied and felt, and fellowship with Christ in his death and sufferings known, according to the doctrine of the apostle; which, those that live in that which made him suffer, know not, though they profess to be saved by His death and sufferings. Much more might be said as to this matter, but I must be brief.

§6. To conclude this chapter, we wonder not that we should be mistaken, misconstrued and misrepresented, in what we believe and do to salvation, since our betters have been so treated in the primitive times. Nor indeed is it only about doctrines of religion; for our practice in worship and discipline have had the same success. But this is what I earnestly desire, that however bold people are pleased to make with us, they would not deceive themselves in the great things of their own salvation: that while they would seem to own all to Christ, they are not found disowned of Christ in the last day. Read the 7th of Matthew. It is he that hears Christ, the great word of God, and does what He enjoins, what He commands, and by his blessed example recommends, that is a wise builder, that has founded his house well, and built with good materials, and whose house will stand the last shock and judgment. For which cause we are often plain, close and earnest with people to consider, that Christ came not to save them in, but from their sins; and that they that think to discharge and release themselves of His yoke and burden, His cross and example, and secure themselves, and comple-ment Christ with his having done all for them (while He was wrought little or nothing in them, nor they parted with anything for the love of him) will finally awake in a dreadful surprise, at the sound of the last trumpet, and at this sad and irrevocable sentence, depart from me ye workers of iniquity, I know you not: which terrible end may all timely avoid, by hearkening to wisdom's voice, and turning at her reproof, that she may lead them in the ways of righteousness, and in the midst of the paths of judgment, that their souls may come to inherit substance; even durable riches and righteousness in the kingdom of the Father, world without end.

Chapter. X. §1. *Of the true* worship *of God in what it stands.* §2. *Of the true* ministry, *that is is by inspiration.* §3. *The Scripture plain in that case.* §4. *Christ's ministers,* true witnesses, *they speak what they* know, *not by report.* §5. *Christ's ministers preach* freely, *it is one of their* marks.

§1. As the Lord wrought effectually, by his divine grace, in the hearts of these people, so He thereby brought them to a divine worship and ministry; Christ's words they came to experience, viz. That God was a spirit, and that He would therefore be worshipped in the spirit, and in the truth, and that such worshippers the Father would seek to worship Him. For, bowing to the convictions of the spirit in themselves, in their daily course of living, by which they were taught to eschew that which was made manifest to them to be evil, and to do that which was good, they, in their assembling together, sat down, and waited for the preparation of this holy spirit, both to let them see their states and conditions before the Lord, and to worship him acceptably; and as they were sensible of wants, or shortness, or infirmities, so in the secret of their own hearts, prayer would spring to God, through Jesus Christ, to help, assist and supply: but they did not dare to awake their beloved before His time; or approach the throne of the King of Glory, till He held out His sceptre; or take thought what they should say, or after their own or other men's studied words and forms, for this were to offer strange fire; to pray, but not by the spirit; to ask, but not in the name, that is, in the power of our Lord Jesus Christ, who prayed, as well as spoke, like one having authority, that is, power, a divine energy and force to reach and pierce the heavens, which He gives to all that obey His light, grace and spirit, in their solemn waitings upon Him. So that it is this people's principle, that fire must come from heaven; life and power from God to enable the soul to pour out itself acceptably before Him. And when a coal from his holy altar touches our lips, then can we pray and praise Him as we ought to do. And as this is our principle, and that according to Scripture, so it is, blessed be God, our experience and practice: and therefore it is we are separated from the worships of men, under their several forms, because they do not found it in the operation, motion and assistance of the spirit of Christ, but the appointment, invention and framing of man, both as to matter, words and time. We do not dissent in our own wills, and we dare not comply against his that has called us, and brought us to His own spiritual worship; in obedience to whom we are what we are, in our separation from the diverse ways of worship in the world.

§2. And as our worship stands in the operation of the spirit and truth in our inward parts, as before expressed, so does our ministry. For as the holy testimonies of the servants of God of old were from the operation of His blessed spirit, so must those of His servants be in every age, and that which has not the spirit of Christ for its spring and source, is of man, and not of Christ. Christian ministers are to minister what they receive. This is Scripture; now that which we receive is not our own, less another man's, but the Lord's: so that we are not only not to steal from our neighbours, but we are not to study nor speak our own words. If we are not to study what we are to say before magistrates for ourselves, less are we to study what we are to say for and from God to the people. We are to minister, as the oracles of God; if so, then must we receive from Christ, God's great oracle, what we are to minister. And if we are to minister what we receive, then not what we study, collect, and beat out of our own brains, for that is not the mind of Christ, but our imaginations, and this will not profit the people.

§3. This was recommended to the Corinthians by the apostle Paul, 1 Cor. 14. that they should speak as they were moved, or as anything was revealed to them by the spirit, for the edification of the Church; for, says He, ye may all prophecy; that is, ye may all preach to edification, as anything is revealed to you, for the good of others, and as the spirit giveth utterance. And if the spirit must give Christ's ministers their utterance, then those that are His are careful not to utter anything in His name to the people, without his spirit; and by good consequence, they that go before the true guide, and utter words without the knowledge of the mind of the spirit, are none of Christ's ministers: such, certainly, run, and God has not sent them, and they cannot profit the people. And indeed, how should they, when it is impossible that mere man, with all his parts, arts and acquirements, can turn people from darkenss to light, and from the power of Satan to God, which is the very end and work of the gospel ministry. It must be inspired men, men gifted by God, taught and influenced by his heavenly spirit, that can be qualified for so great, so inward, and so spiritual a work.

§4. Ministers of Christ are His witnesses, and the credit of a witness is that he has heard, seen or handled: and thus the beloved disciple states the truth and authority of their mission and ministry; 1 John 1. 1, 3. That which we have heard, which we have seen with our eyes, which we have looked upon and our hands have handled, that declare we unto you, that your fellowship may be with us, and truly our fellowship is with the Father, and with his Son Jesus Christ. I say, if Christ's ministers are His witnesses, they must know what they speak; that is, they must have experienced, and passed through those states and conditions, they preach of, and practically know those truths they delare of to the people, or they come not in by the door, but over the wall, and are thieves and robbers. He that has the key of David comes in at the door, Christ Jesus, and has his admission and approbation from Him, anointed by Him, the alone high priest of the gospel dispensation. He it is that breathes, and lays His hands upon His own ministers; he anoints them, and recruits their cruise, and renews their horn with oil, that they may have it fresh and fresh, for every occasion and service he calls them to, and engages them in.

§5. Nor is this all, but as they receive freely, freely they give:

they do not teach for hire, divine for money, nor preach for gifts or rewards. It was Christ's holy command to His ministers to give freely, and it is our practice. And truly we cannot but admire that this should be made a fault, and that preaching for hire should not be seen to be one; yea, a mark of false prophets, when it has been so frequently and severely cried out upon, by the true prophets of God in former times. I would not be uncharitable, but the guilty are desired to call to mind, who it was that offered money to be made a minister, and what it was for; if not to get money and make a trade or livelihood by it; and what answer He met with from the apostle Peter, Acts 8. 18, 19, 20. The Lord touch the hearts of those that are giving money to be made ministers, in order to live by their preaching, that they may see what ground it is they build upon, and repent, and turn to the Lord, that they may find mercy, and become living witnesses of His power and goodness in their own souls; so may they be enabled to tell others what God has done for them, which is the root and ground of the true ministry; and this ministry it is that God does bless. I could say much on this subject, but let what has been said suffice at this time, only I cannot but observe that where any religion has a strong temptation of gain to induce men to be ministers, there is great danger of their running faster to that calling than becomes a true gospel minister.

§1. Obj. But does not this sort of ministry and worship, tend to make prople careless, and to raise spiritual pride in others, may it not give an occasion to great mischief and irreligion?

Answ. By no means, for when people are of age, they, of right, expect their inheritances; and the end of all words is to bring people to the great word, and then the promise of God is accomplished, they shall be all taught of me, from the least to the greatest, and in righteousness (pray mark that) they shall be established, and great shall be their peace. To this of the evangelical prophet, the beloved disciple agrees, and gives a full answer to the objection: these things have I written unto you, concerning them that seduce you: but the anointing; which ye have received of Him, abideth in you, and ye need not that any man teach you but as the same anointing teacheth you, of all things, and is truth, and is no lie and even as it hath taught you, ye shall abide in Him. In which, three things are observable. 1st. that he writ his epistle upon an extraordinary occasion, viz. to prevent their delusion. 2dly. that he asserts a nearer and superior minister than himself, viz. The anointing of grace they had received; and that not only in that particular exigency, but in all cases that might attend them. 3dly. that if they did but take heed to the teachings of it, they would have no need of man's directions, or fear of his seducings. At least of no ministry that comes not from the power of the anointing. Though I rather take the apostle in the highest sense of the words: thus also the apostle Paul to the Thessalonians. But as touching brotherly love, ye need not that I write unto you: for ye your selves are taught of God to love one another. 1 Thess. 4. 9. But helps are useful, and a great blessing, if from God, such was John the Baptist's; but remember He pointed all to Christ. 1 John 1. 26. Lo the Lamb of God! I baptize you with water, but he shall baptize you with the Holy Ghost and with fire, Mat. 3. 11. And so the true ministry does. And while people are sensual, and under such an eclipse, by the interposition of sin and satan, God is pleased to send forth his enlightening servants to awaken and turn them from the darkness to the light in themselves, that, through obedience to it, they may come to be children of the light, John. 12. 36. And have their fellowship one with another in it, and an inheritance at last, with the saints in light for ever.

And as it is the way God has taken to call and gather people, so a living and holy ministry is of great advantage to watch over, and build up the young, and comfort and establish the feeble and simple ones. But still I say, the more inward, the less outward: the more people come to be taught immediately of God, by the light of his word and spirit in their hearts, the less need of outward means, read Isa. 16. 19, 20. Which is held by all to be a gospel promise, and the sun and moon there are generally understood to mean the external means in the Church. Compare them with John 1. 13. Rom. 1: 19. 1 Cor. 2. 11. 15. 1 Thess. 4. 9: 1 John 2. 20, 27. Rev. 21. 22, 23, 24. All which places prove what we assert of the sufficiency and glorious privilege of inward and spiritual teachings. And most certainly, as men grow in grace, and know the anointing of the word in themselves, the dispensation will be less in words (though in words) and more in life; and preaching will in great measure be turned into praising, and the worship of God, more into walking with, than talking of God: for that is worship indeed, that bows to his will at all times, and in all places: the truest, the highest worship, man is capable of in this world. And it is the conformity that gives communion, and there is no fellowship with God, no light of his countenance to be enjoyed, no peace and assurance to be had, farther than their obedience to his will, and a faithfulness to his word, according to the manifestation of the light thereof in the heart.

I say, this is the truest and highest state of worship; for set days and places, with all the solemnity of them, were most in request in the weakest dispensation. Altars, ark and temples, Sabbaths and festivals, etc. are not to be found in the writings of the New Testament. There every day is alike, and every place is alike; but if there were a dedication, let it be to the Lord. Thus the apostle, but he plainly shows a state beyond it, for to live (with him) was Christ, and to die was gain; for the life he lived was by the faith of the Son of God, and therefore it was not he that lived, but Christ that lived in him; that is, that ruled, conducted, and bore sway in him, which is the true Christian life, the supersensual life; the life of conversion and regeneration; to which all the dispensations of God, and ministry of His servants have ever tended, as the consummation of God's work for man's happiness. Here every man's a temple, and every family a church, and every place, a meeting-place, and every visit a meeting. And yet a little while and it shall be so yet more and more; and a people the Lord is now preparing to enter into this Sabbath or degree of rest.

Not that we would be thought to undervalue public and solemn meetings: we have them all over the nation where the Lord has called us. Yea, though but two or three of us be in a corner of a country, we meet, as the apostle exhorted the saints of his time, and reproved such as neglected to assemble themselves. But yet show we unto thee, O Reader, a more excellent way of worship: for many may come to those meetings, and go away carnal, dead and dry; but the worshippers in spirit and in truth, whose hearts bow, whose minds adore the eternal God, that is a spirit, in and by His spirit, such as conform to His will, and walk with Him in a spiritual life, they are the true, constant, living and aceptable worshippers; whether it be in meetings or out of meetings; and as with such, all outward assemblies are greatly comfortable, so also do we meet for a public testimony of religion and worship, and for the edification and encouragement of those that are yet young in the truth, and to call and gather others to the knowledge of it, who are yet going astray; and blessed be God, it is not in vain, since many are thereby added to the Church, that we hope and believe shall be saved.

Chapter XI. §1. *Against* Tithes. §2. *Against all* swearing. §3. *Against* war *among Christians.* §4. *Against the* salutations *of the*

times. §5. And for plainess of speech. §6. Against mixed marriages.
§7. And for plainness in apparel etc. *No sports and pastimes after
the manner of this world. §8. Of observing days. §9. Of care of
poor, peace and conversation.*

§1. And as God has been pleased to call us from an human
ministry, so we cannot for conscience sake support and maintain it,
and upon that score, and not out of humour or covetousness, we
refuse to pay tithes, or such-like pretended dues, concerning which,
many books have been writ in our defence: we cannot support
what we cannot approve, but have a testimony against; for thereby
we should be found inconsistent with ourselves.

§2. We dare not swear, because Christ forbids it. Mat. 5. 34, 37.
and James, his true follower. It is needless as well as evil, for the
reason of swearing being untruth, that men's yea was not yea,
swearing was used to awe man to truth speaking, and to give others
satisfaction, that what was sworn, was true. But the true Christians
yea being yea, the end of an oath is answered, and therefore the use
of it is needless, superfluous and cometh of evil. The apostle James
taught the same doctrine, and the primitive Christians practised it,
as may be seen in the *Book of Martyrs*; as also the earliest and best
of the reformers.

§3. We also believe that war ought to cease among the followers
of the Lamb Christ Jesus, who taught His disciples to forgive and
love their enemies, and not to war against them, and kill them.
and that therefore the weapons of His true followers are not carnal
but spiritual; yea mighty, through God, to cut down sin and
wickedness, and dethrone him that is the author thereof. And as
this is the most Christian, so the most rational way; love and
persuation having more force than weapons of war. Nor would the
worst of men easily be brought to hurt those that they really think
love them. It is that love and patience must in the end have the
victory.

§4. We dare not give wordly honour, or use the frequent and
modish salutations of the times, seeing plainly that vanity, pride,
and ostentation, belong to them. Christ also forbade them in His
day, and made the love of them a mark of declension from the
simplicity of purer times; and His disciples and their followers,
were observed to have obeyed their Master's precept. It is not to
distinguish ourselves a party, or out of pride, all-breeding or

humour, but in obedience to the sight and sense we have received from the spirit of Christ, of the evil rise and tendency thereof.

§5. For the same reason we have returned to the first plainness of speech, viz. thou and thee, to a single person, which though men give no other to God, they will hardly endure it from us. It has been a great test upon pride, and shown the blind and weak insides of many. This also is out of pure conscience, whatever people may think or say of us for it. We may be despised, and have been so often, yea, very evilly entreated, but we are now better known, and people better informed. In short, it is also both scripture and grammar, and we have propriety of speech for it, as well as peace in it.

§6. We cannot allow of mixed marriages, that is, to join with such as are not of our society; but oppose and disown them, if at any time any of our profession so grosly err from the rule of their communion; yet restore them upon sincere repentance, but not disjoin them. The book I wrote of the rise and progress of the people called Quakers, is more full and express herein.

§7. Plainess in apparel and furniture is another testimony peculiar to us, in the degree we have bore it to the world: as also few words, and being at a word. Likewise temperance in food, and abstinence from the recreations and pastimes of the world: all which we have been taught, by the spirit of our Lord Jesus Christ, to be according to godliness; and therefore we have long exhorted all, that their moderation may be known unto all men, for that the Lord was at hand, to enter into judgment with us for every intemperance of excess; and herein we hope we have been no ill examples, or scandal unto any that have a due consideration of things.

§8. We cannot, in conscience to God, observe Holy Days, (so called) the public fasts and feasts, because of their human institution and ordination, and that they have not a divine warrant, but are appointed in the will of man.

§9. Lastly, we have been led by this good spirit of our Lord Jesus Christ of which I have treated in this discourse, according to primitive practice, to have a due care over one another, for the preservation of the whole society, in a conversation more suitable to their holy profession.

First, in respect to a strict walking both towards those that are without, and those that are within; that their conversation in the world, and walking in and towards the Church, may be blameless.

That as they may be strict in the one, so they may be faithful in the other.

Secondly, that collections be made to supply the wants of the poor, and that care be taken of widows and orphans, and such as are helpless, as well in counsel as about substance.

Thirdly, that all such as are intended to marry, if they have parents, or are under the direction of guardians or trustees, are obliged, first, to declare to them their intention, and have their consent before they propose it to one another, and the meeting they relate to, who are also careful to examine their clearness, and being satisfied with it, they are by them allowed to solemnize their marriage in a public select meeting, for that purpose appointed, and not otherwise : whereby all clandestine and indirect marriages are prevented among us.

Fourthly, and to the end that this good order may be observed for the comfort and edification of the society, in the ways of truth and soberness ; select meetings (of care and business) are fixed in all parts, where we inhabit, which are held monthly, and which resolve into quarterly meetings, and those into one yearly meeting, for our better communication one with another, in those things that maintain piety and charity ; that God, who by his grace, has called us to be a people, to his praise, may have it from us, through his beloved Son, and our ever-blessed and only Redeemer, Jesus Christ, for He is worthy, worthy, now, and ever. Amen.

Thus, reader, thou hast the character of the people called Quakers, in their doctrine, worship, ministry, practice and discipline : compare it with Scripture, and primitive example and we hope thou wilt find, that this short discourse hath, in good measure, answered the title of it, viz.

Primitive Christianity Revived, in the Principles and Practice of the People called Quakers.

A Brief ACCOUNT of the *Rise* and *Progress* of the People, call'd QUAKERS.

IN

Which their Fundamental Principle, Doctrines, Worship, Ministry and Discipline are Plainly Declared, *&c.*

By W. PENN.

AN EPISTLE TO THE READER

Reader, this following account of the people called Quakers, etc. *was written in the fear and love of God: first as a standing testimony to that ever blessed truth, in the inward parts, with which God, in my youthful time, visited my soul, and for the sense and love of which I was made willing, in no ordinary way, to relinquish the honours and interests of the world. Secondly, as a testimony for that despised people, that God has in his great mercy gathered and united by his own blessed Spirit in the Holy profession of it; whose fellowship I value above all wordly creatness. Thirdly, in love and honour to the memory of that worthy servant of God, G. Fox, the first instrument therof, and therefore styled by me that great and blessed apostle of our day. As this gave birth to what is here presented to thy view, in the first edition of it, by way of preface to G. F.'s excellent journal; so the consideration of the present usefulness of the following account of the people called* Quakers, *(by reason of the unjust reflections of some adversaries that once walked under the profession of Friends) and the exhortations that conclude it, prevailed with me to consent that it should be republished in a smaller volume; knowing also full well that great books, especially in these days, grow burdensome, both to the pockets and minds of too many; and that there are not a few that desire (so it be at an easy rate) it be informed about this people, that have been so much every where spoken against: But, blessed be the God and Father of our* Lord Jesus Christ, *it is upon no worse grounds than it was said of the old time, of the primitive Christians; as I hope will appear to every sober and considerate Reader. Our business after all the ill usage we have met with, being the realities*

*of religion, an effectual change before our last and great change:
that all may come to an inward, sensible and experimental knowledge of God, through the convictions and operations of the light
and spirit of Christ in themselves; the sufficient and blessed means
given to all, that threeby all may come savingly to know the only
true God and Jesus Christ whom He hath sent to enlighten and
redeem the world: which knowledge is indeed* eternal life. *And that
thou, Reader, mayest obtain it, is the earnest desire of him that is
ever*

    Thine in so good a work, W. P.

A BRIEF ACCOUNT, ETC.
CHAPTER I

*Containing a brief account of diverse dispensations of God in the
world, to the time He was pleased to raise this despised people,
called* Quakers.

Diverse have been the dispensations of God since the creation of
the world unto the sons of men; But the great end of all of them
has been the renown of His own excellent name in the creation and
restoration of man: man, the emblem of Himself, as a God on
earth, and the glory of all His works. The world began with
innocency: all was then good that the good God had made: and as
He blessed the works of His hands, so their natures and harmony
magnified Him their Creator. Then the morning stars sang together
for joy, and all parts of His works said Amen, to His law. Not a jar
in the whole frame; but man in paradise, the beasts in the field, the
fowl in the air, the fish in the sea, the lights in the heavens, the fruits
of the earth; yea, the air, the earth, the water and fire worshipped,
praised and exalted His power, wisdom and goodness. O holy
Sabbath, O holy day to the Lord!

  But this happy state lasted not long: For man, the crown and
glory of the whole, being tempted to aspire above his place,
unhappily yielded against command and duty, as well as interest
and felicity, and so fell below it; lost the divine image, the wisdom,
power and purity he was made in. By which, being no longer fit for
paradise, he was expelled that garden of God, his proper dwelling
and residence and was driven out, as a poor vagabond, from the
presence of the Lord, to wander in the earth, the habitation of
beasts.

Yet God that made him had pity on him; for he seeing man was deceived, and that it was not of malice, or an original presumption in him, but through the subtility of the serpent (who had first fallen from his own state, and by the mediation of the woman, man's own nature and companion, whom the serpent had first deluded) in his infinite goodness and wisdom found out a way to repair the breach, recover the loss, and restore fallen man again by a Nobler and more Excellent Adam, promised to be born of a woman; that as by means of a woman the evil one had prevailed upon man, by a woman also He should come into the world, who would prevail against him and bruise his head, and deliver man from his power: And which, in a signal manner, by the dispensation of the Son of God in the flesh, in the fullness of time, was personally and fully accomplished by Him, and in Him, as man's Saviour and Redeemer.

But His power was not limited, in the manifestation of it, to that time; for both before and since his blessed manifestation in the flesh, He has been the light and life, the rock and strength, of all that ever feared God: was present with them in their temptations, followed them in their travels and afflictions, and supported and carried them through and over the difficulties that have attended them in their earthly pilgrimage. By this Abel's heart excelled Cain's, and Seth obtained the pre-eminence, and Enoch walked with God. It was this that strove with the old world, and which they rebelled against, and which sanctified and instructed Noah to salvation.

But the outward dispensation that followed the benighted state of man, after his fall, especially among the patriarchs, was generally that of angels, as the scriptures of the Old Testament do in many places express, as to Abraham, Jacob, etc. The next was that of the law by Moses, which was also delivered by angels, as the apostle tells us. This dispensation was much outward, and suited to a low and servile state; called therefore by the apostle Paul, that of a schoolmaster, which was to point out and prepare that people to look and long for the Messiah, who would deliver them from the servitude of a ceremonious and imperfect dispensation, by knowing the realities of those mysterious representations in themselves, in this time the law was written on stone, the temple built with hands, attended with an outward priesthood and external rites and ceremonies, that were shadows of the good things that were to come, and were only to serve till the seed came, or the more excellent and general manifestation of Christ, to whom was the promise, and to all men only in Him, in whom it was yea and Amen, even life from death, immortality and eternal life.

This the prophets foresaw; and comforted the believing Jews in the certainty of it; which was the top of the Mosaical dispensation, and which ended in John's ministry, the forerunner of the Messiah, as John's was finished in him, the fullness of all. And then God, that at sundry times, and in diverse manners had spoken to the fathers by His servants the prophets, spoke to men by His Son Christ Jesus, who is heir of all things; being the gospel day, which is the dispensation of sonship; bringing in thereby a nearer testament and a better hope; even the beginning of the glory of the latter days, and of the restitution of all things; yea, the restoration of the kingdom unto Israel.

Now the spirit that was more sparingly communicated in former dispensations began to be poured forth upon all flesh, according to the prophet Joel, and the light that shined in darkness, or but dimly before, the most gracious God caused to shine out of darkness, and the day star began to arise in the hearts of believers, giving unto them the knowledge of God in the face (or appearance) of His Son Christ Jesus.

Now the poor in spirit, the meek, the true mourners, the hungry and thirsty after righteousness, the peace-makers, the pure in heart, the merciful and persecuted, came more especially in remembrance before the Lord, and were sought out and blessed by Israel's true shepherd. Old Jeruslaem with her children grew out of date, and the New Jeruslaem into request, the mother of the sons of the gospel day. Wherefore no more at old Jerusalem, nor at the mountain of Samaria, will God be worshipped above other places; for, behold, He is, by His own Son, declared and preached a spirit, and that He will be known as such, and worshipped in the spirit and in the truth! He will now come nearer than of old time, and He will write his law in the heart, and put his fear and spirit in the inward parts, according to His promise. Then signs, types and shadows flew away, the day having discovered their insufficiency in not reaching to the inside of the cup, to the cleansing of the conscience; and all elementary services were expired in and by Him that is the substance of all.

And to this great and blessed end of the dispensation of the Son of God, did the apostles testify, whom he had chosen and anointed by his spirit, to turn the Jews from their prejudice and superstition, and the Gentiles from their vanity and idolatry, to Christ's light and spirit that shined in them; that they might be quickened from the sins and trespasses in which they were dead, to serve the living God, in the newness of the spirit of life, and walk as children of the light, and of the day, even the day of holiness: for such put on Christ, the light of the world, and make no more provision for the flesh, to fulfil the lusts thereof. So that the light, spirit, and grace, that come by Christ, and appear in man were that divine principle, the apostles ministred from and turned people's minds unto, and in which they gathered and built up the churches of Christ in their day. For which cause they advise them not to quench the Spirit, but to wait for the spirit, and speak by the spirit, and pray by the spirit, and walk in the spirit too, as that which approved them, the truly begotten children of God; born not of flesh and blood, or of the will of man, but of the will of God; by doing His will, and denying their own, by drinking of Christ's cup, and being baptized with His baptism of self-denial; the way and path that all the heirs of life have ever trod to blessedness. But alas! even in the apostles' days, those bright stars of the first magnitude of the gospel light, some clouds, foretelling an eclipse of this primitive glory began to appear, and several of them gave early caution of it to the Christians of their time, that even then there was, and yet would be more and more, a falling away from the power of godliness, and the purity of that spiritual dispensation, by such as sought to make a fair show in the flesh, but with whom the offence of the cross ceased. Yet with this comfortable conclusion, that they saw beyond it a more glorious time than ever to the true Church. Their fight was true, and what they foretold to the churches, gathered by them in the name and power of Jesus, came to pass: for Christians degenerated apace into outsides, as days and meats, and divers other ceremonies. And which was worse, they fell into strife and contention about them; separating one from another, then envying, and, as they had power, persecuting one another to the shame and scandal of their common Christianity, and grievous stumbling and offence of the heathen; among whom the Lord had so long and so marvellously preserved them. And having got at last the worldly power into their hands, by kings and emperors embracing the Christian profession, they changed what they could, the kingdom of Christ, which is not of this world, into a worldly kingdom; or at least styled the worldly kingdom that was in their hands the Kingdom of Christ, and so they became worldly, and not true Christians. Then humane inventions and novelties, both in doctrine and worship, crowded fast into the church; a door opened thereunto, by the grossness and carnality that appeared then among the generality of Christians who had long since left the guidance of God's meek and heavenly spirit, and given themselves up to superstition, will-worship, and voluntary humility. And as superstition is blind, so it is heady and furious, for all must stoop to its blind and boundless zeal or perish by it: in the name of the spirit, persecuting the very appearance of the spirit of God in others, and opposing that in others, which they resisted in themselves, viz. the light, grace and spirit of the Lord Jesus Christ; but always under the notion of innovation, heresy, schism, or some such plausible name. Though Christianity allows of no name, or pretence whatever, for persecuting of any man for matters of mere religion, being in its very nature, meek, gentle, and forbearing; and consists of faith, hope and charity, which no persecutor can have, whilst he remains a persecutor; in that a man cannot believe well, or hope well, or have a charitable or tender regard to another, whilst he would violate his mind, or persecute his body for matters of faith or worship towards his God.

Thus the false church sprang up, and mounted the chair: but though she lost her nature, she would needs keep her good name of the Lamb's bride, the truth church, and mother of the faithful: constraining all to receive her mark, either in their forehead, or right hand; that is, publicly, or privately. But indeed and in truth she was mystery Babylon, the mother of harlots, mother of those that with all their show and outside of religion, were adulterated and gone from the spirit, nature and life of Christ, and grown vain, worldly, ambitious, covetous, cruel, etc. which are the fruits of the flesh, and not of the spirit.

Now it was that the true Church fled into the wilderness, that is, from superstition and violence, to a retired, solitary, and lonely state; hidden, and as it were, out of sight of men, though not out of the world. Which shows that her wanted visibility was not essential to the being of a true church in the judgment of the Holy Ghost; she being as true a church in the wilderness, tho' not as visible and lustrious as when she was in her former splendor of profession. In this state many attempts she made to return, but the waters were yet too high, and her way blocked up, and many of her excellent children, in several nations and centuries, fell by the cruelty of superstition, because they would not fall from their faithfulness to the truth.

The last age did set some steps towards it, both as to doctrine, worship and practice. But practice quickly failed; for wickedness flowed in a little time, as well among the professors of the reformation, as those they reformed from; so that by the fruits of conversation they were not to be distinguished. And the children of the reformers, if not the reformers themselves, betook themselves, very early, to earthly policy and power, to uphold and carry on their reformation that had been begun with spiritual weapons; which I have often thought, has been one of the greatest reasons the reformation made no better progress, as to the life and soul of religion. For whilst the reformers were lowly and spiritually minded, and trusted in God, and looked to him, and lived in his fear, and consulted not with flesh and blood, nor fought deliverance in their own way, there were daily added to the church, such as one might reasonably say should be saved: For they were not so careful to be safe from persecution, as to be faithful and inoffensive under it: being more concerned to spread the truth by their faith and patience in tribulation, than to get the worldly power out of their hands that inflicted those sufferings upon them: and it will be well if the Lord suffer them not to fall, by the very same way they took to stand.

In doctrine they were in some things short; in other things, to avoid one extreme they ran into another: And for worship, there was for the generality, more of man in it than of God. they owned the spirit, inspiration and revelation indeed, and grounded their separation and reformation upon the sense and understanding they received from it, in the reading of the Scriptures of truth. And this was their plea, the Scripture is the text, the Spirit the interpreter, and that to every one for himself. But yet there was too much of human invention, tradition and art that remained both in praying and preaching; and of wordly authority, and worldly greatness in their ministers; especially in this kingdom, Sweden, Denmark, and some parts of Germany. God was therefore pleased in England to shift us from vessel to vessel: and the next remove humbled the ministry, so that they were more strict in preaching, devout in praying, and zealous for keeping the Lord's Day, and catechizing of children and servants, and repeating at home in their families, what they had heard in public. But even as these grew into power, they were not only for whipping some out, but others into the temple: and they appeared rigid in their spirits, rather than severe in their lives, and more for a party than for piety: which brought forth another people, that were yet more retired and select.

They would not communicate at large, or in common with

others; but formed churches among themselves of such as could give some account of their conversion, at least, of very promising experiences of the work of God's grace upon their hearts; and under mutual agreements and covenants of fellowship they kept together. These people were somewhat of a softer temper, and seemed to recommend religion by the charms of its love, mercy and goodness, rather than by the terrors of its judgments and punishments; by which the former party would have awed people into religion.

They also allowed greater liberty to prophecy than those before them; for they admitted any member to speak or pray, as well as their pastor, whom they always chose, and not the civil magistrate. If such found anything pressing upon them to either duty, even without the distinction of clergy or laity, persons of any trade had their liberty, be it never so low and mechanical. But alas! even these people suffered great loss: for tasting of worldly empire, and the favour of princes and the gain that ensued, they degenerated but too much. For though they had cried down national churches and ministry, and maintenance too, some of them, when it was their own turn to be tried, fell under the weight of worldly honour and advantage, got into profitable parsonages too much, and outlived and contracted their own principles: and, which was yet worse, turned, some of them, absolute persecutors of other men for God's sake, that but so lately came themselves out of the furnace; which drove many a step farther, and that was into the water: another baptism, as believing they were not scripturally baptized; and hoping to find that presence and power of God in submitting to this watery ordinance, which they desired and wanted.

These people also made profession of neglecting, if not renouncing and censuring, not only the necessity, but use of all human learning, as to the ministry; and all other qualifications to it, besides the helps and gifts of the spirit of God, and those natural and common to men. And for a time they seemed like John of old, a burning and a shining light to other societies.

They were very diligent, plain and serious; strong in scripture, and bold in profession; bearing much reproach and contradiction. But that which others fell by proved their snare. For worldly power spoiled them too; who had enough of it to try them what they would do if they had more: and they rested also too much upon their watery dispensation, instead of passing on more fully to that of the fire and Holy Ghost, which was His baptism, who came with a fan in His hand, that He might thoroughly (and not in part only) purge His floor, and take away the dross and the tin of His people, and make a man finer than gold. Withal, they grew high, rough, and self-righteous; opposing farther attainment: too much forgetting the day of their infancy and littleness, which gave them something of a real beauty; insomuch that many left them, and all visible churches and societies, and wandered up and down, as sheep without a shepherd, and as doves without the mates; seeking their beloved but could not find Him (as their souls desired to know Him) whom their souls loved above their chiefest joy.

These people were called seekers by some, and the family of love by others; because, as they came to the knowledge of one another, they sometimes met together, not formally to pray or preach at appointed times or places, in their own wills, as in times past they were accustomed to do; but waited together in silence, and as any thing rose in any one of their minds that they thought savoured of a divine spring, they sometimes spoke. But so it was, that some of them not keeping in humility, and in fear of God, after the abundance of revelation, were exalted above measure; and for want of staying their minds in a humble dependence upon Him that opened their understandings to see great things in His law, they ran out in their own imaginations, and mixing them with those divine openings, brought forth a monstrous birth, to the scandal of those that feared God, and waited daily in the temple, not made with hands, for the consolation of Israel; the Jew inward, and circumcision in spirit.

This people obtained the name of Ranters, from their extravagant discourses and practices. For they interpreted Christ's fulfilling of the law for us, to be a discharging of us from any obligation and duty the law required of us, instead of the condemnation of the law for sins past, upon faith and repentance: and that now it was no sin to do that which before it was a sin to commit; the slavish fear of the law being taken off by Christ, and all things good that man did, if he did but do them with the mind and persuasion that it was so. Insomuch that divers fell into gross and enormous practices; pretending in excuse thereof; that they could, without evil, commit the same act which was sin in another to do; thereby distinguishing between the action and the evil of it, by the direction of the mind, and intention in the doing of it. Which was to make sin superabound by the aboundings of grace, and to turn from the grace of God into wantonness; a securer way of sinning than before: as if

Christ came not to save us from our sins, but in our sins; not to take away sin, but that we might sin more freely at his cost, and brought them to an utter and lamentable loss as to their eternal state; and they grew very troublesome to the better sort of people, and furnished the looser with an occasion to profane.

CHAPTER II

Of the rise of the people, their fundamental principle, and doctrine, and practice, in twelve points resulting from it: Their progress and sufferings: An expostulation with England thereupon.

It was about that very time, as you may see in G. H.'s *Annals*, that the eternal, wise, and good God was pleased, in His infinite love to honour and visit this benighted and bewildered nation, with His glorious day spring from on high; yea, with a most sure and certain sound of the word of light and life, through the testimony of a chosen vessel, to an effectual and blessed purpose, can many thousands say, Glory be to the name of the Lord for ever.

For as it reached the conscience and broke the heart, and brought many to a sense and search, so that which people had been vainly seeking without, with much pains and cost, they by this ministry, found within, where it was they wanted what they fought for, viz. The right way to peace with God. For they were directed to the light of Jesus Christ within them, as the seed and leaven of the kingdom of God; near all because in all, and God's talent to all: a faithful and true witness, and just monitor in every bosom. The gift and grace of God, to life and salvation, that appears to all, though few regard it. This the traditional Christian conceited of himself, and strong in his own will and righteousness, overcome with blind zeal and passion, either despised as a low and common thing, or opposed as a novelty, under many hard names, and opprobrious terms, denying, in his ignorant and angry mind, any fresh manifestations of God's power and spirit in man, in these days, though never more needed to make true Christians. Not unlike those Jews of old, that rejected the Son of God, at the very same time that they blindly professed to wait for the Messiah to come; because, alas! He appeared not among them according to their carnal mind and expectation.

This brought forth many abusive books, which filled the greater sort with envy, and lesser with rage; and made the way and progress of this blessed testimony straight and narrow indeed to those that received it. However, God owned His own work, and this testimony did effectually reach, gather, comfort and establish the weary and heavy laden, the hungry and thirsty, the poor and needy, the mournful and sick, of many maladies, that had spent all upon physicians of no value, and waited for relief from Heaven; help only from above: seeing, upon a serious trial of all things, nothing else would do but Christ Himself; the light of His countenance, a touch of His garment, and help from His hand; who cured the poor woman's issue, raised the centurion's servant, the widow's son, the ruler's daughter, and Peter's mother: and like her, they no sooner felt His power and efficacy upon their souls, but they gave up to obey Him in a testimony to His power; and that with resigned wills and faithful hearts, through all mockings, contradictions, confiscations, beatings, prisons, and many other jeopardies that attended them for His Blessed Name's Sake.

And truly they were very many, and very great; so that in all human probability they must have been swallowed up quick of the proud and boisterous waves that swelled and beat against them, but that the God of all their tender mercies was with them in His glorious authority; so that the hills often fled, and the mountains melted before the power that filled them; working mightily for them, as well as in them, one ever following the other. By which they saw plainly, to their exceeding great confirmation and comfort, that all things were possible with Him with whom they had to do. And that the more that which God required seemed to cross man's wisdom, and expose them to man's wrath, the more God appeared to help and carry them through all to his glory.

Insomuch that if ever any people could say in truth, Thou art our sun and our shield, our rock and sanctuary; and by Thee we have leaped over a wall, and by Thee we have run through a troop, and by Thee we have put the armies of the aliens to flight, these people had right to say it. And as God had delivered their souls of the wearisom burdens of sin and vanity, and enriched their poverty of spirit, and satisfied their great hunger and thirst after eternal righteousness, and filled them with the good things of His own house, and made them stewards of His manifold gifts; so they went forth to all quarters of these nations, to declare to the inhabitants thereof, what God had done for them; what they had found, and where and how they had found it, viz. the way to peace with God:

inviting all to come, and see, and taste, for themselves, the truth of what they declared unto them.

And as their testimony was to the principle of God in man, the precious pearl and leaven of the kingdom, as the only blessed means appointed of God, to quicken, convince and sanctify man; so they opened to them what it was in itself, and what it was given to them for: how they might know it from their own spirit, and that of the subtle appearance of the evil one: and what it would do for all those whose minds should be turned off from the vanity of the world, and its lifeless ways and teachers, and adhere to his blessed light in themselves, which discovers and condemns sin in all its appearances, and shows how to overcome it, if minded and obeyed in its holy manifestations and convictions: giving power to such to avoid and resist those things that do not please God, and to grow strong in love, faith, and good works. That so man, whom sin hath made as a wilderness, overrun with briars and thorns, might become as the garden of God, cultivated by his divine power, and replenished with the most virtuous and beautiful plants of God's own right-hand planting, to his eternal praise.

But these experimental preachers of glad tidings of God's truth and kingdom could not run when they list, or pray or preach when they pleased, but as Christ their Redeemer prepared and moved them by His own blessed spirit, for which they waited in their services and meetings, and spoke as that gave them utterance; and which was as those having authority, and not like the dreaming, dry and formal Pharisees. And so it plainly appeared to the serious-minded, whose spiritual eye the Lord Jesus had in any measure opened: so that to one was given the word of exhortation, to another the word of reproof, to another the word of consolation, and all by the same Spirit, and in the good order thereof, to the convincing and edifying of many.

And truly they waxed strong and bold through faithfulness; and by the power and spirit of the Lord Jesus became very fruitful; thousands, in a short time, being turned to the truth in the inward parts, through their testimony, in ministry and sufferings: insomuch as in most counties, and many of the considerable towns of England, meetings were settled, and daily there were added such as should be saved. For they were diligent to plant and to water, and the Lord blessed their labours with an exceeding great increase; notwithstanding all the opposition made to their blessed progress, by false rumours, calumnies and bitter persecutions; not only from the powers of the earth, but from every one that lifted to injure and abuse them: so that they seemed indeed to be as poor sheep appointed to the slaughter, and as a people killed all the day long.

It were fitter for a volume than a preface, but so much as to repeat the contents of their cruel sufferings from professors as well as from profane, and from magistrates as well as the rabble: that it may be said of this abused and despised people, they went forth weeping and sowed in tears, bearing testimony to the precious seed, even the seed of the kingdom, which stands not in words; the finest, the highest that man's wit can use, but in power: the power of Christ Jesus, to whom God the Father hath given all power in Heaven and in earth, that He might rule angels above, and men below. Who impowered them, as their work witnesseth, by the many that were turned, through their ministry, from darkness to the light, and out of the broad into the narrow way of life and peace; bringing people to a weighty, serious and God-like conversation; the practice of that doctrine which they taught.

And as without this secret divine power there is no quickening and regenerating of dead souls, so the want of this generating and begetting power and life is the cause of the little fruit that the many ministries that have been and are in the world, bring forth. O that both ministers and people were sensible of this! My soul is often troubled for them, and sorrow and mourning compass me about for their sakes. O that they were wise! O that they would consider, and lay to heart the things that truly and substantially make for their lasting peace!

Two things are to be considered, the doctrine they taught, and the example they led among all people. I have already touched upon their fundamental principle, which is as the cornerstone of their fabric: and indeed, to speak eminently and properly, their characteristic or main distinguishing point or principle viz. the light of Christ within, as God's gift for man's salvation. This, I say, is as the root of the goodly tree of doctrines that grew and branched out from it, which I shall now mention in their natural and experimental order.

First, repentance from dead works to serve the living God. Which comprehends three operations. First, a sight of sin. Secondly, a sense and godly sorrow for sin. Thirdly, an amendment for the time to come. This was the repentance they preached and pressed, and a natural result from the principle they turned all people unto. For of light came sight; and of sight came sense and sorrow; and of sense and sorrow, came amendment of life. Which doctrine of repentance leads to justification; that is, forgiveness of the sins that are past, through Christ the alone propitiation, and the sanctification or purgation of the soul, from the defiling nature and habits of sin present, by the spirit of Christ in the soul, which is justification in the complete sense of that word: comprehending both justification from the guilt of the sins that are past, as if they had never been committed, through the love and mercy of God in Christ Jesus, and the creatures being made inwardly just through the cleansing and sanctifying power and spirit of Christ revealed in the soul; which is commonly called sanctification. But that none can come to know Christ to be their sacrifice that reject him as their sanctifier. The end of His coming being to save His people from the nature and defilement, as well as guilt of sin; and that therefore those that resist His light and spirit, make His coming and offering of none effect to them.

From hence sprang a second doctrine they were led to declare as the mark of the price of the high calling to all true Christians, viz. perfection from sin, according to the scriptures of truth; which testify it to be the end of Christ's coming, and the nature of His Kingdom, and for which His spirit was and is given viz. to be perfect as our heavenly Father is perfect, and holy because God is holy. And this the apostles laboured for, that the Christians should be sanctified throughout in body, soul and spirit, but they never held a perfection in wisdom and glory in this life, or from natural infirmities, or death, as some have, with a weak or ill mind, imagined and insinuated against them.

This they called a redeemed state, regeneration, or the new-birth: teaching every where according to their foundation, that without this work were known, there was no inheriting the kingdom of God.

Thirdly, this leads to an acknowledgement of eternal rewards and punishments, as they have good reason; for else, of all people, certainly they must be the most miserable; who, for above forty years, have been exceeding great sufferers for their profession; and, in some cases, treated worse than the worst of men; yea, as the refuse and off-scouring of all things.

This was the purport of their doctrine and ministry; which, for the most part, is what other professors of Christianity pretend to hold in words and forms, but not in the power of godliness; which, generally speaking, has been long lost by men's departing from that principle and seed of life that is in man, and which man has not regarded, but lost the sense of; and in and by which he can only be quickened in his mind to serve the living God in newness of life. For as the life of religion was lost, and the generality lived and worshipped God after their own wills, and not after the will of God, nor the mind of Christ, which stood in the works and fruits of the Holy Spirit; so that which they pressed, was not notion, but experience; no formality, but godliness; as being sensible in themselves, through the work of God's righteous judgments, that without holiness no man shall ever see the Lord, with comfort.

Besides these general doctrines, as the larger branches, there sprang forth several particular doctrines that did exemplify and farther explain the truth and efficacy of the general doctrine before observed, in their lives and examples. As,

1. Communion and loving one another. This is a noted mark in the mouth of all sorts of people concerning them. They will meet, they will help and stick one to another, whence it is common to hear some say, look how the Quakers love and take care of one another. Others, less moderate, will say, the Quakers love none but themselves: and if loving one another, and having an intimate communion in religion, and constant care to meet to worship God, and help one another, be any mark of primitive Christianity, they had it, blessed be the Lord, in an ample manner.

2. To love enemies. This they both taught and practised. For they did not only refuse to be revenged for injuries done them, and condemned it as of an unchristian spirit, but they did freely forgive; yea, help and relieve those that had been cruel to them, when it was in their power to have been even with them: of which many and singular instances might be given: endeavouring, through faith and patience, to overcome all injustice and oppression, and preaching this doctrine as Christian, for others to follow.

3. Another was, the sufficiency of truth-speaking, according to Christ's own form of sound words, of yea, yea, and nay, nay, among Christians, without swearing; both from Christ's express prohibition, to swear at all, Mat. 5. and for that they being under the tie and bond of truth in themselves, there was no necessity for an oath; and it would be a reproach to their Christian veracity to assure their truth by such an extraordinary way of speaking; simple and uncompounded answers, as yea and nay, (without asseverations, attestations, or supernatural vouchers) being most suitable to

evangelical righteousness. But offering at the same time to be punished to the full, for false-speaking, as others for perjury, if ever guilty of it: and hereby they exclude with all true, all false and profane swearing; for which the land did and doth mourn, and the great God was, and is not a little offended with it.

4. Not fighting, but suffering, is another testimony peculiar to this people: they affirm that Christianity teacheth people to beat their swords into ploughshares, and their spears into pruning hooks, and to learn war no more, that so the wolf may lie down with the lamb, and the lion with the calf, and nothing that destroys be entertained in the hearts of people: Exhorting them to employ their zeal against sin, and turn their anger against Satan, and no longer war one against another; because all wars and fightings come of men's own hearts' lusts, according to the apostle James, and not of the meek spirit of Christ Jesus, who is captain of another warfare, and which is carried on with other weapons. Thus, as truth-speaking succeeded swearing, so faith and patience succeeded fighting, in the doctrine and practice of this people. Nor ought they for this to be obnoxious to civil government, since if they cannot fight for it, neither can they fight against it; which is no mean security to any state. Nor is it reasonable that people should be blamed for not doing more for others than they can do for themselves. And, Christianity set aside, if the costs and fruits of war were well considered, peace, with all its inconveniences, is generally preferable. But though they were not for fighting, they were for submitting to government; and that, not only for fear, but for conscience-sake; where government doth not interfere with conscience; believing it to be an ordinance of God, and where it is justly administered, a great benefit to mankind. Though it has been their lot, through blind zeal in some, and interest in others, to have felt the strokes of it with greater weight and rigour than any other persuasion in this age; whilst they of all others, religion set aside, have given the civil magistrate the least occasion of trouble in the discharge of his office.

5. Another part of the character of this people was, and is, they refuse to pay tithes or maintenance to a national ministry; and that for two reasons: the one is they believe all compelled maintenance, even to gospel-ministers, to be unlawful, because expressly contrary to Christ's command, who said, freely you have received, freely give: at least, that the maintenance of gospel ministers should be free, and not forced. The other reason of their refusal is because

those ministers are not gospel ones, in that the Holy Ghost is not their foundation, but human arts and parts. So that it is not matter of humour or sullenness, but pure conscience towards God that they cannot help to support national ministries where they dwell, which are but too much and too visibly become ways of worldly advantage and preferment.

6. Not to respect persons was and is another of their doctrines and practices, for which they were often buffetted and abused. They affirmed it to be sinful to give flattering titles, or to use vain gestures and compliments of respect. Though to virtue and authority they ever made a difference; but after their plain and homely manner, yet sincere and substantial way: well remembering the examples of Mordecai and Elihu; but more especially the command of their Lord and Master Jesus Christ, who forbade his followers to call men Rabbi, which implies Lord or Master; also the fashionable greetings and salutations of those times; that so self-love and honour, to which the proud mind of man is incident, in his fallen estate, might not be indulged but rebuked. And though this rendered their conversation disagreeable, yet they that will remember what Christ said to the Jews, how can you believe in me, who receive honour one of another will abate of their resentment, if his doctrine has any credit with them.

7. They also used the plain language of thee and thou, to a single person, what ever was his degree among men. And indeed the wisdom of God, was much seen in bringing forth this people, in so plain an appearance. For it was a close and distinguishing test upon the spirits of those they came among; showing their insides, and what predominated, notwithstanding their high and great profession of religion. This among the rest sounded so harsh to many of them, and they took it so ill, that they would say, Thou me, thou my Dog! If thou thoust me, I'll thou thy teeth down thy throat; forgetting the language they use to God in their own prayers, and the common style of the Scriptures, and that it is an absolute and essential propriety of speech. And what good, alas! had their religion done them, who were so sensibly touched with indignation for the use of this plain, honest and true speech?

8. They recommended silence by their example, having very few words upon all occasions. They were at a word in dealing: nor could their customers, with many words tempt them from it, having more regard to truth than custom, to example than gain. They sought solitude; but when in company, they would neither use, nor

willingly hear unnecessary, as well as unlawful discourses: whereby they preserved their minds, pure and undisturbed from unprofitable thoughts, and diversions. Nor could they humour the custom of good night, good morrow, good speed; for they knew the night was good, and the day was good, without wishing of either; and that in the other expression, the holy name of God was too lightly and unthankfully used, and therefore taken in vain. Besides, they were words and wishes of course, and are usually as little meant, as are love and service in the custom of cap and knee; and superfluity in those, as well as in other things was burdensome to them; and therefore they did not only decline to use them, but found themselves often pressed to reprove the practice.

9. For the same reason they forbore drinking to people or pledging of them, as the manner of the world is: a practice that is not only unnecessary, but they thought evil in the tendencies of it, being a provocation to drink more than did people good, as well as that it was in it self vain and heathenish.

10. Their way of marriage is peculiar to them; and shows a distinguishing care, above other societies, professing Christianity. They say that marriage is an ordinance of God, and that God only can rightly join man and woman in marriage. Therefore they use neither priest or magistrate; but the man or woman concerned, take each other as husband and wife, in the presence of divers credible witnesses, promising to each other, with God's assistance, to be loving and faithful in that relation, till death shall separate them. But antecedent to this, they first present themselves to the monthly meeting for the affairs of the church where they reside; there declaring their intentions, to take one another as husband and wife, if the said meeting have nothing material to object against it. They are constantly asked the necessary questions, as in case of parents or guardians, if they have acquainted them with their intention, and have their consent, etc. The method of the meeting is to take a minute thereof, and to appoint proper persons to enquire of their conversation and clearness from all others, and whether they have discharged their duty to their parents or guardians; and to make report thereof to the next monthly meeting, where the same parties are desired to give their attendance. In case it appears they have proceeded orderly, the meeting passes their proposal, and so records it in their meeting book. And in case the woman be a widow, and hath children, due care is there taken, that provision also be made by her for the orphans, before the meeting

pass the proposals of marriage: Advising the parties concerned, to appoint a convenient time and place, and to give fitting notice to their relations, and such friends and neighbours, as they desire should be the witnesses of their marriage: where they take one another by the hand, and by name, promise reciprocally love and fidelity, after the manner before expressed. Of all which proceedings, a narrative in way of certificate is made, to which the said parties first set their hands, thereby making it their act and deed; and then divers relations, spectators, and auditors set their names as witnesses, of what they said and signed. And this certificate is afterward registered in the record belonging to the meeting where the marriage is solemnized. Which regular method has been, as it deserves, adjudged in courts of law a good marriage; where it has been by cross and ill people disputed, and contested, for want of the accustomed formalities of priest and ring, etc. ceremonies they have refused: not out of humour, but conscience reasonably grounded; inasmuch as no Scripture example tells us, that the priest had any other part of old time, than that of a witness among the rest, before whom the Jews used to take one another: and therefore this people look upon it as an imposition to advance the power and profits of the clergy: And for the use of the ring, it is enough to say that it was an heathenish and vain custom, and never in practice among the people of God, Jews, or primitive Christians: the words of the usual form, as with my body I thee worship, etc. are hardly defensible. In short, they are more careful, exact and regular, than any form now used; and it is free of the inconveniencies, with which other methods are attended: their care and checks being so many, and such, as that no clandestine marriages can be performed among them.

11. It may not be unfit to say something here of their births and burials, which make up so much of the pomp and solemnity of too many called Christians. For births, the parents name their own children; which is usually some days after they are born in the presence of the midwife, if she can be there, and those that were at the birth, who afterwards sign a certificate for that purpose prepared, of the birth and name of the child or children which is recorded in a proper book, in the monthly meeting to which the parents belong; avoiding the accustomed ceremonies and festivals.

12. Their burials are performed with the same simplicity. If the body of the deceased be near any public meeting place, it is usually carried thither, for the more convenient reception of those that

accompany it, to the burying ground. And it so falls out sometimes, that while the meeting is gathering for the burial, some or other has a word of exhortation, for the sake of the people there met togehter. After which the body is born away by young men, or else those that are of their neighbourhood, or those that were most of the intimacy of the deceased party: the corpse being in a plain coffin, without any covering or furniture upon it. At the ground, they pause some time before they put the body into its grave, that if any there should have any thing upon them to exhort the people, they may not be disappointed, and that the relations may the more retiredly and solemnly take their last leave of the body of their departed kindred, and the spectators have a sense of mortality by the occasion then given them, to reflect upon their own latter end. Otherwise, they have no set rites or ceremonies on those occasions. Neither do the kindred of the deceased ever wear mourning; they looking upon it as a wordly ceremony and piece of pomp; and that what mourning is fit for a Christian to have, at the departure of a beloved relation or friend, should be worn in the mind, which is only sensible of the loss: and the love they had to them, and remembrance of them to be outwardly expressed by a respect to their advice, and care of those they have left behind them, and their love of that they loved. Which conduct of theirs, though unmodish or unfashionable, leaves nothing of the substance of things neglected or undone: and as they aim at no more, so that simplicity of life is what they observe with great satisfaction; though it sometimes happens not to be without the mockeries of the vain world they live in.

These things to be sure gave them a rough and disagreeable appearance with the generality; who thought them turners of the world upside down, as indeed, in some sense they were: but in no other than that wherein Paul was so charged, viz. to bring things back into their primitive and right order again. For these and such like practices of theirs were not the result of humour, or for civil distinction, as some have fancied, but a fruit of inward sense, which God, through His holy fear, had begotten in them. They did not consider how to contradict the world, or distinguish themselves as a party from others; it being none of their business, as it was not their interest: no, it was not the result of consultation, or a framed design, by which to declare or recommend schism or novelty. But God having given them a sight of themselves, they saw the whole world in the same glass of truth; and sensibly discerned the affections and passions of men, and the rise and tendency of things:

what it was that gratified the lust of the flesh, the lust of the eye and the pride of life, which are not of the Father but of the world. And from thence sprang in the night of darkness and apostacy, which hath been over people through their degeneration from the light and spirit of God, these and many other vain customs, which are seen by the heavenly day of Christ that dawns in the soul, to be, either wrong in their original; or, by time and abuse, hurtful in their practice. And though these things seemed trivial to some, and rendered these people stingy and conceited in such persons' opinion; there was and is more in them, than they were, or are aware of.

It was not very easy to our primitive friends to make themselves sights and spectacles, and the scorn and derision of the world; which they easily foresaw must be the consequence of so unfashionable a conversation in it: but here was the wisdom of God seen in the foolishness of these things; first, that they discovered the satisfaction and concern that people had in and for the fashions of this world, notwithstanding their high pretences to another; in that any disappointment about them came so very near them, as that the greatest honesty, virtue, wisdom and ability, were unwelcome without them. Secondly, it seasonably and profitably divided conversation; for this making their society uneasy to their relations and acquaintance, it gave them the opportunity of more retirement and solitude; wherein they met with better company, even the Lord God their Redeemer; and grew strong in His love, power and wisdom, and were thereby better qualified for His service. And the success abundantly showed it: blessed be the name of the Lord.

And though they were not great and learned in the esteem of this world (for then they had not wanted followers upon their own credit and authority) yet they were generally of the most sober of the several persuasions they were in, and of the most repute for religion; and many of them of good capacity, substance and account among men.

And also some among them wanted not for parts, learning or estate; though then as of old, not many wise, or noble, etc. were called; or at least received the heavenly call because of the cross that attended, the profession of it in sincerity: but neither do parts or learning make men the better Christians, though the better orators and disputants; and it is the ignorance of people about the divine gift that causes that vulgar and mischievous mistake. Theory and practice, speculation and enjoyment, words and life, are two things. O it is the penitent, the reformed, the lowly, the watchful, the self-denying and holy soul, that is the Christian! And that frame is the fruit and work of the spirit, which is the life of Jesus: whose life, though hid in the fulness of it in God the Father, is shed abroad in the hearts of them that truly believe, according to their capacity. O that people did but know this to cleanse them, to circumcise them, to quicken them, and to make them new creatures indeed! Re-created, or regenerated after Christ Jesus unto good works; that they might live to God, and not to themselves; and offer up living prayers and living praises, to the living God, through His own living spirit, in which He is only to be worshipped in this gospel day.

O that they that read me could but feel me! For my heart is affected with this merciful visitation of the Father of lights and spirits to this poor nation, and the whole world, through the same testimony. Why should the inhabitants thereof reject it? Why should they lose the blessed benefit of it? Why should they not turn to the Lord with all their hearts, and say from the heart, Speak Lord, for now Thy poor Servants hear? O that Thy will may be done; thy great, Thy good and holy will, in earth as it is in heaven! Do it in us, do it upon us, do what Thou wilt with us; for we are Thine, and desire to glorifie Thee our Creator, both for That, and because Thou art our Redeemer; for Thou art redeeming us from the earth; from the vanities and pollutions of it, to be a peculiar people unto Thee. O this were a brave day for England, if so she could say in truth! But alas, the case is otherwise; for which some of thine inhabitants, O land of my nativity! have mourned over thee with bitter wailing and lamentation. Their heads have been indeed as waters, and their eyes as fountains of tears, because of thy transgression and stiffnecked-ness; because thou wilt not hear, and fear, and return to the rock, even thy rock, O England! from whence thou art hewn. But be thou warned, O land of great profession, to receive him into thy heart. Behold, at that door it is he hath stood so long knocking! but thou wilt yet have none of him. O be thou awakened, lest Jerusalem's judgments do swiftly overtake thee, because of Jerusalem's sins that abound in thee. For she abounded in formality, but made void the weighty things of God's law, as thou daily dost.

She withstood the Son of God in the flesh, and thou resistest the Son of God in the spirit. He would have gathered her as a hen gathereth her chickens under her wings, and she would not; so would He have gathered thee out of thy lifeless profession, and have brought thee to inherit substance; to have known His power and kingdom: for which he often knocked within, by His grace and spirit; and without, by his servants and witnesses; But on the contrary, as Jerusalem of old persecuted the manifestation of the Son of God in the flesh, and crucified Him, and whipped and imprisoned his servants; so hast thou, O land! crucified to thy self afresh the Lord of life and glory, and done despite to his spirit of grace; slighting the fatherly visitation, and persecuting the blessed dispensers of it by thy laws and magistrates: though they have early and late pleaded with thee in the power and spirit of the Lord; in love and meekness, that thou mightest know the Lord, and serve him, and become the glory of all lands.

But thou hast evilly entreated and requited them, thou hast set an nought all their counsel, and wouldst have none of their reproof, as thou shouldst have had. Their appearance was too straight, and their qualifications were too mean for thee to receive them; like the Jews of old, that cried, Is not this the carpenter's son, and are not His brethren among us; which of the scribes, of the learned (the orthodox) believe in him? Prophesying their fall in a year or two, and making and executing of severe laws to bring it to pass: endeavouring to terrify them out of their holy way or destroy them for abiding faithful to it. But thou hast seen how many governments that rose against them, and determined their downfall, have been overturned and extinguished, and that they are still preserved, and become a great and a considerable people, among the middle sort of thy numerous inhabitants. And notwithstanding the many difficulties without and within, which they have laboured under, since the Lord God Eternal first gathered them, they are an increasing people; the Lord still adding unto them, in divers parts, such as shall be saved, if they persevere to the end. And to thee, O England! Were they, and are they lifted up as a standard, and as a city set upon a hill, and to the nations round about thee, that in their light thou mayest come to see light, even in Christ Jesus, the Light of the World, and therefore thy light, and life too, if thou wouldst but turn from thy many evil ways, and receive and obey it. For in the light of the Lamb, must the nations of them that are saved walk, as the Scripture testifies.

Remember, O nation of great profession! How the Lord has waited upon thee since the dawning of reformation, and the many mercies and judgments by which he has pleaded with thee; and awake and arise out of thy deep sleep, and yet hear his Word in thy heart, that thou mayest live.

Let not this thy day of visitation pass over thy head, nor neglect thou so great salvation as is this which is come to thy house, O England! For why should'st thou die? O land that God desires to bless! Be assured it is He that has been in the midst of this people, in the midst of thee, and not a delusion, as thy mistaken teachers have made thee believe. And this thou shalt find by their marks and fruits, if thou wilt consider them in the spirit of moderation.

CHAPTER III

Of the qualifications of their ministry. Eleven marks that it is Christian.

1. They were changed men themselves before they went about to change others. Their hearts were rent as well as their garments; and they knew the power and work of God upon them. And this was seen by the great alteration it made, and their stricter course of life, and more godly conversation that immediately followed upon it.

2. They went not forth, or preached in their own time or will, but in the will of God; and spoke not their own studied matter, but as they were opened and moved of his spirit, with which they were well acquainted in their own conversion: which cannot be expressed to carnal men, so as to give them any intelligible account; for to such it is, as Christ said, like the blowing of the wind, which no man knows whence it cometh, or whither it goeth. Yet this proof and seal went along with their ministry, that many were turned from their lifeless professions, and the evil of their ways, to an inward and experimental knowledge of God, and a holy life, as thousands can witness. And as they freely received what they had to say from the lord, so they freely administered it to others:

3. The bent and stress of their ministry, was conversion to God; regeneration and holiness. Not schemes of doctrines and verbal creeds, or new forms of worship; but a leaving off in religion the superfluous, and reducing the ceremonious and formal part, and pressing earnestly the substantial, the necessary and profitable part to the soul; as all, upon a serious reflection, must and do acknowledge.

4. They directed people to a principle in themselves, though not of themselves, by which all that they asserted, preached and exhorted others to, might be wrought in them and known to them, through experience, to be true: which is an high and distinguishing mark of the truth of their ministry, both that they knew what they

said, and were not afraid of coming to the test. For as they were bold from certainty, so they required conformity upon no humane authority, but upon conviction, and the conviction of this principle; which they asserted was in them that they preached unto, and unto that they directed them, that they might examine and prove the reality of those things which they had affirmed of it, as to its manifestation and work in man. And this is more than the many ministers in the world pretended to. They declare of religion, say many things true, in words, of God, Christ, and the Spirit; of holiness and heaven; that all men should repent and amend their lives, or they will go to hell, etc. But which of them all pretend to speak of their own knowledge and experience? Or ever directed to a divine principle, or agent, placed of God in man, to help him; and how to know it, and wait to feel its power to work that good and acceptable will of God in them.

Some of them indeed have spoke of the spirit, and the operations of it to sanctification, and performance of worship to God; but where, and how to find it, and wait in it, to perform our duty to God, was yet as a mystery to be declared by this farther degree of reformation. So that this people did not only in words, more than equally press repentance, conversion and holiness, but did it knowingly and experimentally; and directed those, to whom they preached, to a sufficient principle; and told them where it was, and by what tokens they might know it, and which way they might experience the power and efficacy of it to their soul's happiness. Which is more than theory and speculation, upon which most other ministers depend: For here is certainty; a bottom upon which man may bodly appear before God in the great day of account.

5. They reached to the inward state and condition of people, which is an evidence of the virtue of their principle and of their ministering from it, and not from their own imaginations, glosses or comments upon scripture. For nothing reaches the heart but what is from the heart, or pierces the conscience, but what comes from a living conscience. Insomuch as it hath often happened, where people have under secrecy revealed their state or condition to some choice friends, for advice or ease, they have been so particularly directed in the ministry of this people, that they have challenged their friends with discovering their secrets, and telling their preachers their cases, to whom a word had not been spoken. Yea, the very thoughts and purposes of the hearts of many have been so plainly detected, that they have, like Nathaniel, cried out, of this inward appearance of

Christ, Thou art the Son of God, thou art the king of Israel. And those that have embraced this divine principle, have found this mark of its truth and divinity (that the woman of Samaria did of Christ when in the flesh, to be the messiah) viz. it had told them all that ever they had done; shown them their insides, the most inward secrets of their hearts, and laid judgment to the line, and righteousness to the plummet; of which thousands can at this day give in their witness. So that nothing has been affirmed by this people, of the power and virtue of this heavenly principle, that such as have turned to it have not found true, and more; and that one half had not been told to them of what they have seen of the power, purity, wisdom and goodness of God therein.

6. The accomplishments with which this principle fitted, even some of the meanest of this people for their work and service: furnishing some of them with an extraordinary understanding in divine things, and an admirable fluency and taking way of expression, which gave occasion to some to wonder, saying of them, as of their master, is not this such a mechanic's son, how came he by this learning? As from thence others took occasion to suspect and insinuate they were Jesuits in disguise, who had the reputation of learned men for an age past, though there was not the least ground of truth for any such reflection. In that their ministers are known, the places of their abode, their kindred and education.

7. That they came forth low, and despised, and hated, as the primitive Christians did, and not by the help of worldly wisdom or power, as former reformations, in part, have done: but in all things it may be said, this people were brought forth in the cross; in a contradiction to the ways, worships, fashions and customs of this world; yea, against wind and tide, what so no flesh might glory before God.

8. They could have no design to themselves in this work, thus to expose themselves to scorn and abuse; to spend, and be spent: leaving wife and children, house and land, and all that can be accounted dear to men, with their lives in their hands, being daily in jeopardy, to declare this primitive message, revived in their spirits, by the good spirit and power of God, viz.

That God is light, and in Him is no darkness at all; and that He has sent His Son a light into the world, to enlighten all men in order to salvation; and that they that say they have fellowship with God, and are His children and people, and yet walk in darkness, viz. in disobedience to the light in their consciences, and after the vanity of this world, they lie, and do not the truth. But that all such as love the light, and bring their deeds to it, and walk in the light, as God is light, the blood of Jesus Christ His Son, should cleanse them from all sin. Thus John 1. 4, 19. ch. 3. 20, 21. 1 John 1. 5, 6, 7.

9. Their known great constancy and patience in suffering for their testimony, in all the branches of it; and that sometimes unto death, by beatings, bruisings, long and crowded imprisonments, and noisom dungeons: four of them in New England dying by the hands of the executioner, purely for preaching amongst that people: besides banishments, and excessive plunders and sequestrations of thier goods and estates, almost in all parts, not easily to be expressed, and less to have been endured but by those that have the support of a good and glorious cause; refusing deliverance by any indirect ways or means, as often as it was offered unto them.

10. That they did, not only, not show any disposition to revenge, when it was at any time in their power, but forgave their cruel enemies; showing mercy to those that had none for them.

11. Their plainness with those in authority, like the ancient prophets, not fearing to tell them to their faces, of their private and public sins; and their prophecies to them of their afflictions and downfall, when in the top of their glory. Also of some national judgments, as of the plague, and fire of London, in express terms; and likewise particular ones to divers persecutors, which accordingly overtook them; and were very remarkable in the places where they dwelt, which in time may be made public for the glory of God.

Thus, reader, thou seest this people in their rise, principles, ministry and progress, both their general and particular testimony; by which thou mayest be informed, how, and upon what foot they sprang, and became so considerable a people. It remains next, that I show also their care, conduct, and discipline, as a Christian and reformed society, that they might be found living up to their own principles and profession. And this, the rather, because they have hardly suffered more in their character from the unjust charge of error, than by the false imputation of disorder: which calumny indeed has not failed to follow all the true steps that were ever made to reformation, and under which reproach none suffered more than the primitive Christians themselves, that were the honour of Christianity, and the great lights and examples of their own and succeeding ages.

CHAPTER IV

Of the discipline and practice of this people, as a religious society. The church power they own and exercise, and that which they reject and condemn: with the method of their proceedings against erring and disorderly persons.

This people increasing daily both in town and country, a holy care fell upon some of the Elders among them, for the benefit and service of the church. And the first business in their view, after the example of the primitive saints, was the exercise of charity; to supply the necessities of the poor, and answer the like occasions. Wherefore collections were early and liberally made for that and divers other services in the church, and entrusted with faithful men, fearing God, and of good report, who were not weary in well-doing; adding often of their own, in large proportions, which they never brought to account, or desired should be known, much less restored to them, that none might want, nor any service be retarded or disappointed.

They were also very careful that every one that belonged to them, answered their profession in their behaviour among men upon all occasions; that they lived peaceably, and were in all things good examples. They found themselves engaged to record their sufferings and services: and in case of marriage, which they could not perform in the usual methods of the nation, but among themselves, they took care that all things were clear between the parties and all others: and it was then rare; that any one entertained an inclination to a person on that account, till he or she had communicated it secretly to some very weighty and eminent friends among them, that they might have a sense of the matter; looking to the council and unity of their brethren as of great moment to them. But because the charge of the poor, the number of orphans, marriages, sufferings, and other matters multiplied; and that it was good that the churches were in some way and method of proceeding in such affairs among them, to the end they might the better correspond upon occasion, where a member of one meeting might have to do with one of another; it pleased the Lord in His wisdom and goodness, to open the understanding of the first instrument of this dispensation of life, about a good and orderly way of proceeding; who felt a holy concern to visit the churches in person throughout this nation, to begin and establish it among them: And by His Epistles, the like was done in other nations and provinces abroad; which he also afterwards visited, and helped in the service, as shall be observed when I come to speak of him:

Now the care, conduct and discipline I have been speaking of, and which are now practiced among this people, is as followeth:

This godly elder, in every county where he travelled, exhorted them, that some, out of every meeting of worship, should meet together once in the month, to confer about the wants and occasions of the church. And as the case required, so those monthly meetings were fewer or more in number in every respective county: four or six meetings of worship, usually making one monthly meeting of business. And accordingly the brethren met him from place to place, and began the said meetings, viz. for the poor, orphans, orderly walking, integrity to their profession, births, marriages, burials, sufferings, etc. And that these monthly meetings should, in each county, make up one quarterly meeting, where the most zealous and eminent friends of the county should assemble to communicate; advise and help one another, especially when any business seemed difficult, or a monthly meeting was tender of determining a matter.

Also that these several quarterly meetings should digest the reports of their monthly meetings, and prepare one for each respective county, against the yearly meeting, in which all quarterly meetings resolve; which is held in London: Where the churches in this nation, and other nations and provinces, meet by chosen members of their respective counties, both mutually to communicate their church affairs, and to advise, and be advised in any depending case to edification. Also to provide a requisite stock for the discharge of general expenses for general services in the church, not needful to be here particularized.

At these meetings any of the members of the churches may come, if they please, and speak their minds freely, in the fear of God, to any matter; but the mind of each quarterly meeting, therein represented, is chiefly understood, as to particular cases, in the sense delivered by the persons deputed, or chosen for that service by the said meeting.

During their yearly meeting, to which their other meetings refer in their order, and naturally resolve themselves, care is taken by a select number for that service, chosen by the general assembly, to draw up the minutes of the said meeting, upon the several matters that have been under consideration therein, to the end that the respective quarterly and monthly meetings may be informed of all proceedings; together with a general exhortation to holiness, unity and charity. Of all which proceedings in yearly, monthly, and quarterly meetings, due record is kept by some one appointed for that service, or that hath voluntarily undertaken it. These meetings are opened, and usually concluded in their solemn waiting upon God, who is sometimes graciously pleased to answer them with as signal evidences of his love and presence, as in any of their meetings of worship.

It is further to be noted that in these solemn assemblies, for the churches service, there is no one presides among them after the manner of the assemblies of other people; Christ only being their president, as He is pleased to appear in life and wisdom in any one or more of them, to whom, whatever be their capacity or degree, the rest adhere with a firm unity, not of authority, but conviction, which is the divine authority and way of Christ's power and spirit in His people: making good His blessed promise. That He would be in the midst of His, where and whenever they were met together in His name, even to the end of the world. So be it.

Now it may be expected, I should here set down what sort of authority is exercised by this people, upon such members of their society as correspond in their lives with their profession, and that are refractory to this good and wholesome order settled among them; and the rather, because they have not wanted their reproach and sufferings from some tongues and pens, upon this occasion, in a plentiful manner.

The power they exercise is such as Christ has given to His own people, to the end of the world, in the persons of His disciples, viz. to oversee, exhort, reprove, and after long suffering and waiting upon the disobedient and refractory, to disown them, as any more of their communion, or that they will any longer stand charged in the sight and judgment of God or men, with their conversation or behaviour as any of them, until they repent. The subject matter about which this authority, in any of the foregoing branches of it, is exercised, is first, in relation to common and general practice, and, secondly, about those things that more strictly refer to their own character and profession, and which distinguish them from all other professors of Christianity; avoiding two extremes upon which many split, viz. persecution and libertinism, that is, a coercive power, to whip people into the temple; that such as will not conform, though against faith and conscience, shall be punished in their persons or estates: or leaving all loose and at large, as to practice; and so unaccountable to all but God and the magistrate.

To which hurtful extreme, nothing has more contributed than the abuse of church power, by such as suffer their passion and private interests to prevail with them to carry it to outward force and corporal punishment. A practice they have been taught to dislike, by their extreme sufferings, as well as their known principle for a universal liberty of conscience.

On the other hand, they equally dislike an independency in society. An unaccountableness in practice and conversation to the rules and terms of their own communion, and to those that are the members of it. They distinguish between imposing any practice that immediately regards faith or worship (which is never to be done or suffered, or submitted unto) and requiring Christian compliance with those methods that only respect church business in its more civil part and concern; and that regard the discreet and orderly maintenance of the character of the society as a sober and religious community. In short, what is for the promotion of holiness and charity, that men may practice what they profess, live up to their own principles, and not be at liberty to give the lie to their own profession without rebuke, is their use and limit of church power: they compel none to them, but oblige those that are of them to walk suitably, or they are denied by them: that is all the mark they set upon them, and the power they exercise, or judge a Christian society can exercise, upon those that are the members of it.

The way of their proceeding against such as have lapsed or transgressed, is this. He is visited by some of them, and the matter of fact laid home to him, be it any evil practice against known and general virtue, or any branch of their particular testimony, which he, in common, professeth with them. They labour with him in much love and zeal, for the good of his soul, the honour of God, and reputation of their profession, to own his fault and condemn it, in as ample a manner as the evil or scandal was given by him; which for the most part is performed by some written testimony under the parties hand: and if it so happen, that the party prove refractory, and is not willing to clear the truth, they profess, from the reproach of his or her evil-doing or unfaithfulness, they, after repeated entreaties and due waiting for a token of repentance, give forth a paper to disown such a fact, and the party offending: recording the same as a testimony of their care for the honour of the truth they profess.

And if he or she shall clear their profession and themselves by sincere acknowledgment of their fault, and godly sorrow for so doing, they are received and looked upon again as members of their communion. For as God, so His true people upbraid no man after repentance.

This is the account I had to give of the people of God called Quakers, as to their rise, appearance, principles and practices in this age of the world, both with respect to their faith and worship, discipline and conversation. And I judge it very proper in this place, because it is to preface the journal of the first blessed and glorious instrument of this work, and for a testimony to Him, in His singular qualification and services, in which be abundantly excelled in this day, and are worthy to be set forth as an example to all succeeding times, to the glory of the most high God, and for a just memorial to that worthy and excellent man, His faithful servant and apostle to this generation of the world.

CHAPTER V

Of the first instrument *or person by whom God was pleased to gather this people into the way they profess. His name G. Fox: his many excellent qualifications; showing a divine, and not an human power to have been their original in him. His troubles and sufferings both from without and within. His end and triumph.*

I am now come to the third head or branch of my preface, viz. the instrumental author. For it is natural for some to say, well, here is the the people and work, but where and who was the man, the instrument? he that in this age was sent to begin this work and people? I shall, as God shall enable me, declare who and what he was; not only by report of others, but from my own long and most inward converse, and intimate knowledge of him; for which my soul blesseth God, as it hath often done: And I doubt not, by that time I have discharged myself of this part of my preface, my serious readers will believe I had good cause so to do.

The blessed instrument of, and in this day of God, and of whom I am now about to write, was George Fox, distinguished from another of that name, by that others addition of younger to his name, in all his writings; not that he was so in years, but that he was so in the truth: but he was also a worthy man, witness and servant of God in his time.

But this George Fox was born in Leicestershire, about the year 1624. He descended of honest and sufficient parents, who endeavoured to bring him up, as they did the rest of their children, in the way and worship of the nation : especially his mother, who was a woman accomplished above most of the degree in the place where she lived. But from a child he appeared of another frame of mind than the rest of his brethren; being more religious, inward, still, solid, and observing beyond his years, as the the answers he would give, and the questions he would put, upon occasion, manifested, to the astonishment of those that heard him, especially in divine things.

His mother taking notice of his singular temper, and the gravity, wisdom and piety, that very early shined through him, refusing childish and vain sports and company, when very young, she was tender and indulgent over him, so that from her he met with little difficulty. As to his employment, he was brought up in country business, and as he took most delight in sheep, so he was very skilful in them; an employment that very well suited his mind in several respects, both for its innocency and solitude; and was a just emblem of his after ministry and service.

I shall not break in upon his own account, which is by much the best that can be given, and therefore desire, what I can, to avoid saying any thing of what is said already as to the particular passages of his coming forth : but, in general, when he was somewhat above twenty, he lest his friends, and visited the most retired and religious people in those parts : And some there were, short of few, if any, in this nation, who waited for the consolation of Israel night and day; as Zacharias, Anna, and good old Simeon did of old time. To these he was sent, and these he sought out in the neighbouring counties, and among them he sojourned until his more ample ministry came upon him. At this time he taught, and was an example of silence, endeavouring to bring them from self-performances : testifying of, and turning them to, the light of Christ within them, and encouraging them to wait in patience, and to feel the power of it to stir in their hearts, that their knowledge and worship of God might stand in the power of an endless life, which was to be found in the light, as it was obeyed in the manifestation of it in man. For in the Word was life, and that life is the light of men. Life in the Word, light in men; and life in men too, as the light is obeyed : the children of the light living by the life of the Word, by which the Word begets them again to God, which is the regeneration and new birth, without which there is no coming into the kingdom of God : and to which, whoever comes, is greater than John; that is, than John's dispensation, which was not that of the kingdom, but the consummation of the legal, and forerunning of the gospel times, the time of the kingdom. Accordingly several meetings were gathered in those parts; and thus his time was employed for some years.

In 1652, he being in his usual retirement, his mind exercised towards the Lord, upon a very high mountain, in some of the hither parts of Yorkshire, as I take it, he had a visitation of the great work of God in the earth, and of the way that he was to go forth in a public ministry, to begin it. He saw people as thick as motes in the sun, that should in time be brought home to the Lord, that there might be but one shepherd and one sheepfold in all the earth. There his eye was directed northward, beholding a great people that should receive him and his message in those parts. Upon this mountain he was moved of the Lord to found out his great and notable day, as if he had been in a great auditory; and from thence went North, as the Lord had shown him. And in every place where he came, if not before he came to it, he had his particular exercise and service shown to him, so that the Lord was his leader indeed. For it was not in vain that he travelled; God in most places feeling his commission with the convincement of some of all sorts, as well publicans as sober professors of religion. Some of the first and most eminent of those that came forth in a public ministry, and which are now at rest, were Richard Farnsworth, James Nayler, William Dewsberry, Thomas Aldom, Francis Howgil, Edward Burroughs, John Camm, John Audland, Richard Hubberthorn, T. Taylor, T. Holmes, Alexander Parker, William Simson, William Caton, John Stubbs, Robert Withers, Tho. Low, Josiah Coale, John Burnyeat, Robert Lodge, Thomas Salthouse, and many more worthies, that cannot be well here named; together with diverse yet living of the first and great convincement; who after the knowledge of God's purging judgment in themselves, and some time of waiting in silence upon him, to feel and receive power from on high, to speak in his name, (which none else rightly can, though they may use the same words) They felt its divine motions, and were frequently drawn forth, especially to visit the public assemblies to reprove, inform, and exhort them: sometimes in markets, fairs, streets, and by the highwayside; calling people to repentance, and to turn to the Lord with their hearts as well as their mouths; directing them to the light of Christ within them, to see, examine, and consider their ways by, and to eschew the evil, and do the good and acceptable will of God. And they suffered great hardships for this their love and good-will;

being often stocked, stoned, beaten, whipped and imprisoned; though honest men, and of good report where they lived; that had left wives, children, and houses and lands to visit them with a living call to repentance. And though the priests generally set themselves to oppose them, and write against them, and insinuated most false and scandalous stories to defame them; stirring up the magistrates to suppress them, especially in those northern parts; yet God was pleased so to fill them with His living power, and give them such an open door of utterance in His service, that there was a mighty convincement over those parts.

And through the tender and singular indulgence of Judge Bradshaw and Judge Fell, and Coll. West, in the infancy of things, the priests were never able to gain the point they laboured for, which was to have proceeded to blood; and, if possible, Herod-like, by a cruel exercise of the civil power, to have cut them off, and rooted them out of the country. But especially Judge Fell, who was not only a check to their rage in the course of legal proceedings, but otherwise, upon occasion; and finally countenanced this people. For his wife receiving the truth with the first, it had that influence upon his spirit, being a just and wise man, and seeing in his own wife and family a full confutation of all the popular clamours against the way of truth, that he covered them what he could, and freely opened his doors, and gave up his house to his wife and her friends; not valuing the reproach of ignorant or of evil-minded-people; which I here mention, to his or her honour, and which will be, I believe, an honour and a blessing to such of their name and family as shall be found in that tenderness, humility, love and zeal for the truth and prople of the Lord.

That house was for some years, at first especially, until the truth had opened its way into the southern parts of this island, an eminent receptacle of this people. Others, of good note and substance in those northern countries, had also opened their houses, together with their hearts, to the many publishers, that, in a short time, the Lord had raised to declare his salvation to the people; and where meetings of the Lord's messengers were frequently held, to communicate their services and exercises, and comfort and edify one another in their blessed ministry.

But lest this may be thought a digression, having touched upon this before, I return to this excellent man: and for his personal qualities, both natural, moral and divine, as they appeared in his converse with brethren, and in the church of God, take as follows:

1. He was a man that God endued with a clear and wonderful depth : a discerner of other's spirits, and very much a master of his own. And though that side of his understanding which lay next to the world, and especially the expression of it, might sound uncouth and unfashionable to nice ears, his matter was nevertheless very profound; and would not only bear to be often considered, but the more it was so, the more weighty and instructing it appeared. And as abruptly and brokenly as sometimes his sentences would seem to fall from him about divine things, it is well known they were often as texts to many fairer declarations. And indeed, it showed, beyond all contradiction, that God sent him; in that no art or parts had any share in the matter or manner of his ministry; and that so many great excellent, and necessary truths, as he came forth to preach to mankind, had therefore nothing of man's wit or wisdom to recommend them. So that as to man he was an original, being no man's copy. And his ministry and writings show they are from one that was not taught of man, nor had learned what he said by study. Nor were they notional or speculative, but sensible and practical truths, tending to conversion and regeneration, and the setting up of the kingdom of God in the hearts of men : and the way of it was his work. So that I have many times been overcome in myself, and been made to say, with my Lord and Master, upon the like occasion, I thank thee, O Father, Lord of Heaven and Earth, that thou hast hid these things from the wise and prudent of this world, and revealed them to babes : For many times hath my soul bowed in a humble thankfulness to the Lord, that he did not choose any of the wise and learned of this world to be the first messenger in our age, of his blessed truth to men; but that he took one that was not of high degree, or elegant speech, or learned after the way of this world, that his message and work, he sent him to do, might come with less suspicion, or jealousy of human wisdom and interest, and with more force and clearness upon the consciences of those that sincerely sought the way of truth in the love of it. I say, beholding with the eye of my mind, which the God of heaven had opened in me, the marks of God's finger and hand visibly, in this testimony, from the clearness of the principle, the power and efficacy of it, in the exemplary sobriety, plainness, zeal, steadiness, humility, gravity, punctuality, charity, and circumspect care in the government of church affairs, which shined in his and their life and testimony that God employed in this work, it greatly confirmed me that it was of God, and engaged my soul in a deep love, fear, reverence and

thankfulness for his love and mercy therein to mankind: in which mind I remain, and shall, I hope, through the Lord's strength, to the end of my days.

2. In his testimony or ministry, he much laboured to open truth to the people's understandings, and to bottom them upon the principle and principal, Christ Jesus, the Light of the World; that by bringing them to something that was from God in themselves, they might the better know and judge of Him and themselves.

3. He had an extraordinary gift in opening the scriptures. He would go to the marrow of things, and show the mind, harmony and fulfilling of them with much plainness, and to great comfort and edification.

4. The mystery of the first and second Adam, of the fall and restoration, of the law and gospel, of shadows and substance, of the servant's and son's state, and the fulfilling of the Scriptures in Christ and by Christ, the True Light, in all that are his, through the obedience of faith, were much of the substance and drift of his testimonies. In all which he was witnessed to be of God; being sensibly felt to speak that which he had received of Christ, and was his own experience, in that which never errs nor fails.

5. But above all, he excelled in prayer. The inwardness and weight of his spirit, the reverence and solemnity of his address and behaviour, and the fewness and fulness of his words, have often struck even strangers with admiration, as they used to reach others with consolation. The most awful; living, reverent frame I ever felt or beheld, I must say, was his in prayer. And truly it was a testimony he knew and lived nearer to the Lord than other men; for they that know him most, will see most reason to approach him with reverence and fear.

6. He was of an innocent life, no busybody, nor self-seeker; neither touchy nor critical: what fell from him was very inoffensive, if not very edifying. So meek, contented, modest, easy, steady, tender; it was a pleasure to be in his company. He exercised no authority but over evil, and that every where, and in all; but with love, compassion, and long-suffering. A most merciful man, as ready to forgive, as unapt to take or give an offence. Thousands can truly say he was of an excellent spirit and savour among them, and because thereof, the most excellent spirits loved him with an unfeigned and unfading love.

7. He was an incessant labourer: for in his younger time, before his many, great and deep sufferings and travails had enfeebled his

body for itinerant services, he laboured much in the word and doctrine, and discipline, in England, Scotland and Ireland; turning many to God, and confirming those that were convinced of the truth, and settling good order, as to church affairs, among them. And towards the conclusion of his travelling services, between the years seventy one and seventy seven, he visited the churches of Christ in the plantations in America, and in the United Provinces, and Germany, as his journal relates; to the convincement and consolation of many. After that time he chiefly resided in and about the City of London: and besides his labour in the ministry, which was frequent and seviceable, he wrote much, both to them that are within, and those that are without the communion. But the care he took of the affairs of the church in general was very great.

8. He was often where the records of the business of the church are kept, and where the letters from the many meetings of God's people over all the world use to come: which letters he had read to him, and communicated them to the meeting, that is weekly held, for such services; and he would be sure to stir them up to answer them, especially in suffering cases: showing great sympathy, and compassion upon all such occasions; carefully looking into the respective cases, and endeavouring speedy relief, according to the nature of them. So that the churches, or any of the suffering members thereof, were sure not to be forgotten or delayed in their desires, if he were there.

9. As he was unwearied, so he was undaunted in his services for God and his people; he was no more to be moved to fear than to wrath. His behaviour at Derby, Litchfield, Appleby, before Oliver Cromwell, at Launston, Scarborough, Worcester, and Westminster-Hall, with many other places and exercises, did abundantly evidence it, to his enemies as well as his friends.

But as, in the primitive times, some rose up against the blessed apostles of our Lord Jesus Christ, even from among those that they had turned to the hope of the gospel, and they became their greatest trouble; so this Man of God had his share of suffering from some that were convinced by him, who, through prejudice or mistake, ran against him, as one that fought dominion over conscience, because he pressed, by his presence or epistles, a ready and zealous compliance with such good and wholesome things as tended to an orderly conversation about the affairs of the church, and in their walking before men. That which contributed much to this ill work, was, in some, a begrudging of this meek man the love and esteem he had and deserved in the hearts of the people, and weakness in others, that were taken with their groundless suggestions of imposition and blind obedience.

They would have had every man independent, that as he had the principle in himself, he should only stand and fall to that, and no body else: Not considering that the principle is one in all; and though the measure of light or grace might differ, yet the nature of it was the same; and being so, they struck at the spiritual unity, which a people, guided by the same principle, are naturally led into: so that what is an evil to one, is so to all, and what is virtuous, honest, and of good repute to one, is so to all, from the sense and savour of the one universal principle which is common to all, and which the disaffected also profess to be the root of all true Christian fellowship, and that spirit into which the people of God drink, and come to be Spiritually minded, and of one heart and one soul.

Some weakly mistook good order in the government of church affairs for discipline in worship, and that it was so pressed or recommended by him and other brethren. And thereupon they were ready to reflect the same things that dissenters had very reasonably objected upon the national churches, that have coercively pressed conformity to their respective creeds and worships. Whereas these things related wholly to conversation, and the outward (and as I may say) civil part of the church; that men should walk up to the principles of their belief, and not be wanting in care and charity. But though some have stumbled and fallen through mistakes, and an unreasonable obstinacy, even to a prejuidce; yet blessed be God, the generality have returned to their first love, and seen the work of the enemy, that loses no opportunity or advantage by which he may check or hinder the work of God, and disquiet the peace of his church, and chill the love of his people to the truth, and one to another; and there is hope of divers of the few that yet are at a distance.

In all these occasions, though there was no person the discontented struck so sharply at, as this good man, he bore all their weakness and prejudice, and returned not reflection for reflection; but forgave them their weak and bitter speeches, praying for them that they might have a sense of their hurt, and see the subtlety of the enemy to rend and divide, and return into their first love that thought no ill.

And truly I must say that though God had visibly clothed him with a divine preference and authority, and indeed his very presence expressed a religious majesty; yet he never abused it; but held his place in the church of God with great meekness, and a most engaging humility and moderation. For upon all occasions, like his blessed master, he was a servant to all; holding and exercising his eldership in the invisible power that had gathered them, with reverence to the head and care over the body: and was received, only in that spirit and power of Christ, as the first and chief elder in this age: who, as he was therefore worthy of double honour, so for the same reason it was given by the faithful of this day; because his authority was inward and not outward, and that he got it and kept it by the love of God, and power of an endless life. I write my knowledge, and not report, and my witness is true; having been with him for weeks and months together on diverse occasions, and those of the nearest and most exercising nature; and that by night and by day, by sea and by land; in this and in foreign countries: and I can say, I never saw him out of his place, or not a match for every service or occasion.

For in all things he acquitted himself like a man, yea, a strong man, a new and heavenly-minded man, a divine and a naturalist, and all of God Almighty's making. I have been surprised at his questions and answers in natural things: that whilst he was ignorant of useless and sophistical science, he had in him the grounds of useful and commendable knowledge, and cherished it every where. Civil, beyond all forms of breeding, in his behaviour: very temperate, eating little, and sleeping less, though a bulky peson.

Thus he lived and sojourned among us: and as he lived so he died; feeling the same eternal power, that had raised and preserved him, in his last moments, So full of assurance was he, that he triumphed over death; and so even in his spirit to the last, as if death were hardly worth notice, or a mention: recommending to some of us with him the dispatch and dispersion of an epistle just before given forth by him to the churches of Christ throughout the world, and his own books: but above all, friends; and of all friends, those in Ireland and America, twice over, saying, Mind poor Friends in Ireland and America.

And to some that came in and enquired how he found himself, he answered, Never heed, the Lord's Power is over all weakness and death; the seed reigns, blessed be the Lord: which was about four or five hours before his departure out of this world. He was at the great meetings near Lombard Street, on the first day of the week, and it was the third following about ten at night when he left us; being at the house of H. Goldney in the same Court. In a good old age he went, after having lived to see his childrens' children in the truth to many generations. He had the comfort of a short illness, and the blessing of a clear sense to the last: and we may truly say, with a man of God of old, that being dead, he yet speaketh; And though now absent in body, he is present in spirit: Neither time nor place being able to interrupt the communion of saints, or dissolve the fellowships of the spirits of the just. His works praise him, because they are to the praise of him that wrought by him; for which his memorial is and shall be blessed. I have done, as to this part of my preface, when I have left this short epitaph to his name, Many sons have done virtuously in this day; but, Dear George, thou excellest them All.

CHAPTER VI

Containing five several exhortations, First, general, reminding this people of their primitive integrity and simplicity. Secondly, in particular, to the ministry. Thirdly, to the young convinced. Fourthly, to the children of Friends. Fifthly, to those that are yet strangers to this people and way, to whom this book, (and that it was preface to in its former edition) may come. All the several exhortations accommodated to their several states and conditions; that all may answer the end of God's glory and their own salvation.

And now, friends, you that profess to walk in the way that this blessed man was sent to God to turn us into, suffer, I beseech you, the word of exhortation, as well fathers as children, and elders as young men, The glory of this day, and foundation of the hope that has not made us ashamed since we were a people, you know is that blessed principle of light and life of Christ which we profess, and direct all people to, as the great and divine instrument and agent of man's conversion to God. It was by this that we were first touched, and effectually enlightened, as to our inward state; which put us upon the consideration of our latter end, causing us to set the Lord before our eyes, and to number our days that we might apply our hearts to wisdom. In that day we judged not after the sight of the eye, or after the hearing of the ear, but according to the light and sense this blessed principle gave us, so we judged and acted in reference to things and persons, ourselves and others; yea, towards God our maker. For being quickened by it in our inward man, we could easily discern the difference of things, and feel what was right, and what was wrong, and what was fit, and what not, both in reference to religious and civil concerns. That being the ground of the fellowship of all saints, it was in that our fellowship stood. In this we desired to have a sense of one another, acted towards one another, and all men; in love, faithfulness and fear.

In feeling of the stirrings and motions of this principle in our hearts, we drew near to the Lord, and waited to be prepared by it, that we might feel drawings and movings before we approached the Lord in prayer, or opened our mouths in ministry. And in our beginning and ending with this stood our comfort, service and edification. And as we ran faster or fell short, we made burdens for ourselves to bear; our services finding in our selves a rebuke instead of an acceptance; and in lieu of well done, who has required this at your hands? In that day we were an exercised people, our very countenances and deportment declared it.

Care for others was then much upon us, as well as for our selves; especially of the young convinced. Often had we the burden of the Word of the Lord to our neighbours, relations and acquaintance; and sometimes strangers also. We were in travel likewise for one anothers preservation; not seeking, but shunning occasions of any coldness or misunderstanding: treating one another as those that believed and felt God present. Which kept our conversation innocent, serious and weighty; guarding ourselves against the cares and friendships of the world. We held the truth in the spirit of it, and not in our own spirits, or after our own will and affections.

They were bowed and brought into subjection, in so much that it was visible to them that knew us. We did not think our selves at our own disposal, to go where we list, or say or do what we list, or when we list. Our liberty stood in the liberty of the spirit of truth; and no pleasure, no profit, no fear, no favour could draw us from this retired, strict and watchful frame. We were so far from seeking occasion of company, that we avoided them what we could; pursuing our own business, with moderation, instead of meddling with other people's unnecessarily.

Our words were few and savoury, our looks composed and weighty, and our whole deportment very observable. True it is, that this retired and strict sort of life from the liberty of the conversation of the world, exposed us to the censures of many, as humourists, conceited and self-righteous persons, etc. But it was our preservation from many snares, to which others were continually exposed, by the prevalency of the lust of the eye, the lust of the flesh, and the pride of life, that wanted no occasions or temptations to excite them abroad in the converse of the world.

I cannot forget the humility and chaste zeal of that day. O, how constant at meetings, how retired in them, how firm to truth's life, as well as truth's principles! And how entire and united in our communion, as indeed became those that profess one head, even Christ Jesus the Lord.

This being the testimony and example the man of God, before-mentioned, was sent to declare and leave amongst us, and we having embraced the same as the merciful visitation of God to us, the word of exhortation at this time is that we continue to be found in the way of this testimony, with all zeal and integrity; and so much the more, by how much the day draweth near.

And first, as to you my beloved and much honoured brethren in Christ, that are in the exercise of the ministry: O, feel life in your ministry! Let life be your commission, your well-spring and treasury in all such occasions; else, you well know, there can be no begetting to God, since nothing can quicken or make people alive to God, but the life of God: And it must be a ministry in and from life, that enlivens any people to God. We have seen the fruit of all other ministers, by the few that are turned from the evil of their ways. It is not our parts, or memory, the repetition of former openings, in our own will and time, that will do God's work. A dry doctrinal ministry, however found in words, can reach but the ear, and is but a dream at the best: there is another soundness, that is soundest of all, viz. Christ the power of God. This is the key of David, that opens and none shuts, and shuts, and none can open: as the oil to the lamp, and the soul to the body, so is that to the best of words. Which made Christ to say, My words, they are spirit, and they are life; that is, they are from life, and therefore they make you alive, that receive them. If the disciples that had lived with Jesus, were to stay at Jerusalem, till they received it; much more must we wait to receive before we minister, if we will turn people from darkness to light, and from Satan's power to God.

I fervently bow my knees to the God and Father of our Lord Jesus Christ, that you may always be like minded, that you may ever wait reverently, for the coming and opening of the word of life, and attend upon it in your ministry and service, that you may serve God in his spirit. And be it little, or be it much, it is well; for much is not too much, and the least is enough, if from the motion of God's spirit; and without it, verily, never so little is too much, because to no profit.

For it is the spirit of the Lord immediately or through the ministry of his servants, that teacheth his people to profit; and to be sure, so far as we take him along with us in our services; so far we are profitable and no farther. For if it be the Lord that must work all things in us, for our salvation, much more is it the Lord that must work in us for the conversion of others. If therefore it was once a cross to us to speak, though the Lord required it at our hands; let us never be so to be silent, when He does not.

It is one of the most dreadful sayings in the Book of God, That he that adds to the words of the prophecy of this Book, God will add to him the plagues written in this Book. To keep back the counsel of God, is as terrible; for he that takes away from the words of the book of this prophecy, God shall take away his part out of the Book of Life. And truly, it has great caution in it, to those that use the name of the Lord, to be well assured the Lord speaks, that they may not be found of the number of those that add to the words of the testimony of prophecy, which the Lord giveth them to bear; nor yet to mince or diminish the same, both being so very offensive to God.

Wherefore, brethren, let us be careful neither to out-go our guide, nor yet loiter behind him; since he that makes haste, may miss his way, and he that stays behind; lose his guide. For even those that have received the Word of the Lord, had need wait for wisdom, that they may see how to divide the Word aright: which plainly implieth that it is possible for one, that hath received the Word of the Lord, to miss in the dividing and application of it, which must come from an impatience of spirit, and a self-working, which makes an unfound and dangerous mixture; and will hardly beget a right-minded living people to God.

I am earnest in this above all considerations, as to public brethren; well knowing how much it concerns the present and future state, and preservation of the church of Christ Jesus, that has been gathered and built up by a living and powerful ministry, that the ministry beheld, preserved, and continued in the manifestations motions and supplies of the same life and power, from time to time.'

And wherever it is observed, that any do minister more from gifts and parts, than life and power, though they have an enlightened and doctrinal understanding, let them in time be advised and admonished for their preservation, because insensibly such will come to depend upon a self-sufficiency; to forsake Christ the living fountain, and hew out unto themselves cisterns that will hold no living waters: and by degrees such will come to draw others from waiting upon the gift of God in themselves, and to feel it in others, in order to their strength and refreshment, to wait upon them, and to turn from God to man again, and so make shipwreck of the faith, once delivered to the saints, and of a good conscience towards God; which are only kept by that divine gift of life, that begat the one, and awakened and sanctified the other in the beginning.

Nor is it enough, that we have known the divine gift, and in it have reached to the spirits in prison, and been the instruments of the convincing of others of the way of God, if we keep not as low and poor in ourselves, and as depending upon the Lord, as ever: since no memory, no repetitions of former openings, revelations or enjoyments, will bring a soul to God, or afford bread to the hungry, or water to the thirsty, unless life go with what we say, and that must be waited for.

O that we may have no other fountain, treasure or dependence! That none may presume at any rate to act of themselves for God, because they have long acted from God; that we may not supply want of waiting with our own wisdom, or think that we may take less care, and more liberty in speaking than formerly; and that where we do not feel the Lord by his power, to open us and enlarge us, whatever be the expectation of the people, or has been our customary supply and character, we may not exceed or fill up the time with our own.

I hope we shall ever remember, who it was that said, Of yourselves you can do nothing: our sufficiency is in him. And if we are not to speak our own words, or take thought what we should say to men in our defence, when exposed for our testimony, surely we ought to speak none of our own words, or take thought what we shall say in our testimony and ministry, in the name of our Lord, to the souls of the people; for then of all times, and of all other occasions, should it be fulfilled in us, for it is not you that speak, but the spirit of my Father that speaketh in you.

And indeed, the ministry of the spirit, must and does keep its analogy and agreement, with the birth of the spirit, that as no man can inherit the kingdom of God, unless he be born of the spirit, so no ministry can beget a soul to God, but that which is from the spirit. For this, as I said before, the disciples waited before they went forth; and in this, our elder brethren, and messengers of God in our day, waited, visited and reached us and having begun in the spirit, let none ever hope or seek to be made perfect in the flesh: For what is the flesh to the spirit, or the chaff to the wheat: And it we keep in the spirit, we shall keep in the unity of it, which is the ground of the fellowship. For by drinking into that one Spirit, we are made one people to God, and by it we are continued in the unity of the faith, and the bond of peace. No envying, no bitterness, no strife, can have place with us. We shall watch always for good, and not for evil, one over another, and rejoice exceedingly, and not begrudge at one another's increase in the riches of the grace with which God replenisheth his faithful servants.

And brethren, as to you is committed the dispensation of the oracles of God, which give you frequent opportunities, and great place with the people among whom you travail, I beseech you that you would not think it sufficient, to declare the Word of Life, in their assemblies; however edifying and comfortable such opportunities may be to you and them: but, as was the practice of the man of God, before mentioned, in great measure, when among us, inquire the state of the several churches you visit; who among them are afflicted or sick, who are tempted, and if any are unfaithful or obstinate; and endeavour to issue those things in the wisdom and power of God, which will be a glorious crown upon your ministry. As that prepares your way in the hearts of the people, to receive you as men of God, so it gives you credit with them to do them good by your advice in other respects, the afflicted will be comforted by you, the tempted strengthened, the sick refreshed, the unfaithful convicted and restored, and such as are obstinate, softened and fitted for reconciliation, which is clinching the nail, and applying and fastning the general testimony, by this particular care of the several branches of it, in reference to them more immediately concerned in it.

For though good and wise men, and elders too, may reside in such places, who are of worth and importance in the general, and in other places; yet it does not always follow that they may have the room they deserve in the hearts of the people they live among; or some particular occasion may make it unfit for him or them to use that authority. But you that travail as God's messengers, if they receive you in the greater, shall they refuse you in the less? And if they own the general testimony, can they withstand the particular application of it, in their own cases? Thus, ye will show yourselves workmen indeed, and carry your business before you, to the praise of his name, that hath called you from darkness to light, that you might turn others from Satan's power unto God and his kingdom, which is within. And O that there were more of such faithful labourers in the vineyard of the Lord! Never more need since the day of God.

Wherefore I cannot but cry and call aloud to you, that have been long professors of the truth, and know the truth in the convincing power of it, and have had a sober conversation among men, yet content yourselves only to know truth for yourselves, to go to meetings, and exercise an ordinary charity in the Church, and an honest behaviour in the world, and limit yourselves within those bounds; feeling little or no concern upon your spirits, for the glory of the Lord in the prosperity of his truth in the earth, more than to be glad that others succeed in such service. Arise ye in the name and power of the Lord Jesus! Behold how white the fields are unto harvest, in this and other nations, and how few able and faithful labourers there are to work therein! Your country folks, neighbours and kindred, want to know the Lord and his Truth, and to walk in it. Does nothing lie at your door upon their account? Search and see, and lose no time, I beseech you, for the Lord is at hand.

I do not judge you, there is one that judgeth all men, and his judgment is true. You have mightily increased in your outward substance: may you equally increase in your inward riches, and do good with both, while you have a day to do good. Your enemies would once have taken what you had from you, for his namesake, in whom you have believed; wherefore he has given you much of the world, in the face of your enemies. But O, let it be your servant, and not your master! Your diversion rather than your business! Let the Lord be chiefly in your eye, and ponder your ways, and see if God has nothing more for you to do: and if you find yourselves short in your account with him, then wait for his preparation, and be ready to receive the word of command, and be not weary of well-doing, when you have put your hand to the plough, and assuredly you shall reap, if you faint not, the fruit of your heavenly labour in God's everlasting kingdom.

And you young convinced ones, be you entreated and exhorted to a diligent and chaste waiting upon God, in the way of his blessed manifestation and appearance of himself to you. Look not out, but within: let not another's liberty be your snare: neither act by imitation, but sense and feeling of God's power in yourselves: crush not the tender buddings of it in your souls, nor overrun, in your desires and warmness of affections, the holy and gentle motions of it. Remember it is a still voice, that speaks to us in this day, and that it is not to be heard in the noises and hurries of the mind; but it is distinctly understood, in a retired frame. Jesus loved and chose solitudes; often going to mountains, gardens and seasides, to avoid crowds and hurries, to show his disciples it was good to be solitary, and sit loose to the world. Two enemies lie near your states, imagination and liberty; but the plain, practical, living, holy truth, that has convinced you, will preserve you, if you mind it in yourselves, and bring all thoughts, inclinations and affections, to the test of it, to see if they are wrought in God or of the enemy, or your own selves: so will a true taste, discerning and judgment, be preserved to you, of what you should do and leave undone. And in your diligence and faithfulness in this way you will come to inherit substance; and Christ the eternal wisdom, will fill your treasury. And when you are converted, as well as convinced, then confirm your brethren; and be ready to every good word and work, that the Lord shall call you to; that you may be to his praise, who has chosen you to be partakers, with the saints in light, of a kingdom that cannot be shaken, an inheritance incorruptible in eternal habitations.

And now, as for you, that are the children of God's people, a great concern is upon my spirit, for your good: and often are my knees bowed to the God of your fathers, for you, that you may come to be partakers of the same divine life and power, that have been the glory of this day; that a generation you may be to God, a holy nation, and a peculiar people, zealous of good works, when all our heads are laid in the dust. O you young men and women! Let it not suffice you, that you are the children of the people of the Lord; you must also be born again, if you will inherit the kingdom of God. Your fathers are but such after the flesh, and could but beget you into the likeness of the first Adam; but you must be begotten into the likeness of the second Adam, by a spiritual generation, or you will not, you cannot, be of his children or off- spring. And therefore look carefully about you, O ye children of the children of God! Consider your standing, and see what you are in relation to this divine kindred, family and birth! Have you obeyed the Light, and received and walked in the Spirit, which is the incorruptible seed of the word and kingdom of God, of which you must be born again. God is no respecter of persons. The Father

cannot save or answer for the child, or the child for the father, but
in the sin thou sinnest thou shalt die; and in the righteousness thou
dost, through Christ Jesus, thou shalt live; for it is the willing and
obedient that shall eat the good of the land. Be not deceived, God
is not mocked, such as all nations and people sow, such they shall
reap at the hand of the just God. And then your many and great
privileges, above the children of other people, will add weight in
the scale against you, if you choose not the way of the Lord. For
you have had line upon line, and precept upon precept, and not
only good doctrine, but good example; and which is more, you
have been turned to, and acquainted with, a principle in yourselves,
which others have been ignorant of: and you know you may be as
good as you please, without the fear of frowns and blows, or being
turned out of doors, and forsaken of father and mother, for God's
sake, and his holy religion, as has been the case of some of your
fathers, in the day they first entered into this holy path. And if you,
after hearing and seeing the wonders that God has wrought in the
deliverance and preservation of them, through a sea of troubles,
and the manifold temporal, as well as spiritual blessings, that he
has filled them with, in the sight of their enemies, should neglect
and turn your backs upon so great and near a salvation, you would
not only be most ungrateful children to God and them, but must
expect that God will call the children of those that knew him not,
to take the crown out of your hands, and that your lot will be a
dreadful judgment at the hand of the Lord: but O that it may never
be so with any of you. The Lord forbid, saith my soul.

Wherefore, O ye young men and women, look to the rock of
your fathers: there is no other God but Him, no other light but
His, no other grace but His, nor spirit but His, to convince you,
quicken and comfort you; to lead, guide and preserve you to God's
everlasting kingdom, so will you be possessors as well as professors
of the truth, embracing it, not only by education, but judgment and
conviction; from a sense begotten in your souls, through the
operation of the eternal spirit and power of God; by which you
may come to be the seed of Abraham, through faith, and the
circumcision not made with hands; and so heirs of the promise
made to the fathers, of an incorruptible crown. That, as I said
before, a generation you may be to God, holding up the profession
of the blessed truth in the life and power of it. For formality in
religion is nauseous to God and good men; and the more so, where
any form and appearance has been new and peculiar, and begun

and practiced, upon a principle, with an uncommon zeal and strictness. Therefore I say, for you to fall flat and formal, and continue the profession, without that salt and savour, by which it is come to obtain a good report among men, is not to answer God's love, or your parents' care, or the mind of truth in yourselves, or in those that are without: who, though they will not obey the truth, have sight and sense enough to see if they do that make a profession of it. For where the divine virtue of it is not felt in the soul, and waited for, and lived in, imperfections will quickly break out, and show themselves, and detect the unfaithfulness of such persons; and that their insides are not seasoned with the nature of that holy principle which they profess.

Wherefore, dear children, let me entreat you to shut your eyes at the temptations and allurements of this low and perishing world, and not suffer your affections to be captivated by those lusts and vanities that your Fathers, for the truth's sake, long since turned their backs upon: but as you believe it to be the truth, receive it into your hearts, that you may become the children of God: so that it may never be said of you, as the Evangelist writes of the Jews in his time, that Christ, the true light, came to His own, but His own received Him not; but to as many as received Him, to them he gave power to become the children of God; which were born, not of blood, nor of the will of the flesh, nor of the will of man, but of God. A most close and comprehensive passage to this occasion. You exactly and peculiarly answer to those professing Jews, in that you bear the name of God's people, by being the children, and wearing of the form of God's people: and He, by His light in you, may be very well said to come to His own, and if you obey it not, but turn your back upon it, and walk after the vanities of your minds, you will be of those that received Him not, which I pray God may never be your case and judgment. But that you may be thoroughly sensible of the many and great obligations you lie under to the Lord for His love, and to your parents for their care: and with all your heart, and all your soul, and all your strength, turn to the Lord, to His gift and spirit in you, and hear His voice and obey it, that you may seal to the testimony of your fathers, by the truth and evidence of your own experience; that your children's children may bless you, and the Lord for you, as those that delivered a faithful example, as well as record of the truth of God unto them. So will the grey hairs of your dear parents, yet alive, go down to the grave with joy, to see you the posterity of truth, as well as theirs, and that not only their nature but spirit shall live in you when they are gone.

I shall conclude this account with a few words to those that are not of our communion, into whose hands this may come ; especially those of our own nation.

Friends, As you are the sons and daughters of Adam, and my brethren after the flesh, often and earnest have been my desires and prayers to God on your behalf, that you may come to know your Creator to be your redeemer and restorer to the holy image, that through sin you have lost, by the power and spirit of His Son Jesus Christ, whom He hath given for the light and life of the world. And O that you, who are called Christians, would receive Him into your hearts ! For there it is you want Him, and at that door He stands knocking that you might let him in, but you do not open to him : you are full of other guests, so that a manger is His lot among you now, as well as of old. Yet you are full of profession, as were the Jews when He came among them, who knew Him not, but rejected and evilly entreated Him. So that if you come not to the possession and experience of what you profess, all your formality in religion will stand you in no stead in the day of God's judgment.

I beseech you ponder with yourselves your eternal condition, and see what title, what ground and foundation you have for your Christianity : If more than a profession, and an historical belief of the gospel ? Have you known the baptism of fire, and the Holy Ghost, and the fan of Christ that winnows away the chaff in your minds, and carnal lusts and affections ? That divine leaven of the Kingdom, that, being received, leavens the whole lump of man, sanctifying him throughout in body, soul and spirit ? If this be not the ground of your confidence, you are in a miserable estate.

You will say, perhaps, that though you are sinners, and live in daily commission of sin, and are not sanctified, as I have been speaking, yet you have faith in Christ, who has borne the curse for you, and in him you are complete by faith, his righteousness being imputed to you.

But, my friends, let me entreat you not to deceive yourselves, in so important a point, as is that of your immortal souls. If you have true faith in Christ, your faith will make you clean ; it will sanctify you : for the saints' faith was their victory of old : by this they overcame sin within, and sinful men without. And if thou art in Christ, thou walkest not after the flesh, but after the spirit, whose fruits are manifest. Yea, thou art a new creature: new made, new fashioned; after God's will and mould. Old things are done away, and behold, all things are become new: new love, desires, will, affections and practices. It is not any longer thou that livest; thou disobedient, carnal, wordly one; but it is Christ that liveth in thee; and to live is Christ, and to die is thy eternal gain: because thou art assured, that thy corruptible shall put on incorruption, and thy mortal, immortality, and that thou hast a glorious house eternal in the heavens that will never wax old or pass away. All this follows being in Christ, as heat follows fire, and light the Sun.

Therefore have a care how you presume to rely upon such a notion, as that you are in Christ, whilst in your old fallen nature. For what communion hath light with darkenss, or Christ with Belial? Hear what the beloved disciple tells you: If we say we have fellowship with God, and walk in darkness, we lie, and do not the truth. This is, if we go on in a sinful way, are captivated by our carnal affections, and are not converted to God, we walk in darkness, and cannot possibly in that state have any Fellowship with God. Christ clothes them with his righteousness, that receive his grace in their hearts, and deny themselves, and take up his cross daily, and follow him. Christ's righteousness makes men inwardly holy; of holy minds, wills and practices. It is nevertheless Christ's, because we have it; for it is ours, not by nature, but by faith and adoption: it is the gift of God. But still, though not ours, as of or from ourselves, for in that sense it is Christ's, for it is of and from Him; yet it is ours, and must be ours in possession, efficacy and enjoyment, to do us any good; or Christ's righteousness will profit us nothing. It was after this manner that he was made to the primitive Christians, righteousness, sanctification, justification and redemption; and if ever you will have the comfort, kernel and marrow of the Christian religion, thus you must come to learn and obtain it.

Now, my friends, by what you have read, and will read in what follows, you may perceive that God has visited a poor people among you with this saving knowledge and testimony: whom He has upheld and encreased to this day, notwithstanding the fierce opposition they have met withal. Despise not the meanness of this appearance: it was, and yet is (we know) a day of small things, and of small account with too many; and many hard and ill names are given to it: but it is of God, it came from Him because it leads to Him. This we know, but we cannot make another to know it, unless he will take the same way to know it that we took. The world talks of God, but what do they do? They pray for power, but reject the principle in which it is. If you would know God, and worship and serve God as you should do, you must come to the means He has ordained and given for that purpose. Some seek it in books, some in learned men, but what they look for is in themselves, though not of themselves, but they overlook it. The voice is too still, the seed too small, and the light shineth in darkness; they are abroad, and so cannot divide the spoil: but the woman that lost her silver, found it at home, after she had lighted her candle and swept her house. Do you so too, and you shall find what Pilate wanted to know, viz. truth. Truth in the inward parts, so valuable in the sight of God.

The light of Christ within, who is the light of the world, (and so a light to you, that tells you the truth of your condition) leads all, that take heed unto it, out of darkness unto God's marvellous light. For light grows upon the obedient: it is sown for the righteous, and their way is a shining light, that shines forth more and more to the perfect day.

Wherefore, O friends, turn in, turn in, I beseech you: where is the poison, there is the antidote. There you want Christ, and there you must find him; and, blessed be God, there you may find him. Seek and you shall find, I testify for God. But then you must seek aright, with your whole heart, as men that seek for their lives, yea, for their eternal lives: diligently, humbly, patiently, as those that can taste no pleasure, comfort, or satisfaction in anything else, unless you find him whom your souls desire to know and love above all. O it is a travail, a spiritual travail! Let the carnal, profane world think and say as it will. And though this path you must walk to the city of God, that has eternal foundations, if ever you will come there.

Well! And what does this blessed light do for you? Why, 1. It sets all your sins in order before you: it detects the spirit of this world in all its baits and allurements, and shows how man came to fall from God, and the fallen estate he is in. 2. It begets a sense and sorrow, in such as believe in it, for this fearful lapse. You will then see him distinctly whom you have pierced, and all the blows and wounds you have given him by your disobedience, and how you have made him to serve with your sins; and you will weep and mourn for it, and your sorrow will be a godly sorrow. 3. After this it will bring you to the holy watch, to take care that you do so no more, and that the enemy surprise you not again. Then thoughts, as well as words and works will come to judgment, which is the way of holiness, in which the redeemed of the Lord do walk. Here you will come to love God above all, and your neighbours as yourselves. Nothing hurts, nothing harms, nothing makes afraid on this holy mountain. Now you come to be Christ's indeed: for you are His in nature and spirit, and not your own. And when you are thus Christ's then Christ is yours, and not before. And here communion with the Father, and with the Son you will know, and the efficacy of the blood of cleansing, even the bllod of Jesus Christ, that Immaculate Lamb, which speaks better things than the blood of Abel; and which cleanseth from all sin the consciences of those that through the living faith come to be sprinkled with it from dead works to serve the living God.

To conclude, behold the testimony and doctrine of the people called Quakers! Behold their practice and discipline! And behold the blessed man and men (at least many of them) that were sent of God in this excellent work and service! All which is more particularly expressed in the annals of that man of God: which I do heartily recommend to my readers most serious perusal; and beseech Almighty God, that His blessing may go along with both, to the convincement of many, as yet strangers to this holy dispensation, and also to the edification of God's church in general. Who for His manifold and repeated mercies and blessings to his people in this day of His great love, is worthy ever to have the glory, honour, thanksgiving and renown; and be it rendered and ascribed, with fear and reverence, through Him in whom he is well pleased, His beloved Son and Lamb, our light and life, that fits with Him upon the throne, world without end. Amen.

Says one that God has long since mercifully favoured with his fatherly visitation, and who was not disobedient to the heavenly vision and call; to whom the way of truth is more lovely and precious than ever, and that knowing the beauty and benefit of it above all worldly treasures, has chosen it for his chiefest joy; and therefore recommends it to thy love and choice, because he is with great sincerity and affection,

Thy soul's friend, W. PENN

SUGGESTIONS FOR FURTHER READING

Barbour, Hugh S. (ed.), *William Penn on Religion and Ethics* (Lewiston, Maine, 1991): a very expensive collection of Penn essays accompanied by excellent introductions by Professor Barbour, specialist in Quaker history and theology.

Beatty, Edward C. O., *William Penn as Social Philosopher* (New York, 1939): an early study of the ethical and philosophical beliefs, still used by Penn scholars.

Bronner, Edwin B., *William Penn's 'Holy Experiment'* (New York, 1962): carefully traces the founding of Pennsylvania from the granting of the charter by Charles II to the conclusion of Penn's second visit to the colony in 1701.

Bronner and David Fraser, *William Penn's Published Writings*, Volume 5 of *The Papers of William Penn* (Philadelphia, 1986): an illustrated, interpretive bibliography of Penn's writings, 1660 to 1726, with brief essays about each of 135 titles which he wrote or to which he contributed.

Buranelli, Vincent, *The King and the Quaker, A Study of William Penn and James II* (Philadelphia, 1962): asserts that Penn was always loyal to James, and that he was right in maintaining that attachment.

Dunn, Mary Maples, *William Penn, Politics and Conscience* (Princeton, N.J., 1967): a scholarly examination of Penn's political ideas which emphasizes the reflection of his ethical beliefs in his political writings.

Dunn and Richard S. Dunn (eds.) *The World of William Penn* (Philadelphia, 1986): twenty essays by specialists in British and American history exploring the political, economic, intellectual, religious, and social environment in which William Penn lived and worked.

Endy, Melvin B., *William Penn and Early Quakerism* (Princeton, 1973): emphasizes the religious or spiritual side of this man as reflected in his numerous essays defending Quakers from their opponents, and portraying the beliefs of this movement to outsiders.

Hull, William I., *William Penn: a Topical Biography* (London, 1937): seeks to portray this very complicated man by emphasizing one aspect at a time; a rich source of information, though some of it is outdated.

Illick, Joseph, *William Penn the Politician* (Ithaca, New York, 1965):

discusses the way in which Penn related to the English government, more particularly the men in control of the government, and suggests that his Quaker principles were sometimes compromised in the process.

Peare, Catherine Owens, *William Penn* (Philadelphia, 1956): no one has ever written a completely satisfying biography, but Peare has come closer than anyone else. It is readable, and is still cited by scholars.

Soderlund, Jean R. (ed.), *William Penn and the Founding of Pennsylvania 1680–1684* (Philadelphia, 1983): selections for the common reader from the massive scholarship which went into Volume 2 of *The Papers of William Penn*.

Tolles, Frederick B. and Gordon A. Alderfer (eds.), *The Witness of William Penn* (New York, 1957): selected writings of Penn, including some in this volume, with introductions by Tolles.

van den Dungen, Peter (ed.), *William Penn An Essay Towards the Present and Future Peace of Europe ...* (Hildesheim, Germany, 1983): a thirty-page introduction, tracing the history of this remarkable essay, followed by a facsimile reprint of the first issue of the *Essay* in 1693.